THE RISE OF PACIFIC LITERATURE

MODERNIST LATITUDES

MODERNIST LATITUDES

Jessica Berman and Paul Saint-Amour, Editors

Modernist Latitudes aims to capture the energy and ferment of modernist studies by continuing to open up the range of forms, locations, temporalities, and theoretical approaches encompassed by the field. The series celebrates the growing latitude ("scope for freedom of action or thought") that this broadening affords scholars of modernism, whether they are investigating little-known works or revisiting canonical ones. Modernist Latitudes will pay particular attention to the texts and contexts of those latitudes (Africa, Latin America, Australia, Asia, Southern Europe, and even the rural United States) that have long been misrecognized as ancillary to the canonical modernisms of the global North.

Nergis Ertürk, *Writing in Red: Literature and Revolution Across Turkey and the Soviet Union*

Cate I. Reilly, *Psychic Empire: Literary Modernism and the Clinical State*

Adam McKible, *Creating Jim Crow America: George Horace Lorimer, the Saturday Evening Post, and the War Against Black Modernity*

Hannah Freed-Thall, *Modernism at the Beach: Queer Ecologies and the Coastal Commons*

Daniel Ryan Morse, *Radio Empire: The BBC's Eastern Service and the Emergence of the Global Anglophone Novel*

Jill Richards, *The Fury Archives: Female Citizenship, Human Rights, and the International Avant-Gardes*

Claire Seiler, *Midcentury Suspension: Literature and Feeling in the Wake of World War II*

Elizabeth Outka, *Viral Modernism: The Influenza Pandemic and Interwar Literature*

Ben Conisbee Baer, *Indigenous Vanguards: Education, National Liberation, and the Limits of Modernism*

Aarthi Vadde, *Chimeras of Form: Modernist Internationalism Beyond Europe, 1914–2014*

Eric Bulson, *Little Magazine, World Form*

Eric Hayot and Rebecca L. Walkowitz, eds., *A New Vocabulary for Global Modernism*

Christopher Reed, *Bachelor Japanists: Japanese Aesthetics and Western Masculinities*, 2016

Celia Marshik, *At the Mercy of Their Clothes: Modernism, the Middlebrow, and British Garment Culture*

Donal Harris, *On Company Time: American Modernism in the Big Magazines*

For a complete list of books in this series, see the CUP website.

The Rise of Pacific Literature

DECOLONIZATION,
RADICAL CAMPUSES,
AND MODERNISM

Maebh Long and
Matthew Hayward

Columbia University Press
New York

Columbia University Press
Publishers Since 1893
New York   Chichester, West Sussex
cup.columbia.edu
Copyright © 2024 Columbia University Press
All rights reserved

Library of Congress Cataloging-in-Publication Data
Names: Long, Maebh, author. | Hayward, Matthew (Lecturer in Pacifc literature), author.
Title: The rise of Pacific literature : decolonization, radical campuses, and modernism / Maebh Long and Matthew Hayward.
Description: New York : Columbia University Press, [2024] | Series: Modernist latitudes | Includes bibliographical references and index.
Identifiers: LCCN 2024012057 (print) | LCCN 2024012058 (ebook) | ISBN 9780231217446 (hardback) | ISBN 9780231217453 (trade paperback) | ISBN 9780231561730 (ebook)
Subjects: LCSH: Pacific Island literature (English)—History and criticism.
Classification: LCC PN849.O26 L66 2024 (print) | LCC PN849.O26 (ebook) | DDC 820.9/009120995—dc23/eng/20240603
LC record available at https://lccn.loc.gov/2024012057
LC ebook record available at https://lccn.loc.gov/2024012058

Cover design: Milenda Nan Ok Lee
Cover image: John Pule

For Tom
—Maebh

Vei Lillian, Belinda, Mereoni kei Maciu
—Matthew

CONTENTS

ACKNOWLEDGMENTS   ix

Introduction
Pacific Universities and Modernist Literature   1

Chapter One
Modernism, Pedagogy, and Pacific Writer-Scholars   33

Chapter Two
Decolonizing the Literature Program,
Generating the Niuginian Literary Scene   61

Chapter Three
Traveling Editors and Indigenous Masks:
The Teachings of Ulli Beier   92

Chapter Four
Black Power and Pacific Existentialism:
John Kasaipwalova and Russell Soaba   112

CONTENTS

Chapter Five
Preliminaries and Prologues:
A National Scene in a Regional University   138

Chapter six
Mana on Campus:
New Forms in Pacific Poetry and Prose   160

Chapter Seven
Subramani's Sugarcane Gothic:
Haunting the Regional Dream   189

Coda
The Stories of Multitudes to Come   212

NOTES   225

BIBLIOGRAPHY   259

INDEX   279

ACKNOWLEDGMENTS

This book has its origins in the lecture halls, tutorial rooms, corridors, and cafés of the University of the South Pacific. Over the years, as we designed and taught literature courses at USP, learning from the Oceanian writers and educators upon whose work the university was built, we became interested in the modernist currents that we saw running through both the history of the curriculum and the literary movements of the region. In 2014, with Sudesh Mishra, we founded the Oceanian Modernism project to learn from and with other scholars about the place of modernism in the Pacific. The project led to a conference at USP, two special issues of journals, one edited collection, and numerous talks, panels, articles, and book chapters. *The Rise of Pacific Literature* is the culmination of the project's many hours of deliberating and debating all things modernist and Pacific. It is deeply indebted to the exceptional writers, scholars, and writer-scholars who joined the talanoa, enriching the conversation, revealing our blind spots, and strengthening the weave. They taught these two palagi much: All gaps or errors that linger in this monograph stem only from our inadequacies as students.

There are many teachers we need to thank. In addition to all those who published articles and chapters with the project, we would like to recognize the vital contributions made by colleagues and friends. From USP over the

ACKNOWLEDGMENTS

years, we are ever grateful to Sudesh Mishra, Margaret Mishra, Anurag Subramani, Paula Qereti, Tilisi Bryce, Vilsoni Hereniko, Larry Thomas, Robert Nicole, Frances Koya Vakaʻuta, Susan Sela, Seuʻula Johansson-Fua, Jonathan Ritchie, Fiona Willans, Caitlin Vandertop, and Thomas Vranken. Students and postgraduates drove many fruitful discussions, and we acknowledge in particular Sangeeta Sharma, Jenny Bennett-Tuionetoa, Hilda Kunau, Salanieta Koro, Laisani Lesumaisireli, Sudesh Kumar, and Shagufta Bano.

At Waikato, our thanks go to Keaka Hemi, Apo Aporosa, and the PACIS group, including Alice Te Punga Somerville, Sam Iti Prendergast, Kate Stevens, Jesi Bennett, Wanda Ieremia-Allan, Jess Pasisi, and Hineitimoana Greensill. Collegial support was offered by Sarah Shieff, Kirstine Moffat, Mark Houlahan, Catherine Chidgey, and Tracey Slaughter, as well as Karen Barber, Andreea Calude, Laura Haughey, Fiona McCormack, John Campbell, Michael Goldsmith, Tom Ryan, Keith Barber, and Fraser MacDonald. Student summer research scholarships facilitated the pleasure of working with Kristoffer Lavasiʻi, while Kate Sampson and Robert Gladden afforded helpful assistance through the work-integrated learning program.

In Papua New Guinea we are grateful for the generous involvement of Steven Winduo and Nehemiah Akia. Our thanks to Joanne Wodak, Evelyn Ellerman, Michael Dom of Ples Singsing, and Keith Jackson of *PNG Attitude*.

In Fiji, Subramani, Pio Manoa, Konai Helu Thaman, Satendra Nandan, Vijay Mishra, and Vanessa Griffen—who was Maebh's neighbor for a glorious spell in 2011—have been an inspiration from the start.

In Aotearoa New Zealand we thank Emma Powell, Selina Tusitala Marsh, Erin Carlston, and Jacob Edmond. For their support and encouragement, we also thank Peter Benson, Elizabeth DeLoughrey, Rebecca Hogue, Craig Santos Perez, Douglas Mao, Jahan Ramazani, and the late Susan Stanford Friedman.

At Columbia University Press, we owe much to Paul Saint-Amour and Jessica Berman, brilliant editors of the Modernist Latitudes series, and we are grateful to Philip Leventhal, who has kept us strictly on track.

John Pule, whose art makes such a striking cover, has been unstintingly generous. His artwork made a beautiful poster for our first symposium, and in allowing us to use *Forever and Ever* here, he brings the project's imagery full circle.

We are grateful to the staff at the libraries of USP—particularly their Pacific Collection—UPNG, and Waikato. The National Archives of Fiji, the Harry Ransom Center at the University of Texas at Austin, and Archives New Zealand all provided valuable resources. We thank the Contestable Research Fund of the Division of Arts, Law, Psychology, and Social Science at Waikato and the School of Pacific Arts, Communication, and Education at USP for financial assistance.

Tom and Lillian, we could not have written this without your love and support and your tolerance through the many—many!—days and nights we spent crouched over screens and tied up in Zoom meetings. From Matthew: Belinda, Mereoni, and Maciu, you made it all worthwhile. Grá and love to our families outside the Pacific: Áine, Fin, Ciara, and Gran in Ireland; Diane, Sarah, and Mark in England.

Finally, to the elders we have lost while writing this book—Leo Dawson, Rabbie Namaliu, John Kasaipwalova, Marjorie Tuainekore Crocombe, and Pio Manoa—it was an honor to know you, it was an honor to read you.

PERMISSIONS

A short section in the introduction to this book first appeared in Matthew Hayward, "'Our Own Identity': Albert Wendt, James Joyce, and the Indigenisation of Influence," in *New Oceania: Modernisms and Modernities in the Pacific*, ed. Matthew Hayward and Maebh Long (New York: Routledge, 2019), 81–99. Copyright © 2019 Routledge.

Short sections in chapters 1 and 5 first appeared in Maebh Long and Matthew Hayward, "'For I Have Fed on Foreign Bread': Modernism, Colonial Education, and Fijian Literature," *Modernist Cultures* 15, no. 3 (2020): 377–98. Copyright © 2020 Edinburgh University Press.

Sections of chapter 3 first appeared in Maebh Long, "Being Obotunde Ijimere and M. Lovori: Mapping Ulli Beier's Intercultural Hoaxes from Nigeria to Papua New Guinea," *Journal of Commonwealth Literature* 58, no. 2 (2023): 293–307. Copyright © 2023 Sage Publications. Also in Maebh Long and Kristoffer Lavasi'i, "Travelling Editors, Little Magazines, and Postcolonial Modernism: Ulli Beier, *Black Orpheus*, and *Kovave*,"

Modernism/modernity, Print Plus, 8, no. 2 (2023). Copyright © 2023 The Johns Hopkins University Press.

A paragraph in chapter 6 first appeared in Matthew Hayward and Maebh Long, "Towards an Oceanian Modernism," *Modernism/modernity* 28, no. 2 (2021): 209–28. Copyright © 2021 The Johns Hopkins University Press.

THE RISE OF PACIFIC LITERATURE

Introduction

PACIFIC UNIVERSITIES AND MODERNIST LITERATURE

In his 2012 collection *Ancestry*, Albert Wendt—the "scholarly grandfather" of modern Pacific literature, as one academic descendant puts it—presents a seminar scene in which a group of postgraduates discuss literary representations of sexuality.[1] The students have a range of interests: one is writing a thesis on the Māori author Patricia Grace; another is obsessed with the modernist Henry Miller; a third is studying the poetry of Wendt's Pākehā mentor, James K. Baxter; and another is a "James Joyce addict."[2] The group presents a wide range of views, but it is this last student who, "voice rich with irony," delivers the conversational coup de grâce when he argues for the "basic truth" that "sex and sex and sex are at the core of how we view reality." Engaged in questions of procreation and play, the narrator describes this insertion of sexual frankness into modern literature as "Joyce's ancestry," echoing the collection's title and drawing the Irish patriarch of European modernism into Wendt's exploration of the sexual, cultural, and artistic connections that link people across the book's Pacific settings.

The concept of ancestry or genealogy—gafa in Samoan—is crucial to Oceanian understandings of identity, as another character in Wendt's collection explains: "Her grandmother had believed that every one and every thing was connected through gafa/genealogy right back to the atua, and that gafa was intelligent, and when you maliu-ed—moved on—you became part of that intelligence and the inheritance of your descendants."[3] The tinamatua is not describing here the genealogy of mere succession, but a fluid, sentient process through which the new is absorbed reflexively into the old. Figured thus, as process rather than sequence, genealogy has profound implications for questions of literary growth and is performed in Wendt's *Ancestry* as the practice, to quote the Pasifika poet Karlo Milo, of "finding foreign words, coaxing them / into familiar, into family."[4] Recognizing kinship in that which is different enables Wendt to adopt those of diverse bloodlines into Pacific literary structures, turning the extravagance of Joyce's "sex and sex and sex" into the reproductive pleasures of authorial rebirthing, as varied international modes and generic traits draw new breath as Pacific forms. Wendt is also adept in recognizing the ways that other Pacific writers brought new relatives into the Oceanian family tree. Some decades before the publication of *Ancestry*, Wendt reflected on the encompassing kin line of Oceanian literature, finding the presence of "Eliot, Yeats, Pound, Forster, Auden, Woolf, Faulkner, Hemingway, Wright, Ellison, Lessing and others."[5] This genealogical chart adds palagi modernist authors to Pacific networks, showing Oceanian associations extending across the world, as writers from Fiji, Tonga, Vanuatu, Papua New Guinea, Samoa drew new literary ancestors into their creative dynasties.

Through Wendt's short story, we encounter not only the far-reaching kinship lines traversing Pacific literature but the fundamental significance of the university space. Wendt's collection, with its postmillennial graduate seminar, is the product of a phase of Oceanian writing inextricable from the university campus, a critical period in the 1960s and 1970s where fledgling authors learned new ways of writing the Pacific region. Initially learners on the literary journey, regardless of which side of the lectern they inhabited, they became teachers and then elders, transforming the gafa—what went before and what comes after—through the family ties they formed. As the Māori scholar Alice Te Punga Somerville has recently written, in a chapter taking its cue from Wendt's 1970 poem "Inside Us the Dead," "Genealogies, after all, are not merely endpoints; through them we are connected not only to ancestors but also descendants."[6] Te Punga Somerville is describing literary genealogies, but she too situates this discussion in the classroom, where she locates herself as an intermediary between the ancestral Wendt and "another generation," her students. As she argues, such an

INTRODUCTION: PACIFIC UNIVERSITIES AND MODERNIST LITERATURE

approach to genealogy allows for the reconception of the pedagogic present as a "node" in a "vast, multidirectional network of connections."[7] Thinking in terms of education always means thinking in terms of the longue durée, of gafa, learning from those who came before you and teaching those still to come.

This familial, literary, and pedagogic network, which extends across generations and oceans, is the subject of *The Rise of Pacific Literature*. Identifying modernisms from Europe, North America, and Africa as vital arteries in Pacific literature of the 1960s and 1970s, drawn in through the newly opened Pacific seminar rooms, we trace the influence of the university scene on the growth of Oceanian writing. We map the ways students and pedagogues in decolonizing universities crafted modernist-conversant strategies to construct a regional literature, one developing in tandem with Pacific pedagogies, which were, and are, forward-looking aesthetic and teaching approaches responsive both to the needs of futurity and the experience and outlook of the past. As this is a story of genealogies and inheritances, we necessarily delve into the past to chart authorial legacies, but we concentrate on the period around the birth of two major Pacific institutions, the University of Papua New Guinea (UPNG) and the University of the South Pacific (USP), looking to the dominant pedagogical figures in these institutions and the curricula they established, the students who sat their courses and learned how to respond to texts as well as write their own, and the wider literary forums—extracurricular creative writing workshops, journals and little magazines, and university-adjacent publishers—in which this emerging literature was produced and disseminated. *The Rise of Pacific Literature* tells the story of Pacific writers, teachers, and students who made inventive use of transnational modernist ancestries to produce a literary movement at once globally affiliated and singularly Oceanian.

LEARNING OUTCOMES: RECOGNIZING THE CLASSROOM COMPONENTS OF OCEANIAN LITERATURE

From the University of Papua New Guinea and the University of the South Pacific in the first decades of their foundation arose work of such vibrancy that the Tongan poet and scholar Konai Helu Thaman names this period "the golden age of Pacific writing."[8] There was Pacific literary creativity long before the establishment of these institutions, and it flourishes still today: by invoking Helu Thaman's phrase we do not imply a narrative of a birth and subsequent demise. While anecdotal laments for a post-1980s creative recession within UPNG and USP are not uncommon, we suggest in the coda to this book that it is a case of dispersal rather than decline, with Oceanian literary expression diversifying across the broader artistic vistas that constitute Pacific literature in the twenty-first century. Yet the 1960s to the 1980s remains a special time. During this period, Oceanian literature grew from sporadic publications to a movement that spanned millions of square miles of ocean, across islands and villages and cities. This literary wave, this golden age, is inextricable from the decolonizing drive of the era, but it is equally inseparable from the founding of institutions of higher learning. At universities and university-run workshops, Pacific Islanders who had never written creatively or who wrote reluctantly or occasionally or alone became vocational writers. And it was at universities and through their attendant events and publications that these writers began to see themselves as such—as Anuki writers, as iKiribati writers, as writers of a newly conceived Oceania.

The texts taught at universities and read through the university scene provided Pacific writers with new literary tactics and new uses of familiar forms, which enabled them to turn local, regional, and international expressive trends toward their own contexts and needs. The opportunities afforded by classroom discussions were bolstered by clubs, societies, and recreational spaces that encouraged artists to commit to political activism, define their literary projects, and refine their aesthetic techniques. Educational spaces became—despite varying degrees of institutional reluctance or indifference—literary spaces, and as Oceanian writing made its way into the curriculum and students studied the poetry and prose and plays of their mentors and peers, the universities became major assemblies for the reception of the new literature. In time, the tertiary institutions could be seen as key apparatuses for securing Oceanian writers' legacies, with contemporary literature courses bringing new cohorts of readers each year.[9]

The golden age of Pacific writing is the age of the university. This book retells the rise of Pacific literature as a story of inventive curricula, of writer-scholars and teacher-editors, of student activists, graduate leaders, and subversive staff. It reorients the literature departments of UPNG and USP into a history of radical, decolonizing pedagogy, with the content of the classrooms reframed as literary-curricular projects that not only sustained

INTRODUCTION: PACIFIC UNIVERSITIES AND MODERNIST LITERATURE

the upsurge of Oceanian literature but anticipated the interpretive methods of global modernism. It proposes, with Mark McGurl's *The Program Era* (2009), that as literary scholars we must attend to the "increasingly intimate relation between literary production and the practices of higher education."[10] By admitting into our scholarship sensitivity to the "uncanny affinity between literary work and teaching processes," as Ben Conisbee Baer urges in *Indigenous Vanguards* (2010), we realize, with Rachel Sagner Buurma and Laura Heffernan's *The Teaching Archive* (2020), that across the colonial and decolonizing world the "true history of English literary study resides in classrooms."[11]

The Rise of Pacific Literature recognizes the site of the university, the content of literature courses, and a commitment to education as key components of Pacific literary history, rather than incidental backgrounds or accidental facilitators, and brings into focus the mediated, transnational connections feeding Oceanian writing. The writers of this period sought to articulate Oceanian modernities and Pacific lives, but to do so they drew on a diverse range of sources, approaches, and styles, from Chinua Achebe to T. S. Eliot, existentialism to négritude, fragmentation to heliaki. Identifying the consanguinity between literary output and the curriculum helps contest common, if opposing, desires to present new literatures either as an unmediated outflowing from a pure aesthetic spring—which denies the capacity of Indigenous artists to incorporate other influences—or as a simple, imitative effect of contact with Western forms, which denies the deeper durability of Indigenous art forms through cultural change. To acknowledge the complex threads of this decisive period in the development of Pacific literature is not to undermine the necessary primacy of the homegrown but to show that Oceanian writing, at one of its most productive junctures, was already a complex blend of the local and the transnational.

Of course, such is the diversity of Oceania—where one percent of the world's population has produced around a quarter of the world's languages—that a Pacific writer does not have to venture far before the local is left behind. As Apisai Enos explained in *Kovave*, UPNG's literary magazine, the vast array of languages and cultures in Papua New Guinea alone meant that "although I am a Niuginian, I am at the same time a stranger, an outsider in cultures other than my own, no matter how hard I try. I can never be at home in the diversity of Niuginian cultures and languages."[12] But as Emma Powell points out, evoking the Polynesian concept of the vā—defined by

Wendt as "the space between, the betweenness, not empty space that separates but space that relates"—"how do we make sense of anything if it is not in relation to something else? It is in the space between that we find contrasts and dynamics that are not apparent when the subject is in isolation."[13] The university has long been a space for self-discovery by contrast and comparison—those watchwords for literary assignments worldwide—and the newly designed curricula offered Oceanian writers a range of ways to be between, to stand in new relations. During this period, Pacific writers experimented with the potency of transcommunal, transregional, and transnational alliances, and a significant part of this experiment involved weaving modernist strands into local contexts. It is with this understanding of fundamental interconnectivity, of intricate literary gafa, that we position Oceanian writing within an extended history of global modernism and of modernism as a radical teaching tool.

In tracing the curricular strategies of the two literature departments, we find there to have been a fundamental rehabilitation of literary studies, a reconstitution of the discipline around a Pacific core—a new relationality between the local and the foreign. Allowing for opening years of adjustment and for changes as staff came and went, in both UPNG and USP the Pacific world was presented to students as the ground of literary production and interpretation. Within a few years of the founding of the University of Papua New Guinea, staff within the Department of Language and Literature rolled out a new English literature curriculum. Gone was the Chaucer-to-Coleridge, Hwæt-to-Hardy model ubiquitous in English departments across the globe. Instead of beginning with the Wife of Bath or wind-tossed daffodils, the students began at home, collecting oral narratives from their own villages and comparing them to orature from other parts of Papua and New Guinea—some published by the Papua Pocket Poets series that the English department had founded—and to oral stories and forms from across the world. Orality was followed by courses on new literature from decolonizing countries across Africa and India. Only then did students engage with writing from Europe and America, the majority of which we would understand today as modernist.

UPNG's classes began in 1966; at the University of the South Pacific, founded two years later, the literature syllabus was a little slower in forming, with the English curriculum dominated initially by linguistics. But from the first introduction of literature papers in the early 1970s—two

INTRODUCTION: PACIFIC UNIVERSITIES AND MODERNIST LITERATURE

modernist units, featuring Joyce and Eliot, Katherine Mansfield and Albert Camus—it rapidly came to resemble UPNG, abandoning the familiar chronological trajectory of a traditional literature program for a spatial mapping that began with the newly published literature of the contemporary Pacific, expanded out to the global postcolonial literature that helped inspire it, and finally moved out again to modernism, a major impetus of the postcolonial and Pacific movements alike. By positioning canonical texts of Western modernism after the expressions of modern lives in the Pacific and across the decolonizing world, these syllabuses created a series of interlocking, overlapping explorations of modernity. In jettisoning a curriculum of chronological development, these departments also abandoned the narrative of linear aesthetic progression, offering instead a story of bricolage and imbrication, as the writings of modernity—oral, decolonizing, modernist—that these degree programs set revealed uneven patterns of repetition, influence, and retooling. By the time the students were boarding Conrad's *Nellie* or seeing with Eliot's Tiresias or attending Kafka's trial, they had witnessed allusion, fragmentation, and nonlinearity in Mekeo songs, had encountered alienation, absurdism, and epiphany on Nigerian streets. European and American modernism thus carried both the shock of the new and the serviceability of the familiar, and African, Caribbean, and Indian texts modeled how traditional forms and colonial legacies could be repurposed to decolonizing ends.

Establishing these curricula as the context for Pacific engagements with modernism brings several key affordances. At a hermeneutic level, the claim provides unusually firm ground for the tracing of literary inspiration and adaptation by presenting a particular set of texts read by a particular set of authors in particular pedagogical settings. But more broadly, recognizing the specific position of modernist texts within these curricula—their placement at the outer edge of syllabuses recentered upon the contemporary Pacific—also helps us recall the contingency of the modernist encounter. As we show across this book, student-teacher-writers found all manner of uses for the modernist texts they studied, responding to their various interests and the exigencies of their own cultural situations. But modernism was for these writers a tool, not the telos in a linear evolution of form, and focusing on the uses they found in the service of decolonization avoids the reification of European modernism as some inherently superior mode, the elixir to which colonized writers were ineluctably drawn. Seen against a curricular background where modernist texts were approached via other world literatures, the Pacific incorporation of modernism into its literature appears not as a gesture of obeisance to a peerless style or subject matter, nor a belated catching up with an earlier phase of world literary history, but the putting to good use of tools that students had seen recycled by writers across the world.

In another sense, situating the Pacific engagement with modernism in the university risks diminishing the vanguard spirit of these writers. As an ideological apparatus, the education system may seem irretrievably complicit in maintaining existing conditions and therefore a compromised vector for any truly transformative art form. To encounter modernism through alternative or underground routes, the argument might run, students could experience its countercultural potential, but to become acquainted in an educational setting is to meet a thoroughly tamed version of the rough beast. Yet modernism has long been associated with the tertiary space. As early as the 1920s, undergraduate examinations at Cambridge University featured essays from the *Dial*, *Survey of Modernist Poetry*, and Virginia Woolf's *To the Lighthouse*.[14] Lionel Trilling remarks that it was not until the 1950s that Columbia University reluctantly extended the English department course offerings beyond 1900, but by the end of the Second World War it was possible for most American undergraduates to take multiple courses in modern literature.[15] It is easy to see why. The allusiveness and complexity of a poem such as *The Waste Land* make it eminently suitable for exegesis and analysis; as Gail McDonald suggests, because modernist poetry "repays study, it makes an argument for the value of education *per se*."[16] In the Global North, this marriage between poetry and the professors may indeed have marred modernism's countercultural cachet: according to William Carlos Williams, Eliot's text gave verse "back to the academics" and "returned us to the classroom" just when poetry was "on the point of an escape to matters much closer to the essence of a new art form itself."[17] At the same time, it would be reductive to see accommodation within the institution as mere domestication. Modernism's most stalwart supporters within the universities were often scholarly "'outsiders'—journalists, creative writers, and critics, not philologists and linguists—who posed a threat to the scholarly business as usual."[18] If modernism was co-opted into the university space, this was not necessarily in service of the status quo.

Again, however, context is all, and in regions still suffering under a colonial education system that insisted on the fixed principles of an imposed tradition, modernism presented new and unsettling potentials. As we argue in chapter 1, for Pacific writers—educators and students both—modernist works provided a vital resource in the move from a rote learning system that dictated foreign educational and literary standards to a Pacific writing and learning system that encouraged self-direction and self-actualization. In making this claim, we do not make light of the limitations and biases of modernist texts nor deny the complicity of modernist authors and institutions with the very colonial education systems that Oceanian writers set out to overcome. But in analyzing the interplay between curricula and creative writing of the period, we nevertheless find that modernism, in its many forms, served Oceanian authors who sought not merely to create new oeuvres but to form new ontologies.

Accepting such a conclusion involves recognizing that Pacific teachers, students, and writers developed the agency to make critical use of the pedagogical systems they experienced, but this in turn requires a more reflexive understanding of how curricula operate. If we follow an etymological route from the Latin verb *currere*, as did the educational theorist William Pinar in 1975, we find a conception of "curriculum" as the running of a course, with the stress on the verb rather than the noun. For Pinar, shifting the focus from the course to its running allows us to see teaching and learning not as the uniform repetition of a set track but a journey, taken slightly differently by each individual, enabling an ongoing "complicated conversation" between the self and others.[19] Against a colonizing curriculum that presents one way of understanding the world as the correct and only way, the "conceptual power of *currere* implies newness, creation of things unforeseen, experimentation, expanding of difference and movement."[20] These are resoundingly modernist terms, and it is such a view of learning—with its openness to difference and alternative courses—that we find to have been active among the decolonizing agents of this period. As such, we see the modernist and Pacific courses that ran through Oceanian classrooms and Oceanian texts alike as streams swelling toward decolonizing practices, infused with the openness, the care for the individual as part of a community, and the vision of unfixing identity that Pinar would term *currere*.

The prominence of modernism in the decolonizing university, as we show in chapter 1, was not just coincident with the critical pedagogies of Pinar and his contemporaries but fundamentally performative of their educational principles. The writers of these courses were conversant with the likes of Paulo Freire and Ivan Illich—both of whom spoke at UPNG in the early 1970s, with Illich also speaking at USP—and ideologically allied with works such as "On the Abolition of the English Department" (1972) by Ngũgĩ wa Thiong'o, Henry Owuor-Anyumba, and Taban Lo Liyong, of particular significance since the latter would join UPNG's literature program in the mid-1970s. The design of the literature programs was not so revolutionary, however, that it did away with traditional modes of assessment or wholly undercut teacher-student hierarchies. The first generation of Pacific Island pedagogues was still learning to define and reintroduce Pacific learning methodologies, and many of the visions of decolonization at play in UPNG and USP during these early years were not Pacific-led. Yet the reshaping of literature programs so that they could aid both the national and regional struggles for political independence and the broader ontological prospects of what Walter D. Mignolo and Catherine E. Walsh term *decoloniality*—the drive for other modes of thinking, writing, and being— deserves to be understood as a daring act in a region long constrained by colonial educational apparatuses.[21] The innovation of the educators of the University of Papua New Guinea and the University of the South Pacific lay not in their introduction of modernism to their programs per se but in their routing of modernism into a curriculum prioritizing local relevance and forms, one that treats modernism as a particular if puissant tributary in the rising tide of a contemporary, reciprocal Pacific Island literature.

CONSTRUCTIVE ALIGNMENT: MODERNISM AND OCEANIAN LITERATURE

Given the trajectory and content of the curricula, it is no surprise that Wendt calls upon the postcolonial and the modernist in his genealogical accounts of the rise of Oceanian writing. In *Nuanua* (1995), he notes that the conditions of Pacific modernity—and, we add here, the university syllabuses— placed Pacific writers in intimate relation with other anticolonial writers such as "V. S. Naipaul, George Lamming, Derek Walcott, Achebe, Wole Soyinka, Bessie Head, Ngugi wa Thiongo, and Kwei Armah."[22] Wendt holds the imperial project to account for its depredations upon Pacific ways of life and arraigns colonial missionaries, traders, and educators for their suppression of Pacific forms of artistic expression. Yet his introduction to the collection *Lali* (1980) draws attention to the unforeseen result of this history, arguing that the ruptures of colonialism brought about a new type of art and, importantly, a new type of artist, one "not bound by traditional styles and attitudes and conventions, who explores his craft individually, experiments freely and expresses his own values and ideas, his own mana unfettered by accepted conventions."[23] The new Pacific artists could weave together their own literary project of decoloniality, embracing multiple threads and literary ancestors in "the ongoing serpentine movement toward possibilities of other modes of being, thinking, knowing, sensing, and living" and learning, as Linda Tuhiwai Smith would later term it, to live and write a new "critical pedagogy of decolonization."[24]

The distinctly modernist tones of Wendt's declaration of individuality and decoloniality are bolstered by his direct invocation of modernism to describe the style, form, and temper through which the new artist gave voice to the postcolonial conditions of Oceanian modernity. Looking back at the Pacific literature of the 1960s to the 1980s, he finds that although its plots and ideologies often presented "the colonial and the indigenous as in irreconcilable opposition," the aesthetics and inflections of Pacific writing combined "political and social commitment, with a heavily tragic, pessimistic vision of our times" and express "the other features of modernism too: deliberate ambiguity and complexity, irony, unified structures and characterisation, the search for originality and uniqueness." To these attributes he adds Pacific writers' relationships to the ancestors with whom we began: "Eliot, Yeats, Pound, Forster, Auden, Woolf, Faulkner, Hemingway, Wright, Ellison, Lessing and others."[25]

The Rise of Pacific Literature shows that one of the reasons Pacific literature's family tree includes Eliot and Yeats, Hemingway and Wright, Achebe and Soyinka is because these authors were core components of writers' undergraduate degrees. Of course, many of the luminaries and leaders of the golden age of Oceanian writing were academic staff who designed the literature courses' syllabuses, particularly at USP, and we do not claim that they all read modernist works for the first time during this period. But by bringing modernist novels, poems, and plays together with local, oral, and other postcolonial texts, these writer-scholars presented modernism as a particularly suitable raw material for inscribing a decolonizing Oceania. Recognizing the curricular connections and reconnections in Oceanian writing—modernist and postcolonial, local and transnational—not only enables us to see the effects of course design on a literature but provides a grounding from which to perceive the ways that Oceanian writers drew on the resources at hand to create a corpus at once modern and responsive to Indigenous traditions.

It is important to specify, however, that notwithstanding Wendt's genealogical awareness, modernism as a discourse or aesthetic category receives few direct mentions in essays and critical works by Oceanians in these early years. Pacific writers were directly concerned with inscribing relationships with particular authors—Eliot or Wright, Yeats or Césaire—but less concerned with debating fields of study like modernism or postcolonialism. Arguably, this gave them rather more freedom in their bricolage: by thinking in authorial or textual rather than disciplinary terms, writers were able to disregard broader conventions and expectations, instead incorporating as they saw fit what was useful to a modern Pacific literature. As we show in more detail in chapter 1, if fragmentation is an archetypal modernist technique, in the Pacific this approach was extended so as to fragment modernism itself and reassemble its self-reflective shards. The tendency, during this period of Oceanian writing, to apply rather than classify becomes clearer when we compare it to later discussions around postmodernism. In 2001, the influential Indo-Fijian writer, educator, and critic Subramani complained that Pacific writers were "becoming cosy in Eurocentric discourses—living joyfully in contemporary postmodernism, for example," and signaled Wendt's *Ola* (1991) as particularly at fault.[26] He argued that postmodernism's aversion to meaning and its investment in play and pastiche have "little utility in postcolonial societies, where the real problem is the threat by transnational capital and its capacity to destroy all previously accepted values."[27] In "Decolonizing Pacific Studies: Indigenous Perspectives, Knowledge and Wisdom in Higher Education," Helu Thaman sees similar risks, although she concedes that postmodernism's flexible understandings of truth and knowledge enable a movement away from "the western-dominated, monocultural, assimilationist view of the world [she] had learned at [Auckland] university," freeing up a movement back toward Pacific ways of thinking and knowing.[28]

INTRODUCTION: PACIFIC UNIVERSITIES AND MODERNIST LITERATURE

Perhaps more significant than Subramani's and Helu Thaman's specific views on postmodernism is the fact that they felt the need to publish them at all. Around the turn of the millennium Pacific writers discussed postmodernism much more frequently than they had the category of modernism in the 1960s and 1970s, despite the far deeper exchange with modernist texts and tropes during the earlier time. By the 2000s, Pacific literature was sufficiently well established to allow for internal debates about genre and discipline, disagreements for which there was less oxygen in the early years' rush of literary growth and experiment. Postmodernism was unsettling, that is, because by then there was an articulated Pacific literature to unsettle. In the formative decades of the movement, the focus was on the creation of a literature from the local and international tools available, an approach that was fundamentally pragmatic. As we have suggested, this pragmatism found use in modernist authors' various commitments and associations, which appeared more as a viable toolbox than the fixed "Eurocentric discourse" Subramani finds in postmodernism. As Subramani's comments imply, this is partly because postmodernism was strongly associated with Western economic discourses of late capitalism and globalization, whereas individual modernist authors could be viewed as simultaneously established and countercultural, of the literary present and from a literary tradition whose works could serve as a springboard without weighing too heavily for new literary departures. Modernism, even when not named as such or considered in disciplinary terms, was appropriable and recyclable in ways that postmodernism, for all its celebrated commitment to cosmopolitan hybridities, apparently was not, at least without some soul-searching.[29]

A literature is always made up of complicated genealogies and diffuse ancestry. In *The Rise of Pacific Literature* we trace some of the literary influences from Europe, North America, and Africa woven into Pacific literature, influences that result from the interconnected and fundamentally modern global literary system in which Oceanian writers worked. We show that Pacific writers were working with and within a modernist archipelago, one that shifted with the varying currents of political and educational determination. In Papua New Guinea, writers found ready kinship with Black writers, both Indigenous African and diasporic Caribbean and African American, many of whom were included on the UPNG curriculum when Ulli Beier moved from Nigeria to Port Moresby. The educational and editorial lessons Beier learned in Africa came with him to the Pacific, forming causeways between these two regions. The colonial reshaping of Pacific relationality meant that, in Fiji's case, the nation became an Indigenous space as well as a site for the Indian diaspora, a doubling that brought Fiji's islands into the waters of global narratives around alienation and loss. As a result, writers forged land bridges between Suva and Kolkata—and Roseau and Fort-de-France. But not every archipelago is readily crossed, despite the shared experience of their inhabitants: Indigenous authors from North America, for example, were yet to feature on the literary curricula, and they received few mentions by Pacific writers. At this time in Oceania the representation of Tribal Nations was more likely to be informed by Hollywood westerns than by Indigenous-authored literary works.[30]

Our account in the chapters to come shows that modernism—its aesthetics and politics, its inscriptions and absences and evasions—is an integral part of Pacific literature's genetic code. Does this mean that we present this early movement of Pacific literature as an Oceanian modernism? Or as an Oceanian literature infused with modernism? We trust that this monograph will provide the reader clear evidence of the latter, but we hesitate on the former. The broadest contemporary definitions depict modernism as a field with soft borders and disciplinary characteristics that are always provisional, a category inevitably in the plural: modernisms, that is, where different texts, authors, and periods exist in shifting, partial relationship with one another.[31] Modernism, along these lines, is a loose marker that encourages a range of varied correspondences, bound simply by the idea of a response to modernity, itself an indeterminate and open category. On these grounds there is little doubt that the writing of this period in the Pacific is modernist—as is the African and Indian literature taught in these universities' lecture rooms; as are, indeed, significant elements of the oral forms.

Yet for all the local specificity, adaptability, and openness intrinsic to global modernism, it is difficult for the term and the discipline to cut loose fully from its roots in the literary and critical apparatuses of the Global North. We have elsewhere described modernism as a classificatory tool reshaped by every iteration, more a receptacle than a rule.[32] But as we have also pointed out, it does not require such a sharp shift in perspective to see it as a totalizing discourse that works to subsume other texts and traditions, and this is a particular risk in the Pacific, which has a painful and enduring history of classificatory imposition, where people still live with the effects of colonial disenfranchisement and where Oceanians must still fight for the validity and sovereignty of their own identity.[33] If, then, Pacific literature is a Pacific modernism, the stress must fall on the first term. It must be a *Pacific* modernism, with the adjective taking ownership of the noun, rather than being subordinated to the ever-proliferating catalogue of "*x* modernisms." If Oceanian writing is an Oceanian modernism, it is an indigenized modernism, which means an indigenizing and repossessing of modernism, not a modernizing or Westernizing of indigeneity—an intrusive and unnecessary act, given the cultural self-sufficiency of so many Indigenous modernities. In this way our monograph, while prioritizing critical voices on and from the Pacific, joins wider scholarship that brings together modernism and "Indigenous innovation, adaptation, agency and survival," such as that examined in the essays collected in Kirby Brown, Stephen Ross, and Alana Sayer's *The Routledge Handbook of North American Indigenous Modernisms*.[34] However, colonialization creates complex scenes of relationality, and Indo-Fijian authors' important contribution to the rise of Pacific literature interrupts a simple correlation between indigeneity and Oceania, an unsettling process we explore in the chapters to come, particularly in chapter 7.

In tracing the presence of global literary forms in Oceanian writing, we do not seek to wrest Pacific literature away from itself. We are interested, rather, in the raw materials that go into the construction of a literature and, to channel Teresia Teaiwa, the ancestors that writers choose in forming their works.[35] We see Pacific authors of this period making choices on the understanding that, as expressed by Lewis R. Gordon and Jane Anna Gordon, the master's tools, when used locally, when supplemented with local tools, when turned into new tools, when used to build and build and build again, create new "houses of thought. When enough houses are built, the hegemony of the master's house—in fact, *mastery itself*—will cease to maintain its imperial status."[36] To this we add the fact that the literature programs did much to undermine the very concept of literary tools as belonging to any given master, particularly a foreign one. As Pacific authors and poets writing about the Pacific, for the Pacific, the works they produced are, from our perspective, always and inevitably Pacific, no matter how they relate to or take inspiration from non-Pacific texts. A fale that makes use of concrete is still a fale, a vaka fashioned with fiberglass is still a vaka, an Oceanian poem that borrows from *The Waste Land* is still an

Oceanian poem. Is this Oceanian poem different from an Oceanian poem drawing only on local forms, embedded solely in local conventions—if such a poem is even conceivable under a present-continuous Pacific modernity? Perhaps. But in an age where writers sought to relate and relativize all conventions, neither the repurposing nor the rejection of the global is an absolute marker of quality or identity but only an aesthetic choice among choices.

This starting position does not seek to deny the constraints exerting pressure on the types of choices that are made. From the hard-power effects of primary and secondary education systems that imposed English and elevated European art forms to the soft-power results of English as a convenient lingua franca with a wide market, the landscape in which Pacific writers made creative decisions was shaped by the legacies of imperialism. But the choices made in a colonized terrain, from restricted options, are still choices whose agency deserves to be recognized and whose aesthetics deserve to be taken seriously. In this volume, we focus on unpacking, contextualizing, and interpreting the ways that Oceanian writers chose to engage with modernism, using it as a key through which to analyze the educational origins and investments of Pacific literature. Modernism is an important thread in their works but still one thread among many, and its ontological implications we consider most productive when unfixed. Other scholars have tracked many other connections in Pacific literature: Quito Swan reveals the affinities with a wider Black internationalism, and Michelle Keown is invested in its postcolonial condition. Elizabeth DeLoughrey compares its island associations with those of the Caribbean, and Sina Vaʻai stresses its Indigenous roots.[37] We follow its modernist courses.

So to the question of whether these thematic, tonal, stylistic, and political choices make Oceanian writing modernist we present no final answer, ultimately revealing our commitment to interpretative value rather than some notional disciplinary purity. Instead, if and when it is useful for the reader or scholar, Oceanian literature is a modernism. If and when it is useful, the African literature so important to Pacific literature is a modernism. If and when it is useful, modernism is far wider and more diffuse than its canonical parameters have historically allowed. Our insistence on the pliability of these generic markers demands a certain flexibility in the reader, not least because when we use the term "modernism" in this book it is rarely fixed to a single meaning or point of genesis: in the contexts where

INTRODUCTION: PACIFIC UNIVERSITIES AND MODERNIST LITERATURE

it seems unambiguously global it is haunted by its narrower origins, and in the instances when it seems conclusively canonical it is shadowed by its global reach. If, then, modernism is a thread or a stream or a course, each thread is formed by a plurality of fibers woven together, of rivulets running together, of seminars combining and overlapping. The modernism that influenced Pacific writers was as much African and African American as it was European, its alienated, exiled qualities arising as much from Black existentialism in Chicago or decolonization in Kampala as from the Parisian Left Bank or Jewish Prague.

These archipelagic pluralities and ancestral indeterminacies indicate the contingency of modernism as a category. For us, at this time, in this instance, a modernist framework illuminates certain political and aesthetic choices, enables the mapping of intertextual and transnational nodes, and facilitates the reconstruction of a literary movement's curricular network. But outlining the ways, and the import of the ways, that modernism runs through these two universities and the Oceanian literature they helped produce should not close off any other categories or conversations, and leaves the ontological question—hanging.

FOUNDING THE UNIVERSITIES, ESTABLISHING THE LITERARY SCENES

Before we examine in detail the impact of the two universities on the literary scene, it is useful to rehearse their foundation. UPNG and USP were established as the decolonization of the Pacific Islands was gaining ground. In 1962, Western Samoa had achieved independence from Aotearoa New Zealand, and gradually, across the Pacific, the flags of many of the old colonizing powers began to retreat.[38] But not disappear. Although Indigenous activism grew in Aotearoa New Zealand and Hawai'i, settler dominance remained, and other islands stayed bound in arrangements of "free" association.[39] For much of the region, however, the period from the 1960s to the 1980s was a time of liberation. It is in this decolonizing context that the universities were founded, albeit not without colonial resistance: following decades of underinvestment permitted by Australia's gradualist and paternalistic attitudes to education in Papua New Guinea, it took pressure from communities and the United Nations Visiting Mission to Nauru and New Guinea in 1962 to bring about a Commission on Higher Education in Papua and New Guinea.[40] In 1964, their report, known as the Currie Report, called for a tertiary system that would lead the country into a sovereign future, while not "turn[ing] its back completely on the immemorial cultural traditions of the people."[41] It maintained that

> a vigorous programme of education at all levels can put into the hands and heads of Papuans and New Guineans the means whereby they may themselves choose and shape their own social and political future, but in the circumstances of Papua and New Guinea today, H. G. Wells' dictum that "Civilisation is a race between education and catastrophe" calls an urgent truth; and only the most strenuous, imaginative, and liberal efforts to advance the education of the people will meet the need.[42]

Many of the issues raised by the report would continue to inspire debate by students, faculty, and visiting scholars throughout the first decades of the university. Mirroring the deliberations taking place in universities across the decolonizing nations of Africa, groups at UPNG met to question the purpose of a university—was it to provide an educated workforce as the government envisioned it or to educate for the fulfillment of the individual? How could an educated, typically urban elite remain in touch with those in the villages? Was education to be linked to international standards and trends or remain focused on local values and needs? What was the place of art and literature in a developing nation? The report attempted to tread a careful path between education for the greater good and education for the individual, arguing that higher education is "not only an essential investment for economic growth and political competence; if designed and carried out with imagination and sympathy, it is also an essential investment for the enrichment of social and personal life."[43] It laid an important foundation for the kind of university that UPNG would become, and while its frequent calls for imagination and boldness were undermined by its Eurocentric assumptions—it dismisses Tok Pisin as a university language, for example, considering it to lack range and precision—the Currie Report was effective.[44] Overcoming delays and prevarications, in 1966 the University of Papua New Guinea held its first classes in Port Moresby, attended by forty-two men and six women.[45]

In 1965, as UPNG was being founded, the governments of the United Kingdom and New Zealand established the Higher Education Mission to the South Pacific, commissioned to "investigate the future higher education requirements of the South Pacific area (other than Papua-New Guinea)."[46] The resulting Morris Report, submitted in 1966, recommended the instituting of a regional university, based in Fiji but mandated to serve the English-speaking Pacific Islands and to "carry university studies to towns and villages through the Region."[47] UPNG had to grapple with the extensive range of languages and cultures in Papua New Guinea, but the USP project was still more ambitious in its geographical and administrative scope. As at UPNG, students of the University of the South Pacific would come from communities restricted by limited, often subsistence economies where levels of secondary education were generally low, but USP faced the additional challenge of uniting prospective member countries thousands of miles apart and not always willing to sacrifice national interest for regional solidarity.[48] Nevertheless, with recurrent expenditure to be covered initially by the British and Fijian colonial governments, the project went ahead.[49]

Established under British royal charter at the former New Zealand airbase in Suva, Fiji, the University of the South Pacific accepted its first students to its preliminary program in 1968, with much of the teaching conducted by New Zealand secondary school teachers already in the country. The first students came to Suva from other parts of Fiji, American Samoa, Western Samoa, British Solomon Islands Protectorate, Cook Islands, Gilbert and Ellice Islands (Kiribati and Tuvalu), New Hebrides (Vanuatu), Niue, Tokelau Islands, Tonga, and United States Trust Territory (which included the Marshall Islands, Federated States of Micronesia, and Palau).[50] From 1971, the university began to establish its extension services, with Diploma of Education courses running by distance and new centers opening in Honiara (Solomon Islands), Tarawa (Kiribati), and Nukuʻalofa (Tonga).[51]

In their early days, both universities struggled with the difficulty of reconciling the region's needs for a skilled workforce with the desire to produce intellectuals who could manage political, economic, and educational infrastructures in the islands. Students themselves carried the anxieties born of colonial humiliations: Ken Inglis, the second vice-chancellor of UPNG, recalls that students there struggled to allay their concerns about patronizingly lower standards and "were suspicious about the books they were given. . . . Ernest Hemingway's *The Old Man and the Sea* seemed surprisingly easy to read. Was this the proper version, or one broken down for the likes of them?"[52] They might have been mistaken about the nature of Hemingway's prose—and later in this book we will see the Fijian author Vanessa Griffen remodeling his novella to great effect—but students' concerns about colonial impositions were well founded. During this period, a large percentage of the academic staff were expatriate, and student writing frequently engaged with concerns about cultural loss and the dominance of educational policies and practices of the Global North. In Russell Soaba's "The Victims" (1972), published in *Kovave*, the village women weep for students who return to their villages swollen by foreign knowledge.[53] They lament the profound changes that education causes and on the students' return from university publicly mourn the death of the people they had been.

USP was part of the New Zealand Scheme of Cooperation, which allowed teachers from Aotearoa New Zealand to work and be paid at home salary rates—considerably higher than the salary for local staff—while retaining NZ superannuation benefits. *UNISPAC*, USP's student magazine, condemned the whole operation as a racket: "New Zealanders do the scheming and we do the co-operating."[54] Even within the literature programs the faculty could vary widely in their support for projects of decolonization and literary expression. As we detail in chapter 5, Ken Arvidson, a New Zealander at USP, taught, encouraged, and published on Pacific literature, while Frank Brosnahan, his head of school, remained adamant that creative writing was a free-time luxury with no part in a tertiary institution. Beier, on the other hand, was ceaseless in his efforts to foster Niuginian creativity at UPNG and strongly invested in Indigenous sovereignty, but as we shall see in chapter 3, he also wrote himself surreptitiously into Pacific literary history with a series of Indigenous impersonations. In 1978, one Alan (Albert?) Wendt complained in a poem for the student magazine that USP "still smell[ed] of the colonial stench."[55] There were foreign staff members at both universities who tried to wash that odor from themselves and the curriculum, but they were not always in the majority and had mixed levels of success.

Established by colonial governments, often dominated by foreign staff, and frequently rejecting any formal commitment to the arts, the universities had many flaws and complicities. Yet they also provided a space for engagement with the wider political questions of the region: decolonization,

INTRODUCTION: PACIFIC UNIVERSITIES AND MODERNIST LITERATURE

Western interference and aid, regional unity, traditional culture, changing social structures, and urbanization. They were spaces of learning, unlearning, relearning, resistance, and optimism, facilitating activist movements and feminist groups, and as the number of university graduates from the Pacific increased dramatically, they brought significant and lasting change.[56] Of course, no history tells all sides in equal detail, and in narrating the literary history of this period through two major educational institutions and their teaching archives, we do not discuss the smaller institutions—religious and government-sponsored initiatives, private groups, teachers' colleges, and agricultural colleges—that dotted the Pacific.[57] Many of these contributed to the rise of the new literature, feeding other forums for literary production. In PNG alone, Goroka Teachers College (established 1967) produced creative writers and playwrights, and the Summer Institute of Linguistics (1956), the Papua New Guinean Literature Bureau (1968), the Kristen Pres (1969), Glen Bays's creative writing workshops (1970), and the Christian Writers Association of Melanesia (1972) all provided creative outlets. The Literature Bureau was underfunded and suffered from political meddling, but it established *Papua New Guinea Writing* in 1970 and took over the national literature competitions that Roger Boschman had started in 1968.[58] The national literature competitions were joined by the Waigani Writing Competition in 1969, the Kristen Pres competitions from 1970 to 1973, literary sections in the Port Moresby Eistedfodd in 1970, and, less competitively, a Writers' Day from 1972.[59] Papua New Guinean literature would not exist in its present form without UPNG, but it was not the only site of literary activity.

Nor were UPNG and USP the only universities in the region. The University of Hawai'i was founded in 1907, becoming a university in 1920; the University of Guam, established in 1952, became a university in 1968; and there were many universities in Aotearoa New Zealand and Australia. They had magazines and literary scenes, and Pasifika students and graduates of these institutions played an important role in the Oceanian literary renaissance—indeed, many of the writer-scholars we introduce in *The Rise of Pacific Literature* began their studies there, including Wendt, Helu Thaman, John Kasaipwalova, and Pio Manoa. Joseph Waleanisia argues that it was the contributions to local newspapers from the first generation of Solomon Islanders with overseas tertiary educations that precipitated the development of a local literary scene in the early 1970s, reminding us that

INTRODUCTION: PACIFIC UNIVERSITIES AND MODERNIST LITERATURE

UPNG and USP were not the only drivers of literary activity, even for their member countries.[60] Nevertheless, before UPNG and USP were established, the number of Pacific Island graduates outside of Aotearoa New Zealand and Hawai'i was extremely low.[61] Even in Hawai'i, Kānaka Maoli were underrepresented in university enrollments: by the late 1960s, the student body exceeded 16,000, but Indigenous student numbers were less than 1 percent.[62] For Haunani-Kay Trask, writing about her experiences in the 1980s, the university was simply a "bastion of white power."[63] In contrast, UPNG and USP—for all their limitations—were founded purposely to accompany and facilitate independence, and they altered the region greatly, creating large numbers of Pacific graduates whose journeys through tertiary qualification no longer necessarily required travel outside of the Pacific, or even to the larger, settler-colonial Pacific universities, but could remain closer to home.

That noted, we must not give the impression that the member countries of UPNG and USP, and the writing they produced, represented all the Pacific. French Polynesia receives little attention in our account, as do the countries of Micronesia beyond Kiribati, a USP member. Although Thomas H. Hamilton, the haole president of the University of Hawai'i, was on the governing board of USP, there were few Kānaka Maoli staff or students at USP or UPNG, and since we approach the literature through these institutions, these Pacific peoples remain underrepresented.[64] At the same time, there were Indigenous literary scenes already beginning to thrive in Hawai'i, Australia, and Aotearoa New Zealand, and even when we narrow the lens to view only literary productions associated with UPNG and USP, Indigenous output remains significant. Texts by Māori and Australian Aboriginal and Torres Strait Islander peoples featured on UPNG's oral literature course and on the USP curriculum. Alistair Te Ariki Campbell and Kāterina Mataira attended USP's 1974 Regional Creative Writing Workshop, and Hone Tuwhare, Patricia Grace, and Oodgeroo Noonuccal (Kath Walker) attended the Papua New Guinea Writers Conference in 1976. Tuwhare published in *Kovave*; the Mana project would go on to publish special issues with contributions from many of the key figures from Aotearoa New Zealand, Australia, French Polynesia, and Hawai'i; and these writers' works were reviewed and advertised in UPNG and USP publications.

The partiality of earlier definitions of Pacific Island literature—many of which, it must be said, came from writers and critics associated with the

INTRODUCTION: PACIFIC UNIVERSITIES AND MODERNIST LITERATURE

University of the South Pacific—is the topic of ongoing critical debate, and there is clearly a bigger story to be told about the interrelationship between UPNG, USP, and other institutions in the region, just as there is a bigger story to be told about the multiple, interconnected literatures arising in this remarkably fertile period. *The Rise of Pacific Literature* traces a specific set of routes and leaves many stories untold, but we believe that our framework—premised on the conception of a literature complexly mediated and endlessly intertwined—is one that can be scaled up to include other, larger conceptions of the region.

PEDAGOGIC POLITICS: THE RISE OF PACIFIC LITERATURE

The establishment of the new Pacific universities brought together people, facilities, and anticolonial, emancipatory politics, as well as the energy and momentum to create a collective literary movement. This groundswell led to an exceptional range of creative output, including novels, short stories, poetry collections, literary journals, theatrical works, manifestoes, and critical essays, as university students and staff drew schoolteachers, civil servants, doctors, and, in the villages, farmers and fishers into the writing scene. This has been called the "first wave" of Pacific writing, but while the size of the movement was unprecedented, it was far from the first time that Pacific communities had used the technologies of the printed page.[65] Oral histories of the region go back to the populating of the islands, and Pacific peoples had established complex oratorical and visual forms long before the arrival of the Europeans, but in the nineteenth century, as colonial rule was consolidated and missionaries, traders, and settlers increased in numbers, Pacific Islanders began to write. They transcribed oral narratives; translated religious writing, novels, and other texts into Pacific languages; and recorded accounts of conversion and Indigenous missionary activity, as with Joel Bulu's *The Autobiography of a Native Minister in the South Seas* (1871) and Clement Murau's *Story of a Melanesian Deacon* (1894).

Revealing striking inventiveness in new forms, these early Pacific Island texts provided an important foundation for later creative output. Marjorie Tuainekore Crocombe credits precolonial writing by Indigenous missionaries as a major inspiration in her founding of the Mana project, an endeavor we discuss at length in chapter 6.[66] The autobiographical tradition was maintained across the twentieth century, with key texts including

INTRODUCTION: PACIFIC UNIVERSITIES AND MODERNIST LITERATURE

Ligeremaluoga (Hosea Linge)'s *An Account of the Life of Ligeremaluoga* (1932) and R. T. Kohere's *The Autobiography of a Maori* (1951). Florence "Johnny" Frisbie's *Miss Ulysses from Puka-Puka* (1948) adapted the form into creative nonfiction. Tom and Lydia Davis's *Makutu* (1960) evinces further experimentation, responding to and subverting the long tradition of the imperial medical memoir, a genre they first took up with their 1954 book *Doctor to the Islands*. Longer works were joined by smaller pieces in administration, school, and church magazines, such as *The Papuan Villager* or *O le Sulu Samoa*, with the web of Pacific Island writing expanding into the countries where children and teenagers were sent for boarding school.[67] Wendt, for example, began his sixty-year writing career as a contributor to *The Taranakian*, the student magazine of New Plymouth Boys High School in Aotearoa New Zealand, and published further writing in *Farrago: Annual Magazine of the Ardmore Teachers' College Students' Association* and *Experiment*, Victoria University of Wellington's literary magazine.

But with the founding of UPNG and USP we see the rise of a new Pacific literature, one strengthened by a shared, self-conscious reflection on what it meant to write in and for the decolonizing Pacific. Through lecture rooms, workshops, public readings, and the discursive potential of the printed page, Oceanian writers taught themselves and one another, drawing together local and foreign sources to express the complexities of Pacific modernity. Unsurprisingly, then, the works of this period, like the content of so many modernist canons across the world, were suffused with pedagogical purpose and educational content. As we discuss in more detail in chapter 1, the period's principal manifesto, Wendt's "Towards a New Oceania" (1976), had its first incarnation as a report on the Regional Creative Writing Workshop held at USP in 1974 and then as a paper presented at "Education in Melanesia," UPNG's eighth Waigani Seminar.[68] Novels, short stories, poems, and plays analyze the issue of education from every angle, to the extent that Paul Sharrad finds that "one of the most prevalent images of indigenous Pacific writing is the schoolroom."[69] Ruperake Petaia's much-anthologized poem "Kidnapped" likens the classroom experience to abduction and indoctrination;[70] Vincent Eri's pioneering bildungsroman *The Crocodile* (1970) takes the protagonist from his village schooldays to the theater of the Pacific War; Soaba's *Wanpis* (1977), which we analyze in detail in chapter 4, is an existentialist campus novel; and Wendt's debut novel *Sons for the Return Home*

INTRODUCTION: PACIFIC UNIVERSITIES AND MODERNIST LITERATURE

(1973) depicts a university student straining toward intellectual and cultural independence.

Classrooms and lecture halls were backdrops against which the complex questions of identity in colonized spaces could be explored. Many of the most prominent Pacific writers had some European ancestry, others had spent substantial periods of their lives being educated abroad, and still others were scattered across the Pacific as a result of their ancestors' entrapment in blackbirding and indenture: all were concerned with resolving their positions as highly educated members of communities scarred by colonialism. Aesthetic and rhetorical choices were influenced by writers' differing perceptions of their lineage within Oceania and within Pacific discourses of decolonization and indigeneity. This process was particularly fraught for Indo-Fijians, who, restricted in the outright ownership of land in Fiji, sought security through the shifting sands of schooling and commerce. In "Marigolds," which won the South Pacific Association of Commonwealth Literature and Language Studies' short fiction competition in 1978, Subramani depicts an aging teacher's terrible realization that neither education, employment, family, nor tenancy are guarantors of Indo-Fijian belonging in the decolonized state. The politics of the period were inescapable, and they colored the most innocuous-seeming texts, from the recounting of traditional stories to the crafting of simple tales of fishing or village life. A significant portion of the writing explored internal power structures, from village hierarchies to gender hegemonies to Indigenous paramountcy. "Marigolds," which draws the alienated modernist flâneur into a gothic quest, exemplifies the internal struggles disrupting the kinship of this period, which, as we show in the chapters to come, were frequently articulated through the absurdist, existential, and gothic elements of modernist style and Pacific life.

The same preoccupation with teaching, learning, and identity pervades the region's newly founded literary journals. In the "Mana" pages of *Pacific Islands Monthly*, the Niuginian writer Venantius Tapin and iKiribati poet Maunaa Itaia lament the effects of colonial and foreign schooling on families, Vili Vete explores an instance of traditional community ties in Tonga forestalling the new freedoms afforded by education, and Rejieli Racule's "The Gift" triangulates a young Fijian girl, her love for math classes, and her grandmother's lessons on preparing "perfectly geometrical" masi.[71] Beyond the theme of the particular texts they published, the purpose of the magazines was also presented in terms of instruction and direction. *Faikava*, which was funded by and based at the USP center at Nukuʻalofa, found its genesis in the desire to teach Tongans that new literary traditions could be created by them and for them. To this end it aimed to instill in "artists and audience alike a conscious and analytical awareness of the national literary tradition," as well as of "contemporary writing here and elsewhere, [and] of the many possibilities inherent in literature."[72] Similarly, the regional journal *Mana*, whose links to USP we explain in chapter 6, sought to nurture and promote the untapped talent that "formal education [had] tended to stultify."[73] The first editorial of *Kovave* presents itself as "a workshop magazine" whose "purpose is to encourage young Papuans and New Guineans to write," and Fjii's *Sinnet*, copyrighted to USP's extension services, expressed much the same desire to provide a space in which new writers could grow.[74]

These literary magazines, particularly the "Mana" pages and the independent *Mana* journal, would become vital pedagogic tools, circulating around the Pacific like extensions of USP's satellite and correspondence courses.[75] From 1974 they were also added to the USP literature curriculum, facilitating not only a growth in the creative writing coming from the university but furthering the development of regional narrative styles and discourses. They were joined by the teachable anthologies and schoolbooks that Pacific writers produced. Wendt edited the Some Modern Poets series (1974–1975); Bernard Gadd produced *Pacific Voices* (1977); Francis Mangubhai, *Roots/Waka/*जड़ (1977); Vijay Mishra, *Waves* (1979); and Wendt, *Lali* (1980), which opened Pacific literature to new and wider audiences in and outside of the Pacific and did much to redress the absences in school curricula. The early decades of the universities may not have seen the birth of Oceanian writing, but their staff and students were instrumental in its triumphant, momentous rise.

Steven Winduo coined the phrase "writer-scholars" to refer to Pacific authors engaged in unwriting old colonial narratives, interweaving oral histories and stories, and repurposing the styles of modern novels.[76] The phrase has become a popular descriptor of Pacific writers' authorship of critical and creative pieces, as well as their genre-disrupting tendency to produce scholarship that incorporates elements of the personal essay and creative self-expression. The "scholar" dimension of the "writer-scholar" label signals, if not an inevitable university affiliation, then an approach to

INTRODUCTION: PACIFIC UNIVERSITIES AND MODERNIST LITERATURE

the literary project that holds close the reflexivity, research, and publishing agenda we often associate with scholarship. Embedded in the idea of the scholar is the concept of learning and teaching, and as we will show, the Pacific writer-scholar was also a writer-educator-learner, embodying a creative scholarship in and of the classroom. In *The Rise of Pacific Literature* we extend Winduo's insight to show just how central the scholar/educator dimension is to the history of Oceanian writing.

This centrality is further established when we study the résumés of Oceanian writers. Contemporary commentators worried that political careers would take writers away from their creative practice, but the majority of Pacific writers ended up in educational positions.[77] This should not surprise us—the major figures in Pacific literature during this period were those for whom the education system, for all its failings, worked sufficiently well to give them the skills and the passion to change it. Moved by the desire to provide Pacific students with an education grounded in Pacific perspectives, Wendt became head teacher of Samoa College, pro-vice-chancellor of the University of the South Pacific, and the first Samoan professor of English at Auckland University. Subramani has had a long career as an academic and retired as a professor at the University of Fiji. Pio Manoa, Jo Nacola, and Raymond Pillai began their academic careers at USP's School of Education, as did Satendra Nandan, now emeritus professor at the University of Canberra. Epeli Hauʻofa was a senior tutor in anthropology at UPNG in the late 1960s and became head of the sociology department and founder of the Oceania Centre for Arts at USP, while Helu Thaman became the UNESCO Chair in Teacher Education and Culture, also holding various roles at USP, including director of the Institute of Education and chair in Pacific Education and Culture. Vanessa Griffen, who had undergraduate study at USP and graduate study at UPNG, taught at USP, and Marjorie Tuainekore Crocombe, who also lectured at the University of Auckland, was a vital part of USP's Extension Service, along with Wendt and Mostyn Habu of the Solomon Islands. John Waiko, the first Papua New Guinean to earn a PhD, became a professor of history at UPNG. Soaba and Kumalau Tawali both lectured in literature at UPNG, and Rabbie Namaliu and Bernard Narokobi lectured at UPNG's political science and law programs, respectively. Vincent Eri was a teacher and later became PNG's director of education. John Saunana taught in schools as well as UPNG and later became minister of education and training in the Solomon Islands. In Aoteaora

New Zealand, Witi Ihimaera became a professor and distinguished creative fellow in Māori literature at the University of Auckland, Patricia Grace worked as a teacher in South Auckland, and the Cook Islander Makiuti Tongia lectured at Victoria University of Wellington.

Writer-scholars, then, with the emphasis on "scholar." Yet the works of this period were not concerned only with education in its institutional sense but, more urgently, with the drive to teach Pacific peoples how to read and write differently, how to interpret afresh, and how to see themselves anew. Shifting our perspective to recognize that the politics of the period is a pedagogic politics means recognizing that the literature and the literary spaces of the time were not simply representative of Pacific lives or formative of a resurging Oceanian independence but invested in unlearning—through literature—colonially imposed insecurities and relearning individual and community self-determination. By fostering Pacific voices in workshops, by setting them in classes, and by seeing them into print, editors and educators demonstrated how readers could select their literary ancestors, recall their own stories, and recount them for the generations to come.

NAVIGATION: CHARTING THE COURSES

In the following chapters we propose a new history of the rise of Pacific literature, and to this end we employ a broadly chronological structure to trace the development of the movement. At UPNG, we present a national university producing a national literature, albeit one with an immense array of cultural and aesthetic viewpoints, reflecting Papua New Guinea's position as the most linguistically diverse country on the planet. At the slightly younger USP—a multinational institution established to serve a whole region—we find a literary project conceived in regional terms, drawing national scenes, including that of PNG, towards the pan-Pacificism later celebrated in Hauʻofa's famous vision of Oceania as a "sea of islands."

Chapter 1, "Modernism, Pedagogy, and Pacific Writer-Scholars," considers the impacts of modernism's didactic drive and, by tracing the changing reception of modernist texts and the shifting understanding of modernism as a category, assesses what modernism brought to Pacific lecture rooms of the 1960s and 1970s: how it could be presented as a tool for decolonization, what it taught about the nature of learning and teaching, and why its resistance to rote learning and ready assimilation might have appealed to Pacific writers. We then assess the ways in which Pacific educators such as Konai Helu Thaman and Albert Wendt turned the interrogative stance encouraged by a modernist-informed pedagogy back against colonial education systems. Already beginning to construct the alternative learning models now known as Indigenous pedagogies—models closer to traditional ways of learning, though respondent to Pacific modernities—we find these writer-scholars at work on a parallel literary project, integrating Indigenous aesthetic modes such as the Samoan fāgogo and Tongan heliaki with modernist forms in the creation of a contemporary Oceanian literature.

Chapter 2, "Decolonizing the Literature Program, Generating the Niuginian Literary Scene," considers the impact of a progressive undergraduate literature program, looking at the reception and retooling of modernist writers from Franz Kafka to Ferdinand Oyono in the nascent PNG literary scene. The radical UPNG degree structure first positioned oral forms as modes to articulate the present and went on to disrupt conventional models of literary progress, with courses accessing Europe from Africa rather than Africa after Europe. By drawing on writings from this period at UPNG, with an emphasis on those published in the literary magazine *Kovave* and written by Beier's students, we argue that the program structure created a literary landscape in which Niuginian writers were free to absorb and rework elements of orality, contemporary African works, and modernist techniques with fewer anxieties of colonial influence. This chapter establishes one of *The Rise of Pacific Literature*'s main premises: decolonizing the curriculum liberated Pacific literature.

In chapter 3, "Traveling Editors and Indigenous Masks: The Teachings of Ulli Beier," we balance the political progressiveness of the UPNG curriculum against the complicated figure of one of the men who designed it: Ulli Beier. Beier was a tireless advocate for emerging literary traditions in Africa and the Pacific. However, his service to PNG literature is complicated by the fact that as teacher, magazine editor, and anthologist Beier was able to mold the literary scene according to his preferences. More egregiously, in both Nigeria and Papua New Guinea Beier wrote, published, and staged texts under Indigenous pseudonyms. His surreptitious introduction of a masked European voice into Indigenous literary traditions distorts literary histories and contaminates pedagogic spaces. This chapter unpacks the complex story of men like Beier, whose involvement in the decolonizing moment gave them a power that, for all its seeming ethical rectitude, was underpinned by the white authority that colonialism had created.

Moving from the teacher back to the students, chapter 4, "Black Power and Pacific Existentialism: John Kasaipwalova and Russell Soaba," offers a focused reading of these two influential Niuginian writers. In 1971, Kasaipwalova and Soaba took Beier's creative writing class, which led to Kasaipwalova's long poem *Reluctant Flame* and Soaba's campus novel *Wanpis*. Unmistakably linked to the content and ideologies of UPNG's literature curriculum, particularly modernist writings from Europe, America, and Africa, both texts draw on the wider learnings resulting from campus life. *Reluctant Flame* draws inspiration from Black internationalism négritude, and the UPNG Black Power movement, while *Wanpis* brings Camus and Ralph Ellison to Port Moresby, in part as a direct reply to Kasaipwalova's *Reluctant Flame* and in part, we suggest, as a riposte to Beier. In their very different ways, Kasaipwalova and Soaba wrest Niuginian writing from institutional grasps to redefine what an anticolonial national literature could be.

From the progressive curriculum and literary flourishing of UPNG, in chapter 5—"Preliminaries and Prologues: A National Scene in a Regional University"—we turn to the newly opened University of the South Pacific, where young staff and students had to fight for the place of literature in their studies. We show that in these early days, despite the university's multinational mandate, the nascent creative commitments of the student body were led by Fijians, who drew on the small set of modernist texts—by Yeats and Eliot, Steinbeck and Hemingway—that they encountered in their preliminary courses and the fledgling modernist modules gradually appearing in the undergraduate curriculum. Tracing the adaptations and allusiveness of the Indo-Fijian Anirudh Singh, the part-European Vanessa Griffen, and the Indigenous student Seri, with their teacher Satendra Nandan modeling from the front of the class and on the printed page, we detail the precision with which these budding writers turned stylistic and thematic lessons from a limited range of modernist authors toward the complex realities of Fijian modernity at the moment of independence.

In chapter 6, "Mana on Campus: New Forms in Pacific Poetry and Prose," we move from the nation to the broader Pacific region, linking a newly self-aware Oceanian literature to key developments within and around the regional university: the launch of the USP-affiliated publication *Mana*, the establishment of a regionally representative and creatively inclined teaching faculty, and a series of major regional writers' workshops held on campus. Encouraged by profound changes to the literature program, students from across the region followed key figures such as Crocombe, Subramani, and Wendt into the golden age of Pacific literary creativity. Analyzing a wide cross-section of stories and poems, we show that their experiments with modernist authors and archetypes were galvanized by a renewed attention to both the oral histories and myths and legends circulating across the islands and the national literary scenes recently established in Papua New Guinea and Fiji. What emerges is a triumphant regional literature at once unquestionably of the Pacific and complexly mediated, always in conversation with the modernist courses running through the literature of the decolonizing world.

Our account of the rise of Pacific literature ends with chapter 7, "Subramani's Sugarcane Gothic: Haunting the Regional Dream." We coin the phrase "sugarcane gothic" to name the genre Subramani devises, one whose unique expressions of the lasting trauma caused by indenture in Fiji draw on a network of gothic works extending from the American South to the Caribbean and on global modernist works of estrangement and colonial fracture. Subramani's modernist gothic sensibility reflects the ambiguous place of Indo-Fijians within a new, proudly Oceanian literature premised on a rhetoric of Indigenous ownership and belonging. In important respects excluded from this discourse, we find Subramani developing an unsettling, unhomely narrative form, figured here as a poetics of the unwanted guest. His allusive, fragmentary style, clearly informed by the modernist texts he taught at the university, oblige the reader to proceed provisionally, reenacting the Indo-Fijian relationship with the regional movement. At this momentous point in the development of Oceanian literature and literary studies in the Pacific, we take Subramani's sugarcane gothic as an ominous counterpoint to the major chord of artistic triumph rightly still celebrated today. And as the short coda to the book shows, new generations of Pacific writers have continued to modulate both chord and counterpoint to the strains of the twenty-first century.

Just as we suggest that modernism flows in currents and tides through these universities and this literature, so *The Rise of Pacific Literature* is structured to show patterns swelling and repeating between the two institutions and their separate but interacting scenes. Chapters 2 and 5 lay out the curricular conditions of the two universities, comparing the ways in which the distinct framings of modernism inflect how it appears in their literatures. Chapters 3 and 6 contrast the impact of a significant author-editor-educator in each of these settings: Ulli Beier, a male expatriate at UPNG, and Marjorie Tuainekore Crocombe, an Indigenous woman at USP. Chapters 4 and 7 reconsider the legacies of important authors within the two scenes—John Kasaipwalova and Russell Soaba at UPNG, Subramani at USP—and find a new complexity in their engagement with a modernism channeled through other decolonizing world literatures as well as a critical disruption of the scenes they helped create. Enabling a more nuanced reading than a straight chronology might imply, this structure is intended both to illustrate the conceptual claims we make about modernism in Oceania and to offer new framings of canonical Pacific texts. First, however, we revisit European modernism in the context of education and argue for a pedagogical drive that provoked decolonizing Pacific writer-scholars to define a literature and a pedagogy of their own.

Chapter One

MODERNISM, PEDAGOGY, AND PACIFIC WRITER-SCHOLARS

Oceanian literary movements of the 1960s and 1970s are inextricable from Pacific educational contexts, imperial and anticolonial, which link this literature to comparable projects across the decolonizing world. Yet perhaps less predictably, the educational link also renders them part of a general modernist interest in pedagogy. So many of the writers we associate with modernism in Europe and North America were teachers and lecturers: E. M. Forster taught at King's College, Cambridge, and the Working Men's College. Aldous Huxley's students at Eton included George Orwell, and W. H. Auden taught at the Downs in England and Larchfield in Scotland, where he was "paid to teach English to the sons of Scotsmen— / Poor little buggers."[1] D. H. Lawrence taught in a primary school in Croydon, and Dorothy Richardson was a middle-school teacher in north London and a language assistant in Germany. T. S. Eliot spent time as a University of London extension lecturer in Ilkley, Sydenham, and Southall, where he presented his students with a version of literary history centered on the labor of writing: these classes would lead to *The Sacred Wood*.[2]

Across the Atlantic, Thornton Wilder taught for most of his life, starting as a French teacher in New Jersey in 1921; Marianne Moore taught business subjects at the Carlisle Indian Industrial School; Langston Hughes taught at Atlanta College and the Chicago Laboratory School; and Zora

Neale Hurston taught at Florida Normal College and North Carolina College for Negroes, having also tried to establish a drama school based on "pure Negro expression" in the early 1930s.[3] The Irish expatriates Samuel Beckett and James Joyce both took stints at the top of the classroom. Beckett was a lecteur d'anglais at the École Normale in the late 1920s and a lecturer in French at Trinity College Dublin for a brief period in the early 1930s. Joyce's depiction of Stephen Dedalus as a reluctant schoolteacher in *Ulysses* reflects the author's early efforts in Dublin, and Joyce continued to teach until well into the composition of the novel, including at the Berlitz language school in Trieste, where he taught "the sons of bitches broken English."[4] Virginia Woolf taught history, English composition, and poetry appreciation at Morley College, and her own educational background infused her writing. As Beth Daugherty writes, "Virginia Stephen's struggle to educate herself shaped Virginia Woolf into an essayist who teaches," with the "essay becom[ing] a classroom" in which readers are taught how to read.[5] Much work has been done on the institutions underwriting modernism, from the little magazine and the publishing market to individual and societal patronage.[6] Only recently have scholars begun to pay serious attention to education as another of these foundational institutions.[7] Yet the modernist drive to make it new is not simply a creative impulse but a pedagogic one, as the injunction urged writers to learn new ways to write, readers new ways to read, and people new ways to live.

Often educators in formal settings, European and North American modernist writers were, like their counterparts in the Pacific, frequently critical of the existing educational apparatus. Much of Lawrence's writing on education critiques a system focused on regulation, standardization, and control: in *The Rainbow*, school is presented as a factory where teachers have "the graceless task of compelling many children into one disciplined, mechanical set" and then "reducing the whole set to an automatic state of obedience and attention."[8] Hughes argued that even Black colleges in America "produce[d] spineless Uncle Toms, uniformed and full of mental and moral evasions."[9] In *A Room of One's Own* and *Three Guineas*, Woolf outlines her suspicion that British education indoctrinates men and women into a masculinist, militaristic society, which is also a recurring theme in Joyce's depiction of colonially modeled schools in *Portrait* and *Ulysses*. Auden's years of teaching led to his apprehension that education entrenched rather than eroded social divisions. Describing the school system as a "dope to allay irritation" with one's social position, Auden argued ironically that if a student "is poor . . . better give him something to think about lest he sense the absurd inadequacy of the operations he is made to do, and start to smash. Better teach him enough to read the *News of the World*."[10] Similarly, education was for Wyndham Lewis mere ideological programming, the creation of a state-approved character rather than a freethinking mind. As such, Lewis argued, democracy is a farce because "education and suggestion, the imposition of the will of the ruler through the press and other publicity channels," mean that there is no such thing as the vote of a free citizen.[11]

It is in the spirit of such critiques that Woolf called for a new university, one that would not teach "the arts of dominating other people; not the arts of ruling, of killing, of acquiring land and capital."[12] Instead, she envisaged "an experimental college, an adventurous college," built not of "carved stone and stained glass, but of some cheap, easily combustible material which does not hoard dust and perpetuate traditions."[13] Venerable institutions calcified by long-standing traditions must be replaced by perishable academies dedicated to each generation's new ideas of liberty and innovation: "let the pictures and the books be new and always changing."[14] It was along similar lines that Ezra Pound attempted to form a College of the Arts in London, which would be "a centre of intelligent and intellectual activity, rather than a cramming factory where certain data are pushed into the student regardless of his abilities or predilections."[15]

Such aspirations may sound utopian, but they are not altogether inconsistent with the educational reforms attempted across the decolonizing world, reforms that in a direct sense had roots in the Pacific Islands. In the late 1940s, Clarence Beeby, the former New Zealand director of education and then assistant director-general of UNESCO, spearheaded a global education program based on his experience as an advisor in Western Samoa.[16] In New Zealand educational history, Beeby is noted for his championing of education as a right for all students, not just the privileged or even the most academically gifted, and for a protoconstructionist teaching philosophy—consistent with the vision of the modernists—in which creative thinking was encouraged over the repetition-based learning he had sought to "eradicate in New Zealand."[17] In Samoa, however, Beeby had advocated for exactly the opposite. Claiming it was intended as a temporary measure, he endorsed the rote learning systems introduced by earlier superintendents of education and devised a program intended to build up "an educated elite to staff the civil service, the professions and the higher ranks of industry and the defence services," using scholarships to send a select few to Aotearoa New Zealand under scholarship.[18]

Ostensibly geared toward independence, Beeby's system imposed deeply Eurocentric educational principles. His philosophy, retrospectively formalized in his 1966 book *The Quality of Education in Developing Countries*, explicitly placed Samoan and other colonial and postcolonial schools at the bottom of a four-stage schema, through which all education systems must pass in their journey toward the levels achieved in the "advanced countries of the world."[19] Even Beeby, looking back, accepts—albeit somewhat sardonically—that there is "some measure of justification" for criticisms of his program's "foisting" of Eurocentric ideas and "systems of schooling on defenceless countries regardless of their history and their cultures." Ultimately, however, he argues that this was the only practical solution to these countries' educational needs.[20] From the colonial perspective, it was a success. For the Pacific Islanders drawn into this system, it was a disgrace.

Albert Wendt was one of the first generation of Samoans to be awarded the elitist NZ scholarship, so he had firsthand experience of the educational reforms Beeby had introduced. Looking back on this scheme in his address to the 1974 Waigani Seminar at UPNG, Wendt described it as a "lobotomy operation" that used a disciplinary system of reward and punishment to promote the internalization of colonial ideologies and values: children were "educated away from our own cultures."[21] Deeply critical of the "domesticat[ing]" effect on young Pacific Islanders, he sought to mitigate his complicity as a "minor priest" in the postcolonial educational hierarchy by instituting an extensive, extracurricular arts program at the colonially founded Samoa College, empowering students to "teach themselves whatever craft or art form they are interested in" without "too much teacher participation and domination."[22] With a similar impetus, John Kasaipwalova established the Sopi Arts School in the Trobriand Islands, a "Modern Art School" based on traditional aesthetic concepts. Trained in primary and secondary systems that modeled the internalization of colonial standards in pedagogical techniques of rote learning, Pacific Islanders sought to take ownership of the educational apparatus. Ulli Beier remarked on this trend in a letter to Michael Josselson, who had been commissioned by the CIA to set up the Congress for Cultural Freedom in 1950, explaining that while most good UPNG graduates get "snatched up in highly paid government jobs," the "best don't want a job at all: they want [to] go right back to their village and organise self help movements."[23] Self-help movements that, like Kasaipwalova's, depended on new approaches to teaching and writing. With Wendt's criticism of the "whole education machine" and his depiction of the "factory squeezing students through the examination machine" echoing Pound's views on the "cramming factory" and Lawrence's "mechanical set," we begin to see a continuum of pedagogical critique among writers associated with modernisms old and new.[24]

Tracing the connections between modernism and education, Peter Howarth states it plainly: "literary modernism is unthinkable without pedagogy."[25] He refers to European and American modernism, but the point applies globally and broadly, such that whether we see this period of Pacific writing as modern or modernist, it is inextricable from the project of learning and teaching. Oceanian literature of the mid- to late twentieth century maintains and extends the didactic concerns of European and American modernism, but it also incorporates modernist texts, as educational material, into its pages and its curricula. When lecturers in the Pacific put modernist texts in courses in the 1960s and 1970s, they set texts by writers who were also invested in pedagogy, and if they were not all formal educators, others were "poets at the blackboard," as Hugh Kenner describes Pound and William Carlos Williams.[26] As we map out in more detail in chapters 2 and 5, modernist works were a key component of the English major at both UPNG and USP: in the former, the Western element of the syllabus was composed solely of modernist poetry, drama, and fiction, and in the latter this literature was also a strong feature of the curriculum. Some of these courses were set by lecturers who were not Pacific-born, and we return to the ethical and political dimensions of this fact in later chapters. For now, we ask what lecturers at these founding Pacific universities expected modernism to teach their students. Why did they give it such a prominent position in their courses? Modernism might be marked by a pedagogic drive, but how did it function as a pedagogic tool? And what, importantly, did it leave out?

To consider these questions, we need first to position ourselves in relation to the approaches to modernism and modern literature dominant in the middle of the twentieth century. We cannot be certain about the specific critical texts that influenced lecturers in the Pacific in their formulation of modernism—lecturers such as Beier, Prithvindra Chakravarti, Elton Brash, and Taban Lo Liyong at UPNG and Ken Arvidson, Wendt, and Subramani at USP—though we can be guided by the critical writings these scholars produced and by the course descriptions they provided for their students. Yet to read these documents accurately, we must situate them within the shifting history of modernism as a critical field. The canons and classifications of modernism were fluid long before the dizzying diversification of the field in the twenty-first century, and many of the texts on these courses have been understood in turn as modern, modernist, contemporary, postmodern, and postcolonial. As such, we cannot presume upon a fixed understanding of terms and must always guard against anachronistic framing. In considering the place of these texts within the classroom, we must remember too that they were not introduced in order to further disciplinary discussions of modernism, but to encourage students to consider broader questions of tradition and modernity, the self and society, imperialism and decolonization, ethics and aesthetics. Nevertheless, as the critical context shaped the way in which Beier, Arvidson, Subramani, and the rest conceived these questions, as well as the ways in which they encouraged students to respond, it is important that we keep it in view.

When we consider the publications on modernism between the 1930s and 1970s, much is familiar. Herbert J. Muller's study of modern fiction had emphasized individuality, new modes of representing a changing reality, the importance of psychology, and a general sense of overwhelming disarray within modernist texts.[27] Richard Ellmann and Charles Feidelson's *The Modern Tradition* (1965) described modernism in broadly similar terms. For them, modernism "elevated individual existence over social man, unconscious feeling over self-conscious perception, passion and will over intellection and systematic morals, dynamic vision over the static image, dense actuality over practical reality."[28] Three years later, Frank Kermode attempted to distinguish between the "palaeo-modernism" of the fin-de-siècle and early twentieth century and the "neo-modernism" or early postmodernism of the mid-twentieth century. Although much of his argument hung on the difficulty of defining modernism, the relations he mapped out are recognizable, if not unproblematic: modernism's impersonality against postmodernism's indifference, elitism against anti-intellectualism, newness against plagiarism, fascism against anarchism. Overall, he argued, neo-modernism enables us to "see more clearly that certain aspects of earlier modernism really were so revolutionary that we ought not to expect . . . to have the pains and pleasures of another comparable movement quite so soon."[29]

Unrefined, perhaps, but this picture of an enduring, revolutionary modernism has come back around and is broadly consistent with our contemporary critical frame. In the affective dimension, however, less familiar versions appear. If the academic staff of UPNG and USP took their cues from the likes of Harry Levin, then modernism would have been "one of the most remarkable constellations of genius in the history of the West," after which, as A. Alvarez argued, there had been only descent into humdrum stagnation.[30] The inclusion of Alvarez's *The New Poetry* on the Modern English course at USP from 1972 gives a hint of the direction taken there. Yet if the staff in the literature departments were also, like many of their contemporaries, reading the likes of Irving Howe or Trilling as they planned their modern literature classes, they might have embraced a version of modernism whose world-weariness is bleaker than the one taught today. Howe presents the world of modernist writers as one absent of social conscience, in which "Man is mired—take your choice—in the mass, in the machine, in the city, in a loss of faith, in the hopelessness of a life without anterior intention or terminal value."[31] Modernism, he writes, "forces us into distance and disassociation; it denies us wholeness of response; it alienates us from its own powers of statement even when we feel that it is imaginatively transcending the malaise of alienation."[32] Trilling sees the defining elements of modern literature along similar lines, as "disenchantment of our culture with culture itself" and a "bitter line of hostility to civilisation."[33] Part of this deep sense of disillusionment can be understood through the period's easier inclusion of existential and absurdist texts within the modernist canon, with authors such as Franz Kafka, Bertolt Brecht, Albert Camus, and Fyodor Dostoevsky mentioned more often than they tend to be in current Anglophone discussions of modernism. The inclusion of these writers on the Modern Fiction courses at UPNG and Modern Literature at USP— where they were read under the banner of "literary modernism"—thus makes these modern literature courses more "modernist" to their contemporaries than they might from a later perspective appear.[34]

Once, however, we think in terms of the impact of modernist texts within the classroom, these affective differences begin to retreat. After all, modernism was a core component of the English majors, and even if lecturers felt beholden to contemporary trends, it is unlikely that courses were built around modernist works because of their perceived uselessness. Pacific writers appear inspired by both versions of modernism: the vision of modernity in Wendt, Soaba, and Subramani, for example, is often as bleak as Trilling's, but the excitement of the Pacific movement and the exuberance of its experiments align with Levin's praise. The serviceability of modernism also appears to have extended beyond structural considerations of form and into the realm of political context and import. While the history of Anglophone modernist criticism is conventionally linked to I. A. Richards's practical criticism and the American new critics, Gerald Graff argues that by the 1950s scholars were beginning to blend historical and formal approaches to texts. By the 1960s, Graff comments wryly, the new critics were "the whipping boy of everyone, including some who had actually read their work."[35] In *The Teaching Archive*, Buurma and Heffernan give strong evidence of this blend occurring in classrooms even earlier, with examples from across the twentieth century, and Alice Te Punga Somerville makes a similar point from a Māori and Pacific studies perspective.[36] It is difficult to imagine the politically trenchant Beier subscribing entirely to new critical approaches, and while USP courses included new critical and formalist handbooks such as René Wellek and Austin Warren's *Theory of Literature* (1948) and David Daiches's *Critical Approaches to Literature* (1956), the contemporary critical writings of the lecturers prescribing these texts—as discussed in chapters 5 and 6 of this book—make a depoliticized, highly formalist teaching mode unlikely. A combination is more probable, and indeed a combination that localized the analysis to the Pacific context. Joanne Wodak, who from 1968 to 1970 taught the literature component of UPNG's compulsory preliminary English course, noted in an interview with us that resources on authors or the contexts in which new works were written were not always easy to find, so while classroom approaches often drew on formalist principles, they were also strongly motivated by the consideration of texts' implications for the PNG context.[37] Similarly, while a 1978 *Mana* article reveals new criticism's lingering afterlife at USP, with the expatriate lecturer Alan Barker railing against the "unliterary" concerns with local cultural and historical questions found in the literatures of decolonizing countries, the vehement rejections of this argument by Marjorie Tuainekore Crocombe, Wendt, Konai Helu Thaman, and Pio Manoa, writers and educators all, indicate the contrasting views to which students would have been exposed.[38] As Manoa retorted, echoing Yeats, it is only through writing the "local and national" that Pacific writers may "strive for universality."[39]

Considering these shifting critical and pedagogical contexts and strategies, we can see the value of modernism in Pacific classrooms of the 1960s and 1970s from a number of perspectives. If modernism was taught as a cluster of brilliant writers, their brilliance can be understood in terms of their response to a rapidly changing world. As Levin puts it, modernism's "metamorphic impetus" arose from the writers' "paradoxical state of feeling belated and up-to-date simultaneously, and of working experimental transformations into traditional continuities."[40] Similarly, in 1963 Stephen Spender described the modernists as deeply aware of an "unprecedented modern situation," for which they alter form and idiom by creating "great fusions of present and past."[41] These modernists thus become shining examples of writers forming new worlds and crafting new voices through a complex negotiation of the old and the new. As such, modernism arises as a particularly appropriate movement to teach in decolonizing countries, where students needed above all to navigate and articulate tensions between the traditional and the modern—or more accurately, as we suggest in the final section of this chapter, between multiple traditions and multiple visions of modernity. Modernist texts were useful tools in the basket of Pacific creativity, which the Solomon Islander Mostyn Habu defined as "the ability to see a new possibility in an old situation; a new shape to an old and differently shaped object."[42] No culture can endure without creative responsiveness, as Wendt asserted in his rejection of the expatriate lecturer Barker's colonial gatekeeping: "it is a necessity for the survival of any people."[43] Adapting modernism was one of the ways that Pacific writers formed the advance guard of independence and found the voices of a new Oceanian world.

The political potential lecturers might have found within modernist texts, even in and for a new critical context, appears more clearly when we remember that some midcentury scholars interpreted modernism as a protest literature, with Herbert J. Muller complaining in 1937 of modern writers who "squander much of their energy in incessant protest."[44] Not incessant enough, of course, for some influential figures of the left: Marxist critics of the 1930s, from Georg Lukács to Alick West, were famously opposed to modernism, for its perceived bourgeois complicities, for its preoccupation with form over politics, for its treatment of the human subject in excessively isolated terms.[45] Yet there were strong counterarguments even within Marxist circles—Bertolt Brecht's among the most forceful, but joined by authors such as Richard Wright, who argued in the communist *New Challenge* that Eliot and Stein could provide inspiration for the dissident writer—and outside the party halls the foundation for today's framing of modernism as a subversive political force was already well underway.[46] As Vincent Sherry has argued, Edmund Wilson's *Axel's Castle*, published in 1931, was instrumental in imbuing Eliot, Joyce, Yeats, and Proust with a potent political energy, which, though without a specifically prescribed politics, was leftward leaning.[47]

The politics associated with modernism would continue to shift. After the Second World War, conservatives, particularly in North America, argued that modernist poetry was contaminated by communist politics, while Kenner saw a politics of negation, exemplified in the work of Joyce.[48] For Kenner, reading *Ulysses* as a sustained campaign against the degradations of modernity, the narrative soars above the "hungry sheep" of the Irish metropolis, stultified by their diet of "tenth-hand thinking, tabloids, preprocessed food, predigested sensational news."[49] With a 1960s view of modernism as the countercultural rejection of existing standards and forms, Kermode could declare that "modernism flourishes best in the theatre, where there is more to rebel against," while in 1971 Howe wrote that modern writers worked "at a moment when the culture is marked by a prevalent style of perception and feeling; and their modernity consists in revolt against this prevalent style, unyielding rage against the official order."[50]

Modernism has by turns been read as inherently revolutionary and essentially reactionary, and no doubt this critical cycle will continue. The peak postmodernist complaint of modernist elitism has been effectively silenced by the expansion of modernist studies beyond the men of 1914, but there is no shortage of material to support the counterargument that modernism, particularly as promoted by institutions like the CIA during the Cold War, was emptied of its political dissidence, retuned as a high cultural style produced by self-determining individuals.[51] Yet this is just not the version of modernism that was circulating in Pacific lecture rooms. Even when modernism was presented as a "force of darkness and brutality" in the West, what better way to reveal to students in a colonized country the decay at the heart of colonizing forces, while simultaneously demonstrating modes of articulating modernity's problems and even the potential for changing them?[52] It is surely with such thoughts in mind that Beier defined his paper "Modern Literature II," where students encountered modernist works including *The Waste Land*, *Waiting for Godot*, *The Trial*, Camus's *The Outsider*, and Ionesco's *The Lesson*, as devoted to studying the "rottenness of Western society" and the ways it has led to "alienation, existentialism, and absurdism."[53] As scholars from Abiola Irele to Simon Gikandi have established so convincingly, modernism, for all its limitations, gave writers across decolonizing nations a language, imagery, and form through which to explore the chaos of colonization, the tumult of decolonization, and the uneven development of modernity.[54]

RECITAL AND RESISTANCE: MODERNISM AS A PEDAGOGIC TOOL

The modernist texts read and studied in UPNG and USP were by writers from Europe, North America, Africa, the Caribbean, and India. While we acknowledge uncertainty as to the pedagogical and theoretical approaches that were taken in the classrooms, we accept that, as Selina Tusitala Marsh writes, the "literary-critical research methodologies" employed by foreign lecturers were not in the first instance framed by Pacific concepts like "respect, reciprocity, communalism, collective responsibility, gerontocracy, humility, love, service and spirituality."[55] At the same time, given what Pacific authors have written about the literature they studied and taught, and given the trace of these texts in their own work, modernist literature and its presentation within the classroom clearly offered something to which they could relate and then reshape.

Inside and outside the classroom, modernist writers asked much of their readers, urging them to study complex webs of meaning; to consider abstruse historical, literary, and culture homages, parodies, and departures; and to question the nature of art and society, tradition and the present. The narrative indeterminacy of much modernist writing implies that all is open to question and that there will always be elements of a text that resist alignment into stable, clear, or transmissible meanings. Modernist texts, in different ways, assert the importance of developing individuality, independence, and self-awareness. As we discuss at greater length in the next chapter, they frequently echo oral literature's demonstrations of the multiple ways that time, plot, narrative, and characterization can be expressed. They reveal urban spaces to be zones of anonymity, learning, consumption, and shock and maintain that modernity and alienation and rupture and exile are somehow entangled. They assert that things needed to be made new in the early twentieth century and imply that this imperative has by no means run its course. Modernist works tend to show that experimentation is valuable, that aesthetics and form matter, and that the mode of presentation affects meaning. And they impart again and again the lesson that we need to look further within. The modernist writers studied at UPNG and USP were educators, but they were educators whose works resisted classroom scenes of rote learning and regurgitation in favor of the contingency and unpredictability of constant interpretation. Modernist texts can be understood, as Howarth suggests, as processes of self-education that set readers on an ongoing course of intellectual and emotional experiences in which no stable body of knowledge is transferred and assimilated.[56] Modernism, then, is pedagogic, but it is also resistant to the didactic idea that any core message can be repeatedly and reliably delivered.

This resistance can be seen in the ways that modernist poetry disrupts internalization and assimilation. Much of the Victorian verse presented in midcentury colonial curricula had been retained from the poetry recitation classes that dominated Anglo-American classrooms earlier in the century, and a large swath of these poems featured the well-marked rhythms and regular meters that made memorization a more accessible task. But as students progressed through educational systems in the Pacific, they were gradually, albeit inconsistently and according to the idiosyncrasies of their teacher, examination board, nation, and period of enrollment, exposed to modernist poetry that resisted easy assimilation and mechanical, hyperrhythmical recitation.[57] We can exemplify this transition through the pairing of Felicia Hemans's "Casabianca," first published in 1826, and Elizabeth Bishop's poem of the same name, published in 1946. Hemans's poem was a classroom staple in Britain and across the Empire—Satendra Nandan, for example, recalls that he first heard it in Fiji when a teacher recited the poem in Form IV[58]—as its meter ticks like a metronome and its topic pays tribute to military valor and filial piety: "The boy stood on the burning deck / Whence all but him had fled; / The flame that lit the battle's wreck / Shone round him o'er the dead."[59] Hemans's poem gives a dramatic account of a boy who refuses to abandon his post on a burning ship.

Waiting resolutely for an order that can never come, as his father, the commander, is dead, the boy is killed when the fire reaches the ship's gunpowder and the ship explodes.

Bishop's poem is in free verse, and its meter and message are harder to assimilate. Her version superimposes images of a boy standing alone on a burning deck and a boy burning with anxiety on a "schoolroom platform," both attempting through "stammering elocution" to recite Hemans's "Casabianca."[60] The poem connects death caused by the valorization of suicidal loyalty and the death-like dread caused by the requirements of an education system in which the poem and its ideologies were taught. Yet although Bishop's poem denounces institutions that enculturate the young into terrified obedience, to those caught up in them she directs only love. Eschewing Hemans's single image of honor and devotion, Bishop's reworking diffuses intricate, ambiguous versions of love throughout her overlapping scenes. As we move from Hemans's flagship to Bishop's, we move from the straightforward to the complex, which brings to mind another modernist ship—Conrad's *Nellie*—and the famous distinction Conrad offers between the sailor's tales and the narratives told by Marlow, which has come to stand for the modernist project as a whole. If the "yarns of seamen have a direct simplicity, the whole meaning of which lies within the shell of a cracked nut," Conrad writes, for Marlow "the meaning of an episode was not inside like a kernel but outside, enveloping the tale which brought it out only as a glow brings out a haze."[61] If Hemans's poem is a neat whole, Bishop's poem is a series of fragments whose linkages and separations flicker unresolved, like Marlow's hazy tales. It is full, as Conrad's admirer Eliot said great writing should be, of "flashing phrases which never desert the memory," but if the mind, with little effort, can retain and recall Hemans's regular verses in their entirety, it is only with conscious and deliberate exertion that Bishop's may be retained in more than glinting shards.[62]

Eliot writes that "poets in our civilisation, as it exists at present, must be *difficult*." In an increasingly varied and entangled world, a "poet must become more and more comprehensive, more allusive, more indirect, in order to force, to dislocate if necessary, language into his meaning."[63] Complex poetry can rhyme, and labyrinthine meaning can be found in regular meter: Auden, for example, put traditional meters to refined use. Yet as students accustomed to rote learning and recitable verse encountered modernist poetry, which frequently uses free verse, might its resistance to assimilation have been part of its appeal? In other words, if modernism presents poems that are, without unusual effort, memorable in fragments rather than stanzas, did their formal intransigence appeal in correlation with the rebellious content and attitude? As students encountered modernist poetry, they moved from narrative verse like Hemans's to texts with a knottier, frequently plural presentation of voice and perspective, and together with an irregular meter, this demanded a slower engagement with the lines. Readers could not skip from iamb to iamb but were asked to shuffle, with due hesitancy, through works that presented meaning, positionality, and ideology in less accessible ways. Such a process of reading would perhaps have appealed to students used to slogging through colonial poetry, whose meaning—if overtly legible, formally—remained alien and recalcitrant to their lived experiences. The breaks, gaps, and aphasic glitches of so many modernist works might also have resonated with students learning, and authors writing, in English as a second or third language. These attributes led to the frequent recycling and reassembling of the shored fragments, broken images, and butt-ends of the modernists into new Pacific wholes.

In addition, much modernist verse resisted the received conventions of poetic recital and could not be declaimed in the same formal way, requiring new modes of elocution. As Kamau Brathwaite writes, it was Eliot who introduced "the notion of the speaking voice, the conversational voice" to Caribbean poetry. When Brathwaite and his fellow poets listened to the BBC recording of Eliot's reading of "The Love Song of J. Alfred Prufrock"—a recording that Subramani would use in his own teaching in Fiji in the 1960s—they heard in his "dry, deadpan delivery" rhythms that reminded them not of the forced diction of poetry recitation but the jazz and dislocations of "Bird, Dizzy and Klook."[64] This was a subversive force, Brathwaite explains, for people who have had "to recite "The boy / stood on / the burn / ing deck" for so long" that they are "unable to express the power of the hurricane" or the specifics of the world around them. As we will outline in more detail in what follows, Manoa's relocation of phrases from "Prufrock" to the Fijian vanua suggests that it served a similarly liberating function for Pacific poets, though as our tracing of modernist courses in this book suggests, they were inspired too by the creolizations and innovations of other postcolonial poetries freed from the rigid regulations of an outdated colonial prosody. In Port Moresby as in Bridgeton, Suva as in Port of Spain, modernism encouraged new experiments with sound, rhythm, and voice.

The unlearning of entrenched repetition-based systems was a huge project, conducted in multiple spaces across several generations. As late as the 1990s, the Samoan poet Sia Figiel would stage a humorous response to the rote learning of Wordsworth's "I Wandered Lonely as a Cloud," a permanent fixture of the Pacific classroom. Beginning with the repetition—the recitation—of the poem's first verse, the next stanza interrupts Wordsworth's regular meter with a baffled, provocative outburst—"I wandered / I wandered / I wondered / What the fuck is a daffodil?"[65] Joining Caribbean authors such as Michelle Cliff and Jamaica Kincaid in picking the daffodil as a fitting emblem for a rote learning system imposing foreign standards across the colonial and postcolonial world, Figiel plays with a declamatory style, defying the prescriptions of classroom poetry recital with frisky free verse and fragmented rhymes.[66] Figiel was born in 1967, just as Pacific Islanders such as Manoa were turning the fragments and the fragmentariness of the European modernists against the edifice of the colonial education system. For these and other Oceanians, modernist poetry was part of a rite of passage, a movement from the childish verse of earlier school systems into advanced classes and the university. Its sounds, foreign as they may have been, open up intonations much closer to home: its openness makes room for them to echo and distort; its resistances allow for productive dissonance.

As such, we find affinities between critical pedagogy, modernist form, and modernists' critiques of education. Critical pedagogy has been interpreted in many ways since Paulo Freire's *The Pedagogy of the Oppressed* was published in 1968—and since his Pacific trip in 1974, when he spoke at UPNG's Waigani Seminar and at the Conference on Education for Liberation and Community, held in Fiji—but at its core it focuses on the relations between education and power.[67] Critical pedagogy contends that education can, as Lawrence, Lewis, and Auden argued and as Pacific writers and educators knew from experience, perpetuate existing relations of control and oppression, or it can be instrumental in creating a society that privileges social justice. Beyond this basic binary, critical pedagogy is a philosophy of education that encourages close analysis beyond surface impressions, dominant narratives, and embedded suppositions to look deeply at ideology, context, causes, and consequences.[68] Too much education, as Freire puts it, depends on a banking model in which education is an act of depositing knowledge into passive students who "patiently receive, memorize, and repeat."[69] We end this chapter by noting that Wendt entered quite literally into dialogue with Freire, but we are not the first to connect critical pedagogy to modernist literary projects. Rod Taylor finds it in Woolf's attempt to create a malleable space of learning that is filled with critical inquiry and dedicated to addressing social injustice. Jonathan Heron and Nicholas Johnson see the same potential for critical pedagogy in Beckett's works, unlikely as that may sound, since the qualities of play, openness, fallibility, silence, and resistance in his scripts manifest Freire's "epistemological curiosity," in which students/readers are not "content to merely learn about things, but also about what underlying frame makes them important, worth knowing, or even knowable in the first place. Subtraction, stillness, absence, and void are apt rebukes to a banking model of education."[70] Against such a model, Woolf, Beckett, and Freire call for an education that asks students to think critically, to grow and change. For them, as for so many modernists, education is never neutral, and while it can inculcate the young into dominant systems, it can also give students the tools to transform their world.

"NEW OCEANIA": PACIFIC POETICS AND PEDAGOGIES

We have framed modernist pedagogy as a project of radical critique. If—as we argue here—the value of modernism in the Pacific classroom is the space it establishes for self-education and its adaptability to local contexts and political needs, it could not be accepted unquestioningly, especially given the pernicious, if often hidden, lessons it smuggled into the classroom. Despite the many rehabilitations attempted for modernism in recent decades, there is no denying that key modernist authors and works were complicit with racism, xenophobia, sexism, classism, ableism, and fascism. Conrad's stories of the Pacific are as susceptible as his African tales to Chinua Achebe's complaint that a vast and diverse region exists for the author only as backdrop for the "breakup of one petty European mind";[71] Joyce could riff on stereotypes of Fijian cannibalism to depict cheap, imperial food products in *Ulysses*;[72] and Lawrence—whose works featured prominently on modules at both UPNG and USP—wallows in the mire of anti-Pacific racism in his review of Melville's *Typee*, describing the region as "a vast vacuum, in which, mirage-like, continues the life of myriads of ages back," while taking as axiomatic the cultural hierarchies of Empire: "far be it from me to assume any 'white' superiority. But they are savages."[73] The more typical European modernist response to the Pacific, however, was to ignore it altogether. The intensity of their preoccupation with one side of modernity could be domineering, while their emphasis on the individual could further the displacement of students from communally oriented cultures that began with the mission schools of the nineteenth century. We have argued that the modernist texts on the courses at UPNG and USP presented students with a curriculum of unlearning whose message, as Woolf wrote in *The Common Reader*, was to "take no advice...follow your own instincts...use your own reason...come to your own conclusions."[74] Liberating as these injunctions sound and moldable as they may have proven for a decolonizing movement, the atomization of agency to the individual scale was at odds with the relational, often hierarchical structures of many Pacific communities, and as we trace how Pacific writers drew on modernism to transform a decolonizing Oceania, we cannot disregard the ways that modernist texts inculcated troubling ideologies of their own.

Yet if, as we have outlined, modernism's principal lesson was that everything is up for question, so, it follows, was European modernism: it could not lay claim to the last word or be readily crammed for exam regurgitation. When Pacific writer-scholars took up the modernist text, therefore, they did so with the dissector's knife and not the novitiate's zeal. In "Recall" (1968), the first published poem by the Fijian poet Pio Manoa, the speaker sets out to recover a relationship with the motherland the poet left to study in Australia. The poem's free verse begins boldly with a line from Eliot— "Do I dare"—and, as in "The Love Song of J. Alfred Prufrock," the repeated phrase opens into a series of self-interrogations:

Do I dare
dip my bread
in the old, old wine?
Do I dare
suck dewdrops
out of early dawn?[75]

In Manoa's hands, the line becomes a provocation toward a first act of literary self-affirmation. Invoking the pedagogical injunction of a colonial education system predicated on rote learning—recall, recite, recount, repeat—Manoa responds to the challenges set by Eliot's poem, the education system that taught it, the colonial project as a whole, and the independence drive opposing it by repurposing an imposed language and using it to examine a native and distinctly uncolonized Fijian territory, a Fiji of Indigenous inheritance:

> Do I dare sail
> an ancient river
> and draw my life
> from my primal mother,
> still shuffling down
> from dark, dark hills
> in her native summer?[76]

The optimism expressed in Manoa's poem is not unqualified. The triumph of the act of "recall" in the creation of an Indigenous art form in English, with its implication that each interrogation of the speaker's daring is to be answered in the affirmative, is tempered by the melancholy cry that closes the poem:

> For I have fed on foreign bread,
> sipped foreign wine;
> I have sailed a foreign river,
> felt foreign earth:
> I forget my mother . . . ![77]

Such ambivalences run through the literature of the period. By the mid-1970s, when Manoa was firmly ensconced in the USP literature program that he helped to modernize, he would identify the feeling of cultural "loss" as an initial stage in the growth of Pacific poetry: in the essay "Singing in Their Genealogical Trees," published in a 1976 *Mana*, he relates this dispossession to the sense "that schooling is an enforced process" that makes "the captive *whiter*."[78] Yet if the title of this early poem, "Recall," can be read ironically to denote his recollection of particular lines memorized from

English poetry—an act compelled in the secondary classroom—it also describes how the poet in the tertiary institution writes his way back into the land as site and subject of postcolonial literary resistance. Through the recollection of Eliot's lines, Manoa recalls them to a new purpose, one that revokes the colonial past.

While Eliot's text is undoubtedly part of the "foreign" cultural estrangement Manoa describes, the refrain "Do I dare" is finally more enabling for his speaker than it is for Eliot's hand-wringing Prufrock. As Manoa would observe in his 2010 essay "Retrospective," his "successful" poem set the pattern for his "subsequent effort and avocation" as poet. Against all of the "various names" for the imperial project, "Progress, Civilization, Religion, Science, Education, and the latest one, Development," Manoa works to reclaim the "multivalent hinterland concept" of the vanua, the land, which for Fijians includes the surrounding waters. As Manoa explains, reclaiming the vanua as the site of postcolonial Fijian identity helps sustain its social and sacred values of belonging, stability, and reciprocity, "never really fully understood or appreciated in the process of subjugation or conversion."[79]

Accessible in fragments rather than as matter for blind recitation, modernism seems to have enabled critical responses to the educational systems preceding the Pacific university. However, we must keep in mind that while modernism was a prominent component of the tertiary curriculum, the writer-scholars of UPNG and USP had also been schooled in a more traditional syllabus. As we have detailed elsewhere, modernist texts may have been creeping in to examination questions posed by the Cambridge, New Zealand, and various Australian examination boards—the boards most commonly taken by Pacific school leavers and university hopefuls—but they were a distinct minority and could be avoided if teachers so chose.[80] When students started writing, then, they had to navigate the various poetic forms they had encountered to present contemporary Oceania as a space recognizable as both modern and Pacific. Our contention is that modernism helped guide this navigation, in Oceania as elsewhere. Nathan Suhr-Sytsma has drawn on the work of Pascale Casanova to explain how poets such as Christopher Okigbo and John Pepper Clark-Bekederemo of the University of Ibadan—where Beier taught before his relocation to UPNG— used modernism to refashion "the literary present held out to them by their education in order to create credible, legitimate idioms for themselves."[81] Yet it would have taken sustained study to determine which of the works taught at school were part of the literary present, and if English idioms of the eighteenth and nineteenth centuries had been presented to students from an early age as poetic language, rather than the poetic language of a particular time and place, then the appearance of dated phrasing in local inscriptions of modern Lagos, Port Moresby, or Apia is to be expected.

And it is there to be found. In the 1950s, the PNG poet Alan Natachee was writing lines such as "O race of mine" and "Hark and behold, our stone age is swaying," apostrophes and exclamations with biblical overtones and pre-twentieth century poetic sources.[82] What are we to do with such examples? Against modernism's overbearing newness, it would be easy to dismiss such poetry as immature. Yet context is key, and in some situations there may be good reasons for the adaptation of archaism, as well as sophisticated ways of doing so. For example, the Indigenous Tongan poetic tradition, best known outside of the islands through the poetry of Queen Sālote Tupou III (1900–1965), retains a deliberately elevated style with marked formal conventions.[83] Heliaki is a notable feature, an elaborate figurative mode through which the subject is addressed indirectly, either for ornament, allusion, or—especially in the treatment of royal or divine subjects—to avoid a directness that could, by Tongan custom, affront.[84] Heliaki is often culturally specific, involving detailed genealogical and historical allusion, and can appear as what Tēvita O. Ka'ili describes as "metonymic heliaki," where, for example, an "endemic bird of an island is a representation for the whole island."[85] Without some understanding of this tradition, Tongan poetry in English is subject to misreading, particularly when approached with English poetic conventions in mind. Peni Tutu'ila Malupo's "Tonga, Blessed Land" celebrates the "pride and dignity" of the sovereign state and is striking both for its nationalist sentiment and its seemingly old-fashioned English diction: "Her kingly line is still continuous; / And ruled by law constitutional."[86] Inversions of syntax ("law constitutional") and, in other lines, archaic syncope ("O'erbrim'd with passion") invoke English verse conventions of the previous century, which, from the perspective of the English poetic tradition, appear out of place.

Similarly, the extended flower imagery with which Malupo opens his poem—"Tonga is the equal of flower garden / Languorous odours and pervading scents"—appears anachronistically romantic for modern postcolonial verse.[87] Yet flowers play an important part in heliaki and form an expected part in Tongan poetry. As Futa Helu explains, kakala (literally "flower" or "perfume") conveys rich significance in Tongan culture, as a flower with sacred origins, "a mythical perfume that has burst its mythical shell and come down to us in historical times."[88] Significantly, kakala is specifically and exclusively an Indigenous bloom: recent introductions like roses are not kakala because they are "not of mythical origin and have not been hallowed by time."[89] When Tevita 'O. Helu works kakala into his poem through the use of heliaki—"let me taste the fragrance from Pulotu of prime kakala / That I may render it to grace circles at Pangai on a day of celebration"—the cultural specificity obviously situates the poem within a deeper Tongan tradition.[90] Yet with the distinction between Indigenous and introduced flowers in mind, his verse simultaneously declares its independence within the English tradition it also joins. Kakala are emphatically not Wordsworth's daffodils.

Beier at UPNG found no place for "distracting archaism" in postcolonial verse from Africa or Papua New Guinea, but given the importance of the high, formal strain for treating notable figures or concepts respectfully in the Tongan poetic tradition, the introduction of English archaism here served a useful function, approximating a traditional register within a new linguistic frame.[91] Against Beier, we can read this maneuver not as an unfortunate anachronism but as an inventive and knowing use of England's literary past within Tonga's literary present. And if colonial verse seems an incongruous source for the anticolonial imperatives of 1970s Oceanian literature, it is important to remember Tonga's historical peculiarity as a Pacific Island that was never formally colonized. Though this distinction may be qualified by the seventy years for which Tonga was counted as a British protectorate (1900–1970), the country's uninterrupted monarchy, aristocracy, and associated land ownership present enduring cause for celebration, as Malupo's encomium to Tonga's "kingly line ... continuous" shows: "She is our pride and dignity / On this we glory, on this we triumph."[92] It is thus, perhaps, that some Tongan poets felt able to harmonize the voice of the high colonial period in British poetry to their own, late-twentieth-century nationalist sentiment.

This is just one example within a diverse range of interconnected contexts, but the important point is that the writer-scholars and student poets turning to the page in the 1960s and 1970s had simultaneous access to multiple traditions: the diverse oral and new written literatures of the Pacific region; the English, often colonial writing upon which they had been examined at school; the modernist literature they studied in their university courses; and postcolonial writing from what was still called the Commonwealth, itself mediating multiple traditions, many of them modernist. Pacific writers shuttle back and forth between these different traditions and in this movement scramble received heuristics. The archaic turn of Malupo and Helu can be explained in this context as a transposition of the higher strain of the Tongan tradition, but what about instances where archaic English phrasing appears without any obvious correspondence to alternative traditions? Salochana Devi's "Man" is a free-verse poem that appears modern in form and in much of its phrasing—"he knows / he stinks / like puke"—yet antique exclamations repeatedly intrude—"Oh, but within," "But alas"—as do dated contractions: "E'en worse."[93] Since the theme, on the folly of man, is conventional and there is little rooting the poem in either the Indian or Fijian contexts or traditions, it is hard not to read these archaisms as imitations of the colonial poetry that made up at least part of the curriculum in Fijian high schools.[94]

In the English tradition, such archaisms were the mark of bad poetry in the 1910s, let alone the 1970s. They may be the mark of bad poetry here too, but classification is harder once multiple traditions are brought into play. As we have seen, the archaic turn may translate traditional elements in Indigenous poetics. Alternatively, it may invoke the biblical register, as in the Cook Islander Harry Ivaiti's "Tangaroa," where the speaker addresses the atua of the sea: "Oh! Idol of the great blue sea / Oh! Tangaroa my God to be. / . . . / My life and fate are in thy hands."[95] As with the Tongan examples, the archaisms indicate respect for a dignified subject, but they also carry a political charge, turning the linguistic markers of the Christian Bible away from the religion brought by the colonial missionaries and toward the forbidden atua, ancestral and yet still "to be." More stridently still, the biblical or colonial register may be evoked as a metonym for colonialism itself and dismissed in turn. Such appears to be the case in the PNG poet Joseph W. Sukwianomb's "Where Are the Green Leaves." It opens with a stilted, formal style:

> The alarming sounds of prodigious intensity . . .
> Amidst thy despicable wants
> Despoils and detaches and deteriorates
> the green, green leaves.[96]

With its arrangement in quatrains, its archaic pronouns ("thy"), and the use of palilogia, or affective repetition ("green, green leaves"), this stanza reads as old-fashioned verse, but as the poem progresses, the formal register breaks down. Upon an exclamation, "Goddamn machines," the speaker contrasts the "lifeless and boastful" architecture to the traditional home—"kunai huts / Mud walls / Gardening lands"—and the "Plumbed in air" of the foreign buildings to the "Cool / Clean / breeze." The contrived verse of the poem's opening gives way to short, simple lines, often comprising only one or two words, and the archaisms of the first half of the poem fall away. Sukwianomb thus figures at a formal level the rejection of the "alien and extravagant luxury" of colonial development, and in the final stanza the speaker is freed to stage a frank dismissal of the foreign, through the acceptance of the homely: "Get the hell out of here, / let me breathe my native air / like my native husband / who will caress me plainly."

In new poetries combining panoplies of images and phrases—archaic, modern, mythical, oral, written—from disparate traditions, the collision of registers in verse arising from these Oceanian universities ultimately appears as an aesthetic strategy in itself, an expression of the contest between, but also on behalf of, the multiple, seemingly incommensurable voices and ideologies in the decolonizing Pacific. In short, the poems appear modernist even where older or alternative features come to the fore—even, perhaps, when they seem at their most straightforward. To take a very different example from the Tongan context, the opening line of Helu Thaman's "Resistance"—"We are like songs"—uses the first-person plural to invoke community and the musical image to suggest continuity with a Pacific art form.[97] These accordances, however, are immediately stripped in the lines that follow: "Sung out of tune / You and I." The harmonious musical image becomes one of discord, and the collective pronoun is split to indicate interpersonal separation. As soon becomes clear, the speakers of the poem are elders who, enjoying the perquisites of modernity in the form of "Beer and whisky," spend their time lamenting the social shifts that threaten the "petty customs" underwriting their privileged way of life and dreaming of "lives / that are not ours." The "resistance" of the title resurfaces not as an anticolonial struggle against outside forces but as elders' reaction against the new ways in which "imagination / And change" threaten the older entitlements "Of birth."⁹⁸ Here and elsewhere, Helu Thaman's principal tool is irony, probing and revealing all-too-modern compromises within traditional rhetoric, hierarchy, and appeals to indigeneity.

Helu Thaman is particularly attuned to the ways that women are caught in a double bind between restrictions and enfranchisements that are both traditional and modern. Her first and still best-known poem, "You, the Choice of My Parents," presents a woman addressing the man she is to marry. The suitor has been chosen by her parents for the "wealth and prestige" he will bring, with his modern accomplishments, his "Western-type education / And second-hand car."⁹⁹ Yet as again becomes clear, this is not a straightforward complaint against a contemporary, consumerist debasement of Pacific ideals. The arranged marriage itself represents Tongan custom—one far more restrictive for the woman than an education or a car—and thus tradition is troubled as a viable ground from which to present a stand against the encroachments of a commodifying modernity. Hence the ceremony is presented as a sacrifice: when the priest has left the altar and the dancing has begun, the speaker sees herself "dying, slowly / To family and traditions; / . . . / Alienated from belonging."¹⁰⁰

In the final stanza of the poem, as the speaker attempts to secure an integral self behind the "mere act of duty," she invokes the land, the "ironwood tree" and the "weeping willows along the shore."¹⁰¹ These trees are cleverly chosen. The weeping willows sound like a transplant from English verse, and the tree is indeed an introduced species. Yet as Helu Thaman has elsewhere explained, it is a tree that is commonly found in the inner lagoon of Tongatapu, signaling the point at which "the soul goes to rest in *pulotu* (paradise)."¹⁰² The introduced tree has been "hallowed by time," which has given it entry to the mythical repertoire. The ironwood, or toa, is by contrast an indigenous tree. Yet it was also one of the primary items of early Tongan trade, and thus—"herald[ing] strangers / To the land of my ancestors"—it also symbolizes the incursions of commodification to which the speaker of the poem falls victim. Imbricating indigeneity with exploitation, invasion with internalization, these trees embody the contradictions portrayed across the poem at large.

Clearly, we must at one level distinguish Helu Thaman from the nationalist Tongan poets discussed earlier. Her contemporary English register is a long way from the cultivated archaisms of Helu and Malupo, and her use of free verse and the quintessentially modernist techniques of irony, contradiction, and impasse signal a critical distance from the appeal to tradition. Yet as a form of indirect address, irony can also be read in relation to heliaki, approaching criticism through implication rather than direct statement, suggesting shared wellsprings. Similarly, her treatment of the trees in "You, the Choice of My Parents" presents an extension rather than a repudiation of heliaki. From this perspective, the social bind described in the poem is resolved at the mythical level, in pulotu, "where there are no conflicts and contradiction."[103] For all the differences, then, Helu Thaman shares with Malupo and Helu a rooting within the mythical bedrock, and her poetry is better approached as a development within rather than a reaction against the Tongan poetic tradition. The encoded Polynesian references create what Paul Sharrad terms an exoteric/esoteric doubling, as knowledge available to all readers of literature is interlaced with knowledge commonly only available to those of Tongan heritage.[104]

It is significant that this maneuver can also be seen in her teaching. Helu Thaman is as well known for her contributions to pedagogy as for her long poetic career, and she recalls that her first forays into verse came when she tried to broaden students' receptiveness to literature by translating Tongan poetry into English and then using the imagery and symbolism of Tongan poetics to teach the ubiquitous (and at this stage compulsory) Wordsworth, Shelley, and Byron.[105] This overlap between poetic and pedagogical strategies supports our contention that modernism's preoccupation with tradition and futurity served as both a critical lesson and a lesson in critique for Pacific writer-scholars, and the development of pedagogies more responsive to Oceanian needs—turning back against the methods of the colonial education system—can be read in relation to the theories of critical pedagogy associated with Freire. The Pacific-born educators we study in this chapter and this book as a whole, from Subramani to Manoa, Helu Thaman to Wendt, were taught by scholarships in the twilight of the British Empire, and as they rose to independence in the Pacific university, they examined the system they inherited.

So Satendra Nandan, the first Indo-Fijian literature teacher at the University of the South Pacific and a prominent poet—we return to his poetry in chapter 5—lamented the colonial education system's imposition of foreign standards as the norm and its disregard of valid local modernities: "Fiji, according to our expatriate and local teachers, had neither history nor geography. And as for culture: we were told 'agriculture' was the most we could aspire to."[106] So John Waiko complained that the educational system he encountered in PNG was decidedly "not geared towards encouraging literature that is based on the culture of the people of this country."[107] And so Helu Thaman would devote her long career at USP to "decolonizing formal education," a process that she sees as requiring the acceptance of "Pacific perspectives, ways of knowing, and wisdom, and encouraging efforts by staff and students alike to reclaim indigenous knowledge as well as philosophies of teaching and learning that encompass the multiple experiences of Oceanic peoples."[108] Writing at the turn of the millennium, Helu Thaman notes that this project remains an ongoing struggle against the coercions of pedagogical globalization, and it would be misleading to suggest that USP or UPNG—universities developed in this globalizing context—were at every level united in their defense of Indigenous ways of seeing and being. It would take time for Pacific pedagogies to be thought through, worked out, and reconnected to an Indigenous history that colonial education systems had spent generations working to eradicate. Yet if the coherent framework outlined in, say, Linda Tuhiwai Smith's monumental *Decolonizing Methodologies: Research and Indigenous Peoples*, now in its third edition, was not yet established in the Pacific classroom, the roots are still there, roots that can be seen both in Pacific writing about education and in the creative and critical writing of Pacific Islanders.[109]

As with other key figures in the golden age of Pacific literature, these writer-scholars move between the critique of imposed literary standards and the critique of an imposed educational scheme, and in their pedagogies as in their poetics they find ways of interweaving and opposing elements from multiple traditions in the development of self-reflexive systems. Across *The Rise of Pacific Literature*, we shift between the literature produced by these Pacific leaders and that of their students, who were learning to write in the decolonizing systems these educators produced. We end this chapter by reconsidering the pedagogical dimensions of Wendt's landmark essay "Towards a New Oceania." First published in *Mana* in 1976, just as the USP literature curriculum was entering its zenith, and much-anthologized since, most recently in Alys Moody and Stephen J. Ross's *Global Modernists on Modernism*, "Towards a New Oceania" can be read as the summation of the Pacific literary and pedagogical project we chart in this book. It is at once a critique of the stultifying effects of colonial education, a redefinition of Oceania as a perpetual integration of the traditional and the modern, and a manifesto for the new literature that Wendt sees as the vehicle for this integration and decolonization of education. Observing that the formal colonial education systems were designed not for personal or national development but to produce "minor and inexpensive cogs . . . for the colonial administrative machine," Wendt asserts that to begin any serious project of self-determination, Pacific Islanders must take control of education, to "train our own people" in an act of "creative nation-building."[110] For this, he suggests, Oceania must be newly conceived, avoiding the false dichotomy of Pacific-traditional versus foreign-modern. Wendt's vision is throughout predicated on "the vitality of our past, our cultures, our dead," but he rejects the view—colonial in origin and maintained by a self-serving elite—that this past must be preserved at the expense of the present. "No culture is ever static," he declares, and elements once "considered *foreign* are now authentic pillars of our cultures."[111] Pacific societies, like all societies, have always been in a state of growth and adaptation, persisting through the prolonged assault of colonialism, and the quest for the Pacific educator is to continue to cultivate this growth. "Our quest," he resolves, "should not be for a revival of our past cultures but for the creation of new cultures . . . based firmly on our own pasts. The quest should be for a new Oceania."[112]

Importantly, as an act of creativity, this is for Wendt as much an aesthetic project as an educational one, and he calls for a comparable artistic approach interlarding the new and the old, the imported and the autochthonous. Indigenous forms present "a fabulous treasure house of traditional motifs, themes, styles, material," but these are to be used and not "preserved," integrated toward "contemporary forms to express our uniqueness, identity, pain, joy, and our own visions of Oceania and earth."[113] Celebrating the experiments in form that had arisen from UPNG and USP across the last decade—many of which we analyze in the chapters that follow—Wendt suggests that the educational and the aesthetic dimensions are each part of the same political project: "across the political barriers dividing our countries," he concludes, "an intense artistic activity is starting to weave firm links between us. This cultural awakening, inspired and fostered and led by our own people, will not stop at the artificial frontiers drawn by the colonial powers."[114]

Illustrating our argument that the pedagogical program initiated by Pacific Islanders in the Oceanian universities can also be understood as a modernist enterprise, "Towards a New Oceania" brings together the various strands, curricular and extracurricular, traced in *The Rise of Pacific Literature*. Wendt's manifesto is inseparable from the USP milieu in which he wrote, taught, and compiled curricula. It synthesizes ideas about the role of literature in the decolonizing Pacific presented by Crocombe in "Mana," and though it does not name "modernism" explicitly, it is of a piece with Wendt's other accounts of literary studies and education at this time, such as his comment in a 1977 interview that he does not see much value in reading texts from before 1900, or his later comment, discussed in our introduction, where he associates this golden age of Pacific literature with a strong modernist imperative.[115]

More concretely, the article itself—epoch-defining as it has been in the critical picture of the Pacific, in and outside of the region—began as a modest report on the USP- and UNESCO-sponsored Regional Creative Writing Workshop held at the university in 1974, a correspondence that has until now gone unremarked. And lest the stress upon USP seems to marginalize the Papua New Guinean scene that preceded it, Wendt not only quotes liberally from Niuguinian writers such as Kasaipwalova, whom we return to in chapter 4, but draws from and participates in the intellectual space of UPNG: it is an infrequently noted fact that Wendt presented an intermediate version of "Towards a New Oceania" at the eighth Waigani Seminar, held at UPNG in 1974 on the subject of education in Melanesia. This paper, "A Sermon on National Development, Education, and the Rot in the South Pacific," rehearses many of the details worked out in "Towards," but unlike that essay it culminates in a detailed prospectus for a decolonizing Pacific education system, involving the "abolition of all external examinations; complete reform of the curriculum to suit our students . . . with an emphasis on Pacific studies . . . reinforcement of the principle of co-operation and group effort, the basis of our way of life."[116] Reflections on the exigencies of Pacific pedagogy were thus central to the genesis of Oceania's most celebrated literary tract, and the keynote speaker at this conference was none other than Paulo Freire—whose idea of critical pedagogies, discussed earlier, affords such productive ways of writing modernist strategies back into the decolonizing educational project that is the subject of this monograph. Both education in general and the University of Papua New Guinea specifically are thus important contexts in the history of Wendt's momentous publication; it is to the University of Papua New Guinea that we now turn.

Chapter Two

DECOLONIZING THE LITERATURE PROGRAM, GENERATING THE NIUGINIAN LITERARY SCENE

In Kama Kerpi's short story "Kulpu's Daughter" (1975), Mark, a second-year arts student at the University of Papua New Guinea, returns to his highlands village for a family wedding. Before the festivities begin, his father and the village elders ask him to enter into a politically expedient marriage with a young woman from a neighboring village, the titular Kulpu's daughter. Mark is already dating Carol, a young woman who attends Sogeri Senior High, and is horrified at his father's suggestion that he take Kulpu's daughter as his "village wife" and keep Carol as his "educated wife."[1] Mark's strong response to his father's suggestion, which he denounces as "the ravings of a madman" (12), shows how far removed from village customs he has become. Polygamy has become impossible for him, and as his education has taught him to think in terms of personal rights and individual choices, he struggles to put aside his own beliefs for the communal good. But despite his strength of feeling and the privileged position his education gives him, Mark finds himself incapable of an empowered response to his father and the other men. His schooling might have taught him modern, Westernized ways, but it has not equipped him to be "a man among our people" (10). Mark has, he realizes, been put on trial and found wanting. Overwrought by his inability to resist or respect village obligations, he walks away from the village and, believing he hears Carol's voice ahead of him, steps off a cliff and falls to his death.

There are no winners in Kerpi's story—the village loses a beloved son, and Mark loses his life—but unlike many renditions of the tradition/modernity conflict, it is not village culture that "Kulpu's Daughter" places on a precipice but the educated youth. The "educated man," Kerpi writes, "becomes a victim of change," as "once he is assimilated to live like a Western man" (9) his home is no longer a refuge but a place made unfamiliar, whose logic and purpose no longer seem true. For Mark, clan protocol has become "like an invisible shadow": separate from him, and often unseen, but from which he cannot escape. His death enacts the fatal tension between the old ways and the new: the village's "distinct hierarchical structure" looms over him, "united like a silent hill" (10), and it is from this height, as much as the physical cliff, that Mark plummets. Yet Kerpi's killing of his protagonist is neither a condemnation of the traditional nor a repudiation of the modern but an expression of the sense that for the educated Papua New Guinean navigating a decolonizing modernity, all that is solid has melted into air. For young people such as Mark, the old ways have become insubstantial, invisible shadows that haunt them, and new attestations of independence leave nothing secure under their feet.

Crucially, this fraught path is explicitly joined to the inroads and byways of a global literary modernity. Kerpi's description of Mark as a "man among our people" (13) is an allusion to Achebe's novel *A Man of the People* (1966), which was taught in the Department of Language and Literature at the University of Papua New Guinea, and as Mark walks away from the meeting, he thinks about *Song of Lawino* (1966), a "long poem of lament" by Okot p'Bitek, a Ugandan poet he—and Kerpi—studied at UPNG. And perhaps afterward met in person, as Okot attended the Papua New Guinea Writers' Conference in 1976.[2] In Okot's epic poem, Lawino, a traditional village woman, protests against her educated husband's rejection of customary practices and laments his obsession with Western culture. Ocol, Lawino's husband, has taken an urbanized and educated second wife, who fuels his fascination with Western dress, technology, and lifestyles, as well as his increasing distaste for local customs. In Kerpi's story, Mark recalls the discussions he and his friends had about the poem and worries that if he marries Kulpu's daughter he will be cast as "the educated black-white husband Lawino was lamenting over" (13). This realization is a pivotal point in the story, as Mark decides that regardless of whether the community considers him a villain or a fool, regardless of the lamenting his Lawino might do for him, he will not marry based on village demands. In a merging of old and new religions he vows to God, the stars, the moon, and spirits of the darkness: "I am the master of my soul and body. And I curse those who deny this God-given freedom" (13). This affirmation of his agency is followed swiftly by stress-induced hallucinations, however, until Mark follows phantom sounds off the edge of the cliff.

The woman Mark is asked to marry is never named; she remains Kulpu's daughter and is described only through her beauty and her expensive brideprice. Mark's education took place outside his community, an experience shared by most Papua New Guineans receiving post-primary education during this period, and this separation ruptured his connection with the village pride and values that might make her beauty and price important to him. Alienated from his community and bereft of a personal investment in the proposed marriage and its political ramifications, he substitutes a literary one: Okot's *Song of Lawino*. A colonial education structure had removed him from his village, but an anticolonial university had given villages back to him, albeit villages scattered across the postcolonial world rather than located on a single mountain. Mark's classes in a literature department committed to world literatures and anticolonial ideologies provided a means through which the estranged youth could imagine how his village and a village woman might view him, so he relates to his home by superimposing an Acoli village on a Niuginian one and turning Kulpu's daughter into Lawino's double. The department's attempt to mitigate long years of colonial education and exploitation embeds Mark in global discourses of postcolonial modernity, and by exposing him to the alienation portrayed by modern writers across the world attempts to provide him with the tools for contemplating and advancing his own position. Within the narrative, these tools are helpful but inadequate, and Mark loses his way. With the text "Kulpu's Daughter," however, published in the literary journal *Kovave*, which was founded at UPNG, Kerpi presents newly learned orientations for a generation navigating modern Papua New Guinea.

The layered setting of Kerpi's story makes it a perfect exemplar of the connections wrought by and through education systems in postcolonial modernities: a Papua New Guinean author examines a local tension between the modern and the traditional by drawing on a Ugandan poet he encountered at university, whose own works voice the clash between the local and the foreign by drawing on sources from "friends, enemies, school."[3] Okot's poem is a cry for nativist pride, and it is often understood as more locally traditionalist in form and approach than the works of Wole Soyinka and Christopher Okigbo. However, as Oga Ofuani and Jahan Ramazani have argued, even in his traditionalism Okot draws on techniques and styles that blend the African and the Western. Okot's translation of *Song of Lawino* into English "combines the long Western dramatic monologue in free verse with the repetitions and oral urgency of Acoli songs; its diction intertwines Acoli words and semi-translated proverbs with a robustly Africanized English; and its anti-Western localism is informed, ironically, by Okot's Western anthropological training."[4] The version that students at UPNG studied was a modernist-receptive work: when reading *Song of Lawino* in English, they read a Ugandan poem castigating Western intrusions through the repurposing of Western poetics. In this way Okot retooled modernist aesthetics to his own ends. This recycling clearly resonated with Kerpi: in addition to his remodeling of Okot for "Kulpu's Daughter," he causes his protagonist to argue that when creating art and molding society a man must choose "the parts that are sweet to his tongue" (9), as it is the individualism and suitability of his choices, not an adherence to an illusory untouched purity, that renders works, and societies, unique. An unattributed article in the student magazine *Nilaidat*, possibly written by the literature student John Waiko, makes a similar point: "If we are mature, we need not fear outside influences—in fact, we need visits from Australian producers, Russian novelists, German musicians, and so on. Drawing on what we see as the best in all of these, and avoiding what we dislike in them and what we see as inappropriate to us, we can develop and strengthen our own ideas and expression."[5] For Kerpi and his contemporaries at the University of Papua New Guinea in the 1960s and 1970s, the sweetest parts seem often to be found in the globally routed courses of the literature curriculum. In tracking these delicacies, however, we cannot ignore the ways that global routes and international movement are bound up in racial and colonial hierarchies: while students at UPNG read Okot's poem, they could not read his DPhil in anthropology, which the University of Oxford had failed twice on problematic grounds.[6]

In this chapter, we follow the logic of UPNG's pioneering literature and creative writing program, covering the major courses in the order that students took them, to consider the entangled presentation of modernist texts and the impact of this entanglement on UPNG's student writers. These writers drew on the thematic preoccupations, rhetorical devices, and political investments of writers they encountered at university, with the African texts on the syllabuses providing a notable source of inspiration. As outlined in our introduction, the UPNG degree structure was innovative: it began with oral literature, which was followed by the literatures of decolonizing countries and then by modernist literatures, with an emphasis on Europe. As such, the degree program concentrated on expressions of contemporary life, be they based on oral aesthetics, embedded in decolonizing politics, or imbued with literary and philosophical experimentation. This subversive course structure undercut the primacy of canonical Western literature by rejecting both the content of the Beowulf-to-Brontë format and its pattern of chronological development. Instead, much of the oral literature studied was both contemporary and historical. The emerging literature courses had some early-twentieth-century texts by writers such as R. K. Narayan, Rabindranath Tagore, and Aimé Césaire but primarily engaged with texts from the 1950s and 1960s by writers like Chinua Achebe and Alex La Guma, and the modern literature courses began in the late nineteenth century with Fyodor Dostoevsky and Joseph Conrad and moved across the twentieth to the present with writers such as T. S. Eliot, D. H. Lawrence, Franz Kafka, V. S. Naipaul, and Kōbō Abe.

We map out the importance of beginning with oral forms, but of particular interest in this chapter is the impact—to the students and to contemporary modernist scholarship—of a curriculum that positioned a select corpus of European and American modernism after contemporary works from Africa and India. By exposing students at UPNG to texts that drew on Indigenous forms and European modernists to express modern life in decolonizing countries—and to condemn colonial rule—Pacific students encountered models, like that offered by Okot, of the ways that the local and the Western could be grafted together to form aesthetically minded and politically focused texts. As difficult as it is to wholly overturn the hierarchies instilled at school, the pedagogic trajectory of the department's degree structure interrupted colonial mapping of lines of influence, thereby decentering the imperial hub, as the modern literature courses were organized such that they approached Europe from Africa, say, rather than Africa after Europe. This structure would, most appropriately, have followed the path that many European and American modernists took when they themselves found inspiration in Africa and the East. The students, having already had some exposure to modernism in school syllabi, thus accessed European and American modernism via African modernists, who were themselves motivated by Western modernists, who had been motivated by African arts. Approached from this direction, which is to say from multiple directions simultaneously, the syntheses and the new trajectories of innumerable modernist writings and writings of modernity would have been readily visible, and global literary history recognized as a pattern, albeit an uneven one, of diverse influence and reworking.

The most prolific writers from UPNG drew upon techniques from European, American, and African writers, techniques that contemporary scholarship associates with modernism. Whether the UPNG staff and students saw the content of the emerging and modern literature courses as modern or modernist is a question of greater interest to modernist scholars than it was to them: while the question of what constituted modern writing in Africa or the Pacific was a point of frequent debate by UPNG writers, the distinction or overlap between modern and modernist writing was not a source of concern. The driver of developments in the UPNG curriculum was not disciplinary upheaval but a national project of agency and independence. It sought to undo the limitations of colonial curricula on personal, political, and aesthetic development by opening students up to the oral forms, novels, poetry, and plays that could inspire a literary revolution in Papua New Guinea. In so doing, however, Beier and the rest of the UPNG staff saw the value of texts we would see as "canonically modernist" to lie in their various modes of writing and critiquing modern life. By tracing, through juxtaposition, transnational webs of interconnecting explorations of the modern world from Africa to India, the curricular projects at UPNG and, slightly later, USP foreshadow the approaches of what would come to be called global modernism. The revelatory result for the modernist scholar reopening the course books of the decolonizing world is the realization that pedagogic spaces like those at UPNG and USP created the conditions for the new modernist studies to arise.

As we argued in the previous chapter, modernist writing, be it from Harlem or Accra, appealed in the Pacific because it resonated with the rhythms and sounds of modernity, rebellion, and revolution; because it gave voice to familiar struggles with confusing, alienating spaces; because it came with overtones of intellect and reflection; because it was bound up with decolonization; and because, we suggest, it carried echoes of oral traditions. The oral literature courses presented orature, histories, and mythologies that were similar to the narratives that students heard at home. Kirsty Powell's interviews of PNG playwrights in the 1970s show that while most felt alienated from their communities, particularly because of the educational opportunities that had taken them far away, few seem to have been so removed as to have forgotten their homes' literary traditions in chants, songs, and dances.[7] By following classes on orature with modern African and Indian literature that articulated the contemporary via a compound of traditional elements and international literary forms, the seeming obsolescence of traditional tales was belied by their use in works full of the material markings of the present—clothes, technology, politics, transportation, and so on—and by their continual applicability. While these texts may not have been considered modernist during the 1970s, they were clearly seen as explorations of postcolonial modernities that frequently and overtly drew upon European and North American modernism. Students thus encountered and reencountered various forms of modernism across their schooling. Importantly, however, within the tertiary setting, they approached African and Caribbean writers' assimilations and recastings of modernist forms and themes *before* classes on modernism in Europe. Modernism was thus already an involved form, replete with reinscriptions and alterations.

ON THE INAUGURATION OF THE ENGLISH DEPARTMENT: READING THE SYLLABUS

When Beier accepted a position as a lecturer in phonetics at the University of Ibadan in 1950, he found it a colonial university whose linguistics courses served little purpose beyond giving students "an English upper class accent." He thought of transferring to literature, but their courses followed syllabi set in London and were, he argued, little better than "exercise[s] in colonialism."[8] He moved instead to the extramural department, and within its more flexible teaching environment became an important force in the Nigerian literary scene. In 1966, he and his wife, Georgina, an artist who would involve herself with Papua New Guinean art, moved to UPNG. The faculty at the Waigani campus's Department of Language and Literature—Beier,

Prithvindra Chakravarti, and Frank Johnson, with Taban Lo Liyong, a poet and academic from South Sudan, Elton Brash, Michael Greicus, and Adeola James joining in the late 1970s—sought to move away from a literary education bound by anxious adherence to the Western canon and tried instead to instill in their students a passion for local literary traditions and anticolonial ideologies. They hoped that students could think of English as a useful tool they could control, mold, and change to their own needs and desires, rather than a language of calcified norms determined by a colonial authority.[9] So they designed an ingenious degree program that, while subject to alterations as staff came and went, commenced "with a study of oral literature and the literature of developing countries in English," then studied "modern world literature in English." As the department grew, more courses were offered, including literary criticism, drama, advanced folklore studies, and special studies of selected authors and nations, but the basic pattern remained.[10] Beier and later Chakravarti also offered creative writing courses, but these were available to a small number of second- or third-year students by invitation only.[11]

A quick overview of the English major in the late 1960s and early 1970s provides important insights into the works the students read and the implications of the order in which they read them. The inclusion of oral material was a bold decision: some years before he would work at UPNG, Liyong joined forces with Ngũgĩ wa Thiong'o and Henry Owuor-Anyumba to write the polemical piece "On the Abolition of the English Department," whose suggestions included repositioning oral traditions as the root of literary studies in Africa.[12] This approach was already being implemented for the Pacific context at UPNG, an innovation that connects UPNG firmly to the history of radical pedagogy and literary studies. In their first courses, students studied folklore from around the world, with a strong emphasis on Africa, India, and Oceania, the latter primarily through the Papua Pocket Poets series and specially stenciled copies of local origin stories.[13] Beier's *The Origin of Life and Death: African Creation Myths* (1966) and Chakravarti and Beier's *The Oral Poetry of Bengal* were frequently used. Obotunda Ijimere's *The Imprisonment of Obatala* (1966), Beier's *Five New Guinea Plays* (1971), and Tutuola's *The Palm-Wine Drinkard* (1952) were drawn on to demonstrate modern African experiments with oral traditions—a pedagogic exercise troubled by the fact that, as we detail in the next chapter, Ijimere and M. Lovori (whose work was included in *Five New Guinea Plays*) were not Nigerian or Niuginian playwrights but some of the Indigenous identities fabricated by Beier. Gradually more works from the Papua Pocket Poets series were included, along with Beier's and Chakravarti's collections, such as their coedited *Sun and Moon in New Guinea Folklore* (1974). In this way peers and near-peers were included in the curriculum, showing students how their publications could become pedagogic material and be the subject of focused classroom analysis and inspiration. We will see an intensification of this strategic use of local, contemporary authors in the USP curriculum in chapter 5.

The students followed the oral literature course with courses on New Writing in English from Emerging Nations, with a concentration on Africa and India. The African course presented authors from across Africa, many of whom Beier had published in *Black Orpheus*. In 1971, for example, students read Césaire, p'Bitek, Achebe, Soyinka, Camara Laye, Gabriel Okara, Ferdinand Oyono, Alex La Guma, and Andrew Salkey, as well as anthologies of modern African poetry and prose, and négritude poetry edited by Beier. In the course on new writing from Asia students read V. S. Naipaul, Thakazhi Sivasankara Pillai, Bhabani Bhattacharyn, Rabindranath Tagore, and a host of anthologies of shorter fiction and poetry. However, as we will see in our discussion of student writing below, it is the material from Africa that seems to have resonated most strongly in UPNG at this time.

Students then moved on to courses that looked at "important literary and philosophical trends in modern literature."[14] Staying with 1971, Modern World Literature I paid particular attention to the relationship between the individual and the community by moving "from the problems of colonialism and independence to direct and indirect handling of European preoccupations with war and personal responsibility."[15] The reading list was extensive: Joseph Conrad, Bertolt Brecht, Jean-Paul Sartre, George Orwell, Max Frisch, Erich Maria Remarque, and Boris Pasternak were taught alongside works by Peter Shaffer, Raja Rao, Peter Abrahams, and V. S. Naipaul. In the same year, Modern World Literature II focused on European and American literature, and the course description gives a clear indication of the approach: "in this part, moral choice will be considered in more philosophical detail. From the expression of the 'primitive' in man, the rottenness of Western society as a whole will be considered leading to ideas of alienation, existentialism, and absurdism on behalf of individuals."[16] The students engaged extensively with modernist authors: Lawrence, Eliot, Kafka, Allen Ginsberg, Samuel Beckett, Albert Camus, Eugène Ionesco, Harold Pinter, Saul Bellow, Carson McCullers, Jean Genet, as well as Dostoevsky, William Golding, John Whiting, Arthur Miller, and Kōbō Abe. Over the years the texts changed, but these courses are broadly representative of the content that recurred. There is a significant lack of women across all courses—although Oodgeroo Noonuccal (Kath Walker) gave the keynote lecture at the 1976 Papua New Guinea Writers' Conference and spoke to the students—and of African American voices in the modern fiction reading lists, although in 1973 Modern World Literature II included *Black Fire: An Anthology of Afro-American Writing*, edited by LeRoi Jones and Larry Neal. It should also be noted that course records are apparently not exhaustive; John Kadiba, for example, has recently described the powerful impact of James Baldwin's *Another Country*, which he was taught at UPNG but which is not listed on the official records.[17] Yet the records as we have them give a clear sense of course content and emphasis, allowing us to trace in some detail the progressions and juxtapositions between texts that students encountered.

By 1971 the degree offered at the Department of Language and Literature was not only progressive but deeply modern, in that it was dedicated to different ways of writing the contemporary: traditional Niuginian ways of expressing the present, African and Indian ways that commingled the conventions of local traditions and Western modernism, and European and American ways whose modernist approaches incorporated traditional elements. It was also strongly political, as an anticolonial agenda pervaded its choices of and approach to the texts. In presenting European and North American texts after the literatures of colonized countries, the program invited students to consider the political responsibility of the West while also reflecting on the aesthetic potential but not inevitable dominance of the West's literary output. The importance of politics is unsurprising. The Department of Language and Literature operated in a decolonizing space where, in addition to lectures, the intellectual climate was stirred by the Waigani Seminars, Niugini Arts Festivals, and Writers' Conferences, as well as student groups such as the Politics Club, the Black Power movement, the Drama Society, and the Melanesian Action group. As we will see in chapter 4, groups such as these were also vital components of the literary scene.

DECOLONIZING THE LITERATURE PROGRAM

"TANGLED STRANDS AND WEAVING KNOTS": ORALITY AND MODERNISM

The folklore paper did not merely study published oral accounts but established an important practical component: students recorded, transcribed, translated, and analyzed orature from their own villages, exploring the literary devices employed by their own communities. Importantly, as Beier remarked elsewhere, students were not "'recording' the folklore of a dying and foreign culture" but showing themselves to be active parts of a living tradition: "story*tellers* rather than *collectors*."[18] For Beier, as he insisted in *Words of Paradise: Poetry of Papua New Guinea* (1972), poetry was a "*living* tradition in New Guinea," with older and contemporary compositions alike only different instances of a dynamic art form. All the poems in the collection, he argues, are "*traditional* in the sense that they are part of a group of cultures whose roots go very far back and that they still use ancient forms," but some are also "*modern* in the sense that traditional forms are often used to describe or celebrate contemporary events."[19] Beier asserts that the oral literature that students studied was, first, part of a long literary tradition and, second, that this living literary tradition was wholly capable of depicting modern Papua New Guinea on its own terms. Students could choose to bring the literary traditions of their parents into conversation with the literary traditions that they were taught in schools, but this blend was not their only access to representations of the contemporary. The necessary aesthetic and conceptual tools had already been given to them at home.

Kovave, which Beier founded at UPNG, contains numerous interpretative, creative acts of collection, as oral stories were inscribed on the printed page. Kumalau Tawali contributed "Three Tales from Manus" (1969), Leo Hannett published "Creation: The Creation Story of the Nehan People" (1970), and Arthur Jawodimbari recorded and transcribed his father's telling of "The Migration of the Girda Tribe" (1970). From his mother's people Jawodimbari transcribed the tale of how the sun was initially taken away from a community but finally released to shine in all people. This transcription was published in Beier and Chakravarti's *Sun and Moon* as "The Owner of the Sun" but was first given a theatrical reworking as *The Sun* (1970) in *Kovave*. Bringing dances, songs, drums, flutes, and conch shells on stage, Jawodimbari's play draws on the techniques of repetition and elaboration found in various modes of prose-poetry in Niugini and running through the works in *Kovave*: "A man walks proudly in the sun / a man walks angrily in the warmth ... A man walks proudly in the sun / he is going to offend an orphan ... A man walks angrily to the orphan."[20] These techniques also embed *The Sun* in the UPNG curriculum, as they are found too in the works of Obotunda Ijimere—Beier's Nigerian avatar whose *Imprisonment of Obatala* was on the oral literature course—and the Yoruban playwright Duro Ladipo, with whom Beier had collaborated and with whom in 1974 Jawodimbari would work.[21] *The Sun* is thus a simultaneously local and transnational work, born of the village and the urban university.

The adaptations of oral stories were joined by original and popular works that played with the tensions between the modern and the traditional. John Waiko's "The Old Man and the Balus" (1970) presents an account of a villager's first time in an airplane, while Addie Odai translated from the Graged language a song about a woman going to Madang because she wants "to take an X ray."[22] Russell Soaba's "The Villager's Request" (1974), which was republished in "Mana" and included in the USP literature curriculum, is presented as a student's transcription of a narrative recorded from an elder, but instead of a traditional tale, it offers an all-too-modern account of an old man's failure to traverse contemporary Port Moresby. The man's lack of money prevents him from taking buses, and his unfamiliarity with written languages means that he cannot follow road signs. He is unable to navigate as he cannot see the stars, and when he is finally arrested for wearing "indecent" traditional clothing, the policemen's mockery defies customary protocols respecting age.[23] Although the motif of a transcribed oral account might imply a point of communion between the elder and the youth, the "young lad" translating the story shows little empathy, and the old man assumes that the boarding school and university have turned him into "one of those quiet but polite gentlemen produced by Western education."[24] The student is a reluctant listener, and in his eagerness to board a bus and visit his girlfriend he draws the old man's account to a hurried close. Against Beier's assertions about the value of UPNG assignments in the documentation of orature, Soaba's story of an old man's humiliation, barely attended to by his student recorder, suggests that the narrative rapprochement these exercises foresee may itself be fictional. Orality, Soaba suggests, may well be able to tell tales of the present, but this is a present that frequently refuses to accommodate the lives of its traditional tellers, thereby misrepresenting and disrespecting their experiences.

DECOLONIZING THE LITERATURE PROGRAM

Presenting a traditional voice decrying modernity through the guise of a modern university exercise on traditional narratives, Soaba calls to African criticisms of colonial modernity within supposedly tradition-oriented works. In *The Palm-Wine Drinkard* (1952), read by students at both UPNG and USP, Tutuola uses local storytelling traditions to subvert the literary expectations of colonial education systems. As Dan Izavbaye has argued, this technique reveals an "African alternative to the realist conventions of the rationalist tradition."[25] Tutuola's deployment of Yoruba folktales and oral modes encouraged the book's reception in Europe and America as primitivist and decidedly nonmodern, yet as Izavaye and others have shown, its seeming timelessness is rooted within a decolonizing Nigerian modernity. The "white tree" episode, for example, features photographs, Technicolor lights, hospitals, a dancing hall decorated with one million pounds, injections, cigarettes, high-heeled shoes, and orchestras. The white tree is a place of control, financial exchange, and surveillance, and thus, in the middle of a surreal West African tree-being, Tutuola inserts an interchange drawing in the totems of modernity and capitalism.[26] Yoruba storytelling traditions and modern life become conjoined in ways that the students would encounter again, albeit in modified forms, in Soyinka and p'Bitek, and the erosion of imperially introduced bulwarks between an Africanist past and a colonialist future would prove valuable in the Papua New Guinean literary context. The novel worked its way into Niuginian writing: although Kadiba's autobiographical account of "Growing Up in Mailu" in the *Kovave* pilot issue deals with the loss of his mother, the opening pages recounting his early life and his version of the story of how the coconut first came to his village are clearly indebted to Tutuola's tone, style, and humor.[27]

Despite these examples of Papua New Guinean writers engaging with questions of tradition, Beier recorded his disappointment with his students' lack of interest in exploring contemporary issues in textual modes based directly on oral traditions.[28] We can speculate on the reasons for this perceived neglect—the legacy of a school system and social context that encouraged students to look away from traditional forms, the desire of young people to write in their version of the literary present and embrace future-oriented forms, the commitment of young people to modes they think conducive to political change. But whatever the case, they undoubtedly absorbed the idea presented in the oral and developing literature courses of bringing vernaculars into their texts. *Kovave*'s pilot features Leo Hannett's

"Em Rod Bilong Kago," and Rabbie Namaliu published two plays in Tok Pisin: *The Good Woman of Konedobu* (1970), which brings Brechtian allusions to local contexts, and *Maski Kaunsil* (1968, published in *Kovave* in 1975).[29] John Kasaipwalova's "The Magistrate and My Grandfather's Testicles" (1972) makes raucous use of slang and non-standard English, as does "Betel Nut Is Bad Magic for Aeroplanes" (1971). This short story is based on a one-man demonstration that Kasaipwalova staged at Port Moresby's airport, where he protested the banning of betel nuts in the building by standing under a "no betel nuts" sign and pointedly chewing. When he was asked to stop, he pointed out that white people were allowed to scatter cigarette butts everywhere.[30] His story, which won first prize in the 1971 short story competition, shows a university student besting the various levels of a colonial administration. Told to spit out the betel nut as there are "plenty plenty white people inside the terminal," the narrator and his friends are passed from local employees, through their white bosses, to the upper echelons of colonial law enforcement.[31] The story closes with victory for Kasaipwalova's narrator, who stoutly asserts his rights one last time: refusing inconvenience as he refused the guards' demands, he and his friends are driven from Boroko Police Station back to the university, "chewing our betel-nut on the way."[32]

Framing the story's modern locations—the airport, a place of connectivity and infiltration; the police station, a place long associated with a law indifferent to Niuginian needs; the university, a place of empowerment, albeit one tainted by colonial association—is the chewing of betel nut. Betel nut, we are reminded by the narrator and a female university student who sides with the group, is an inextricable part of Papua New Guinean modernity but also part of a culture that existed long before colonial powers arrived. Such social practices as "chewing plenty buwa [betel nut] like civilised people" will, the story suggests, long outlast foreign administrations and their cultural biases.[33] The narrator's success in obliging modern PNG to accommodate long-standing Niuginian cultural preferences is predicated on his ability to switch between linguistic registers—his narrative and his arguments draw on Tok Pisin, Motu, and English—as well as his knowledge of the law. Although the story is told in a rich indigenized English whose grammar and syntax is heavily informed by Niuginian creoles—"We was standing about thirty of we, waiting to catch our things"—when the narrator counters the security guards and the police he does so through fluent legalese supported by standard English: "They are political terms which I often ascribe to persons committing injustice."[34] In this way the narrator protects his native culture by wielding the native language of the administration against them, using the knowledge of the law and English that his colonial schools and university gave him to overturn the administration's prejudices. In this short, humorous piece that abounds with linguistic play, Kasaipwalova pits Black Power against white supremacy—and wins. In so doing, he pushes back against the founding document of the university. The Currie Report, which had led to the formation of UPNG, had patronizingly rejected Tok Pisin as a potential lingua franca for the university, stating that while Tok Pisin could be "ingenious and at times delightful," it could not articulate "even quite simple abstract concepts with elegance, precision and economy. Efforts to demonstrate its range, say by translating Shakespearean speeches, fall into the category of literary curiosities—entertaining certainly, but as certainly trivial."[35] Student writers like Kasaipwalova and Namaliu proved the report wrong, certainly.[36]

Encouraging the writing of tradition into modernity, the first cluster of courses in the department's degree structure worked, we propose, to render the experimentalism of European and American writers amenable to local contexts. A typical English literature program introduces modernism as a late development, stressing its radical departures from the literary conventions of the nineteenth century. As any literature lecturer knows, these departures can be bewildering for students, and it is often only when their disruptive functions are explained in the context of literary history that techniques such as fragmentation, nontemporality, and bricolage begin to appear meaningful. When introduced after local and African orature, however, this contextualizing reading is itself disrupted, and new affinities are revealed: disjunction, fragmentariness, and mythical interplay may appear more familiar, continuities rather than radical departures.

Apisai Enos notes that the time sequence in Papua New Guinean oral literature is of lesser importance than experience and sensations, and the "non-sequential perception" found in oral traditions "creates a distorted reality" full of temporal leaps that do not necessarily seek to form a rational picture. The supernatural and the natural interconnect and fuse, and these works are full of symbols and allusions.[37] Such modes of storytelling, found across the Pacific, partake in what has been called "spiral time," a completely different basis for narrative.[38] As Selina Tusitala Marsh explains, the "spiral's structure confronts and defies the Western linear hierarchical way of thinking, urging the mind's eye toward a centre that allows for the possibility of multiple centres; it 'looks' back even as it progresses forward, hence embracing the common Polynesian adage: 'We face the future with our backs.'"[39] Spiral time in turn evokes the Polynesian concept of the vā, a spatial and relational concept that Caroline Sinavaiana Gabbard interprets as a "dynamics of space-time continuum, in which both space and time always already operate inseparably and simultaneously."[40] A complex sense of perspective and relationality is met with the use of repetition, or the variation of a recurring phrase, as an aesthetic choice that layers meaning and enables the plot to progress in steps.[41] As Waiko, a UPNG student during this period, later wrote regarding Binandere oral traditions, myths and legends are deeply complex forms, and even when they have a specific moral to impart, they consist of "myriad tangled strands and weaving knots passing one on top of the other, mingling sacred and secular values, and leaving the listeners to unravel a small part of the mystery of right behaviour."[42] Ideas of collage, anonymity, and a chorus of responses—all elements easily associated with modernism—are present within orature, and there is also much implied and encoded information. A naïve listener, Waiko insists, would struggle with the layers of meaning.[43]

The sense of familiarity for UPNG students engaging with modernism might have been increased by European modernism's own investment in oral traditions, folklore, and mythology. Faber and Faber's decision to publish *The Palm-Wine Drinkard* immediately brings the book into Eliot's circle and the sphere of modernist interest, but modernism was from the start embroiled with traditional forms.[44] In his 1923 review of *Ulysses*, Eliot drew attention to Joyce's manipulation of "a continuous parallel between contemporaneity and antiquity," famously comparing his use of myth to Yeats's "way of controlling, of ordering, of giving a shape and a significance to the immense panorama of futility and anarchy which is contemporary history."[45] By using the *Odyssey* as a frame on which to hang a story shot through with other mythic allusions, Joyce gives substance to modern lives while preventing that substance from fixing or closing meaning. In the same way, Robert Hampson argues, Conrad layers *Heart of Darkness* with myriad mythic quests and journeys of enlightenment, from the Buddhist Jatakas to Dante's *Divine Comedy*.[46] Eliot's use of fertility myths and anthropological works, like Lawrence's ethnological pretensions and his desire to recover lost origins, speak to the modernists' awareness of a modern world embedded in the past.[47]

J. G. Frazer's *The Golden Bough* offered modernist writers a means through which to reconfigure the dominance of Christianity and thereby recognize the legitimacy and interrelatedness of other worldviews. Once Christianity is understood as a borrower and assimilator of other religious beliefs, it becomes less the source of absolute truth and more a master in creative collage. Myth becomes that which is already present in Christian faith and that which can relativize its importance.[48] We can trace the impact of this position in Beier's approach to creation stories. For Beier, as he writes in his introduction to *African Creation Myths*, creation stories showed the range of "answers given by man to the problems and mysteries of life and death," and he refused a hierarchy that positioned Christian origin stories as truth and other accounts as myths.[49] His position rightly serves to put "Christian mythology into its proper place," but in so doing it also treats all origin stories as either social documents that explain cultural knowledge and belief rather than truth, or as "pure literature."[50] In approaching all creation accounts as epistemology and art but deprioritizing narratives' theological and genealogical aspects, the department's methodologies were progressively Western but not Pacific.[51] It would be left to students such as Soaba to find local ways to decenter Christianity in fiction, though he was joined by autobiographical accounts such as Hannett's "Disillusionment with the Priesthood" (1970). In his play *Scattered by the Wind* (1972), Soaba blends the bible stories of the Prodigal Son and Cain and Abel with existential tropes, Brechtian choruses, and Anuki songs and dance. The play, like much of Soaba's writing, sees living—and in this play, dying—with painful, alienating truth morally superior to a life calcified by the false comforts of doctrine. The play suggests that dogmatic belief systems like Christianity have not only led to the death of freethinkers such as James, the play's protagonist, but of entire communities, "whose past is a long story of this very land" yet whose future is "nothing but dead silence."[52] Against a life of doctrine and deceptive compliance, which causes brother to kill brother, are the possibilities of other ways, which fuse an individualist choice of Anuki and Western practices.

The Literature of Oral Traditions course included Frazer's *Folklore in the Old Testament: Studies in Comparative Religion, Legend, and Law*, a text that works to similar ends as *The Golden Bough*. UPNG students read oral works and Frazer's grammar of the human imagination and later read modernist works inspired by Frazer, thereby encountering both the exposition of interconnectedness and the literary manifestations of this exposition. From such a starting point, the texts in the emerging and modern world literature courses must have appeared less alien, more akin to local traditions, and more available for appropriation to the students of UPNG than they might appear to their European or American counterparts. Of course, while Frazer's works may have enabled an important awareness of the recurring nature of rituals, narratives, and symbols, his work was bound up in the same assumption of developmental hierarchies that Pacific Islanders were forced to contend with in their struggle for decolonization. Frazer saw humanity as progressing away from the lives lived by many Papua New Guinean students' families. This means that in the classroom, students were confronted with writing and analysis that simultaneously reinforced and undercut Western dominance and that closed certain doors to modernity to them even as it opened others. Lewis Nkosi, the South African writer whom UPNG students read in their emerging literature courses in 1973, puts it forcibly: "much of Modernism is driven by negative impulses, even hatred of modern society and its arrangements, even without a reincorporation of excluded elements from dominated societies."[53] Yet even with this exclusion, the very fact of the negative impulse allows its manipulation toward anticolonial ends. "Eurocentric Modernity," Nkosi concludes, "contains within itself enough critical resources to undo what it set up."[54]

LIVES LIKE OURS: AFRICAN MODERNISM

After their studies of orality, students turned to New Writing in English from Emerging Nations, works that showed UPNG students African and Indian versions of lives close to their own. As Tawali recounts, "most of the novels I had read before I came to the University were written by Europeans." But at university, he continues, "I started reading African literature and I found that it illustrated the life of the villagers," men and women who lived similar lives to Niuginians.[55] The novels' and plays' explorations of colonial encounters and political revolution offered portals to their own and their communities' possible futures. The early years of the protagonist Mhendi in Peter Abraham's *A Wreath for Udomo* (1956), which they encountered in Modern World Literature I, would have been both familiar and inspiriting: "The missionaries had picked out the brightest boy in a little village in Africa and set about educating him. Education had brought awareness. The boy had then examined the world in which he lived and found it wanting by the very standards the missionaries had given him. He had turned against them then and struck out on his own."[56] The authors that the literature students encountered were, like them, educated colonial subjects who felt the cleavages and interruptions that displaced them within their traditional communities. The most educated Africans may have been the most alienated from traditional structures, but they were also the most disillusioned with colonialism. In a reading of *A Wreath for Udomo*, Simon Gikandi argues that the modern African individual was formed in the act of negotiating and reworking both tradition and colonialism, an act of self-formation rather than the erasure of an authentic self behind the masks of Frantz Fanon or the mimicry of Homi K. Bhabha.[57] These acts of self-formation were represented and advanced in novels, poetry, and plays, which both fueled the anticolonial movement at home and—on the other side of the world—gave students at UPNG a literature of displacement, trauma, and degradation, as well as resistance, humor, and hard-won dignity. And also anger, as we see in Tawali's "The Bush Kanaka Speaks" (1970), a poem that derides the rage and ignorance of the Kiaps, district officers who were traveling representatives of the British and Australian governments in colonial PNG. Each stanza of a rural dweller's quiet description of local knowledge is punctuated with a chorus describing the Kiap's excessive aggression: "The kiap shouts at us / forcing the veins to stand out on his neck / nearly forcing the excreta out of his bottom." Yet all the officer's anger and insistence on the perceived inferiority of Niuginian life is simply a failed attempt, Tawali's speaker maintains, to hide the fact that "these white men have no bones."[58]

Given the emphasis on African writers in accounts of world literature at the time and the prevalence of allusions to African works in UPNG writers' fiction and drama, we concentrate here on the African component of the Emerging Literature course. These writings showed the lure of modernity (*Houseboy*) and the alienation of the educated, political elite (*A Wreath for Udomo*). They portrayed the rot caused by colonization (*Notebook of a Return to the Native Land*) as well as the potential for postindependence corruption, authoritarian leadership, and community decline (*A Man of the People, Kongi's Harvest*). They demonstrated ways of critiquing Christianity

(*The Road*); of satirizing colonial paternalism (*The Old Man and the Medal*); of using oral forms to comment humorously on the daily difficulties of modern, colonial life (*Song of Lawino*); and of experiments with pidgin (*The Voice*). They ranged from absurdism in *A Man of the People* to angry, naturalist tragedy in *A Walk in the Night*.[59] Studied across the semester, they showed new ways of conceptualizing modern African nations, the grammar of which could be mapped to modern Pacific contexts.

In their introduction to *Modern Poetry from Africa*, Gerald Moore and Beier reflect on their selection processes for the volume. They acknowledge that their understanding of the modern is "difficult to define" but attempt to explain it in terms of value and voice: "In part it is simply a matter of quality; hence the exclusion of the rather tractarian verse of the West African pioneers. In part it is a matter of the poets' awareness of the modern idiom in European and American poetry. It is this awareness that enables them to use their respective languages without distracting archaism and in a way that appeals instantly to the contemporary ear."[60] In the previous chapter, we showed that Pacific uses of archaism trouble the straightforward grounds upon which Beier and Moore reject it in an African context, and "quality" is of course a hopelessly subjective marker. But Beier's choices for the Emerging Literature course at UPNG echo the choices made for *Modern Poetry from Africa*: authors whose depiction of Indigenous languages and lives also reflect an easy familiarity with modern Western poetics. For Moore and Beier, a contemporary writer in Africa was an Afropolitan writer, and we see that blend of the local and the cosmopolitan reflected in the works of UPNG authors.[61] This blend was aided by newly forged connections: Kasaipwalova's *Reluctant Flame*, which we analyze in detail in chapter 4, was published in 1971 under both the Papua and the Pan African Pocket Poets series, and in 1974 Jawodimbari visited Nigeria and spent time with the University of Ife Theatre Group. Later, while Liyong was chair of English, both Soyinka and Achebe would visit UPNG. Yet before all else, the exchange between Africa and Papua New Guinea was textual.

Take, for example, Oyono's *The Old Man and the Medal* (1956, translated 1967), from the New Writing in English from Emerging Nations course, which moved Jawodimbari to write *The Old Man's Reward* (1971). "If they can do it," Jawodimbari said of African writers, "so can we," and so he did, on the page and, by founding PNG's National Theatre Company, on the stage.[62] In Oyono's novel, which was set in Cameroon, written in French, and read by UPNG students in English translation, the protagonist Meka gives his land to the French colonial administration and permits his sons to fight and die for the French forces in the First World War. In Jawodimbari's play, set in PNG and written in English, the protagonist Danuba gives his land to the Australian administration and permits his sons to fight and die for Australian forces in the Second World War. Both men are rewarded by their administrations with medals, both undergo a ceremony designed with no thought to their comfort or culture, and both end up imprisoned, humiliated, and deeply disillusioned. Jawodimbari's remodeling not only shows the impact of modern African literature on students at UPNG but illustrates the ways students, through this literature, wrote themselves into a transnational anticolonial literature. *The Old Man's Reward* tells Pacific audiences that hope in administrations will only end in further shame and that this shame has been shared by colonized nations across the world. In refusing to reduce colonial humiliation to the actions of specific individuals or administrations, Jawodimbari uses the global literary networks he encountered at university to show that the ignominy caused by Pacific colonization is inherent to imperialism: despite differences in names, languages, or locations, there will not be a better experience for villagers, there will not be kinder colonizers, and there will not come a day when administrations harmonize with local customs: colonization, be it French, Australian, English, or Japanese, will always be a force of abasement and imposition.

When heard in unison, the two texts use local traumas to cry out against global power structures. They are joined by a third in "The Healer" (1970), a story published in *Kovave* by the Cook Islander Marjorie Tuainekore Crocombe, who took classes with Beier at UPNG and—as we show in chapter 6—played a central role in the establishment of USP's literary culture. "The Healer" concentrates on the power and eventual failure of Mata, a village ta'unga, but scenes such as the account of her husband's involvement in Anzac Day parades echo Oyono's *The Old Man and the Medal*.[63] The majority of the texts studied in the emerging literature courses evince the pull of local poetics and narrative forms, and UPNG students were often exposed to what Irele refers to as an "aesthetic traditionalism" in African literature, where authors adapted from the Western literary tradition to reflect African oral traditions, current idioms, and imagination.[64] But as African scholars and writers have recognized, there are equally strong correspondences between this literature and European and North American modernism. Césaire was an important surrealist, and Soyinka was among the poets criticized by Chinweizu, Onwuchekwa Jemie, and Ihechukwu Madubuike in *Towards the Decolonisation of African Literature* (1980) as producing work beset by "Hopkinsian syntactic jugglery, Poundian allusiveness and sprinkling of foreign phrases, and Eliotesque suppression of narrative and other logical linkages of the sort that creates obscurity in 'The Waste Land.'"[65] Gabriel Okara's *The Voice* (1964) contains modernist-inspired experimentalism, and Alex La Guma was spurred on by Hemingway's stylistic experiments.[66] Gikandi sees Oyono as a writer of modernist disenchantment, arguing that such alienation does not make sense outside the "orbit of enchantment with modernity that shadows and ultimately determines the story of the African as a modern subject."[67] Nkosi stated that it was the "writers of the Harlem Renaissance, W. E. B. Du Bois, Claude McKay, Langston Hughes, Countee Cullen among them, who kindled among black South Africans of my generation the desire to write."[68] The voices of African American modernism, also often drawing strongly on folkloric traditions, were an important source of inspiration across Atlantic and Pacific passages alike. And even where the African literature read by UPNG students appears realist, when we consider this style alongside the authors' influences and agendas, we recognize a realism whose minute scrutiny of the stresses of contemporary life leads frequently to what Irele described as "a general and resolute experimentation with form, based largely upon the application of the procedures of European modernism in the creation of what are manifestly parables of the African condition."[69] In the African literature the students encountered they saw a considered, creative use of European and American modernist styles and themes to write a modern Africa into being.

As such, we realize that, for Papua New Guinean students, a vibrant, productive aspect of the literary present they encountered at university was the localization, refashioning, and indigenization of early-twentieth-century literature as well as the modernizing of traditional elements. In *Moving the Centre* (1992), Ngũgĩ explains that even though he became increasingly troubled by Conrad's relation to imperialism, he saw much potential for African expression in Conrad: "[Conrad] was Polish, born in a country and a family that had known only the pleasures of domination and exile. He had learnt English late in life and yet he had chosen to write in it, a borrowed language, despite his fluency in his native tongue and in French. And what is more he had made it to the great tradition of English literature. Was he not already an image of what we, the new African writers, like the Irish writers before us, Yeats and others, could become?"[70]

If Ngũgĩ saw his future in Conrad and Yeats, did UPNG students see these authors as his past? That is, if European modernism is approached after contemporary postcolonial literature, does it seem foundational, or might it seem belated? Although many of the UPNG writers had read and studied European and North American modernists in school, the school systems in the Pacific Islands, as well as in Aotearoa New Zealand and Australia, still prioritized a more traditional approach to the literary canon. It was not until university that Niuginian writers engaged in detail with modernist texts as movements collectively responding to a changing world, but when they did so their courses on European and American modernism came after their courses on oral traditions and postcolonial, modernist-inflected literature. The students at UPNG thus read the works of those subverting and rewriting European modernists before they engaged in detail with these writers themselves. Eliot thus becomes reminiscent of Soyinka, Conrad contains echoes of Ngũgĩ, and Yeats calls to Achebe. Modernist alienation on the streets of London had been seen earlier, and more poignantly, on the streets of Cape Town, and yearnings to build and represent new worlds came to students fresh from reading the texts of colonial modernity. The African texts afforded students a powerful version of modernism not bound to the ideology of art for art's sake but to a commitment to community and self-determination: a pedagogic modernism constructed by those whose intellectual background gave them the breadth of literary knowledge, the immediate familiarity with colonization, the political impetus, the deep awareness of a crisis of identity, and, to an extent, the financial security to write an African modernity and imaginary into being. As such, not only did European and American modernism become more available for appropriation, but African writers seemed, as such, to do the modern most successfully.

"I MAKE UP MY MIND TO TAKE THIS OR THAT": MODERNIST MIXES

After an influential engagement with African literature, supplemented by writing from India, the Caribbean, and Australia, with a select few students chosen for the creative writing classes we mention further in the next chapter, students took the modern literature courses, which focused on the individual, community, war, colonization, politics, and, as quoted earlier, the alienation, existentialism, and absurdism caused by the "rot" in Western society. These courses introduced European and American material for the first time, but even in these courses the West was not presented in isolation but through broad temporal and geographical interchanges. Modern World Literature I mixed *Heart of Darkness* from 1899 with Abrahams's *A Wreath for Udomo* from 1956 and Raja Rao's *Kanthapura* from 1938 with Max Frisch's *Andorra* from 1961. In Modern World Literature II, Kōbō Abe's *The Woman of the Dunes* from 1962 was taught alongside *The Waste Land* from 1922, and Arthur Miller's *The Crucible* from 1953 was set against Kafka's *The Trial* from 1925. Naipaul was taught in both the emerging literature courses and modern world literature courses. If the progression across the English major positioned European and American modernists after writers they inspired, within the final courses timeframes and lines of influence were further disrupted as modernist literature was shown to arise across the world and the twentieth century. Modernity in its various forms recurred and recurred, as even authors within the oral tradition courses were wrestling with modernity—Tutuola's *The Palm-Wine Drinkard* might be, as Gikandi writes, a "fantasy of the unmodern," but its fantasy is "constantly haunted by the claims of the modern it seeks to foreclose," including urban spaces and capitalism.[71]

One of the most striking aspects of the modern world literature courses is the dominance of the theater of the absurd, a phrase Martin Esslin had popularized in 1961. For Esslin, the works of Beckett, Ionesco, Genet, Frisch, and Pinter, alongside elements within writings by Brecht, Sartre, and Camus, all of whom featured on the modern literature courses, strove to express "a world deprived of a generally accepted integrating principle, which has become disjointed, purposeless—absurd."[72] If the theater of the absurd marks a post-traumatic condition, the staff of the Department of Language and Literature also found it apt for ongoing trauma. In Ionesco's *The Lesson*, for example, a professor does not just cram knowledge into his students' heads but also empties them, sucking their vitality and finally disposing of their lifeless bodies. Within the PNG context, *The Lesson* operates as an extreme repudiation of the regressive aspects of many a colonial classroom and a deliberate reminder of what the tertiary system was

DECOLONIZING THE LITERATURE PROGRAM

working against. The relevance of absurdism is reflected in the students' published work: stories such as Kadiba's "Tax" (1969) and Kasaipwalova's "The Magistrate and My Grandfather's Testicles" (1972) might adopt a largely realist style, but their presentation of government levies as obscure, baffling payments that must be made to a shadowy administration associates their works with the oppressive opacity of bureaucracy in Kafka's *The Trial*.[73] When Kiaps such as those in Waiko's *The Unexpected Hawk* (1969) make impenetrable, seemingly vindictive decisions and villagers in Jawodimbari's *The Old Man's Reward* endure endless waiting for white administrators to arrive, we can see the ways in which Pinter and Beckett resonated.

As we will show in chapter 4, Soaba's long-standing love for Camus was well supported by the works taught in these papers, and his corpus reveals a fascination with existentialism and absurdism. "A Portrait of the Odd Man Out" (1971), which was Soaba's first contribution to *Kovave*, presents a protagonist from "nowhere" who struggles to articulate his rejection of conformity.[74] "A Glimpse of the Abyss" (1972) plays on similar themes, presenting a hitchhiker who has turned his back on old certainties in favor of a permanent journey to nothingness.[75] "The Victims" (1972) begins by telling readers that "*An ignorant animal is one which is enclosed in the dark, windowless prison of its own being*," which also evokes *The Waste Land*'s "each in his prison."[76] Calling for "Applause!" and then cuing "Dialogue!," Soaba presents his short story in theatrical terms: he reminds the reader of Shakespeare's claim that all the world's a stage but explains that those who do not like the parts that life has given them become the victims in life's drama. One such actor/victim is Stephen, the "first native martyr," who, echoing Joyce's protagonist in *Portrait*, will embrace "silence and ignorance" and journey "into the darkness of his own being only to return later to do nothing but destroy."[77] Stephen will be martyred by the colonial system, but he will also crush everything it has created, including the Indigenous groups who have profited from colonial rule.

The absurd world created by colonization is one that, for these young Niuginian writers, consolidates the traditional threat of village sorcerers, supernatural encounters, and raids by distant tribes with the modern threats of arcane bureaucratic systems and power structures that appear erratic but absolute. As such, Niuginan absurdism frequently draws on the horror and gothic dread contained within modernist canons, be they European,

American, or African, elements that we see refined in Subramani's sugarcane gothic, discussed in chapter 7. Kasaipwalova's play *Kanaka's Dream* (1971) is a case in point, as he combines a cosmopolitan absurdism with a rural gothic to depict the complexities of a colonized PNG. Dikodiko's white "masta" insists on strange, incomprehensible rules such as only taking two sugars in his coffee on Wednesdays, and as the play progresses, Dikodiko feels increasingly lost, an existential anguish caused by his own lies, the spells of village sorcerers, and the demands of white urban bosses: "I cannot separate the dream from the nightmare," he says, "because the two of us do not know which is the true me."[78] Unlike many of Soaba's texts, however, Kasaipwalova's play offers a resolution marked by greater hope and dynamism than the theater of the absurd usually provides: Dikodiko rouses himself against both the dark magic and against his white employer. The theater of the absurd pillories an "inauthentic, petty society" and in Europe arose as a response to the mid-twentieth century's traumatic loss of certainties about humanity's purpose.[79] In colonized contexts, absurdist sensitivities offered a means through which colonization, the cause of much inauthenticity, trauma, and loss, could be explored. But the presence of a foreign administration that was already retreating, of which many countries were ridding themselves, also implies an end date to their oppression. This fact grounds the majority of the works in *Kovave* in greater realism and satire, securing it where Western absurdist theater casts itself adrift and giving a clearer explanation for trauma than European absurdism usually allows.

Poetry took up a much smaller percentage of the modern world literature courses, but the students studied major works; in 1971 Eliot's *The Waste Land* was set alongside Ginsberg's *Howl*. The students came to these texts with a solid foundation: the emerging literature courses contained Okot's *Song of Lawino*, Moore and Beier's edition of *Modern Poetry from Africa*, Césaire's *Notebook of a Return to the Native Land*, Beier's edited collection of poetry dedicated to Okigbo, an anthology of négritude poetry that Beier put together for the emerging literature courses, and various collections, including Papua Pocket Poets editions, of modern poetry from Bengal, Indonesia, and India. We do not doubt that the degree's movement from Césaire and Okigbo to Eliot and Ginsberg attempted to offer a corrective to colonization: if the texts of a new world literature decried the effects of imperialism in colonized countries, the modern world literature course showed those complicit with colonization to have created their own waste lands and peopled them with the "starving hysterical naked."[80] Such a progression makes a clear political point about the ends of empire while also serving to decenter the West as the site of literary production without dismissing its legacies of control. Framed as such, the curriculum sequence positions Western literature within other literary histories and infuses political value judgments with aesthetic ones.

In this way the degree progression is, once again, intriguingly unorthodox in the associations it enabled. In 1963, C. L. R. James compared Césaire's *Notebook* to Eliot's *Four Quartets*, noting that both works counter a fragmented, divided world with acts of poetic unification: "it is the Anglo-Saxon poet," James writes, "who has seen for the world in general what the West Indian has seen concretely for Africa. . . . Mr. Eliot's conclusion is 'Incarnation'; Césaire's, Negritude."[81] The potential for comparison rather than contrast between Eliot and Césaire has rarely been taken up, but recently Mara de Gennaro placed *The Waste Land* and *Notebook* together to argue that despite their political differences, when read side by side we can hear in their omissions and silences, as well as their intertextuality, multilingualism, discursive shifts, and extensive parataxis, sustained engagements with the inadequacies of inherited discourses and the insufficiencies of educated speakers to give voice to equivocal situations. If we concentrate only on the political differences between Césaire and Eliot, we miss the possibilities for poetic as well as existential connections.[82] At UPNG, European and American modernism was presented after a swath of politically engaged, modernist-influenced global writing whose politics arose from the same colonizing modernity that allowed European and American modernism to come into being. From within these complex folds, students found the means to apportion political blame but also to recognize aesthetic symmetries and poetic potential.

Symmetries and confluences between literary traditions resound in the original verse published in *Kovave* and the Papua Pocket Poets series, which includes Kasaipwalova's *Reluctant Flame*, examined in detail in chapter 4. The poetry in these UPNG publications draws in elements from oral and modern poetic traditions, which can be read as the euphony of amenable forms rather than the conjunction of two disparate aesthetics: much of what modernist verse prized—and had borrowed—was found in oral styles. Consider an extract from James Kaputin's translations of Tolai songs:

Jump up and dance, dance To Cabang,
jump up higher and dance in silence.
There are no drums to beat
so no one will hear you,
there are no drums to beat
so no one will hear you.[83]

Now consider Kerpi's original work "Song of Lament":

Our ways, our paths are retiring,
Uchimakona,
The white bear whispers songs of departure,
Dried blood of Ochimakona...
Aia! Aia!
I have dreamed,
A terrible dream.
Two horrible white termites have eaten
Your shield.[84]

Kerpi's original work contains less repetition than the Tolai song, but so much that the surrealists, imagists, and expressionists sought is present in both the original and translated verses. Across *Kovave* and the Papua Pocket Poets series, much of the verse is stripped down, the language is clear and evocative, the images precise. The fusion between traditional forms and modern verse we find in UPNG poets is made more complex by the fact that much avant-garde poetry was invigorated by the use of traditional forms and by the fact that those translating from traditional forms were aware of the conventions of modern verse. Since there was much formal accord in the verse studied across the years of their degree, the students also had a long period of engagement with such styles. Thus the traditional becomes more "modern," while the modern itself was based on the traditional.

One negative ramification of this correspondence was that the variety of influences could be more easily overlooked, allowing some reviewers to read the poetry produced by UPNG writers through primitivist lenses, in terms of instinctive urge rather than measured craft. This attitude saturates Nigel Krauth's consideration of Kumalau Tawali's verse. Krauth, who taught in the literature program in 1973 and 1974, argues that the clarity of poetic vision sought by the likes of Wallace Stevens and E. E. Cummings, which they had painstakingly honed to declutter their aesthetics, came naturally to Tawali. "Modern New Guinean poets don't have to work to establish this poetic attitude," he writes, as "they inherited it when they were born."[85] Tawali's verses owe much to traditional literature, and we readily acknowledge the importance of birth rights and inheritances, but describing his poetic forms as congenital implies organic, unthinking instinct rather than carefully woven art form. It also ignores the exposure that Tawali had to Western as well as Niuginian forms, whose correlations shine in lines across the poem.

Although the poetry published in *Kovave* and Papua Pocket Poets demonstrates the harmony of the traditional and the modernist, the original fiction written during the early years of UPNG tends, like the fiction in *Black Orpheus*, toward social realism. The difference between the seeming experimentalism of the poetry and the seeming conservatism of the prose can appear surprising. On first glance, it appears as though the parts that were sweetest to the writers' tongues, to call back to Kerpi's short story with which this chapter began, were the poetics of modernist verse, close as it was to the intricacies of oral poetics, and the thematics of modernist prose, which resounded across the emerging and modern literature courses, but not the prose register of the modernists. This may be the case, but we can complicate this reading when we break out from a unilinear model of literary history, bearing in mind that in any system writers take inspiration from a wide range of overlapping and contrasting sources. The first point to note, then, is that the African literature that inspired the writers was often realist or at least played with realist form. Although students' private reading was varied, the literature courses did not include Woolf or Joyce, and the style of the set Lawrence texts were, if ornamented, broadly realist in their depiction of human experience. Modes of realism were thus common across the literature program, though not always the realism of a remote Victorian age.

Second, the prose arising from this period rarely conforms fully to the realist criteria of the European tradition, being frequently interrupted by strained dialogue and inconclusive endings. We can see this as a flaw, and it is inevitable that in any literary scene, particularly one featuring junior writers surrounded by the distractions and disruptions of student life, standards will be mixed. We can also, however, think in terms of the literary and cultural context of these supposed flaws. Awkward dialogue and open endings are techniques often drawn on in dialogic theater, absurdist works, and modernist fiction, and they were present in the literature taught at UPNG. These techniques are ways of narrativizing social upheaval, and we can read Niuginian stories and plays as using the abrupt, the unspoken, and the disjointed to reveal, as Kalyan Chatterjee suggests, that "incompleteness has become [Niuginian] society's self-consciousness."[86] Similarly, Paul Sharrad reminds us that the lack of closure can be linked to a sense of communal identity, which may tend to "impose unconscious open-ended structures" on fiction, as "the rise and fall of an individual is not regarded as the be-all and end-all of corporate existence."[87] We can further suggest that the competing narrative expectations and contrasting ontologies that the authors had to navigate did not merely affect stories' conclusions but contributed to the uneven texture of many of the stories, as alienation and clash is not merely a theme but the condition of their creation. The stories not only bear witness to the writers' difficulties in representing identity but in forming their own. In the successful stories, different worldviews and expository styles synthesize in complex, intriguing ways, but the disjunction of the less harmonious stories does not render them any less the products of a complex, alienating modernity.[88]

Niuginian writers drew innovatively on the African, North American, and European modernist authors they encountered, instantiating an increasingly well-documented global process whereby postcolonial writers recuperated the styles, trends, and thematics of modernism to protest Western impositions and chart their decolonizing worlds. Its imagery, cross-cultural blends, rejection of strict meter, disjunctive symbolism, and scattered allusions made modernism from Europe and Africa a valuable tool for protest and a ready component of an aesthetics melding the local and the foreign. Authors associated with UPNG made use of the imagery available to them, be it from the aesthetic traditions of their communities or the literary traditions they encountered during their schooling. So Enos evokes Eliot even as he calls for action against the assimilation of Western ideologies: "the wheel is turning so fast that before we know where we are, we will be just hollow men."[89]

We do not claim that without the specific program structure offered by the Department of Language and Literature the writing arising from PNG would have been of lesser quality, lesser quantity, or even necessarily less in conversation with modernisms. But where there is a demonstrable modernist mechanism in the university and a demonstrable modernist engagement in the literature that arose, it is reasonable to infer that the program helped make modernism—understood both in its canonical and global formulations—more obviously appropriable. When studied after and alongside global writings, the anxieties and preoccupations of Anglo-American writers must have appeared useful rather than universal, with some of their tropes and themes applicable outside of their contexts, and some solely the concerns of British and European cities. The alienation of London and Paris might have seemed aesthetically well wrought and emotionally familiar but lacking the devastation of the colonial experience expressed in African texts and experienced in PNG. The degree structure in the Department of Language and Literature presented European and American modernism as already appropriated by decolonizing writers: a contrivance that writers had repurposed as they wished, rather than a literary standard to be imitated slavishly but never equaled. Furthermore, seeing African literature as retooling European and American literature means that African works could themselves be more easily refashioned. In this spirit Leo Hannett brought together Sartre and Malcolm X in a paper on religion in PNG, and in 1968 the University Arts and Drama Society staged Brecht's *The Exception and the Rule* (1930) alongside Ama Ata Aidoo's *The Dilemma of a Ghost* (1965).[90] As Jawodimbari said: "I have no sense of conflict between Melanesian and Western traditions.... Blending, cross fertilisation, will produce something unique, stronger. I know I have this strong Melanesian spirit but I need Western elements to help me stylise and to adapt to the stage.... I make up my mind to take this or that."[91] Jawodimbari's sense that he "needs" Western forms is a discordant note in an otherwise affirmative statement about creative choices, though in the end he resolves upon a principle of utility rather than essential quality. In the next chapter, we complicate the progressive story of the UPNG literary and pedagogic scene by focusing on another discord, one arising from the shifting, thorny presence of one of its major teachers, editors, and instigators: Ulli Beier.

Chapter Three

TRAVELING EDITORS AND INDIGENOUS MASKS

The Teachings of Ulli Beier

John Waiko's semiautobiographical play *The Unexpected Hawk* (1969), one of the earliest dramatic works by a UPNG student, presents a forceful statement on the power that schooling can provide. Waiko's play tells the story of a community whose homes are burned down by the administration when they refuse to move into the village of their traditional enemy. Faced with such a violent response to civil disobedience, a mother, who had initially resisted her son's pleas to attend school, realizes what can be gained by his attendance:

MOTHER: We do not understand them, and they do not try to understand us. But every tree has its roots deep down in the ground. . . . I want you to go to school, so that you can dig out their roots. Do not hesitate to uproot their tree and drink their wisdom.
SON: . . . I will not give up, until I dig up the root. . . . I must learn how to plant the seed and I must return with the secret and plant it here.[1]

The point is reframed in "Seduction," a short story in *Kovave* by the New Hebridean arts student Maurice Thompson. "You must be successful at school, so that you can live by writing in an office, and not like us," says an elder to a youth. "We do all these things for the white man, and still we do not understand him."[2] Finding the space within a system to subvert the system requires a maturity and self-awareness few schoolchildren can be expected to attain, however. In practice, most pupils were too embedded within school rules and life to undermine their institutions' colonial commitments. Even Albert Maori Kiki, who debated political issues in the "Bully Beef Club" at the Administrative College and was a founding member of the Pangu Pati, a political party dedicated to national independence, noted the difficulty of such activism at school.[3] As he recounts, "there was no political consciousness yet, nor did we think at all about racial discrimination. This question simply did not arise because our Australian teachers were there on one level, and we were on another, and it did not even occur to us that we might aspire to the same level."[4]

As we have seen, it was the higher educational institutions that provided spaces in which power structures and identity could be debated with passion and determination. The writers in PNG in the 1960s and 1970s would draw upon the literature they studied in school as they reflected on their schooling, but it was the freedom of the tertiary setting, and the political and literary ideas that circulated there, that enabled their work. Symposia such as the Waigani seminar series provided intellectual spaces in which national and regional issues could be vigorously explored, including questions of the purpose of education itself. UPNG students began to break down entrenched social boundaries, dressing casually, drinking in places usually reserved for white people, and having relationships across racial lines.[5] Political activism and literature coincided: the Niugini Black Power group, a "Fanon-inspired African Negritude" movement, was formed in 1970 and consisted of twelve passionate members—many of whom, like Waiko, Leo Hannett, Rabbie Namaliu, Leo Morgan, and John Kasaipwalova, were in Ulli Beier's creative writing classes.[6] For Quito Swan, such activism on campus makes UPNG "an influential nexus of Black modernity."[7] As Renagi R. Lohia wrote in *Nilaidat*, "When you were at a primary or secondary school, you depended very much on the teacher to give you the facts, and your task was to learn them by heart. At the University level you are regarded as your own ruler."[8]

Although the university is undoubtedly the institution of modern letters in PNG and produced writers who "considered themselves the ombudsmen of progress and barometers of society," this chapter troubles Lohia's idealistic enthusiasm by examining the ways in which the university's space of self-rule was mitigated by foreign control.[9] In studying the work produced by the students and graduates of UPNG, we engage with the creative labors of talented and inventive writers, and chapters 2 and 4 show how inventively these writers took control of the literature they were taught. However, in examining the relationship between the students and the institution, we cannot ignore the constraints they faced and the political contexts in which the literature department operated. The PNG literary movement was spurred by a hastily assembled process of decolonization, as the Australian administration rushed to prepare Papua New Guinea for its withdrawal. Tracey Banivanua Mar rightly warns against repeating the biases of colonial powers by presuming that political unrest was introduced and fed solely by foreign academics and residents, but it is still important to note the presence of foreign change agents—"people who specialized in transferring western social institutions to newly independent states"—who were involved in the transfer of power alongside local actors.[10] In the following chapter we will look at the ways in which Indigenous writers resisted and responded to these change agents, but for now we attend to the complex figure of Ulli Beier, a German man who came to UPNG's Department of Language and Literature from the University of Ibadan, Nigeria.

As we have seen in previous chapters, many of Beier's contributions to UPNG were positive. The intellectual space that his literature and creative writing classes created was one in which Tok Pisin and Indigenous languages were valued, in which traditional cultural forms were viewed as literary and rich, and where wider conversations between international texts could take place without oppressive hierarchies or too many automatically imposed standards. Beier insisted on the aesthetic value of Indigenous forms and advocated loudly and repeatedly for respecting the voices of burgeoning literary traditions. His service to PNG literature is complicated by a number of factors, however. As a teacher, magazine editor, and anthologist, Beier was able to shape the direction of the literary scene according to his tastes and ideologies. Compounding this control, in both Nigeria and Papua New Guinea Beier wrote, published, and had performed texts under Indigenous pseudonyms. What appeared to be works by local playwrights were by a European, and what seemed to be analysis by Indigenous critics was in fact the guiding of ideas by an expatriate. External conversations masqueraded as internal ones, as a disguised hand was shaping form, tastes, and responses. While Nigerian and Niuginian writers were trying to construct a national identity through literature, Beier's Western interference concealed itself behind a local name.

Beier, who was born in Germany in 1922 and later studied at the University of London, took a job teaching phonetics at the University of Ibadan in 1950. He found, on arrival, that the education system in Nigeria served only "to turn Nigerians into British gentlemen, able to play cricket and to quote Tennyson," and so switched to the extramural department, which was based on the British Workers' Educational movement. From there Beier started teaching courses in African rather than English literature and subsequently founded and edited the hugely influential *Black Orpheus: A Journal of African and African American Literature* (1957–1975).[11] From 1957 to 1967 Beier edited twenty-two issues of *Black Orpheus*, giving early recognition to writers such as Wole Soyinka, Ama Ata Aidoo, and John Pepper Clark-Bekederemo and presenting Francophone writers such as Aimé Césaire and Leopold Sedar Senghor in translation, often for the first time. In addition to an impressive list of publications on African art and literature, in 1961 Beier, Chinua Achebe, Soyinka, and others founded the Mbari Writers and Artists Club, and a year later Beier and Duro Ladipo opened the Mbari Mbayo club in Osogbo. When the Biafran War broke out in 1967, Beier and his wife Georgina moved to PNG, where Beier taught literature and creative writing at UPNG and became, in Steven Winduo's words, "the patron of creative literature in Papua New Guinea."[12] There, as Epeli Hau'ofa puts it, the Beiers were "responsible for the birth of the new contemporary arts in Papua New Guinea," influencing both Marjorie Tuainekore Crocombe's establishment of the "Mana" project at USP and Hau'ofa's later founding of the Oceania Centre for Art, Culture, and Pacific Studies at USP.[13] Beier launched the Papua Pocket Poets series, which published twenty-five volumes between 1968 and 1970, as well as *Kovave: A Journal of New Guinea Literature*, Papua New Guinea's first literary magazine. He later established and edited *Gigibori: A Magazine of Papua New Guinea Cultures*. He worked with Albert Maori Kiki on *Kiki: Ten Thousand Years in a Lifetime*, the first Papua New Guinean autobiography, and with Vincent Eri on *The Crocodile*, the first Niuginian novel. He helped organize and judge writers' festivals and awards and in 1974 became the first director of the Institute of Papua New Guinea Studies. As Rabbie Namaliu, one of Beier's students, describes him, Beier was an empowering "pioneer" who "shattered the old shibboleth that Niuginians can only be evoked as objects, but that they can't write." Beier saw "potential, he encouraged our talents, and over a period of four years, Niugini had its own literature written by its own artists."[14]

This literature, however, was guided, edited, and published by a single, foreign figure. It is difficult to separate Beier's behavior as a teacher, editor, and instigator of a literary hoax: all three roles are closely interlaced. Nonetheless, the following sections attempt to tease out their different implications for the UPNG literary scene. Since the Department of Language and Literature was described in detail in the previous chapter, we give just a brief overview of Beier's educational role, before examining his importance as a travelling editor and a fraudster.

EDUCATOR

In his reflections on his time at PNG, Beier presents himself as strongly invested in anticolonial ideologies and with a deep commitment to a literary education unburdened by anxious adherence to the Western canon. He had felt constrained by the University of Ibadan's emphasis on British literary traditions and standards, and when he saw that UPNG was looking for someone to teach a course on "New English Literature from Developing Countries," he applied eagerly.[15] Elton Brash argues that before Beier's arrival, the major features of the literary scene were bleak, as creative works and commentary emphasized the "disruption and decay of Traditional forms of Oral Literature," mourned the "understandable reluctance of New Guineans to express themselves through English or English Literary forms," and lamented the "exploitation of the New Guinea scene by foreign writers in search of romantic and exotic material for popular literature."[16] For Brash, the "most significant direct encouragement of creative writing in New Guinea" came from Beier, as he quickly discovered potential writers and artists, opened channels for the publications of their works, and established creative writing courses.[17] Beier's anticolonial politics extended outside the classroom—articles in the UPNG student magazine *Nilaidat*, for example, speak of "the mass vocal outburst and enthusiastic clapping" that met his pointed questioning of Johan Maree, South Africa's high commissioner to Australia, during Maree's trip to PNG.[18] Beier's actions and teaching caught the eye of the Australian Administration, who blamed him for "motivating and mobilising indigenous students to protest and demonstrate."[19] Concerned that he encouraged his students to see themselves as a "powerful pressure group," the Administration worried that the literary works they produced could be "subtle and . . . effective" in undermining Australia's authority.[20]

As a teacher, Beier encouraged his students to recognize and respect the literary value of local forms. He had decided early in his time in Nigeria that he needed to know the literature his students had grown up with, and he asked them "what kind of songs did they sing as children? What forms of poetry were they acquainted with and who had recited it? What stories were they told by their grandmothers? Who were their heroes?"[21] He made oral literature a core component of the qualification, brought new African authors to the students' attention, and presented modernist texts after postcolonial encounters. He was also instrumental in creating a creative writing stream. In a review of a book on Yirawala, an Aboriginal Australian artist, Beier stresses the importance of giving artists the personal freedom to create.[22] He appears to have acted on this belief in the classroom, as the playwrights and authors who worked with him said that he had a light editorial touch and did not impose ideas of form or structure on them.[23] For John Kadiba, Beier "taught with great passion," and through him students discovered ways of "experimenting with creative writing connected to their immediate world," inspired greatly by Black writers and those from other decolonizing nations.[24] Crocombe, who "had the wonderful good fortune to enrol in Professor Ulli Beier's course in creative writing" at UPNG, saw him as aiding students to let their "potential emerge and grow."[25] Russell Soaba found Beier's importance to lie in "the spirit in African art and literature that he tried to convey," although Soaba did express concern that his teacher's commitment to the rapid creation of a Papua New Guinean literature gave writers insufficient time to invent a literature on their own terms.[26] In an intriguing aside in an interview he gave with Chris Tiffin, Soaba says that he "secretly feared that he [Beier] was a mean politician," and he complained elsewhere that Beier's classes were frequently too focused on the anticolonial.[27] There is little doubt that Beier was invested in nurturing nascent literary scenes and that he was committed to decolonization. And yet, even a teacher opposed to the teaching of "Beowulf, Chaucer, Dryden, Milton and Wordsworth—daffodils and all!" retains a position of authority within the classroom.[28]

Beier stood firm on his right to hand pick a small group of talented students for his creative writing classes.[29] As Ellerman notes, "by instituting privileged access to creative writing classes, Beier acted from the outset as a gatekeeper to the development of literature at UPNG."[30] His gatekeeping within the private pedagogic space extended to public literary places: he created an echo chamber that amplified his influence on the early shape of Niuginian writing. In *Black Writing from New Guinea* (1973), we find, as Paul Sharrad puts it, "Beier selecting from Beier [*The Night Warrior* (1972)] selecting from Beier [*Kovave*] selecting from source material," with that source material being most commonly his students' texts.[31] One effect was the exclusion of women: none of the Papuan Pocket Poets volumes is by a woman, and despite the growing body of female students at UPNG, Ellerman argues that Beier's classes were male dominated.

In "Literature in New Guinea," Beier repeatedly dismisses as "pathetic" writers whose style and content emulate Western tastes.[32] Across his critical essays, he tends to admire, first, engagements with Indigenous forms that produce work seemingly untouched by Western influences. Second, he encourages original, personal responses to Indigenous practices that draw inspiration innovatively from both local and international sources. In the first instance, then, he respects purity, and in the second, a knowing hybridity. In *Decolonising the Mind*, Beier robustly condemns the effect of the colonial education system on the Papua New Guinean poet Allan Natachee, as its grip turned him into a man "hopelessly confused between two irreconcilable worlds and trying to express himself in a language whose music, rhythm, and subtler meanings he did not understand."[33] It was, Beier writes, only when he asked Natachee to translate songs from his village that he "shed the pompous diction of his Tennyson-inspired poetry and ... captured the simplicity and dignity of this ancient chant."[34] Yet despite Beier's argument that he inspired Natachee's move from imitation to thoughtful interpretation, Natachee had published translations of Mekeo sing-sings in Oceania in 1951, some sixteen years before Beier arrived in Papua New Guinea. It should further be noted that Allan Natachee is a pseudonym: as Beier explains, Avaisa Pinongo "was nicknamed Natachee after the hero of a cowboy-and-Indian story that was the young boy's first introduction to fiction."[35] This use of a pen name, Beier implies, is an additional indication of the poet's sad loss of identity and his desire to embrace the values taught to him by the nuns. An odd position for a man drawn to cross-racial pseudonyms of his own.

TRAVELING EDITOR

The importance of the little magazine in modernisms across the world is long established, and periodicals such as *Mana* and *Kovave*, Tonga's *Faikava* and Fiji's *Sinnet* played an integral part in the Pacific's literary and pedagogic scenes. These periodicals not only provided publication opportunities and spaces for shared conversations around literature, but, as they were also used in classrooms and lecture rooms, enabled Pacific school and university students to study contemporary Pacific literature. In the USP chapters we will see the impact of magazines that had Pacific editors, but while Niuginian writers eventually moved from supporting to central positions on the *Kovave* editorial board, the founding and early issues of *Kovave* were very much controlled by one German scholar. What new light is cast on the relations between global literary scenes, and the way power plays out within them, if we follow the movement of a figure we term the "traveling editor," and in particular one who was born in the Global North but founded magazines in the Global South?

Both *Black Orpheus* and *Kovave* were invested in promoting local expression while fostering translocal or regional links. The first editorial of *Black Orpheus* states the magazine's aim of providing Africans with a greater body of work by translating writers from across the continent. Similarly, *Kovave*'s first editorial describes the periodical's purpose as "encourag[ing] young Papuans and New Guineans to write and to show them what their colleagues in other parts of the country are doing."[36] When we consider the presence of Beier, however, we are reminded that these local agendas were envisioned, and connected, by an editor on the move. An awareness of the tension between local fashionings and foreign impositions within Beier's circles is not new. In 1975, William Wyckom Jr. wrote to *African Arts* from Southampton, New York, to comment on the "curious sameness" of the works produced by Osogbo artists working with Ulli and Georgina Beier.[37] In a subsequent issue, Michele Gilbert wrote from London to add that the Beiers, now resident in PNG, were teaching artists there to produce work that in technique and in approach was "practically identical" to the works they developed in Nigeria. The "style and taste of the Beiers," she wrote, is "reflected in the work of the artists which they have chosen to promote from both these areas" to a "striking extent."[38] Two years earlier, Peter Livingston had reviewed Beier's edited collection *The Night Warrior and Other Stories* in the pages of *Pacific Islands Monthly* and had made much the same complaint. Beier, Livingston claimed, had "established precisely the same assembly line in Papua New Guinea as he had previously in Africa," with the result that despite different names and different settings, the content reflects "the same old Ulli Beier transmitted to the writers by Ulli Beier's efficient process."[39] Beier the educator may have shared the modernist distaste for the university as cramming factory, yet as editor, it seemed to some, he had established a similarly soulless, mechanistic model.

In the following issue of *Pacific Islands Monthly*, Kirsty Powell robustly critiqued Livingston's inability to recognize variety and idiosyncrasy in the collection and described Livingston as "a deaf man who hears only the confusion of sounds," comparing him to "the white man who complains that all black men look the same."[40] Powell's concerns regarding the narrow-mindedness and prejudice of many white responders to African and Pacific creativity are well founded, yet transnational repetitions were noted by appraisers more astute and insightful than Livingston. In a review pointedly titled "Papuan Parallels," Abiola Irele, who had become the editor of *Black Orpheus* in 1968, assessed the literary output arising from Beier's move to Papua New Guinea. *Kovave*, he observes, was "obviously meant as an equivalent of *Black Orpheus*," and he finds Beier to be "repeating his efforts in Nigeria" to the extent that the "parallels between the new literature in English coming out of Papua New Guinea with developments we have known in this part of the world are many and striking."[41] Similarly, Sharrad has argued that we can recognize a formula in Beier's magazines, one of "historical reconstruction . . . folktale preservation . . . transcriptions of taped memoirs . . . [and] overwhelmingly autobiographical element[s]" that repeats across magazines, anthologies, and countries.[42]

In considering Beier's role as a traveling editor we observe how easily Western interference can be hidden in plain sight. Although scholarship rightly treats *Kovave* as a Papua New Guinean magazine, it is also in another sense a Nigerian magazine, built on Beier's experience and replicating much in terms of tone and appearance. The original aims of both magazines were similar, their short stories tended toward realism interspersed with more experimental work, their poetry was in general slightly more complex, they mixed creative with critical pieces, and they shared very similar layouts. The visuals were related intimately to Beier: his first wife Susanne Wenger provided the cover art for much of *Black Orpheus*, and his second wife Georgina Beier provided quite similar art for much of *Kovave*. *Black Orpheus* and *Kovave* are many things—storehouses of talent, sites of experimentation, places of learning, exemplars of nascent literary scenes—but they are also, importantly, examples of the Global South as envisioned by a European, who fostered local scenes while also making them part of a denationalized cosmopolitanism.

Peter Benson writes that Beier's *Black Orpheus* was invested in promoting a "universalism" in Nigerian writing, whose "standards and themes were unconsciously predicated on contemporary Western aesthetic preoccupations."[43] When we see the pieces in *Kovave* exhibiting a similar tendency, we are witnessing editorial practices swayed by a Western-influenced understanding of Indigenous writing as raw authenticity. Thus, Beier's magazines are Pacific and African magazines but are also European magazines. To further complicate their local specificity, in 1961 the Congress for Cultural Freedom (CCF) began funding Beier and *Black Orpheus*, offering a grant of two thousand pounds, which continued annually.[44] In 1966, it was revealed that the CCF was controlled by the CIA, and while the CCF seems not to have had a policy of manipulating content or political agenda, *Black Orpheus* was also in part an American magazine and a product of the Cold War.

There are many reasons why *Black Orpheus* and *Kovave* have similarities, and for many of these instances Beier, as the white, traveling editor, is a symptom of repetitive structures rather than a direct cause. The contributors to his magazines were responding to decolonizing modernities, and with colonization and modernity deeply embedded in the singular phenomenon of global capitalism, modes of influence and control are repeated across territories.[45] Colonial education systems instilled similar attitudes to literary language, expression, and merit, and across all corners of the planet they institutionalized learning to delegitimize the education taking place outside school walls. Decolonizing politics in many countries were also, however, driving an increased interest in oral traditions and local literary techniques, as well as self-expression in first languages. Given the contexts in which the contributors to *Black Orpheus* and *Kovave* were writing, correlations are unsurprising. Similarities might also, as we showed in chapter 2, reflect deliberate engagement with African forerunners by Niuginian authors, thanks to Beier's work in Africanizing the UPNG literature curriculum. This too, however, necessitates an awareness of the mediating role of Beier, as he was the editor of many of the African texts he taught. Perhaps we cannot, to paraphrase Yeats, separate the contributors from the context, the periodical from the power structures, or the Western editor from the wider colonial narrative, inclusive of its decolonizing throes. But we can consider the ways that control is mediated and be impressed by the innovation of the magazines' writers—many of whom would become major literary and political figures—while also remaining cognizant of how an editor can channel and position innovation. If a medium such as a little magazine shapes content and form and an editor has sizeable authority over that medium, then we have to recognize that the editor, as a gatekeeper, can regulate the creative arena. By traveling with Beier between nations and regions, we remind ourselves of the transnational web within which local contributors wrote and of the ways in which little magazines are embedded in large global flows.

It is telling that Beier would describe the 1960s and 1970s, the period of *Black Orpheus* and *Kovave*, as a time during which "we ... were blissfully ignorant of borders," an ignorance "that gave me and still gives me my irrevocable sense of belonging."[46] Far from Beier's cosmopolitan experience of borderless belonging, for many writers in *Black Orpheus* and *Kovave* borders, nationhood, and regional identity were of deep importance. This is not to claim that contributors to these magazines sought only to articulate the local or be considered solely within the confines of regional literary scenes. As the next chapter shows, Soaba in Papua New Guinea was forming a Pacific existentialism that owed much to Albert Camus and Richard Wright, while the Nigerian writer Christopher Okigbo once declined a prize at the Festival Mondial des Arts Nègres in Dakar on the grounds that he wrote literature, not Black literature.[47] These positions, however, arise from careful attention to the implications of borders, not blissful ignorance of them. The sense of unawareness is less the reality of contributors to *Black Orpheus* and *Kovave* and more the fantasy of a traveling editor who facilitated Indigenous scenes but who also wrote himself into them, covertly and overtly.

FRAUDSTER

While Beier was repeating formulae for authenticity and individuality across continents, he was also continuing his practice of literary fraud. In 1966, Heinemann published *The Imprisonment of Obatala and Other Plays* by a Yoruba playwright named Obotunde Ijimere. Wole Soyinka was impressed by Ijimere's work and in *Myth, Literature, and the African World* (1976) offered Ijimere's *The Imprisonment of Obatala* as an excellent example of authentic Yoruba perspectives and language use.[48] The biographical notes to the Heinemann edition said that Ijimere began writing plays while attending Beier's writers' workshop in Osogbo, but Beier did not simply influence or encourage Ijimere: Beier was Ijimere. Beier wrote *The Fall of Man* (1965), *The Bed: A Farce* (1965), *The Suitcase* (1966), and *Born with a Fire in His Head* (1967) as Ijimere, as well as the three plays in the Heinemann edition: *The Imprisonment of Obatala*, *Woyengi*, and *Everyman*. The critical articles and reviews in the early issues of *Black Orpheus* were likewise dominated by his writings under names such as Omidiji Aragbabalu and Sangodare Akanji, the latter a name he also used to translate Tchikaya U Tam'si's poetry collection.[49] He then published this volume, *Brush Fire* (1964), through his Mbari Publications. Beier also reviewed cultural activities in Nigerian newspapers under different names.[50] Beier continued this habit in Papua New Guinea, where he wrote and had staged two plays, *Alive* and *They Never Return* (1969), under the Niuginian name M. Lovori. In his essays on Papua New Guinea, Beier repeatedly outlines local writers' desires to wrest control of their representation away from European pens, yet by writing under Indigenous names he conceals Westerner-authored texts in their midst.

How can we relate M. Lovori to Beier's pedagogy? In *Decolonising the Mind*, Beier describes *Alive* and *They Never Return* as educational tools. He claims that he hoped to broaden his students' repertoire beyond anticolonial protest by showing that their communities' oral traditions could provide fertile ground for dramatic works.[51] He explains that he thus wrote two plays based on the folklore students brought back from their villages—Waiko collected the plot for *Alive* and Moeka Helai that for *They Never Return*. There was, then, a collaborative element to the construction, although Waiko confirms that Beier alone had written the script for *Alive* and that Waiko had not wanted coauthorship, as the words were not his.[52] In its publication in *Five New Guinea Plays* the piece is subtitled "A Fantasy in Eight Scenes by M. Lovori, based on a folk tale collected by John Waiko." For Powell, Beier was "at one and the same time creator and amanuensis: he both expressed his own original creativity in writing the plays and wrote down the original creative contributions of others."[53] And, for her, the pedagogic aim was fulfilled; even if the students continued to be focused on anticolonial themes, they did absorb the idea of bringing vernaculars into their English texts. But if the students in the 1968 class got to experience Beier's demonstration of the process of creating modern drama from traditional tales, what was the pedagogic element once the play was written? Perhaps it provided them with material proof that such plays could be written, but if this were so, why use a pseudonym? Why, indeed, publish them at all?

Although Beier might have presented Lovori as a hybrid figure in the 1970s, by the time he wrote *Decolonising the Mind* this was a pseudonym for him alone, and he brushes past his appropriation: "I actually wrote two plays based on Papuan myths, which the students had collected for our literature class."[54] A similar oscillation between the collaborative and the egoistical can be found in Beier's descriptions of Ijimere. In *The Return of Shango*, Beier writes that his early plays were inspired by the oral poetry he had been sourcing, translating, and transcribing with the help of Yoruba scholars and poets and that to use his own name would have implied that the plays were the work of one man.[55] Yet his descriptions of the alias and of Ijimere's writing processes repeatedly center Beier and the pedagogic inspiration he supposedly provided: he may deny that the plays were the work of one person, but he nonetheless maintains that they were the result of one teacher.

Alive and *They Never Return* are stories of the forbidden movement across the boundaries between life and death. In *Alive*, the protagonist Ada murders her husband, but overcome with regret she follows him into the world of the dead. There, in an intriguing parallel with Beier's racial pretences, Ada covers herself in lime to make her skin look pale and deathlike: Beier presents himself as a living author of color; his character pretends to be fatally white. Boundary crossing, surreptitious or otherwise, was an incorrigible habit for Beier. Ogundele describes Beier's tendency to move between academic, creative, and community settings as a skill in "raid[ing] territories that do not belong to him, disregard[ing] the border set up between them": despite a clear desire to exonerate Beier from wrongdoing, the metaphor is telling.[56] Perhaps Beier's students understood the irony, but it is unclear how aware they could have been of the extent of Beier's other identities. Ijimere's *The Imprisonment of Obatala* and Beier's *Five New Guinea Plays*, which contained his work as Lovori, were taught in the UPNG literature courses. Did Beier and later lecturers teach these as texts by an Indigenous or expatriate author, and how were they approached by the students? To add further confusion to the scene, in the 1968 UPNG course handbook, Ijimere is listed variously as "Mary Ijimere" and "Bondi Ijimere."[57] Intriguingly, Camara Laye also featured in the English courses, but both his *L'enfant noir/The Dark Child* and *Le regard du roi/The Radiance of the King* have been beset with speculation regarding their true author. It has been suggested by some, including Mongo Beti, that the first was written by a team of ghostwriters who were part of the French colonial propaganda machine and the second possibly by a white Belgian man called Francis Soulié.[58] Achingly appropriately, in *Black Orpheus* Beier reviewed *The Dark Child* as Sangodare Akanji.

A literary hoax is "a metafiction, a fiction about a fiction. It is designed not merely to tell a story, but to weave a lie around that story: a lie about the status of the story, its origins, its authenticity, and mostly, its authorship. It is the lie that constitutes the hoax."[59] Whom was Beier deluding? Beier's creative writing classes of 1968 knew the identity of Lovori, as Beier says: "I wrote it [*They Never Return*] while students looked over my shoulder."[60] Ed Brumby, an Australian who studied literature at UPNG, says that it was "fairly common knowledge on the Waigani campus and elsewhere that the playwright M. Lovori was, in fact, Ulli Beier—if only because no-one ever managed to meet this Lovori person."[61] When Beier accompanied Albert Maori Kiki to a sing-sing held by his clan, people there likened Beier to Kiki's deceased uncle Lovori and referred to Beier by that name. Kiki made this information available to readers beyond his village when he published the anecdote in his autobiography.[62] Similarly, Ogundele argues that within the Nigerian context Ijimere's identity was hardly a secret, as "primary and secondary school kids in and around Osogbo in those days knew who the bearer of such an implausible name was."[63] Were the hoaxes, then, perpetrated only on those outside of Beier's communities? Charles Larson writes that Heinemann was understandably upset by the deception,[64] and it is tempting to presume that the joke was being played on audiences and publishers outside of Africa and the Pacific, who had a romanticized notion of exotic writers. Interpreted along these lines, Lovori and Ijimere become in-jokes between Beier and the communities in which he worked, pranks that put those communities in positions of knowledge and discernment. Foreigners are deceived because their unfamiliarity with local forms means that they need the illusion of a local name, whereas locals are free to judge the work on its own terms.

And yet, less immediate audiences within Nigeria and Papua New Guinea could hardly be thought to be in on the joke, especially as Ijimere was given a printed backstory. *The Imprisonment of Obatala and Other Plays* featured a photograph of Ijimere—not Beier, but a Nigerian man—as well as a biography that gave fake details of Ijimere's year and place of birth, his schooling, and his relationship with Beier. In a letter to the Transcription Centre in 1965 Beier promotes his translation, as Sangodare Akanji, of U Tam'si's *Brush Fire* and a performance of a Yoruba version of Ijimere's *Everyman*, describing Ijimere as "a new Yoruba author who had his plays accepted by Heinemann."[65] When Bernth Lindfors asked him about his pseudonyms in *Black Orpheus*, he confirmed them but wrote "let's *not* reveal it."[66] Legon 7, a student drama group at the University of Ghana in the late 1960s and early 1970s, toured with Ijimere's *The Fall*, which James Gibbs of the group described as "the Biblical story retold with wit and intelligence by Nigerian playwright Obotunde Ijimere."[67] In *Three Nigerian Plays* Beier describes Ijimere as "the pen-name of the author" but doesn't specify that the author in question is himself, or mention his authorship when telling Maxine Lautré of the Transcription Centre that Madang Teachers College will stage *Everyman* by Obotunde Ijimere at the arts festival in Port Moresby.[68] Similarly, in his introduction to *Five New Guinea Plays*, which include Lovori's *Alive*, Beier writes that the "plays in this volume were produced by students in the creative writing class of the University of Papua and New Guinea," although he notes that "the theme of *Alive* was suggested by the teacher."[69] There is no evidence that schools and colleges in PNG staging Ijimere's and Lovori's plays knew they were performing works by a German playwright. The names Beier used might have contained clues to his identity, but they nonetheless appeared to have fooled many, including academics. In the Pacific context, while most histories of Pacific literature present Beier as a major player, few authors apart from Powell and Ellerman refer to his use of

TRAVELING EDITORS AND INDIGENOUS MASKS

cultural masks. Excusing his deception as one designed only to trick the colonizers simply does not convince.

For those students who did know the identity of Lovori, Beier's Indigenous alter ego did more than demonstrate the dramatization of mythology. Beier-as-Lovori modeled the appropriation of identity and continued the normalization of half-concealed white authority and interference in decolonizing spaces. Did a perceived lack of authenticity in the pedagogic space feed into Kasaipwalova's diatribe against white people's duplicity and their "cold bloodless masks" in *Reluctant Flame*?[70] Ellerman presents Beier's masking as part of the overthrowing of colonial structures: "The practice sometimes occurs during decolonization, when European mentors try to transfer the institutions and values of western literature to colonized peoples who have no previous literary tradition. Beier was not alone in adopting a 'native' mask in order to persuade student writers and others that the 'native' could write."[71] However, it was precisely the knowledge of such masking that fed racist narratives about Indigenous communities' inability to write without white assistance. Lovori's plays were written at a time when Australians in PNG were deeply skeptical of the authenticity and autonomy of Niuginian writers' work, and Beier's students may well have seen parallels between expatriate doubts and Beier's actions. Beier recounts that when *Kiki* was published, members of the expatriate community were sure that Kiki "had been 'instigated' to write it by a left-wing rabble-rouser called Ulli Beier, and others doubted that a Bush Kanaka could have conceived a book at all." As Beier continues: "They claimed it was a kind of forgery on my part."[72] Such racist assumptions are unambiguously offensive, but despite the obvious risk of jeopardizing Indigenous claims to originality, Beier nevertheless decided in the following year to continue the practices he had started in Nigeria and committed a real act of literary forgery in Papua New Guinea. So much of what the Black Power movement was doing on campus was to mitigate precisely the attitudes that Beier's impersonation could have fueled.

In an article published in a *Meanjin* special issue on Papua New Guinea, Beier criticized the cathedral in Port Moresby for sporting "a mock *haus tambaran*, a crude imitation of a Maprik initiation house, the traditional designs copied onto the concrete walls by a European hand."[73] In what ways are the plays of M. Lovori different from the mock haus tambaran created by European hands? Did Beier presume that his plays were not "crude" and therefore authentic pieces rather than mock works? Ijimere's works were praised by Soyinka, and his plays were reviewed positively nationally and internationally.[74] In Papua New Guinea, Beier wrote his plays as a relatively recent arrival, with far less cultural knowledge and investment than he had developed in Nigeria. Nonetheless, Beier had Lovori's plays performed in Australia, Papua New Guinea, and Nigeria, and they were generally well received. Don Laycock's review of the 1969 performance criticized Lovori's attempts "at a poetic style, with a result that sometimes sounds a little odd to an English audience."[75] However, Judith McDowell's early article on "The Embryonic Literature of New Guinea" described Lovori's *Alive* as the best play in *Five New Guinea Plays*.[76] Similarly, Irele's review in *Transition* singles out the "marvellous short play, *Alive* by M. Lovori," for particular praise, seeing it as "redeem[ing] the volume" in which it was published.[77]

We thus have the work of an experienced European writer and teacher masquerading as work by a Niuginian student writer and by comparison making the actual student writers seem amateurish. *Alive* might have been written as an exemplar of and for Niuginian writers, but it does so through a lie, which, in effect if not necessarily by intent, allowed for the critical denigration of the incipient Indigenous work it infiltrated. Its publication does not provide a record of Niuginian drama but of what a European, versed in African drama, thought a Niuginian play should look like. A text that seems local is cosmopolitan, but with its European connections concealed. Irele's review described *Alive* as a "dramatisation of a local myth which has close and immediate affinities with the African tradition, and whose appeal for us is thus obvious." There are kinships between African and Pacific traditions that cause each to charm practitioners of the other, but we cannot ignore the fact that *Alive* also appeals to Nigerian tastes because the author was long resident in Nigeria. Nor the fact that the play exhibits close and immediate affinities with the African tradition because it echoes the Yoruba plays Beier wrote under a Nigerian name. Blurring Irele's ability to unpack the correspondences between Nigerian and Niuginian traditions is the figure of Ulli Beier and his masked interpretations of the dramatic conventions of both.

If the works, then, appear to have been valued by both local and global audiences, we arrive at the old question caused by the uncovered hoax: does the true identity of the author really matter, or should the works stand alone? Continuing a long history of white men pretending to be writers of color, in 1988 a white, male, middle-class English vicar named Toby Forward wrote a collection of short stories about the lives of young Asian people in Britain and submitted them to Virago Press as a young woman called Rahila Khan. When the hoax was revealed, Forward's response called indignantly to the freedoms of fiction: "The unspoken assumption behind most of this [criticism] was that all imaginative literature, all fiction, is autobiographical. Later I was to be accused of pretending to occupy a position I didn't hold, to speak with a voice that wasn't mine. I had thought that that was the purpose of art."[78] Phillipe Lejeune has described the "autobiographical pact" as the implicit understanding between author and reader that the protagonist within an autobiographical work is the person named on the book's cover.[79] We tend to extend this pact beyond pure autobiography into works of fiction, and we do this most consistently with writers from marginalized communities. Works of "minority" literature are, Jaime Hanneken argues, commonly "construed by producers, marketers or consumers to be somehow representative of a marginalised group, whether or not their content or the conditions of their production bear out such interpretations."[80] To an extent this means, as Spivak might put it, that the subaltern—or those impersonating them—cannot write a novel, as only those privileged with normalized positions of power have the luxury of authorial remove from their fictions. The autobiographical imperative can place a grave burden of representation on writers outside of the white, male, Western preserve, but while it infuriated Forward when his perceived right to fiction was interrupted, the inextricability of a voice from its community is a burden that many Oceanian authors assumed, whether gladly or by necessity. For the vast majority of Pacific writers during this period, the primary function of writing was not art for art's sake but art, as Albert Wendt put it, "for man's sake."[81] For authors who see the value of art in its ability to speak intimately to and about a community and enable that community to understand and conceptualize the changes it is undergoing, the countersignature of one who is from within the community is extremely important.

Beier was not of Lovori's or Ijimere's communities, despite the familiarities he fostered. The autobiography he brings to the texts is a wholly different one: he did not suffer the same insecurities or anxieties about who could write and about what. As invested in the communities as he may have been, he had opportunities, contacts, and freedoms not available to them.

Privileged authors cannot pretend to be from minority groups even in order to bolster that community's body of work, as the deception simply extends the platform held by those with power. A fake that fools is still a fake, and it still has the potential to harm, to enable the privileged to benefit, and to shape, distort, or interrupt the development of a literary tradition. Beier had numerous avenues of publication open to him, and his deception was by no means one of necessity. A publisher's desire to provide opportunities for Indigenous writers should not be met with the simulation of Indigenous identity.

This does not mean that Beier's, Ijimere's, or Lovori's works should be written out of literary histories. Instead, they should be recognized for what they are: works of colonial mimicry written from a position of power, as Beier was a white, Western educator miming Indigenous identity, secure in his right and ability to do so. His adoption of Indigenous names performs a fantasy of intellectual ownership and assimilation—of knowing another culture so well as to appear from it. There is an arrogance and paternalism to Beier's acts that is exacerbated by the inventive aspects of his mimicry: in many instances he was not copying a preestablished body of Indigenous work but demonstrating new paths to be taken. What Beier presented was another white version of local identity and its literary future. Beier's reviews and essays repeatedly condemn racism and imperialism, but his Lovori and Ijimere avatars are in some sense figures of colonization: of mapping, leading, controlling, owning. If Beier decided to be Lovori on the seemingly positive grounds that you cannot be what you cannot see, what the people saw was counterfeit.

Beier is a troubling representation of the white lecturer involved in decolonizing academic spaces—one whose apparently genuine ideological commitments to Indigenous independence is offset by his belief in his position of intellectual leadership and his right to speak knowledgably on behalf of Indigenous communities. His writings and his classes show that he wanted no part in daffodils and Shakespeare, and he worked hard to encourage African and Pacific voices of protest and sovereignty, but he also saw this position as permitting him to appropriate, impersonate, and direct. As scholars neither from Nigeria nor Niugini it is perhaps not our place to condemn a man that Ogundele repeatedly describes as a "German-born Yoruba" writing creatively or academically about a community of which he is part. Nevertheless, identity matters, and names matter. Beier was persecuted for his Jewish heritage; in the 1930s his father's money was confiscated by the Nazis, and in the 1940s Beier was interned by the British as an enemy alien. His privilege may be mitigated by these experiences of persecution: when home is made precarious, it is easy to understand why one would seek belonging elsewhere. However, one can belong without impersonating, and as we will see in chapter 7, there were other communities in the Pacific who were at this time being forced to confront their unbelonging, without any of the luxury of choice.

Embedded in processes of transition from colonization to reacquired independence across the world are liminal figures who straddle the old colonial ideologies and new self-governing ideals. One such figure is Ulli Beier. In a letter critiquing a review of *The Night Warrior* in *Pacific Islands Monthly*, Powell asks us to reflect on Beier's place within the history of Niuginian and Melanesian literature: "Should that role be seen as catalytic or determinative; as a phenomenon of the last days of colonialism, or of the first days of independence?"[82] Beier's role lies precisely in the difficult progression between these periods: he is a white anticolonial retaining a colonial-inspired position of authority, a European promoting Indigenous literature by concealing himself behind Indigenous masks.

Whatever Beier's pretensions, the Indigenous writers surfacing from the UPNG scene found their own ways of extending and critiquing his assumptions and assertions. In the next chapter, we turn to two of Beier's students, John Kasaipwalova and Russell Soaba, whose works exemplify the mix of influences, inspirations, and grievances Beier and the department of English galvanized.

Chapter Four

BLACK POWER AND PACIFIC EXISTENTIALISM
John Kasaipwalova and Russell Soaba

In this chapter we turn our attention from the deeds and misdeeds of the teacher-editor and look instead to two influential student-writers, John Kasaipwalova and Russell Soaba. In 1971, while taking Beier's creative writing classes, Kasaipwalova and Soaba made their first appearance in *Kovave*, Kasaipwalova's long poem *Reluctant Flame* was published in the Pacific and Africa via the Papua Pocket Poets series and the Pan African Pocket Poets series, and Soaba worked on his novel "The Village Idiot," which was finally published in 1977 as *Wanpis*.¹ Traces of the content and ideologies of UPNG's literature courses are unmistakable in Kasaipwalova's poem and Soaba's novel, but their works are never overwhelmed by individual or institutional influence, as both draw strongly on Black authors not on the UPNG syllabuses. *Reluctant Flame* and *Wanpis* also abound with lessons that the university, and the colonial administration, had not intended to teach. In particular, both writers saw the potential limitations of a university designed, as Kasaipwalova puts it, as "an exotic hothouse plant, fashioned in the likeness of Australian universities."² Although we consider Kasaipwalova and Soaba here in relation to UPNG, the successes of their works cannot be subordinated to the tertiary institution, particularly as both writers abandoned their degrees, although Soaba did later return to complete his. *Reluctant Flame* and *Wanpis* remind us that a university is more than its departments or dominant figures, and that the new literatures of the Pacific go far beyond the universities from which they emerged.

Beier argues, somewhat patronizingly, that the writers of this period did not consider their literary efforts to be "an intellectual entertainment or as a sophisticated exercise, but rather as an urgent task that had to be fulfilled."[3] There is no denying their sense of urgency, and Kasaipwalova and Soaba also demonstrate intellect and sophistication, but the ends to which each put his energy and commitment differ substantially. Soaba's novel and Kasaipwalova's poem both present a modern Papua New Guinea striving for economic growth, political independence, personal development, and social advancement, but Soaba avers the indispensability of individual expression for personal and national prosperity, while Kasaipwalova sees the individual raised up only through community connections. Ian Howie-Willis has argued that "the very existence of a Papua New Guinean state depended on the presence of an educated elite who would hold together an otherwise sedimentary agglomeration of disparate ethnic and regional groupings."[4] In Soaba's *Wanpis* and Kasaipwalova's *Reluctant Flame* we see two of the educated elite propose radically different ways of supporting a diverse, modern PNG. One is primarily emotional, one intellectual; one is focused on unity, one on individualism; one is populist, one elitist. *Reluctant Flame* draws inspiration from Black internationalism and négritude, while *Wanpis* brings Albert Camus to Port Moresby, in part as a direct reply to Kasaipwalova's *Reluctant Flame*, in part to the Black Power movement on UPNG's campus, and in part, we suggest, as a riposte to Beier. If, as Kasaipwalova wrote, "national consciousness is the unifying spirit among black people of Niugini in the stand for the right to determine their own destiny," for Soaba national consciousness can only arise from the realization of individual consciousness.[5] If *Reluctant Flame* calls for a modern Pacific illumined by a fire passed between "beautiful black hands," then *Wanpis* suggests that only when individuals find their own spark can a country progress.[6] Against Kasaipwalova's brother flames, Soaba presents Camus's recognition that in the "burning and frigid, transparent and limited universe in which nothing is possible but everything is given, and beyond which all is collapse and nothingness," one must embrace the "pure flame of life" in all its absurdity.[7] Each, however, draw on a variety of modernist texts—European, North American, and African—to forge a new Papua New Guinea within the university and urban space. Whether the flames of a burning new world come from individual sparks or a community bonfire, both writers find use for foreign kindling.

THE POETRY OF BLACK POWER: *RELUCTANT FLAME*

John Kasaipwalova was born in 1949 on Kiriwina Island in the Trobriand Islands. He moved from a Catholic boarding school in Milne Bay District to St. Brendan's, a Catholic school in Queensland, Australia, where he read voraciously from the library.[8] His record at high school in Australia was impressive—in his final year he was school captain, and his grades earned him a Commonwealth Scholarship. At the University of Queensland he enrolled in veterinary science but soon switched to arts/law; there he became an avid reader of Fyodor Dostoevsky, Herbert Marcuse, Jean-Paul Sartre, James Baldwin, and Eldridge Cleaver while also an active member of the New Left Movement.[9] His investment in Black nationalism grew, which led to his arrest in 1970 during a demonstration in support of Bougainville.[10] His activism distracted him from his studies, however, and when his failed examinations caused his scholarship and visa to be revoked, he returned to Papua New Guinea and enrolled at UPNG. There he ran a leftwing, Black Power bookstall and became a charismatic and idiosyncratic president of the Student Representative Council (SRC).[11] With enthusiastic student support he declared presidential rule and ignored the elected council to create ministers of love, happiness, and freedom, as well as more conventional ministerial roles of transport and finance. His vision was riotous and exciting but unsustainable. His initiatives failed, his flouting of convention eventually caused him to lose popularity, and there were suspicions of malpractice with the SRC finances.[12]

When we consider the function of educational institutions in the formation of literary movements, we must also acknowledge that the commitment required for a degree may be impossible in the decolonizing context or may seem remote from other needs: in the middle of 1972, Kasaipwalova dropped out of university to enter Trobriand politics and reform the Kabisawali Association, a self-help movement with aspirations for political, economic, and social self-sufficiency for the Trobriand Islands.[13] Yet this was not a rejection of education or of creative endeavors: Kasaipwalova went on to establish the Sopi Arts School, a "Modern Art School" modeled on traditional aesthetic concepts, and he later wrote a series of modern dramas based on the Kesawaga, an Indigenous ballet.[14] Controversy followed him, however, and in 1976 and 1977 he was accused three times of stealing funds from government and cultural grants: in 1977 he spent nine months in jail before being cleared of those charges.[15]

At UPNG, Kasaipwalova had elected to continue his studies in law, but he failed his exams at the end of his first semester because he chose not to answer the questions set for constitutional law. Instead, he wrote a long essay challenging the basis of the exam and arguing that constitution-drafting legitimizes those in power. The examiners deliberated on how to grade his submission; one thought it was a worthy piece, but in the end the faculty failed him for a rubric violation, as he wrote only one essay, rather than the four required.[16] In protest, Kasaipwalova threw himself into anti-colonial politics, switched to arts, and joined Beier's classes in 1971. His move to literature and creative writing was thus from the start a deeply political act, and his activism suffuses his writings: he wrote *Reluctant Flame* while a dynamic member of the university's Black Power group, many of whom, like Kasaipwalova, were in Beier's creative writing classes. For these students, politics and aesthetics were bound together, and Beier described Kasaipwalova's poem as offering "the kind of healthy, exuberant, explosive exposure of colonialism that Papua New Guinea surely needed."[17] A long, intimate, angry text, *Reluctant Flame* pits the warmth of Black lives against the coldness of white imperialism, using the imagery of a fog's occluding, shape-shifting whiteness to figure the spread of colonization across Papua New Guinea. The fog's cloaking effects become the means to reveal colonial powers' shrouding of local traditions and diminishing of local pride, as well as their camouflaging of colonial rapacity. While obviously concerned with Niuginian lives, Kasaipwalova's poem is also an extended dramatic monologue whose address incorporates conversations with the global modernist texts that Kasaipwalova encountered at university, such as Aimé Césaire's *Notebook of a Return to the Native Land* and Chinua Achebe's *Things Fall Apart*. *Reluctant Flame* might not, like *Wanpis*, set itself on campus, but it is unmistakably the product of UPNG in the 1970s—its politics, its concerns, its literature classes.

In *Reluctant Flame*, colonial modernity has turned people into "Black stooges yessarring whitishly to make paper our destiny" (6)—people whose lives are bound by money, controlled by qualifications, and managed by documents that are, like the fog, powerful but insubstantial. The poem accepts that much offered by the Western world can seem appealing, but when people long for the indistinct trappings of a fog-bound modernity, their real worth is lost, and their "aspirations will forever lie lost in the mess of paper status" (6). This chimes with Kasaipwalova's concerns, published in *Nilaidat* in 1971, that the paper degrees offered by universities, even those in PNG, produce "white flesh in a black skin," as graduates simply fit themselves into the roles and lives mapped out by colonial structures.[18] White paper, like white fog, masks and controls, shaping and changing realities. The real and familiar are replaced with a haze that blankets the land, such that "eyes are dimdimed and in your enemy you see your friend" (4). Playing on the Tok Pisin word for a white person—dimdim—for Kasaipwalova Western exploitation is an acidic mist that renders everything shadowy, lifeless, and deceptive: white.

Within the fog of white-led modernity, religion captures Black souls "for the ransom of an amen" (2), while the lure of technology turns proud Black men into servants clamoring for cars (6). The imposition of white cultural norms makes Niuginian men no longer see beauty in their villages and instead "painfully shout out for a white vagina" (2).[19] The colonial chill imposes regulation, and spontaneity dies as "motion is timed" (1). Even the wind blows to the ordered beats of modernity's clock. The alienating haze turns Niuginians into mimic men—"Black bodies madly showing off white long stockings shirt and trousers" (6)—who put their energy to Western tasks and their aspirations into colonial structures. The land has likewise been infected by capitalist modernity, and though the mountains are still green, their uniform greenness stems from the cultivation of cash crops, not their natural lushness. However, while these factory mountains "boast their size and their foreverness" (3), the poem asserts their contingency, promising that one day the flame's "volcanic pulse will tear the green mountain apart" (4).

With the vigor of volcanoes and fires, the poem moves toward a reclamation of Black love and pride through connectivity. Colonial and territorial structures were planted to control lives with education and paper, and it was the "cold pale seed" (1) that caused the poem's speaker to "drop the bush knife for the pen" (2). Yet *Reluctant Flame* also shows how the white page can be commanded by black ink and the pen be wielded as a cane knife. Written works and musical compositions by Black artists will ally "brother flames" across the world and burn into the "icy centres" (4) of white supremacy. In a rejection of a white-centered history of the arts, the best white music is credited to Black artistry: "Chubby Checker gave Elvis the twisting flame to throw / Ray Charles gave the Beatles the explosive pulse to shake the total stiffness" (4). Within *Reluctant Flame*, Chubby Checker and Ray Charles are not the victims of theft or appropriation but active teachers, conduits through which the flame "now creeps obviously into the pale coldness" (4) and wakes even white musicians to its warmth. Linking the flame that pulses within the speaker to the smoldering resistance to slavery and poverty across the world, the poetic voice imagines the flame spreading like lava and drawing cities from Johannesburg to New York into the conflagration.

By the end of the poem, the speaker envisions the sun burning off the white, suffocating mist to reveal a Niugini in which modernity is not abandoned but indigenized. At the Palm Tavern, the local and the international join, as wantoks dance together to music played on guitars, ukuleles, and tins and bond with betel nut while sharing rides in passenger trucks. The creation of this space of Indigenous modernity requires the flame to burn hot and transform systems of law enforcement, capitalism, land ownership, and political control, as well as Black estimations of self-worth, with a destruction born of love and self-regard:

> Firm beautiful black hands stoning police thugs
> Proud feet kicking off the liar's cargo on high roads
> Determined wills pulling out the devil's claims
> Voices slapping their faces to tell them "white bastards"
> Smashing the glassy window shows of the thief.
>
> (7)

Papua New Guinea cannot, as Kasaipwalova writes elsewhere, be frozen in an imagined version of the past but must allow for life to be in a constant state of flux, "always changing within the context of black people consciously deciding what they wish to hold as their values." Inextricable from this constant change are the arts, which provide "a mirror for self-examination, where the inconsistencies and situations of human oppression could be expressed ... with a view to enlightening and transforming our society."[20]

Kasaipwalova was one of the twelve staunch members of the Niugini Black Power movement, and his poem is deeply bound up in their activism. The group formed at UPNG, as Leo Hannett writes, during "one of the many anti-colonialist hate sessions" they used to have at night.[21] The group was aware of the importance of engaging with institutions for change: in March 1971, they made a submission to the visiting UN mission, calling for an all-Black House of Assembly, self-government by 1972, and the removal of English as the standard language of university instruction. Many of the members of the group were, as we have noted, in Beier's creative writing classes, and they were cognizant not only of their ability to counter white dominance but of the value of literature in the process. As such, Beier writes, their "motivation was not too dissimilar from that of the African *négritude* writers of the forties and fifties, but they were less romantic and more down to earth than their Francophone colleagues."[22] The connections were not merely literary and political: as négritude was arising in the 1930s it stemmed from Black student groups and from Césaire's journal *L'Étudiant Noir* (The Black student), and both Césaire and Léopold Senghor were training to become teachers during this period.[23]

The Black Power group's knowledge of what education and literature could accomplish, however, also made them sensitive to its misuses. Waiko called for educators to "destroy the present basis of the education system" and lead a "cultural revolution" by establishing vernacular schools that would study subsistence agriculture in order to improve farming, as well as the traditions and languages of the people in order to create a common literary tradition.[24] Similarly, Hannett argued that when "a Niuginian receives western oriented education, he learns the language that is heavily biased against his cultural values. It is ironic that the more education a Niuginian receives, the more he becomes divorced from his own cultural values, at the same time achieving proficiency in the language of self-condemnation." Too many educated Niuginians, he claimed, prove how "'sophisticated', 'westernised' or 'civilised'" they are by vociferous rejections of traditional values such as tribalism and polygamy: it takes "a man of black pride to see positive values in such terms."[25]

Like Kasaipwalova, Hannett writes of the need for Black pride in a "world infested and dominated by ... whites," who try to keep Black people subservient with discourses of inferiority and the promise of trips and trinkets.[26] For Hannett, who was also a strong spokesperson for the Bougainville secession movement, Black Power was not a foreign import but was as innate and as "relevant to Niugini as a betel nut," as full of fiery "ginger, pepper and limestuff."[27] National pride and claim to ownership does not preclude influence or adaptation, and throughout the literary and political writing of the period we see the texts studied in the classroom repurposed as authors saw fit. Both *Reluctant Flame* and Hannett's essay on UPNG's Black Power movement, which featured together in an Australian-published book on racism, draw on T. S. Eliot and Césaire, depicting the Black body as at risk of becoming "an empty man filled with straw, an ape or a parrot at that, with no cultural soul."[28] The "cold seed" of *Reluctant Flame* appears in Hannett's essay as a "cancerous growth," but the effect, which makes each Niuginian a "captive victim of white power," is the same.[29]

No author creates a voice ex nihilo; the student writers of UPNG moved between the literary styles presented to them at school, universities, and in their communities to devise literary responses to their circumstances. That their choices so frequently drew on modernist writers from Europe and Africa is evidence, as we suggested in chapter 1, of the adaptability of modernist prosody, allusiveness, concision, and collocation to a range of colonial experiences. When students were taught Eliot and other modernists, they were given models of techniques such as collage and cross-cultural reference and were shown that such techniques were considered educationally valuable. European and North American modernism's frequent brashness, its invocation of the new, and its fascination with alternative ways of viewing the world gave stylistic exemplars for direct and incisive engagement with a very different, decolonizing space, exemplars that were realized in African texts. Modernism was a ready tool for inventive remodeling by innovative thinkers, and *Reluctant Flame* draws on modernist collage, the blending of form and voice, and oral call-and-response techniques to create a new register for Papua New Guinean verse.

As such, Kasaipwalova's poem converses with, rather than cowers before, works such as Césaire's *Notebook of a Return to the Native Land*. Taught in the emerging literature courses and drawing on schoolroom imagery of exercise books, the repetitiveness of grammar drills, and the uncertainty of developing identities, *Notebook* is replete with symbols of colonial oppression and militant Black liberation, bringing together surrealism and Black consciousness movements.[30] The prose poem shares tone, open rhythm, and rhyme with *Reluctant Flame*, as well as kindred imagery and linguistic play. As Abiola Irele wrote in Beier's *Introduction to African Literature*, Césaire's "picture of destruction is reinforced by images drawn from the natural world, of fire and its many variations, of serpents, and poisonous plants and dangerous animals, and from the human world bullets, poisons, knives and the like."[31] *Reluctant Flame* could be described in near-identical terms. Both poems are invested with a strong social purpose, which in *Reluctant Flame* stems from concerns about the pain of "splitting-two" (3) and which Irele describes as *Notebook*'s drive "to render back to the West Indian that sense of pride in his racial origin which is necessary for him to reconcile the two parts of his divided self."[32] The call for the dancing flame with which *Reluctant Flame* ends—"BURN INTO MY HEART A DANCING FLAME" (7)—shares the vitality of the life-affirming dance in *Notebook*: "rally to my side my dances . . . / the it-is-beautiful-good-and-legitimate-to-be-a-nigger-dance / Rally to my side my dances and let the sun bounce on the racket of my hands."[33] In *Reluctant Flame*, Kasaipwalova continues, with fewer ambiguities and uncertainties than the *Notebook* contains, Césaire's rejection of shadowy assimilation, bringing a poetry of vibrant and unconventional imagery to a Niuginian revolt against colonialism. As Irele writes in a review of *Reluctant Flame*, "it might well be that Aime Cesaire of Martinique has found a true heir in far-away Papua."[34]

Kasaipwalova's poem is a political, intertextual collage that brings together voices of Black Power across the world, while working in occasional white voices that strike the right chord. The poem contains twisting flickers of possible connections, and Kasaipwalova's references are as elusive as Eliot's in *The Waste Land* or Pound's in *The Cantos*. Voices are invoked in ways that bring echoes of origins and interrelations without reifying specific paths of influence, as his structure does not include direct cut-outs and quotations but paraphrases and intimations. The speaker's realization that the "unseen enemy has the poisoned knife to my throat!" (5) evokes a line from Achebe—"he has put a knife on the things that held us together and we have fallen apart"—itself adapting a line from W. B. Yeats.[35] The distaste for a "paper . . . destiny" calls to the "paper experts" and "paper achievements" disparaged in Peter Abraham's *A Wreath for Udomo*, which was also taught at UPNG.[36] And the penultimate section, where Kasaipwalova "give[s] the warn for flame next time" (7), gleams with Baldwin's forewarning of a general inferno: "If we do not now dare everything, the fulfillment of that prophecy, recreated from the Bible in song by a slave, is upon us: *God gave Noah the rainbow sign, No more water, the fire next time!*"[37]

Throughout the poem flash images from Richard Wright's *Native Son*: the "white mountain looming behind" Black men, the figuring of white power as a white haze and as "mountains, floods, seas: forces of nature."[38] Bigger Thomas's dread, like the fear that sometimes besets the speaker in *Reluctant Flame*, is caused by the sheer oppressiveness of white authority, and in his alienation he yearns not only for a sense of self no longer defined by fear but for a community of people similarly free: "If his heart were a battery giving life and fire to those hands, and if he reached out with his hands and touched other people ... would there be a reply, a shock? ... But just to know that they were there, and warm!"[39] Wright's concentration of Bigger's hatred, fear, and attraction into his conflicted desire for Mary Dalton reappears in Eldridge Cleaver's hateful desire for the white woman, "the Ogre, rising up before me in a mist," and Kasaipwalova's speaker's self-loathing cry for a "white vagina": in each of these texts, racial humiliation is closely bound up with images of sexual violence against women.[40] Cleaver's invocations of Black nationalist fire across *Soul on Ice* (1968), particularly in the chapter "Notes on a Native Son," present an important stage in the passing of the flame from the African diaspora to Papua New Guinea and contributes to Kasaipwalova's elemental imagery.

Kasaipwalova's speaker's cry—"I hate you as a panther hates a motherfucker" (2)—is an overt reference to the American Black Panther Party, with overtones of LeRoi Jones/Amiri Baraka. Baraka was not taught in the literature department while Kasaipwalova was studying there, but the addition of LeRoi Jones's and Larry Neal's influential *Black Fire: An Anthology of Afro-American Writing* (1968) to the Modern World Literature II course in 1973 shows that Baraka's work was known in PNG at the time. A more direct link to the syllabus lies in the inspiration the poem takes from Ginsberg, whose work was studied in Modern Literature II. Ginsberg's depictions of the destruction of the "best minds of [his] generation," who "broke down crying in white gymnasiums naked and trembling before the machinery of other skeletons," suffuse *Reluctant Flame*, making it, as Chris Tiffin wrote in 1978, "a magnificent farrago of scarcely controlled energy in the style of Ginsberg's *Howl*."[41] For John Beston, it is precisely this "vitality," this "tumultuous abundance, almost in disarray," that makes *Reluctant Flame* stick "in one's mind more lastingly than a more technically perfect poem."[42]

Nor do the poem's international conversations detach it from national discourse. Most scholarship on Kasaipwalova connects his work with male international writers, and there is little doubt that *Reluctant Flame* is a deeply masculine, transnational poem. Yet Lynda Thomas, who would later marry Kasaipwalova, published "Volcano" in 1971, a poem that also strives to fight whiteness with heat and vibrancy: "We'll force our way through you / like a volcano."[43] Her voice and the focus of her poem interrupt the masculinist space of *Reluctant Flame* and *Kovave* by adding a local, female writer to Kasaipwalova's extended text. *Reluctant Flame* also responds to the English department's encouragement of local languages: Kasaipwalova includes lines in Tok Pisin and with ready poetic force disregards the rules of standard English grammar. He uses language creatively and with New Guinea pidgin inflections—"passion logic," "my looking face," "masks stare me," "my vagueness dreaming," "I hazily wink my attention." English is thus bent to Niuginian will: in a poem resisting the suffocating nature of white fog, poetry's kinship with orature is prioritized while the written word is reclaimed. Kasaipwalova owns the white page: English is his tool, not that of the colonizers.

Yet despite this poetic declaration of independence, Kasaipwalova came under fire for making his interconnections too plain. His modernist-inspired bricolage was, as Nigel Krauth explained in 1977, "criticised for being derivative of African Negritude poetry and Black American revolutionary verse."[44] The anxiety of influence that often besets commentators on new Pacific writing is neatly encapsulated by Ken Goodwin's growing unease with the poem. In a 1972 review in *Kovave*, Goodwin described Kasaipwalova's writing as "a highly personal expression of black anger, remarkable in its avoidance of the clichés of black America ('whitey' is not once used), of *negritude*, and of Caribbean creole." By 1978, however, he lamented that "Kasaipwalova's specific observation of the local scene is occasionally displaced by the conventional borrowed rhetoric of United States and Third World Black Power."[45] This change in perspective typifies foreign critics' demand that writing from Africa and Oceania espouse an impossible authenticity, a demand inextricable from a Western reification of concepts of primitivism. The glorification of the authentically homegrown meant that the intertextual poetics of *Reluctant Flame*, which was a cry for Black relationality and community, was misunderstood as imitative. Kasaipwalova was also not immune to local criticism, and Soaba also dismissed *Reluctant Flame* as overly mimetic, but as we will see, this judgment was based less on a romanticization of primitivism than a vastly different view of the relations between individual and community.

The prejudice that Niuginian authors encountered is powerfully encapsulated in a 1969 *Nilaidat* article: "A native can't write anything intellectual, he must always have been influenced by whites. If ever he writes anything radical it must be communist-inspired or negro-inspired. If ever he hates he must be under the influence of evil white men. If ever he writes anything thoughtful it must have been thought out by others."[46] While student writers at UPNG were aware that some audiences were skeptical of the authenticity and autonomy of Niuginian writers' work, they did not consider intertextual relations a denial of their individuality and originality. As their degree structure showed them, insecurities around influence and authenticity only conceal the borrowings and responses that take place in all texts, and ignoring *Reluctant Flame*'s allusions misunderstands the purposeful ways in which the poem conjoins the Niuginian experience of Western exploitation with the experiences of racial oppression across the world.

Reluctant Flame performs the global spread of protest movements through the mingling of modern sources to create an impassioned call for Black love and pride that "IS the unseen vibrant rhythm from my pulse deep down down inside" (5). Kasaipwalova's work is not quietly imitative of international works but takes—and tells us that it is taking—"fuel from these brother flames" (4) to foster local and global growth: if the colonizing fog draws power from its international reach, a revolutionary flame can too. These literary and political flames never overwhelm *Reluctant Flame* but sustain Kasaipwalova's poem, underscoring its passionate, personal outburst through a fragmented, defamiliarized chorus of voices. The concerns of *Reluctant Flame* are the isolation and diminishment of Black lives: voices raised together in revolution are a virtue, not a deficiency. From this modernist anthem of Niuginian and international Black Power, we turn to Soaba's existentialist work of individual determinism.

THE NOVEL OF INDIVIDUAL CONSCIOUSNESS: *WANPIS*

Russell Soaba was born in 1950 in Tototo, Milne Bay Province. He attended four different primary schools—the Anglican mission school at Pem, then administration schools in Divinai in Milne Bay and Losuia in Trobriand Islands, and finally an Anglican school at Tarakwaruru. From the age of thirteen he attended Martyrs' Memorial School, an Anglican secondary school in Popondetta, where he stayed for four years and which formed the basis for the fictitious All Saints' in *Wanpis*.[47] From there he won a scholarship to attend Balwyn High School in Victoria, Australia. In an interview he explains that the inspiration to write, and specifically to write in English, came from his "excellent English teachers who were predominantly English and 'English' Australians. Hence, the unconscious eagerness in choosing to write in English."[48] School was predictably full of the classics—Tennyson, Blake, Byron, Shelley—but his regular depression during this period abroad caused him to read widely of "'outside' writers": Bertolt Brecht, Thornton Wilder, John Arden, Robert Bolt, Albert Camus, James Joyce, Samuel Beckett, Eldridge Cleaver, and James Baldwin.[49] His early loneliness and his feelings of isolation and cultural loss echo through his works. In his short story "The Next Resort" (1974), a father describes youths who were "brought up on a foreign soil" as having "lost their beginnings," while in "Natives Under the Sun" (1973) Soaba writes that Anukis, who were "scattered, disorganised by Europeans," respond to the new dislocation of their lives by moving into cities, where continued alienation leads to their deaths. That, Soaba writes, is "our sickness."[50] Yet Western education and life abroad could not wholly erase the sense of identity his grandmother had provided him: "I had managed to learn a great deal about my family history, the history of the Anuki, my social status, etc., during those first eight years of my life which, according to the traditional educational practices of the Anuki, were spent exclusively in the house of my grandmother, who was then also my excellent teacher."[51]

The majority of the literature written in PNG during the late 1960s and 1970s critiqued colonization and affirmed Pacific agency; both *Reluctant Flame* and *Wanpis* continue this agenda, seeing literature as a catalyst for social change.[52] Unlike *Reluctant Flame*, however, *Wanpis* is not a text designed to rouse a nascent Black nation but to stimulate individual consciousness, and it is fundamentally opposed to impassioned calls to arms: while resounding with challenges to educational and civil structures, it is suspicious of collective revolt, seeing it as replacing loyalty to one structure with blind adherence to another. Soaba was unconvinced by the transparent attacks on colonizers found in many of his fellow students' writings, because the authors who used them "hated, through their writings, but did not pause to reflect on the nature of their hatred for the white man.... Is he really worth the trouble of us hating him? If so, to what purpose?"[53] For Soaba, much of the protest literature produced by his fellow students failed even to serve a cathartic purpose. Importantly, however, his novel is not opposed to Black Power but to a version of Black Power that becomes authoritarian and restrictive. Soaba would have been much in agreement with Hannett's version of the Black Power movement on campus, which attempted to marry a "complete antithesis to all 'virtues' upheld by the established institutions in the Territory" with a dedication to ensuring each member believed in their right to "dignity, self respect as an individual person equal to anyone."[54]

As such, within *Wanpis*, protest awakens a nation to the evils of colonization only to demand subservience to the nationalist program. Papua New Guinea's first campus novel is mistrustful of many aspects of the university in which it originated and in which it was set: neither radical groups nor university authorities are seen as offering paths for individual advancement. It is, as such, an anticampus campus novel. The Black Power movement is shown to facilitate authoritarianism and corruption, and academics within the university are equally bent on figuring the arts as a tool for reductive national aims and propaganda. As one lecturer puts it—the only lecturer in the novel, tellingly a scientist rather than a literature scholar—"a writer's duty is to provide national consciousness, to stimulate national unity; to educate the village masses; to guide those promising young writers who are lost to come back to the right path of creative writing; to go through the right kind of training and ultimately take over from their expatriate counterparts as the future literary leaders of his country; to make one plus one equal two and not five or ten."[55]

These comments, which combine remarks made by the administrator of Papua New Guinea, Leslie Johnson, at the 1971 National Writers Day with the founding documents of UPNG, reveal Soaba's position that neither educational, political, nor traditional social structures within modern Papua New Guinea can be trusted to better lives within the community.[56] Even literary expression is presented as contaminated when institutionally controlled, which infuses the passage with an implied criticism of Beier. The literature lecturer would never have supported the kind of restrictive control that forbids inductive leaps—sometimes one plus one can lead to five—but Beier did seek to guide promising young writers back to creative writing, with the "right path" one that he determined and controlled. Against, then, the strictures and controls of the university, *Wanpis* places its hope in individual self-consciousness and in those who will embrace critical self-reflection and loneliness to live an authentic life.

This focus on self-reflection places *Wanpis* in extended dialogue with French existentialism through Camus and with Black existentialists such as Baldwin and Ralph Ellison.[57] In Ellison's *Invisible Man* (1952), a campus and city novel that has a clear influence on *Wanpis*, a literature professor quips that Stephen Dedalus's problem in *Portrait of the Artist* is not "one of creating the uncreated conscience of his race, but of creating the *uncreated features of his face*. Our task is that of making ourselves as individuals. The conscience of a race is the gift of its individuals who see, evaluate, record."[58] The real assignment faced by decolonizing students and countries, Soaba agrees, is not the development of national consciousness and predictable outcomes but of personal identity, for all its unpredictability and irrationality. The modernist project that moved Soaba is before anything else an individualist, existentialist one, and *Wanpis*'s story of awakening consciousness draws on international testaments of the discordance and alienation that follow colonial and independence projects alike. As realized by the protagonist of Cameron Duodo's *The Gab Boys* (1967), a Ghanaian novel Soaba places on his protagonists' shelves alongside works by Baldwin, Alan Paton, Peter Abrahams, Richard Wright, and Eldridge Cleaver in "Natives Under the Sun" (1973), personal and national transitions to independence require that each citizen think of him or herself not as a "member of a *group*" but as "a member of a *very large collection of individuals known as humanity*."[59]

Laura Doyle argues that modernism appeals to many postcolonial writers because they "recognise and mean to signal the way that 'their own' history lies at the back of canonically modernist aesthetics," and we see this vividly in the way Pacific writers such as Soaba and Albert Wendt respond to Camus.[60] Existential philosophy argues for the essential absurdity of human existence and focuses on uncovering what is unique to each individual to help them live an authentic life. Camus's *The Stranger* (1942) and *The Myth of Sisyphus* (1942), along with Sartre's *Being and Nothingness* (1943), were published during the Second World War, when established philosophical, political, and social systems seemed incapable of producing meaning and identity amid such devastation and disillusionment. As Michelle Keown notes, colonization involves much of the trauma of direct warfare, as Indigenous cultures suffer assaults to their ways of being and become "refugees in their own country, faced with the problem of (re)building a viable sense of identity from the ashes of the colonial holocaust."[61] When Wendt read Camus he was moved; *The Stranger* was "the book, the testament, I'd been looking for to help understand myself."[62] Not only did Camus's stripped-down style appeal to Wendt, but Camus articulated "a way of life, of enduring and finding 'hope' in a world that seemed absurd, of creating my own meanings through my writing to sustain myself in a planet without God."[63]

Soaba had the same sense of homecoming when he read Camus in high school. Camus's hostile landscapes were familiar to a reader born in the Great Anuki Savannah, described by Soaba as a place of "isolation, emptiness, abandon," where one sees "nothing but burnt out and naked trees clawing desperately for an empty sky that pays no attention whatever to all that is dead and silent beneath."[64] Anticipating Doyle, for Soaba reading the French Algerian's works enabled him to "re-live what had already been my past, my inheritance."[65] So close did Soaba feel to Camus that when he realized the author was dead, and had died many years before, he too felt that he had died, and celebrated his own symbolic demise in exile in a Western city.[66]

Soaba's existentialist bildungsroman tracks his characters' journey from a Westernized boarding school to a decolonizing university and on to employment in a semisovereign urban space. The novel's three sections map stages of identity, from that of a "lusman," a loser or rootless loner, to a "split-egg nostalgic" who thinks that all contemporary ills can be healed by a return to the village, to "wanpis," one who realizes that neither the traditional past nor a Westernized modernity can provide easy answers, and instead finds difficult answers on his or her own.[67] A wanpis, as Soaba elsewhere explains, "professes self-hood, commitment and social responsibility in his style of living"—an existentialist.[68] Not every character completes the journey, as not all can understand or tolerate what is required to live authentically and responsibly in modern Papua New Guinea. Their failure, from the novel's perspective, is unsurprising, as there are few refuges: stagnation and death have become "part of the village atmosphere" (41), and the city is a huge factory, with dusty conveyor-belt roads on which humans are "manufactured, shaped, moulded by the very vehicles" they drive (88). Even ideas of social responsibility are tainted by a public service that destroys more lives than it saves. Hope lies only in those brave enough to drive off the roads, or—like the novel's protagonist, Anonymous—reckless enough to fling themselves off buses to share the pavement with those who have embraced life's irrationality. These people have become "custom-stripped village idiots whose virginity had been deprived through urban nets of confusion, no longer fearing the world that surround us, no longer wanting, no longer yearning for ways to compensate the traditional rules we had overlooked" (89). Fulfillment, in *Wanpis*, lies in moving from selfish isolation to responsible selfhood by recognizing the absurd, chaotic complexity of contemporary life and trying to respond to it as it is, rather than the fabricated, sanitized versions given by governments, educators, or clergy.

Wanpis's three main characters represent three possibilities for authentic life in modern Papua New Guinea: Jimi Damebo, who renames himself James St. Nativeson, so as to live with poetic commitments; Joseph Bikman, who becomes Just Call Me Joe and embraces political commitments; and the narrator Abel Willborough, who sheds the names given by his absent white father and his Anuki mother to live with philosophical commitment as Anonymous. Just Call Me Joe fails because he exploits the system and tries to turn the Black Power movement to his own advantage; James St. Nativeson dies because the system has no place for a voice that is searingly true. Of the three men, only Anonymous's story ends with affirmation, as he reclaims his name, accepts his life, and writes the story we read as *Wanpis*.

Soaba's portrait of the artist as a young Niuginian existentialist takes the reader back to the narrator's school, All Saints', a place of pleasant exile that cocooned students "in the silence of its atmosphere, down in a valley and walled in by several hills" (13). As for so many students in the Pacific, the school separated them from their communities, and as they traverse its cruciform layout, the school molds their imagination and rhetoric. "You know, when I was in Form One," Anonymous explains, "I used to think of my home as having 'green isles' and 'bonnie banks' with rich pastures where sheep roamed, with my imaginary father as the shepherd" (75). A microcosm of elite, Western-style education, the learning offered at All Saints' is restricted and controlled: local languages can be spoken only at the weekends, traditional culture is reduced to decoration, and reading outside of the prescribed curriculum is possible only when James St. Nativeson smuggles in books. Soaba's criticism of the system is clear: the elite that the school produces "are educated without having been educated" and incapable of recognizing talent that is not Western or traditional: "if a Papuan wrote something down on paper the other Papuans never bothered to read it" (106). When Anonymous finally leaves school he realizes that All Saints' has robbed him of a home: when he returns to his village, he finds his mother long dead, his sister unrecognizable, and his native Anuki displaced by English. Traditional life provides no refuge. The villages surrounding the school are impoverished and look fruitlessly to All Saints' students for future aid. A headman tells the students, who react arrogantly to his gift of the last of his green coconuts, that he cannot afford to send his son to the school and hopes that someday the students will help and guide them (32). Yet his hopes are in vain, and the novel presents clerkships and jobs in the civil service as utterly without value.

The fictional All Saints' was founded by Archibald William Goldsworth, a reworking of Ellison's Founder from *Invisible Man* into an imperial, paternalistic Australian benefactor. Goldsworth's plane was shot down during the war, and as a token of gratitude that parodies Australia's appreciation for Papua New Guinea's wartime commitment, he decided to open a school. Asserting that "a strong united nation" stems from the "economic, social, political and perhaps cultural and religious integrity" of the young, Goldsworth seeks to determine the course of PNG's future by forming them in an image that he has ordained (59). He preaches to Anonymous that "a twig alone can be easily broken; but where there are more than twenty twigs gathered together and bundled together it will be hard to break" (56). Presumably intended to convey the old Aesop fable of strength in unity, this adage also betrays the confining, homogenizing, controlling nature of Goldsworth's vision. As the word "fascism" derives from the Latin for a bundle of sticks, Soaba's point is particularly forceful: behind Goldsworth's seeming benevolence is a dangerous authoritarianism. Goldsworth imagines the new Papua New Guinea wholly as he decrees it and, until its actual power is shown, is patronizingly tolerant of Indigenous self-assertion in the university's Black Power group, seeing it merely as a youthful passion that will be outgrown: "Reminds me of my own academic years when the students at the university I went to could divide themselves into different groups of Rightism, Leftism, this and that, aha, ha, ha" (59).

If lives at All Saints' are controlled by repetitive lessons and monotonous schedules, at university control is effected through play, with Soaba eschewing classroom scenes to show how power is discussed and negotiated in dorm rooms and bars. Anonymous and J. C. M. Joe are invited to a party at Goldsworth's, whose house Anonymous describes as the "Garden of Eden" (66, 69) but that also recalls Homer's tales of Circe, as well as the "Circe" episode of *Ulysses*. Neither Eden, Aeaea, nor colonized cities encourage clear, rational thought—Eden keeps people as innocent as animals, Circe turns men into them, and colonization treats them as such. Goldsworth's lavish party is designed to trap attendees within Australian munificence and power, and as Anonymous is plied with food and drink he, the existentialist, feels the lure of thoughtlessness and wonders if peace and tranquility can be found there. But the party can neither dull Anonymous' individuality nor prevent racial violence, and the spell is finally broken, Circe's bondage destroyed, by the eloquence of the Black Power movement. Just Call Me Joe recognizes how white Australians try to turn Black people "into another group of whites" (68), and following a powerful speech by J. C. M. Joe, Goldsworth is left standing like a failed enchanter: "I saw Mr Goldsworth extend two powerful arms far in front of him, his face twisted into contours of pain supported by a popping pair of blazing eyes" (69). The night, however, is no longer his to command.

Although Just Call Me Joe can strike blows at colonial powers, it is his own taste of power that undoes him. J. C. M. Joe's story is one of betrayal, but he ultimately betrays himself: the first time when he is lured by the power of adulation and success and the second when he fails to use that power for any social good. At the beginning of their time at university, Anonymous and Just Call Me Joe become dedicated members of the Black Power movement, and Soaba gives J. C. M. Joe moments of great eloquence. J. C. M. Joe ends the party at the Goldsworths when, "his body quivering with the poetry of Negritude," he argues that "the black man that is of the soil is stripped, his youth far molested, cursed and gripped by a slow, smouldering fire of colonial hell.... Why? Because of the perennial greed of the white man that helps to do nothing but chop him down like a tree" (70). But the story of J. C. M. Joe turns out to be one of plagiarism and selfish ambition, and *Wanpis* asks readers to be wary of groups that press the priority of the party over the individual and even more mistrustful of those who use party doctrine to their own ends.

Like Soaba, Anonymous's detachment and individualism means that he cannot commit to group ideologies—he is punched by a senior Black Power member for making statements that "'proved contradictory' to the movement's 'well-thought-out policies'" (86). Just Call Me Joe, however, learns to take advantage of groups and tries to turn Goldsworth's fascist bundled twigs to his advantage. At a thousand-strong Black Power rally—an idealized representation of UPNG's student numbers—J. C. M. Joe takes a measured, cautious speech by Anonymous, full of "truth and implications... bluff and protests... parody and contradictions" (91), and turns it into trite slogans hung from banners. As Anonymous watches the crowd react to Joe's anaesthetizing passion, each feeling that the speech was speaking personally to him or her, he feels himself "melt into a single pool of horror" as he realizes the betrayal of his ideals. He has become a writer of platitudes who, much like the politicians parodied in *The Gab Boys, A Wreath for Udomo,* and *A Man of the People,* conjures the "WHOLESOME BLACK INDIVIDUAL, WHO WILL IN TURN CONSTITUTE AN ENLIGHTENED NATION" (91–92). J. C. M. Joe's metamorphosis into a "potential black dictator"[69] is marked by his adoption of an oversized "Afro-Asian cloak" (93)—recalling the flamboyant theatrics of Ellison's Ras the Exhorter—and his shrewd attention to particular members of his audience, "mostly whites who showed signs of understanding his studentship political aspirations" (92). When Anonymous questions his friend's newfound wealth, J. C. M. Joe tosses the narrator a magazine. One source of his affluence is the royalties from a speech he had stolen from Anonymous: "I found a photograph of him with a clenched fist, and a column of printing under it whose words, apart from the caption, were definitely mine" (95). The crime of plagiarism is not merely literary but existential, as J. C. M. Joe becomes a fake who mouths the words of others rather than finding his own. The sin of being a "black bourgeois copyist" is condemned throughout Soaba's works as an absolute betrayal of the self, and it marks the ethical end of J. C. M. Joe.[70]

Finally, J. C. M. Joe's grand political visions come to nothing, and he takes one of the much-despised jobs in the public service, becoming a man consumed with "executive meetings and constitutional meetings and law reform meetings and ombudsman committee meetings" (141). These meetings serve no social purpose, and though, like Anonymous/Abel, Just Call Me Joe eventually returns to his original name, it signifies no self-realization or responsibility to his community: he "deliberately forgot his village, his parents and relatives" (140). In a final mark of his blindness, his response to the news of James's imminent death is to offer money, and nothing else. With that, the novel leaves him to his life of self-deception and bad faith.

The novel's counterbalance to J. C. M. Joe is James St. Nativeson. Joe and James are extremes—one self-interested and dictatorial, based on campus, one self-sacrificing and messianic, who does not go to university—with the imperfect complexity of Abel/Anonymous positioned in between. Against J. C. M. Joe's theft of other writers' ideas stands James, the subject of other writers' works. During a conversation on Sartre, James says that "quite frankly, the Frenchman is just paining himself writing of me; I am the reality of his unintended intentions" (119). Soaba thus restructures literary inspirations and subjects: Pacific students were never the expected readers of the novels they read at school, university, and at home, and Sartre did not visualize a Papua New Guinean poet as his literary subject. Yet Soaba suggests that St. Nativeson, a Papua New Guinean man, is the epitome of the lives Sartre strove to articulate. St. Nativeson lives Sartre's words and has the potential to be the apotheosis of international works, internalized to Niuginian modernity. If they avoid the self-interested inauthenticity that J. C. M. Joe indulges in, then Pacific writers, *Wanpis* argues, need feel few anxieties of influence: they are not restricted to works designed with them in mind but can draw on any text they choose to express selfhood. The novel ends with Anonymous embracing an existential life, but the price of Anonymous's decision to live and to write is St. Nativeson, who dies alone, the perfectly alienated lusman. The novel tells us that James St. Nativeson went knowingly to his death.[71] As Anonymous says, seeing James's battered body on the dusty road, "No one else but James St Nativeson . . . would choose to die like this" (111). James's death is a suicide that is also a sacrifice—a violent demise accepted not solely in affirmation of the virtues of the self, as Winduo puts it, but also in order that others might write.[72] Soaba explained in an interview with Chris Tiffin that only James could have written the novel of the nation, one that was not the voice of the comfortable, educated, urban elite but that spoke for, without homogenizing, Papua New Guinea's proliferation of languages, traditions, races, needs, and agendas. Yet Soaba suggests that the country was not ready for such complexity, and so in some sense hope for the perfect work "died with St. Nativeson."[73]

The hero who outlives St. Nativeson does not write the story of the country but his own bildungsroman, an allegory of the unique, developing individual, and shows that perfect failure is outlasted by an imperfect compromise with the absurdity of one's surroundings. It is a universal fact, Soaba argues, that writers "are martyrs of the societies in which they are born and bred," and Anonymous does not live on without suffering and loss.[74] He does, however, manage to reconcile a form of martyrdom with survival: the deathly loss he suffers is losing James, as James martyrs himself on all writers' behalf. If James St. Nativeson was the perfect writer that only a perfect PNG could embrace, Anonymous is the writer that the living, messy, imperfect PNG gets, even the writer it needs. Soaba has described St. Nativeson as "the internal strife or fate of Abel": Anonymous/Abel can live on because he manages to concede some of James's detached perfection.[75] Anonymous survives to become Abel because he accepts that to live authentically in modern PNG is to be complicit and to choose to find belonging in a self-aware, responsible state of impurity.

Reluctant Flame calls for Black Power to come from the literary and political union of "brother flames," and Soaba too presents his version of a self-sacrificing Black Power in the poet whose names are an international hybrid yet whose voice is utterly Niuginian. Jimmy Damebo's new name connects him to Baldwin through "James," while "Nativeson" links him to Richard Wright's *Native Son* (1940) and Baldwin's reply, *Notes from a Native Son* (1955), writers that Kasaipwalova also draws on. But the "saint" between these names calls to his always inevitable martyrdom, and James St. Nativeson becomes a messianic condition of literary possibility. That is, he dies so that others like Anonymous and like St. Nativeson's girlfriend Vera might write, and Soaba hopes that his infinitely imminent return keeps them writing.[76] As we see in Soaba's later poem "Return of St. Nativeson," James is the writer who is continually "definitely coming today" and whose always impending yet endlessly delayed return allows writers the "afternoon[s] bare with native anguish" that enables them to write.[77] Who but a deific native son could hold the promise of the perfect Niugini novel? And who, Soaba asks, but a mixed-race, semianonymous, semiestranged insider-outsider like Abel could give that promise flawed, human realization? James St. Nativeson becomes the redeemer whose perfect failure opens up the space for other writers' imperfect successes.

CAMPUS ROMANS À CLEF

In an interview Tiffin asked Soaba if *Wanpis* is a roman à clef, and Soaba acknowledged that it contains many autobiographical elements: "I was thinking of the people with whom I had gone to school and university." But immediately, unprompted, he brings up Kasaipwalova: "It wouldn't be entirely true to say that Just Call Me Joe is someone like Kasaipwalova. No. That would be a little too much. But it would be true ideally that J. C. M. Joe would be anyone of us who were getting ourselves involved in politics and making sure we got our independence through as soon as possible."[78]

J. C. M. Joe represents the lust for power that can destroy every movement, and as such he functions as Soaba's warning of the potential dark fate waiting for any of the student activists in UPNG. Yet it is hard not to hear the fire of *Reluctant Flame* or Kasaipwalova's 1970 talk "Why We Should Hate Whites" in J. C. M. Joe's early speeches, hard not to see in Joe's ill-gotten gains an allusion to Kasaipwalova's suspected indiscretion with finances, and hard not to associate Joe's sartorial flare with Kasaipwalova's tendency to dress "theatrically in African nationalist style."[79] Joe's fate also enacts a quiet conversation with *Hanuabada*, Kasaipwalova's 1972 poetry collection, in which a poem called "Cow Boi" is followed directly by one called "Public Servant," which details the deadly monotony of the civil service. For Soaba, Kasaipwalova's *Reluctant Flame* was, like J. C. M. Joe's speeches, too obvious, too didactic, and too indulgent of its readers' easy ideologies.[80] The poem also came damningly close to Joe's plagiarism: "Kasaipwalova's poetry certainly sold out in New York. But is Kasaipwalova himself aware that the thought content of all that prolific writing was nothing new to Western ears; that the poetry he has written was merely a footnote to the Anglophone and Francophone excitements of the 50's and 60's? And is he capable of repeating such a creative writing venture today?"[81]

Soaba writes Kasaipwalova's passionate cries into *Wanpis* and dismisses them as conformist copies—drawing a clear line between his own dialogue with international texts and Kasaipwalova's. James St. Nativeson might represent the conditions of possibility for Pacific writing, but he does so by dying: contained in his real and symbolic death is not only the calcifying lure of perfection but the names of Baldwin and Wright, writers who gave searing articulations of complex Black lives. Soaba might not kill all his darlings—it is significant that there is no sign of Camus's execution—but he does martyr the literary heroes who overlap with the Black Power movement. With this literary crucifixion, Soaba clears the space for Anonymous/Abel, and Soaba himself, to create a novel that stands as a productive, dynamic new venture. Any new venture remains tangled up in everything that came before, and the messianic space that enabled Anonymous/Abel to write is an involved, knotted space of birth/resurrection, but it is, Soaba insists, no footnote, even to literary greats.

Given that *Wanpis* is a campus novel filled with fledgling authors, the complete absence of creative writing classes or anyone teaching them is a provocative omission. This is perhaps attributable in part to Soaba's own reservations about university education. That noted, why would a book about student writers omit their teacher, and particularly one that so many Niuginian writers have acknowledged as a founding figure? Soaba's position on Beier has always been more ambiguous than those of his peers, and his secret fear that Beier was "a mean politician" has already been mentioned.[82] Soaba also expressed concern that Beier's commitment to the rapid creation of a Papua New Guinean literature meant that he gave writers insufficient time to invent a Niuginian literature on their own terms.[83] Perhaps Soaba found it difficult to square Beier's commitment to existential authenticity with his Indigenous masks, and so, in the pages of fiction, he gifts Niuginian writers the space and freedom he felt Beier denied them. *Wanpis* thus presents a version of UPNG without foreign lectureship, in which students' writing is self-led and their literary heroes self-discovered. Colonial control remains in the Territory, but the university space becomes, if not Edenic, then at least dominated by local students, not foreign staff.

Alternatively, perhaps the charge against Beier is included in the text surreptitiously, his importance within the literary and publishing scene making direct censure unwise. Could it be that Soaba critiques Beier through the figure of Goldsworth, who becomes representative of troubling educational engagements at the tertiary as well as the secondary level? Like James St. Nativeson, Goldsworth's surname is a literary amalgam: Oliver Goldsmith and William Wordsworth. By representing Beier through authors that were part of the colonial education system, particularly he of the infamous daffodils, Soaba could signal Beier's camouflaged conservatism: despite Beier's commitments to decolonization and independence, he retained aspects of the colonial system's control. The pecuniary Goldsworth also perhaps alludes quietly to the monetary references in the homophones Beier/buyer and like Goldberg or Goldmayer has vague Jewish overtones— Beier was Jewish. Noting the fascistic implications of Goldsworth's bundle-of-twigs speech, it is also possible that Goldsworth is a reference to George Orwell's Emmanuel Goldstein, a supposed figure of rebellion in *1984* who is most likely an invention of the dystopian state. Beier chose to teach Orwell on the modern fiction courses, but given the interplay of fascistic and Jewish allusions at work here, we might note Orwell's antisemitism, of which Soaba may or may not have been aware.

In the repeated urges to remember that Goldsworth is "a wonderful man, a great man" (12) to whom everything is owed, we hear not only criticism of a system that demands gratitude toward Australian colonial forces but criticism of the reverence with which Beier was regarded. Goldsworth's party recalls the frequent social gatherings that Beier and Georgina held, which means that the triumph of J. C. M. Joe is a ritualistic disruption of all white spaces and white authority, Beier's included.[84] The "White Fatherism" that Joe denounces can then be read as a general rebuke to all white men involved in educational and political fields in Papua New Guinea. Goldsworth-Beier thus not only alludes to Ellison's Founder but to Mr. Norton, Ellison's white college trustee (68). After all, when Ellison's anonymous protagonist brings Norton to the Golden Day, a bar filled with psychiatric patients and sex workers, the trustee is told that to some he is "the great white father, to others the lyncher of souls."[85] We are left, then, with two possibilities: that Soaba's campus roman à clef writes Beier out of the educational and literary scene or that he anonymizes him to suggest that he is interchangeable with any other colonial educational figure. Removed or rebuked, Soaba's novel excoriates Ulli Beier.

In their contrasting ways, Russell Soaba and John Kasaipwalova, alongside the other student writers of *Kovave* and the Papua Pocket Poets, responded to the literary and political scenes of the university and of Papua New Guinea. Their writings take inspiration from global sources— movements such as négritude, philosophies such as existentialism, techniques such as bricolage—drawing on sources encountered in classrooms, others from different spaces of learning, and blending these with local literary traditions and knowledges to write a new Niuginian literature into being. Their writing was nurtured by their teacher-editor Beier, but their innovations and experimentations pull Niuginian writing firmly from his grasp to redefine what anticolonial PNG writing could be. Across the water, meanwhile, students at the University of the South Pacific were engaged in a rather different struggle. Where the challenge for Kasaipwalova and Soaba was learning to work beyond the constraints imposed by their literature teacher, at USP the challenge was to have literature included on the curriculum in the first place. It is to these students that we now turn.

Chapter Five

PRELIMINARIES AND PROLOGUES
A National Scene in a Regional University

In Vanessa Griffen's 1979 story "A Double Life," a mature Fijian student reflects on the challenges he has faced in reconciling the conflicting requirements of family and university. An in-service teacher sent by the government to undertake tertiary study, he is humiliated in class by his feeling of ineptitude: "I did not know it was possible for me to be so ignorant. In the village where I was teaching, I was the 'qase ni vuli', the schoolteacher.... But at the university, I was the stupid one."[1] The Fijian term helps indicate the source of the man's embarrassment. Translated accurately within the text as "schoolteacher," a position of status and authority in Fijian society, a literal translation is closer to "elder of learning." Yet in the new university setting, his seniority in the village hierarchy is meaningless: not only must he sit alongside students fresh out of high school, who appear to him quicker and better able to adapt to university life, but even his lecturers are younger than he. Meanwhile, at home, the student experience isolates him from his community. When he tries to discuss the things he learns with his friends and family, he finds little shared ground: "They shake their heads and say 'Dina? True?', or nod at me and say, 'Yes, many strange things they teach at university'" (16). In this story, higher education is before all else a dislocating experience.

The narrator accepts his humbling as part of an initiation into a higher order—"when I graduate I shall be a new man"—and values the knowledge he trusts his lecturers to provide, young as they are: "After years of teaching in a primary school, it was a pleasure to be a student and be taught by others much more learned than myself" (18). Yet for all his faith in the worth of his studies, he is forced to conclude that the wisdom of his teachers may not be altogether accurate, at least in relation to his own culture. When a sociology lecturer from New Zealand holds a class discussion on Fiji's "different system, the extended family, where you have greater interaction with your relatives," the narrator dutifully joins his peers in listing the features they know the teacher presupposes: "We talk about how our people are seldom allowed to go starving, how the old are taken care of and not left to grow old alone, or put in old people's homes, 'which is what Europeans are more likely to do' the lecturer says with a smile" (17). For the narrator, however, it seems as though "no one talked from experience" (14). Against the essentialisms of the foreign sociologist, who projects a simplified view of a contented people maintaining a traditional communality, the narrator perceives the tensions these traditions bring in the urban context of the university city, where he struggles to feed the children his relatives lodge with him for schooling, and cannot find the space to study: "My home is crowded and small.... But even with a bigger house, it would still be crowded, because our relatives would come here. That is our family way of life. Yet in tutorials none of us talk of these things when we discuss the family" (16–17). Sitting through class and "nod[ding] knowingly" as the "bright young ones talk," he keeps his lived experience to himself: "I don't let anyone know... I even curse to myself my relatives; I have many worries to feed them all" (17). Hence his sense of a "double life": "at university... I left my family behind, and at home, I left university behind" (14).

Lecturing on a unified way of life in Fiji, the foreign academic fails to recognize its "doubleness" for the Fijian student, a split caused by the conflicting modes and models that must be negotiated by the postcolonial learner. And writer. For this is also a story about writing, both within and beyond its setting in the University of the South Pacific, unnamed within the text but unmistakable in context. Initially, for the narrator, writing is an unwelcome imposition—"on the many things we were asked to write about, we had no thoughts at all" (12)—which serves only to augment his embarrassment: "Nothing is more terrible to me than to receive back my essays. It is a very private and painful thing.... At first my grades used to make my stomach lurch. It is something terrible for a man my age who has been a teacher to see D, or D– on his paper, on an essay which I read many books to prepare" (15). However, despite his mortification, writing comes to yield the student teacher a space to explore feelings otherwise inexpressible within the patriarchal strictures of Fijian society, where only women are expected to be "voluble in their emotion" (11). "Many times . . . I have felt like crying," he confesses within the story: "It is a shameful thing to admit. . . . I can only write it here because we have been taught not to fear to express ourselves, to bring these things out" (15).

Ultimately, beyond the personal growth it allows, this narrative form provides a space for the Fijian writer—the narrator within the story, the author Griffen through the text—to contest both received expectations within Fiji and constraining stereotypes imposed from the outside. The narrator uses the written page to correct the lecturer's assertions, which dominate the verbal discussion in the classroom. In doing so, he also challenges a range of other outside discourses, from the tourist guidebook resembling the attitude of the sociologist—"happy go lucky we are called, at least by the tourists that pass through here"—to colonial historiography: "Yet in the history books, we were once the most savage people in the Pacific" (11). Within his own narrative space, he can reject these accounts for their ignorance of the intricacies of a Fijian modernity that is both troubled by colonial legacies yet culturally rooted in a rich and complex tradition.

The complexities requiring negotiation in the postcolonial educational situation multiply for the student writer. Family and community expectations both encourage and thwart individual endeavor and achievement. The teacher must humble himself in order to learn and then assert himself to question his new learning. The university demands the suppression of cultural identity—"I left my family behind"—yet enables new potentials: "The university was a free place in social terms. We had no identity there except the identity we made" (13). It calls for new and unfamiliar forms of verbalization and interpretation—in English classes they "broke up the language and . . . talked about the psychology of the characters"—but these allow the expression of previously unspeakable shades of emotion and experience, in defiance of Fiji's gender norms. And the alien narrative form permits the writer to contest the discursive frames and assumptions imposed by the foreign lecturer, the foreign history book, the foreign tourist brochure.

Articulating the adjustment to a new educational setting, "A Double Life," published in the last year of the 1970s, reflects on the challenges faced by the writers—students and teachers both—who arose from and around USP in this remarkably productive decade. Like Griffen's unnamed narrator, the earliest USP students met with a curriculum that was largely foreign, for the most part produced and arranged by educators with little direct understanding of Pacific cultures and traditions. In English as in their other classes, they were set texts that remained external, exclusive, and, in their position as set texts, superior; as the historian and USP graduate Brij Lal writes of the Fijian education system more generally, "we were taught to learn, not to question, the values of colonial education."[2] Unlike UPNG, where students were invited to place their orature at the start of their readings in global and modernist literature and encouraged in literature and creative writing classes to approach the local through a wide range of intertexts, the USP English curriculum in these early years had no local component, no creative writing, and indeed hardly any literature at all. With the bachelor's degree dominated by linguistics, until 1972 it was only at the preliminary level that students encountered literary texts, and these were almost exclusively British and North American. As the undergraduate program began to include more literature, this material remained, and across the decade the strong emphasis on Anglo-American modernism endured, even as the curriculum opened up to the global literatures in English that were foregrounded so productively at UPNG in the previous decade.

Correspondingly, the early writing arising from USP frequently converses with Anglo-American modernism. As we show in this chapter, the students and young Fijian staff at USP in its earliest days saw compelling images in John Steinbeck, adapted narrative techniques from Ernest Hemingway, found their poetic voice with W. B. Yeats, and developed allusiveness from—and with allusions to—T. S. Eliot. Much of this might be seen as apprentice work, but it was not merely imitative, nor was it directed outward, oriented to a foreign lodestar. The techniques developed from core modernist texts were in every case turned back to the local environment to engage with issues core to Fijian modernity: the ramifications of the colonial enterprise upon Indigenous culture, the particular effects on the lives of Fijian women brought by a globalized consumer economy, the divisions within divisions that constitute the Indo-Fijian experience. As in "A

Double Life," the university allowed not only for new forms of expression but the expression of uncharted forms of encounter; by developing the earlier modernists into components of contemporary Pacific texts, these Fijian writers established a shared literary voice with which to speak collectively of and to the newly independent state. As in "A Double Life," too, it was the teacher as well as the student who learned to sing with this new voice. Teachers such as Satendra Nandan, whose academic progress at USP was punctuated with periods of study abroad, returned with new references and ideas, ready to draw new ways of working the curriculum to local needs. Yet the role of the students in shaping the curriculum must not be downplayed. As will be seen, it was the agitations of USP's first undergraduates, including Vanessa Griffen, that helped create the space for literary studies and creative writing within the university, even within the English program.

Together, local staff and students produced the conditions necessary for the thriving, regional literary scene that would soon appear. In the next chapter, we will consider the various elements that came together in that flowering: the arrival from outside of Fiji of established and rising stars of Pacific writing, such as Albert Wendt and Konai Helu Thaman; the major revision of the curriculum, which now placed a radically contemporary Pacific literature at the very start of the program; the inauguration of formal and informal creative writing classes, inviting a truly regional participation; the launch of "Mana" in *Pacific Islands Monthly*, which took the writing emerging from the university—much of it from these very creative writing classes—to some ten thousand homes each month, in and beyond Oceania. This is by now an almost mythic period in the literary history of the Pacific Islands: tracing it through the classrooms and corridors of USP affords new ways of appreciating its cultural triumph. In this chapter, however, we look more closely at the period just preceding, when USP was at once full of the excitement of a new tertiary space in the dawn of Pacific independence yet limited by its reliance upon a largely foreign staff, a foreign curriculum that left out literature at the undergraduate level, and a Fiji-centrism at odds with the university's regional aspirations. As this chapter shows, no matter how limiting this early scene may have been, it was still a moment of great originality and expedience, when students and staff together drew upon a narrow range of texts to forge stylistic and technical devices that would, along with the more globally routed work of the UPNG set, be turned to a broader range of Pacific cultural concerns in the decade to come.

PRELIMINARY SUBJECTS:
STUDENTS IN SEARCH OF A CURRICULUM

In the early years of USP, literature was not the driving anticolonial force that Ulli Beier and his colleagues presented to UPNG students. From 1968 until 1972, literature at the undergraduate level was notable for its absence, as the English stream of the BA program consisted only of the linguistics courses deemed necessary for trainee teachers. However, the literary components in the compulsory preliminary program meant that all USP students studied at least some novels before they proceeded to undergraduate study.[3] These works were clearly influential, as their presence can be traced in the early writing produced by students at the university. As such, the first writings at USP can be seen as preliminary excursions: student-led literary initiatives that utilized the sources available to them in the absence of a devoted literature program.

The preliminary program at USP was headed and partially staffed by teachers employed under the New Zealand Scheme of Cooperation, an old colonial system allowing New Zealanders to teach in Fiji with the incentive of higher salaries and superannuation rates. We have already noted the resentment felt within the university at the inequalities introduced by this "self-perpetuating" racket, but the scheme also reflected the alignment of the preliminary program to the New Zealand University Entrance qualification, with the first of the two year-long courses required for any students who had not sat that examination and the second a "post-University Entrance level" course also based on the NZUE, compulsory for all students.[4] Despite the prominence of the NZ "schemers," however, the program also served as a proving ground for local teachers entering academia. On the team in 1970 were Nandan, an Indo-Fijian who had schooled in Nadi, traveled to Delhi for his degree and returned a teacher, and Jo Nacola, an iTaukei man who had also traveled abroad for his tertiary study, returning with a master's degree from the University of Waikato. Each contributed significantly to the literary culture developing around USP.

In these earliest years, the preliminary English courses featured twentieth-century British and American novels: Aldous Huxley's *Brave New*

World (1932), John Steinbeck's *The Pearl* (1947), Ernest Hemingway's *The Old Man and the Sea* (1952), William Golding's *Lord of the Flies* (1954), Harper Lee's *To Kill a Mockingbird* (1960).[5] There was a temporary diversification in 1971, with Preliminary II divided into separate streams for students entering "Arts-oriented" and "Science-oriented" programs, and the reading list was adjusted to provide a stronger emphasis on Africa: nearly half of the novels studied in this year were by African writers, including Chinua Achebe, Amos Tutuola, Cyprian Ekwensi, and Ngũgĩ wa Thiong'o.[6] It is not clear what caused this change, but in the following year there was a reversion to "recognised authors," which meant that texts were again largely British and American.[7]

As we have said in earlier chapters, there are few remaining records of how this literature was taught, whether it was African, American, or British. The course handbook for 1970 states that "controversial topics are presented as a stimulus to further discussion, reading and critical study of chosen texts," so it was evidently not entirely apolitical. But with the New Zealand staff turnover high, with Nandan and Nacola traveling in the early years of the decade to further their studies—Nandan away for 1971 completing a master's at the University of Leeds and Nacola studying drama at the University of Exeter in the same period—and with the preliminary program designed as a preparatory course to fit students for undergraduate study across a range of disciplines, it is unlikely to have presented the resolute ideological commitment of UPNG's Department of Literature and Language.[8] At such a small scale, and without a dominant figure like Beier controlling the political direction of the program, the experience for USP students in this period was clearly incomparable with that of their Papua New Guinean counterparts.

There was also no creative writing component, but this did not prevent a small set of student writers from publishing poetry and short stories in *UNISPAC*, the university magazine. Early editorials celebrated the regionalist ideals upon which the university was founded—"the birth of a New Era in the Pacific," as one enthusiastic student put it—but the creative work appearing in the magazine did not yet reflect the regional paradigm.[9] The self-styled "U.S.P. Literary Figures" were principally Indo-Fijian: Shashikant Nair, Anirudh Singh, and Raymond Pillai each served in editorial positions and published across multiple numbers.[10] In our introduction to this book we pointed out the significance of education for Indo-Fijian families denied secure land ownership after indenture: as Lal puts it, "schooling offered an important avenue of upward mobility" for a community "emerging from a history of political and economic servitude and indifference of the colonial government to its basic social and economic needs."[11] The disparity between Indo-Fijians and Indigenous Fijians in educational success was a subject of political contention from the same early period, and in the 1970s the postindependence government introduced a contentious "educational affirmative action" scheme, awarding a higher number of USP scholarships per capita to iTaukei students.[12] If Indo-Fijian students were quicker to put pen to paper at USP, this corresponds with a documented educational overachievement across much of the twentieth century.

Contemporary student articles in *UNISPAC* engage directly with the difficult issue,[13] but accounts of these early years in "Mana"—written in the service of a broad Pacific regionalism intended for but not yet established at the university—tend to downplay the Indo-Fijian literary initiative. When Marjorie Tuainekore Crocombe describes a 1972 poetry reading as consisting "mostly of poets from overseas, but including . . . two Indian poets from Fiji," the ethnic specification serves as much to stress the unrepresentative nature of the local participants as to praise their enterprise in taking part.[14] The troubled place of Indo-Fijians in a largely Indigenous movement has endured in the literary history of the region. As we argue in chapter 7, an author such as Subramani was able to turn this displacement to productive use in his writing of Fijian modernity; indeed, as writer, educator, and editor, Subramani would in some ways come to define USP's literary-pedagogical scene in the latter part of the 1970s. Yet while Subramani's critical legacy may be assured, it is less often noted that even before his arrival in 1975, Indo-Fijian students had done much to establish USP's literary scene.

These students wrote primarily about issues faced by Indo-Fijians: racial difference, dispossession and the quest for belonging, domestic violence within the community, and the changes to Indian traditions wrought by indenture, religious conversion, and Western-style education. Without the organized ideological, aesthetic, or pedagogical direction an established literature program might provide, they do not evince the political urgency of the decolonizing literature produced at UPNG, and—enrolled before the first introduction of African writing into the preliminary curriculum in 1971—their writing does not reflect such a wide range of reading. Yet the texts they studied clearly resonated, as their writings repurpose forms and phrases from their preliminary studies. A 1971 *UNISPAC*, for example, which Nair and Singh helped edit, takes for its cover page a quotation from Steinbeck's *The Pearl*—"God punished Kino because he rebelled against [the way] things are"—and images and themes from Steinbeck's novel recur in stories published in the student magazine by these authors.[15] In "The Screaming Man" (1970), Singh isolates the climactic scene where Kino discovers the fatal pearl—"He put back his head and howled. His eyes rolled up and he screamed"—and creates from this a strange, fabular image of a man, "created by the modern age," who cannot stop screaming.[16] Recalling the "God punished Kino" line taken for the *UNISPAC* epigraph, Singh's unnamed protagonist blames God when he is hounded and abused by his fellow citizens for refusing to conform. In Steinbeck's story, when Kino accepts the misfortune that the pearl has brought him, "his eyes were hard and cruel and bitter."[17] Singh's protagonist responds similarly to his persecution—"his eyes were bitter"—and, pursued like Kino at the end of *The Pearl*, he is ultimately killed by his tormentors: "Before he died, he let out one last scream. A long scream, a very long scream, and a lone scream, a very lone scream."[18]

Nair's "That Hour" (1970) presents a disaffected young man who, rejecting a local fantasy of finding treasure in the colonial town, flees society and attempts to forget both past and future in drink.[19] Without the direct echoes employed by Singh, the story nevertheless engages with themes from Steinbeck's "parable" of a novel, including the social ruptures wrought by colonialism and the alienation accompanying the pursuit of materialist gain. The foreword to Steinbeck's tale is thus fitting: "If this story is a parable, perhaps everyone takes his own meaning from it and reads his own life into it."[20] Turning elements of the story to their own context, Nair and Singh put forward preliminary versions of the modernist theme of urbanized alienation that would come to the fore at USP later in the decade. Like many of his fellow students, Singh did not extend his literary career much beyond his university years, though he did play an important academic role at the university as a physicist and in Fiji at large as a human rights activist. It is a cruel irony of Fijian history that, like his protagonist, Singh would in real life be victimized brutally by his peers, in an infamous instance of military torture following the 1987 coup.[21] Yet if this violent event has received more recent press coverage than his short-lived career as a writer, he nevertheless played a significant if minor part in the development of Pacific literature, along with other early Indo-Fijian writers such as Nair and, especially, Raymond Pillai.

Pillai was prolific, publishing in *UNISPAC* and then "Mana" stories that combined a light comic touch with a realist attention to the concerns of the Indo-Fijian community. Collected in *The Celebration* (1980), these stories satirized superstition and staged conflicts between Indian religions and Christian conversion under Fiji's colonial state ("A Case of Diabolical Possession"), explored the dislocations wrought through foreign education ("The Funeral"), depicted the humiliations and exclusions of strict arranged marriage customs ("To Market, to Market"), and examined the perpetuation of cruelty and violence across generations within the patriarchal Indo-Fijian household ("The Celebration"). Less formally experimental than other Indo-Fijian authors of the period, Pillai could be reactionary in his commentary on the Pacific literature developing later in the decade. "We manifest our 'Pacificness' through content rather than form," he declared, with a jab at the avant-gardism of Wendt, and asserted that while "regional English may be introduced into the dialogue," there is "little call otherwise to deviate from Queen's English."[22] Yet he was a pioneer in Pacific Island fiction—Subramani credits his stories in the Suva Grammar School magazine as a key inspiration—and his stories are, at times, more exploratory than these critical comments suggest. In "Muni Deo's Devil," for example, published in a 1971 issue of *UNISPAC*, he presents an appalling story of domestic violence and murder, framed through the oral accounts of a village shopkeeper and following the powerful effects of the spoken word in a rural Fijian setting. This working of orality into the written text was a key innovation in the burgeoning regional movement, and Pillai's depiction of a brutal, bloody experience at the heart of a postindenture modernity—"his head was left impaled on the gate-post of his father's compound; the rest of his body was found in a cane field, wrapped in a sugar bag"—can be read productively alongside Subramani's "sugarcane gothic," discussed at length in chapter 7.[23]

Despite the prominence of these writers in the early years, it would be wrong to present the USP scene as an Indo-Fijian coterie. There were several other student writers involved heavily with *UNISPAC*, including the Samoan Ata Maʻiaʻi, Neal Engledow from American Samoa, and Griffen, a Fijian of European heritage. Griffen in particular stands out from the

UNISPAC set, not only as a female student who wrote from the start about issues faced by Fijian women, nor only as a rare exception to the Indo-Fijian majority, but also by the quality of her commitment to the new movement—as editor, contributor, and campaigner for the introduction of literary studies at USP—a commitment matched in these early years only by Pillai. Upon graduation in 1973, Griffen spent a year in Papua New Guinea on a creative writing fellowship and became one of the most prolific Fijian short story writers. But she is still perhaps best known for her first story, "Marama," much reprinted and anthologized but first published in the same 1971 *UNISPAC* issue as Pillai's "Muni Deo's Devil." On the surface a simple story of a woman out fishing, "Marama" is in fact a complexly intertextual piece, presenting a Fijian, feminist reworking of Hemingway's Cuban novella *The Old Man and the Sea*—like *The Pearl*, core reading on the preliminary program in 1970 and a staple text for much of the decade.[24]

Against Hemingway's masculinist epic of an idealized man driven to fish too far out and catch a fish too large, Griffen presents the daily, common struggle of a marama ("woman")—every Fijian woman fishing on every urban sea wall—performing a traditional female task made harder by urbanization, pollution, and overfishing. The woman sits with "endless, timeless patience" amid signifiers of both permanence and change: the reef, water, and sea birds, as well as ferries, cars, and foreigners.[25] Griffen's piece contains little extraneous detail and limited development of plot; it is, like much of Hemingway's short fiction, invested in presenting a sharp image of a particular moment in time, unburdened by background or circumstance, always in medias res. Mirroring the protagonist's care as she sits and silently fishes, the story stays with the woman quietly, and with deceptive simplicity, watching her watch the reef. The dramatic loss suffered by Hemingway's old man may be contrasted against the woman's quiet failure, as Santiago's enormous fish is replaced by her small catch, and while his defeat means that he will die with noble tragedy, her inability to land enough fish for her family forces her to capitulate to a cash economy, using what little money she has to purchase rather than catch food.

Within Griffen's domestic adaptation, Santiago's devoted acolyte is replaced by a hungry grandchild, and the Fijian woman's lonely struggle with nature is broken far more immediately by the problems of a commercial modernity, symbolized by passing cars, streetlights, a shop and its canned provisions. These trappings of a changing world are joined by its beneficiaries in the figures of a passing European couple, who represent colonial history and received, racialized power imbalance. Their dog sniffs inquisitively at the woman's fish, but she curbs her desire to strike it when she sees the identity of his owners. The woman, until now so dignified and self-possessed, at once adopts a nonthreatening mask: "Instantly, a wide, shy, good-natured grin spread across her face."[26] The Europeans and their pet move on, but they leave pestilence behind them in a swarm of flies that hover over the fish. The sharks that surround and consume Santiago's catch become contaminating flies, as fearsome nature is replaced by the insidious contagion of domestic pests. The smaller scale of Griffen's story, with its hero who cannot reach Santiago's fateful depths, undercuts Hemingway's tale, presenting the equally noble though less elemental struggles of a woman and the everyday while localizing the universalist appeal of *The Old Man and the Sea* in a particular modern context, cleft if not foreclosed by the inroads of colonial and neocolonial relations.

While students were, without encouragement, finding ways to publish and, without guidance, finding ways to apply their limited curriculum to their context, they were also working actively to bring more literature to the curriculum. Griffen told us that she felt "immensely distressed" when after her preliminary year in 1970 she felt she "had to quit English," since the entire program seemed to consist only of linguistics courses.[27] In 1971, she and thirteen other students, including the incoming *UNISPAC* editor Pillai, published an article criticizing what they saw as the limited scope of an English program that covered only the "uninspiring intricacies of the English language."[28] Their main complaint was that teachers emerging from this system, while literate, would lack the creativity fostered by literary studies. Accepting that the university is mandated to contribute to the national development of its member countries, an obligation that was the subject of much debate at UPNG, the students argued that this should not be at the cost of individual growth and that in any case, utilitarian conceptions of national development, "unless supplemented in some way by the creative arts," will be "merely material; culturally, the country will be bankrupt."[29]

The university's only professor of English, (Leonard) Frank Brosnahan, an African languages specialist from New Zealand, replied at length in the following issue, dismissing the article on several grounds. He argued that creativity is not a special concern for an English program; that the "academic study of literature" is, like linguistics, analytical and "tends to discourage and inhibit literary talent"; that creative writing is not something that can be taught; and that USP's students should feel grateful rather than complain, being the "lucky few" to have got into the university.[30] As the School of Education was already planning to expand the literary side of the English program through the appointment of Ken Arvidson for the 1972 academic year, Brosnahan's dismissiveness is odd, perhaps driven more by a personal defense of his discipline than any genuine engagement with the students' requests. Revealing the very different creative support on offer at USP compared to UPNG—the exclusive enrollment requirements of Beier's creative writing classes notwithstanding—this exchange neatly captures the difference between attitudes to literature at the two universities in these early years.

Thus, between 1968 and 1972 the newer university had no literature program to speak of, and as students encountered literary texts only in preliminary courses intended primarily to strengthen their literacy, this period exhibits a nascent, student-led literary scene, born of sorely limited literary studies. At UPNG, Beier offered empowering if problematic guidance, but at USP the small body of young writers—Nair, Singh, Pillai, and Griffen, as well as Sister Mary Stella, Karuna Prasad, Sulochana Devi, Udaraj Prasad, John Haydon, and Neal Engledow, a group largely but not exclusively Indo-Fijian—had to find their own ways of relating and responding to the texts they studied and discover their own ways of seeing these responses into print. Publishing in the university magazine, they had none of the international exposure brought to UPNG student writers by Beier's marketing nous. As the student body was still small, it could be said that the "U.S.P. Literary Figures" constituted their own audience in these earliest years. This situation would change dramatically in 1973, when "Mana" launched new publishing routes across the Pacific, creating a massive new readership. But other institutional changes were also afoot, changes that would help USP writers take advantage of the new publishing opportunities.

"O, WHOSE NATIVITY?":
LITERARY STUDIES, MODERNISM, AND FIJIAN VERSE

The appointment of Arvidson in 1972 brought the first of many expansions to the curriculum. A well-known poet and scholar who had published alongside Wendt in Aotearoa New Zealand in the 1960s, Arvidson introduced two new first-year literature courses, Modern English I and II, with set texts including Eliot's *Selected Poems* (1930), James Joyce's *A Portrait of the Artist as a Young Man* (1914), Katherine Mansfield's *The Garden Party and Other Stories* (1922), Albert Camus's *The Outsider* (1942), and Yeats's *Collected Poems* (1933).[31] The literary content of the USP curriculum would ebb and flow across the decade: the program would be restructured, the discipline framed and reframed, and particular texts introduced or removed, according to the preferences and practices of the staff who came and went. The year 1973 would see the first Commonwealth literature module, heavy on Australian and Pākehā New Zealand writing initially, though by the mid-1970s this course was reoriented to an incipient postcolonial literature, with a particular emphasis on the Pacific. This Pacific orientation would prove the most productive for the student writers of USP, but the initial modernist emphasis of the literary studies program would remain. Yeats and Eliot served as mainstays, and from the early 1970s, when literary studies at USP finally began, it was to their poems that USP's writers were drawn.

This is particularly so for the Fijians—iTaukei and Indo-Fijian—who made up the majority of the student body, and, through Nacola and Nandan, constituted the only local component of the teaching faculty. As literary studies took shape within the bachelor's program, the broader range of texts and genres taught was accompanied by greater participation in the creative writing scene, and the ethnic imbalance seen at the start of the decade was soon redressed with publications by Indigenous Fijians. iTaukei writers tended from the start toward poetry, as Pillai observed in the essay "Prose Fiction in Fiji: A Question of Direction," published alongside Griffen's "A Double Life" in a 1979 *Mana*. Noting that the poets of the period were more apt to follow up their debuts with further submissions and suggesting that short stories, though greater in number, were often too short to "really merit serious consideration as prose fiction," he concludes that poetry is the mode most akin to Indigenous oratorical traditions: "The poet . . . fares much better in Fiji because he is seen as a romantic figure operating within a native tradition of seers and composers, of mekes and chants, so his poetry, even if it be imperfect or naive, takes on an almost oracular significance. The prose writer, on the other hand, is seen as operating within a Western (and therefore heretical) tradition."[32]

This impression is not without its problems. It does not factor the equally "native tradition" of italanoa and itukuni, spoken narrative forms recounting historical, mythic, or allegorical stories. It draws a narrow definition of what constitutes a short story, which—in excluding "legends as not being original creations"—itself betrays a "Western" classificatory system. Arguing that even bad poetry takes on "oracular significance," it implies a certain lack of discernment in oral traditions. It also ignores the complex engagements with "Western" literature performed in both poetry and prose. Yet it is true that Indigenous experiments appearing in print during this period were predominantly poetic.

These Indigenous experiments correspond with the introduction of modernist poetry into the curriculum. We are duly cautious about confusing causation and correlation, but it is a statement of fact that—at least in copies that have survived at the University of the South Pacific—there are no contributions to *UNISPAC* by iTaukei writers before 1972, when the literary program began.[33] And when iTaukei student publications do begin, they enact a notable dialogue with modernist poets. Perhaps, as we suggested in chapter 1, modernist verse resonated because of its overt experiment in blending old and new forms, negotiating incommensurate worldviews. Perhaps it was attractive in its cynical treatment of the version of Western civilization that had been celebrated in colonial Pacific classrooms for generations. Perhaps it was appealingly difficult, drawing the reader into the construction of meaning and resisting any fixed interpretation. Perhaps, as elsewhere in the decolonizing world, it enticed young poets with its rebelliousness, its fragmentariness, its exercises in sound, rhythm, voice. Whatever the reason, modernism struck a chord.

Pio Manoa was engaging with the modernists from the late 1960s, alluding to Eliot's *The Waste Land* and Yeats's "The Second Coming" in poetry published while he studied in Australia.[34] Manoa would not join USP's teaching faculty until 1975, but the iTaukei poet Seri seems to have arrived at a similar point independently while at the university, announcing himself with aplomb in "Prologue," a long poem published in the second appearance of "Mana" in April 1973 but presumably completed before the launch of the new title. Here Seri mythologizes the colonial encounter, invoking the shark-god Dakuwaqa to castigate the "lost race" who sold the land for "Trinkets" and presenting the sold birthright in terms of human sacrifice: "Doom'd, / garlanded to fast in lovo flames."[35] If the archaic contraction seems to call back to an earlier, outmoded English tradition, its use in a single-word line pulls it into the contemporary, while the image of the lovo (the Fijian earth oven) and the salusalu evoked by "garlanded" localizes it culturally. The rich, loaded images that follow—"honeycombed wormwoods / dead and dry / Speak shark-teeth to my cenotaph"—are closer to the symbolism of early-twentieth-century European modernist verse than to the English lyric verse of the previous century, which Seri's archaisms might seem to evoke, or to the Fijian poetic tradition of serekali, which typically records or anticipates specific events, from fishing expeditions and battles to births and deaths. Nevertheless, there is something of the mystical claim at work in "Prologue," as Seri fuses the personal and the national in a vision of cultural betrayal, presenting the poet as seer speaking "prophetic warnings": "I see in mud pools the mirage / of a lost race purchased / Coughing bamboo crackers."[36]

Yet this mystical strain can be approached from other cultural routes. Apocalyptic in tone, and with a terrible birth scene—"O, whose nativity? O, whose delight?"—"Prologue" can also be read as a Fijian "Second Coming," signaling the loss of "innocence and beauty" in the arrival of colonial modernity:

> Salty balolo juice to
> reptiles cocktail mix
> oozing lavender harbours the scent
> A woman's spread
> Legs a straddle to semi-recumbent
> Posture,
> Wriggling thick-lipped monster.

The imagery is as vivid as in Yeats's poem, and throughout "Prologue" particular words and phrases call back to "The Second Coming." Seri's "estuary of Blood" echoes Yeats's "blood-dimmed tide"; his "cruel sun" recalls Yeats's "pitiless... sun"; the "wriggling... monster" of Seri is akin to Yeats's "rough beast."[37] With echoes such as these, Seri's "mirage" is evidently related to the Irish poet's "vision." Continually, however, these images are rooted back into the Fijian context. Sometimes this rooting is unmistakable, as with the apostrophe "FIJI," a single-word line in block capitals. Elsewhere it is subtler, as with the uneven couplet—"Gone. / No lullabies to soothe"—which can be read both in correspondence with Yeats's violently "rocking cradle" (20) and as a local, bilingual pun: "gone" is the Fijian word for "child."[38]

If Yeats provides a model of the poet as visionary, the way that Seri combines images, piling one startling scene upon another, often at the expense of clear narrative sequence, is closer to Eliot's *The Waste Land*. There are lucid flashes: where the speaker castigates his kawa (ancestors) for exchanging "Papalagis' pearl / Trinkets, trappings, trash, ash-tray glass / With your land," or where a degraded modernity is figured through the trope of the Westernized woman, with "Miniskirted bums—grass skirts discarded." But overall, as with Eliot, it is the accretion of images that creates mood and meaning, performing its sense of cultural ruin while establishing itself as a poetic monument. Or, rather, "cenotaph"—if not for the ancient "lecherous fools," who invoked the anger of the ancient gods by letting in the "Cancerous beach-combers," then for the contemporary "Melanesian / Submerged" in the polluted "Blood lagoons." Or, finally, as the title suggests, for their inheritors. As a prelude, "Prologue" suggests at once the Romantic-modernist promise of the poet-prophet's career, the birth of a Fijian poetic tradition to succeed, revive, or complement the serekali, and the advent of a perilous new age.

Course records for the period of Seri's enrolment show that Modern English I set the *Selected Poetry of W. B. Yeats*, edited by A. Norman Jeffares, which included "The Second Coming," and Modern English II featured Eliot's 1954 *Selected Poems*, which contained *The Waste Land*.[39] We do not have records to confirm how these texts were framed and taught within the classroom, but some insights can be gained from an essay by Arvidson, published in the same year as "Prologue," where he invokes Yeats to commend the preoccupations developing in Pacific literature. Quoting the Irish poet's famous comment that "one can only reach out to the universe with a gloved hand—that glove is one's nation"—Arvidson argues that it is by embracing the national and regional singularities of Pacific cultures that a sustainable literature will appear.[40] Arvidson acknowledges both the established writing of Wendt and "the remarkable upsurge of writing in Papua New Guinea," but spends much of the essay praising the newer writing emerging from USP, including that of Seri, Griffen, and Nair. He focuses on those elements that seem to him most distinctively Pacific and accepts that the primary critical measure for the evaluation of this literature will need to come from the region itself.[41] Yet with this and other quotations from Yeats, he acknowledges his own "preconceptions" while suggesting that regional literatures need not close themselves off from other movements to maintain their cultural uniqueness. As a Pākehā New Zealander, Arvidson was already invested in adapting the precepts of a distant Anglo-American tradition for new national contexts. During this period, Yeats featured prominently in the development of modern Pākehā verse and, by some accounts, of Māori verse too.[42] Arvidson's essay confirms that in 1973 he was already considering how this adaptive process could be extended to the decolonizing Pacific, and it is reasonable to suppose that this attitude informed his approach to Yeats and others in the classroom.

If Arvidson's critical writing perceives affinities between European modernism and Pacific literature, his Indo-Fijian colleague Satendra Nandan performs these affinities with his poetry. Newly returned from England, with a master's degree and a promotion to teach literature courses at undergraduate level, Nandan inaugurated his long literary career with the poem "My Father's Son." Like the student writer Seri in "Prologue," Nandan addresses the disjunctions of Fijian modernity, though with a very different focus and depth of field. Seri presents the long history of colonial collision, beginning with the arrival of the European beachcombers and ending with the Indigenous Fijians disoriented under modernity. Nandan begins with the more particular though no less momentous event of indenture in Fiji—where the British transported Indian laborers to work sugarcane in the colony—and ends with an Indo-Fijian ascendancy under independence, with the civil servant son "secure in a sinecure."[43] Seri works on the mythical scale, transmuting historical events into an oracular vision of the future. Nandan works in the other direction, presenting history by synecdoche, through the personal stories of a father and son. Significantly, neither poet includes the other ethnic group within their vision of Fijian modernity. Though the iTaukei and Indo-Fijian populations were roughly equal in number at this time, and though the groups were fatally wedded in the bind of postcolonial modernity, as the events of the 1987 coup would prove, it would be left to other writers to find synthesis between the two subject positions. Yet Seri and Nandan played significant roles in the creation of a modern poetic idiom to figure the complexity of Fijian modernity, and they did so, in no small part, with reference to the poetry of the European modernists. In particular, as Nandan was a writer-scholar furthering the Fijian poetry scene while teaching literature courses, we can infer a link between his poetic practice and his pedagogy, suggesting that he found modernist writers on the syllabus useful instruments for presenting the fractures and contradictions of modern Fiji.

The opening sections of "My Father's Son" establish three historical stages of Indo-Fijian experience embodied through the life of the speaker. The period of high indenture is recalled from his father's terse account of the traumatic passage to Fiji, a "narak" (hell) not survived by all.[44] The postwar, preindependence period—still centered around sugarcane for many Indo-Fijians, though the airport and "a few hotels on the landscape" signal a changing order—is figured in the speaker's boyhood in a dilapidated village in the west of Fiji.[45] Finally, the speaker is placed in the urban, postcolonial present as he stands in a "conditioned office" overlooking the island where his father had been quarantined on his arrival from India (presumably Nukulau, close to the capital, Suva). Against this broad background, Nandan presents a series of tableaux depicting the civil servant's experience of his father's death: the call from his brother with the news, interrupting his bourgeois pleasures in the city; his return to the village, where he takes the only chair and appears "too well-fed" among the "toothless, faceless, nameless" villagers; the funeral, in the shadow of the international airport, which brings home the incongruity of the old rites in the modern Fijian setting. The funeral scene is full of contradictions, with the speaker pouring the sacred lota (cup, pot) while comparing the old man to Christ, recalling the biblical phrase "ashes to ashes" while reciting "om shantih, shantih, shantih" and administering "pure australian ghee," whose cultural purity is ironically undermined by its Australian, consumerist origin.[46]

In the final section, failing to find meaning at the seashore, the speaker returns to his city life: "i flew back to my retreat. / it's different here."[47] Most obviously, "here" is Suva, and the difference is from life in the "peasant" village with the other children, "teeth beaming with stolen sugarcane," and life "on a swivel chair" in the civil service, where human attachment consists only in adjacency with "the woman in my bed." Thus, the movement is from the country to the city, from poverty to wealth, from connection to alienation, from one generation to the next. But given the father's earlier description of his transformative journey from India—"the passage of one life into another"—"here" is also Fiji. Himself passing from one life into another, the civil servant at once estranges himself from his father and fulfills the dream of improvement that had brought the laborers from India a generation earlier, leaving behind "the cows grazing beside the 'mandir' / and my friends playing 'gullidanda.'" The civil servant is indeed his "father's son."

Modernism presents a fitting frame for these ideas of rupture and continuity, and it is appropriate that Nandan should contract Eliot for his poetic treatment of the theme, introducing numerous echoes from *The Waste Land*. Consistent with the other remodelings of modernist verse we have discussed in Papua New Guinean and Fijian poetry, these are typically fragmentary: the quotation from the Order for the Burial of the Dead references "The Burial of the Dead," the title of Eliot's opening section; Nandan's "Neither the living nor the dead" gestures to Eliot's "He who is living is now dead"; Nandan's "drowned son" stands for Eliot's "death by water"; Nandan's "red hill" for Eliot's "red rock."[48] Occasionally an echoed phrase is turned to similar thematic ends, as where Eliot's line—"I sat upon the shore"—is drawn into the civil servant's search for meaning: "the sea beat against the shore . . . while i sat." Other echoes are formal, such as the division into numbered sections and the calculated use of rhyme. "My Father's Son" is free verse, and for the most part unrhymed, but for the scene in which the civil servant is called back to the funeral—"worse, such dinners are so rare / with the permanent secretary's wife / with so promiscuous an air"—Nandan follows the method of Eliot's "The Fire Sermon" section, introducing a whimsical rhyme scheme to paint the materialistic attitude to sex in a tawdrier light.

With echoes from Eliot reverberating through the text, the mantra that ends the funeral scene—"om shantih shantih shantih"—reads rather differently. In the context of the Hindu funeral it may appear an authentic close to the ritual. To the modernist-conversant reader (or student) summoned by Nandan with his recitals from Eliot, it invokes rather the famous closing line from *The Waste Land*—"Shantih shantih shantih"[49]—and in this sense presents the textual equivalent of "pure australian ghee" imported back into a dislocated Indian context from a foreign, appropriative source. And yet, Nandan suggests, this might be the correct move for a culture no longer at home with its inheritances. The civil servant looks gauche in the village as he "mumbles 'ram ram,'" but he is not the only one who feels disconnected from the Vedas, as shown at the funeral, where the pundit reads "a few 'mantras' from a red book / which neither the living nor the dead understood." In its reference to Anglo-American modernist poetics, an alien language for the community described in the poem, "My Father's Son" performs the disjointing it describes. But it can also, in some sense, be read as a reclamation. For a displaced community—"it's different here"—a manifestly intertextual mode may make the most sense, accepting fragments and phrases from a multitude of sources, toward new and unfixed futures, without special reverence for any single given tradition.

Focusing on the correlations between the curriculum and the published output of staff and students in USP's earliest years helps clarify both the limitations and the potentials of the university's literary scene. The most obvious limitation is cultural. It was principally a Fijian scene, and even as iTaukei writers like Seri began to participate more actively, the scope did not extend beyond the national level. A second limitation is textual. With a narrow literature curriculum, initially available to students only during their preliminary studies and after 1972 in the dedicated literature courses, students relied largely upon English and American modernist writers for model and for allusion, in contrast to their counterparts at the University of Papua New Guinea. At the same time, this limitation forced USP's budding writers to teach themselves how to adapt this material to the local context. Hemingway provides a narrative frame and a principle of repetition, not phrases to be repeated, while Eliot is important for his mixed register and fragmentary form. As we suggested in chapter 1, the tendency for modernism to dislocate conventional rote learning pedagogies, to reveal the fractures within texts and render themselves susceptible to disassembly and reassembly, may explain why they were so productive within postcolonial contexts. But whatever the nature of the adaptation, the important point is that this course material was adapted—not imitated—and put to new uses for the society in which these students and teachers wrote.

Another valuable lesson from this early period was that teachers and students could, to an extent, appear together as peers, or at least fellow pioneers. For all of Beier's progressiveness in accepting and validating non-Western literatures, accounts from UPNG leave no doubt that he presented himself as very much the instructor, guiding Papua New Guinean tyros. While the lack of a creative writing program at USP was mourned by the students, it also necessitated a self-directed approach. And while Nandan may well be one of the lecturers Pillai remembers to have been "willing to offer encouragement and advice,"[50] perhaps his greatest gift to USP's fledgling writers was the model he presented of a local poet attuned to the courses of a global literature. In this new literary venture, as in "A Double Life," the teacher is also the student, and as both students and teachers sought to bridge differences through a shared vocabulary, modernism provided a library of images, styles, and forms aiding the establishment of a literary collective. Seri and Nandan might each write works featuring but one of Fiji's two major population groups, but their shared uses of modernism showed the potential for conversation, understanding, and appreciation across the cultural divides entrenched by colonial practices.

Each of these elements—the discovery of the plasticity of model texts and their applicability to local settings as well as the leveling effect of a largely student-driven national movement—proved essential to the more expansive and solidary regional movement heralded by the launch of "Mana" in March 1973. As will be seen, this marked a period (and periodical) of immense literary productivity and coincided with the rapid expansion of the literature curriculum and the arrival of key writers, teachers, editors, and students. It is these components that came together to create a diverse literary movement and to drive a radical recentering of the literary canon upon a Pacific present.

Chapter Six

MANA ON CAMPUS
New Forms in Pacific Poetry and Prose

In Nihi Vini's "The Thing" (1973), islanders on the Cook Islands atoll Penrhyn (Tongareva) are going about their daily work when the calm routine is shattered by a "thing in the water" that "hoist[s] itself on to the reef."[1] Mesmerized by the thing's strangeness, the islanders surround the alien shape, cutting off its retreat and spearing it to death. Following ceremonial rituals over the catch, the islanders cook and eat their "pieces of the dead thing," but although "it was good," gradually those who dined begin to fall sick and die.[2] When the survivors later congregate, they decide that "the next time such a thing came to their shores" it would be treated with respect and, tragically, "made king of all the island."[3] "It," the narrator eventually confirms, was a European castaway who had fled his ship as it passed the atoll. Perhaps the European had brought disease to the island, perhaps his killing had offended some god: the result is that the islanders commit to major social change.

Vini, a Cook Islander who had graduated from USP's teaching program, presents his tale as a retelling of the best-known version of an oral history describing the arrival of the first white man on Tongareva. The event is said to mark a symbolic turning point for the island through two pivotal events: the end of anthropophagy and the heralding of European rule. In Vini's telling, however, a different set of concerns arise. While this may be an oral history, it is clear from the opening lines that we are reading a text conversant with the European short story form. It opens with a concrete, specific location—"the island was Penrhyn, the date the early 1840s"—and uses picturesque language to establish the setting—the sky was "decorated by strokes of different colours."[4] More arrestingly, Vini makes marked use of defamiliarization in his depiction of the European. While an opening vignette, centered on an unnamed passing ship, describes "someone" slipping into the water, the subjective narration then shifts to the perspective of the community, who perceive only "something." Not until the final section of the story is the "thing" given a personal pronoun and revealed to be a man.

The function of this stark objectification is not to characterize the Tongarevans as barbarous. Though the islanders renounce such killings, the narrator approaches their story as an insider and accepts their actions and their worldview as the norm, both before and after the event. In othering the castaway, Vini can instead be seen to reverse the frame of the European adventure story, which consistently objectifies the colonized other under the imperial gaze. To take a well-known example taught in Pacific classrooms, R. M. Ballantyne's *The Coral Island* (1857) presents three English boys who wash up on and take possession of a Pacific Island they deem unnamed and uninhabited. "Liv[ing] on our island in uninterrupted harmony and happiness," they are shocked by the arrival of warring tribes from neighboring islands.[5] The Pacific Islanders are mistaken first for "black seagulls" and "whales" and as they wage war on the beach are presented as "incarnate fiends," "terrible monster[s]," "wretched creature[s]," "more like demons than human beings."[6] Vini would not have needed to know this particular book, popular as it was, to have understood the narrative frame of the imperial encounter tale, which may be practically defined by its dehumanization of colonized people. In "The Thing," Vini reverses the frame, centering Pacific people as the subjects of the narrative—who learn and develop and respond to change—and a European as the alien, objectified other, whose only role is that of catalyst for the islanders' continued growth.

Vini thus defamiliarizes not only the figure of the European colonizer but also, in flipping the narrative viewpoint, the colonial adventure tale through which that figure is normalized on Oceanian shores. Defamiliarization, of course, has a storied modernist legacy. Though defined by

Viktor Shklovsky with reference to nineteenth-century realist narrative techniques, the aesthetic idea of renovating mundane perceptions through art has parallels in Ezra Pound's old diktat "Make It New."[7] As a literary technique, it can be seen everywhere from Samuel Beckett's belabored slowness of thought and action, to James Joyce's freewheeling cycles through style, to Virginia Woolf's estrangement of the processes of apperception, to the famous "delayed decoding" of Joseph Conrad's descriptions. It is this last that presents the most useful comparison for Vini's use of defamiliarization in "The Thing," one that moves us from a reading of the story as a simple riposte to nineteenth-century adventure tales to a more complex exchange with Conrad's *Heart of Darkness* (1899), another classroom staple that unsettled received ideas about both the colonial mission and the colonial adventure genre.

Ian Watt coined the term "delayed decoding" to describe Conrad's depiction of the temporary bewilderment of an individual consciousness, during which a particular character experiences unexpected events more quickly than they can be processed and understood.[8] Vini deals with the group and not the individual, but his prolonged defamiliarization functions in a similar way, with the European depicted only as the Tongarevans perceive him: "something was coming towards them," "the thing finally hoisted itself on to the reef," "the thing . . . began to skim the shore with its eyes," "it suddenly turned around and plunged swiftly into the sea," "there it lay dead on the beach."[9] As with the "Inferno" scene in *Heart of Darkness*, where the identity of the "black shapes" found dying in the grove is decoded only with Marlow's horrified realization of their human suffering, it is only in the final part of Vini's story that the European is described as a man, when the community comes to perceive their shared humanity.[10] As such, Vini's story, assembled and transcribed from oral sources, meets Conrad's story, which—like *Lord Jim* (1900) and *Under Western Eyes* (1911), also on the USP curriculum from this time—plays with the idea of assembled and transcribed oral accounts. Both "The Thing" and *Heart of Darkness* deal with the colonial encounter: Conrad dimly foreshadows an end to Empire, while Vini, still living under its shadow, looks back at a colonization yet to come. Both use a defamiliarizing horror in their treatment of the other: Conrad to strip away sentimental ideas about colonial progress, Vini to stress the contingency of the European arrival. Both overturn the generic expectations of the imperial adventure tale: Conrad by defeating the purpose of the colonial quest, Vini by reversing the frame to make Pacific Islanders the questers.

Vini's islanders, however, are as a social unit capable of cultural transformation in a way that Conrad's individuals are not. Achebe would famously complain of the "preposterous and perverse arrogance" in "reducing Africa to the role of props for the breakup of one petty European mind."[11] With Penrhyn as the center, it is less arrogant for Vini to move from the individual to the group and describe a community's decision to make lasting social change. The author does not sidestep the implications of this momentous decision to embrace future European arrivals: in presenting the people's resolution to make the next "thing" the "king of all the island," he presents a more complex version of colonization than the simple equation of European occupation with Pacific passivity allows. Colonial history tells us that disenfranchisement will occur, but Vini writes an act of enfranchisement into its origins. He also does not suggest that the perspectival reversals of "The Thing" can overturn the real power structures under which he wrote and with which the oral history deals. Yet his story retains a clear political charge: locating colonial history in the accidental arrival of a single, vulnerable castaway, he demystifies the reified image of inevitable European authority. Holding the focus on the community and their response to this arrival, he allows them agency in bringing about a cultural shift, as calamitous as this may have been.

Published less than a decade after the attainment of self-government in the Cook Islands—subject even today to the Realm of New Zealand, albeit in "free association"—this sense of agency was as important in 1974 as in the early 1840s. And published in "Mana," the newly launched "vessel" for the "upsurge of creative talent ... breaking forth across the whole Pacific," Vini's text helped redefine both the narrative form of Oceanian literature and the breadth of the community to which these narratives could speak.[12] Here we trace the ways in which the regional nature of this new publication, the establishment of a regionally representative teaching faculty, profound changes to the literature curriculum, and the extracurricular writers' workshops hosted at the University of the South Pacific led to the growth of a mature writing scene—from a small, modernist-inflected and Fiji-dominated circle to a self-sustaining literary system spanning the university region and spilling into the wider Pacific.

REFITTING THE REGIONAL CANOE: THE LAUNCH OF MANA

In or around March 1973, Pacific literature changed. An eight-page literary segment appeared under the heading "Mana" in *Pacific Islands Monthly*, an Australia-based magazine founded in 1930 to share news and information across the colonial territories of the Pacific Islands. Although the magazine had been refitted to make returns on the decolonizing spirit of the second half of the century, a skim through the cover pages of the 1970s—the "canoe-full of lovelies"; the "winsome Niue Island girl, with the sly side glance"; the topless adolescent dancing to the "intoxicating rhythm of the pounding stones"—reveals the magazine's cultural frame.[13] Yet despite this compromised vessel, a group of Pacific Island writers succeeded in establishing in *PIM* a hold for a regional literature offering a very different representation of Oceania. These "Mana" pages would lead to *Mana*, an independent title whose ambition and scope makes it the most significant regional literary publication in Pacific Island print history and one of the most enduring, albeit through a complicated series of iterations.[14]

Histories of Pacific literature have tended, as elsewhere, to privilege the major international publications of men: Albert Maori Kiki's *Kiki: Ten Thousand Years in a Lifetime* (1968), Vincent Eri's *The Crocodile* (1970), Witi Ihimaera's *Pounamu, Pounamu* (1972), Albert Wendt's *Sons for the Return Home* (1973). Yet "Mana" was spearheaded by a woman, the Cook Islander Marjorie Tuainekore Crocombe, and while Wendt's "Towards a New Oceania" is often read as the manifesto of the new literature, it is Crocombe who first declared its regionalist ideals. These are clear from the first "Mana" editorial and are maintained through to her 1977 retrospective, "Mana and Creative Regional Cooperation," where she identifies three factors inspiring her pan-Pacificist vision. The first was a transformative encounter with early Pacific Island writings all but ignored by the colonial historical and educational record—including nineteenth-century texts written by the pre-colonial Rarotongan missionaries Ta'unga and Maretu—which convinced her of the importance of "recording our own histories" and "developing our national literatures, to offset the dominating viewpoints of foreign writers."[15] Crocombe would cement her commitment to Pacific writing past as well as present by editing these missionaries' works: her edition of *The Works of Taʻunga: Records of a Polynesian Traveller in the South Seas, 1833–1896*, which she edited with her husband, Ron Crocombe, was published in 1968, while her edition of Maretu's *Cannibals and Converts: Radical Change in the Cook Islands* was published by the Institute of Pacific Studies at USP Press in 1983. The second factor informing Crocombe's founding of "Mana" was her firsthand experience of the new literary scene in PNG, where she lived for most of the 1960s and enrolled in Beier's creative writing course. Praising the vision of the university in establishing an academic post and credit-bearing course in creative writing, Crocombe writes vividly of the rich writing scene it helped establish and the numerous print journals it supported; as we saw in chapter 2, she contributed to this scene herself, publishing prose pieces in *Kovave*.[16]

Here we have the discovery of an older, precolonial literary tradition legitimizing Pacific writing as an Indigenous rather than imitative endeavor and a contemporary model proving that a modern Pacific literature could be viably produced and sustained. With tradition and model in place, the third element Crocombe identifies is a growing collective creative spirit, exemplified by the inaugural South Pacific Arts Festival, hosted at USP in Suva in May 1972. Featuring almost four thousand performers, with some two-thirds coming from outside of Fiji, the festival showcased Pacific art forms of all kinds: visual art and handicraft in wood, shell, bone, tapa, and pottery; countless forms of dance; and various dramatic forms, including contemporary plays from PNG and Samoa—the latter, *Come the Revolution*, written by Wendt (not himself in attendance) and performed at Laucala campus by Samoan students.[17] Like many observers, Crocombe hailed the South Pacific Arts Festival as an event of major cultural significance, a performance of the pride and self-determination of the rapidly decolonizing Pacific.[18] As she put it in her first "Mana" editorial, the festival expressed "a new wave of confidence among the Islands peoples," bringing to light "visions which formerly lay dormant."[19]

Crocombe is careful to separate USP as an institution from the artistic movement that followed, drawing attention to the host's failure to facilitate any serious contribution from staff or students to the activities of the festival, particularly the literary events. With the exception of the Samoan play and a pair of poetry readings, Crocombe states that "there was no USP participation in dance, poetry reading, and drama despite a student and staff body which then numbered about a thousand people from all over the Pacific and beyond."[20] It is thus that she describes the university—pre-"Mana"—as "an institution without a Pacific soul," bearing no comparison with the vibrant scene she experienced at UPNG. The gulf separating the neighboring tertiary institutions was symbolized at the festival by the impressive display of books published by Papua New Guineans between 1967 and 1972. As she recalls, this display "brought home most clearly to many of us at USP that any meaningful attempt to encourage creative writing in the University's catchment area of the South Pacific region had to be done predominantly by islanders."[21] So the South Pacific Creative Arts Society (SPCAS) was born, and from this society came "Mana."[22]

In spite of the institutional indifference, USP remained central to the new publication, not least as a base of operations. The SPCAS president and vice-president, Jo Nacola and Raymond Pillai, were USP literature teaching staff, and around half of the "Mana" editorial committee members were affiliated with the university, either as lecturers—Satendra Nandan, Sione Tupouniua, and Ken Arvidson, with Wendt set to join the following year—or as students, including Vanessa Griffen, Neal Engledow, and Ata Maʻiaʻi, all of whom had transitioned from editorial roles with *UNISPAC*. More importantly, the university brought together in one place students from across the region, and these students played a major part in the "Mana" movement, contributing somewhere between two-fifths and a half of the texts published in the *PIM* period. In turn, "Mana" brought out the best of the students in relation to the university's regional aspirations. As we saw in chapter 5, contributors to *UNISPAC* were almost all from Fiji. "Mana," by contrast, was truly inclusive, and though Fijians still made up the largest group of writers, contributing some 40 percent of the total pieces published for the *PIM* run, this figure is roughly in line with the Fijian proportion of the student body as a whole. As limited as USP's investment in SPCAS or "Mana" may have been, the regionalism invoked by Crocombe is both physically enabled by the university's infrastructure and ideologically consistent with the founding principles of an institution spanning some thirty-three million square kilometers of ocean.

Conversely, the regional movement animated by "Mana" brought about a corresponding set of changes within the institution, with the half-decade following the launch of "Mana" in 1973 seeing the flowering of the USP scene into a self-supporting literary environment. With the arrival of key literary figures from the region upon the staff roll, including Wendt, Helu Thaman, Subramani, Pio Manoa, Mostyn Habu, and Crocombe, and the introduction of first extracurricular and then credit-bearing creative writing classes, the new literature was produced as part of a fruitful interaction between Pacific Island mentors and students. At the same time, the literature modules on the English syllabus proliferated, connecting the existing modernist components to what was then called Commonwealth literature and, more specifically and more experimentally, to the literature of the region as it appeared in "Mana." By the end of this period, the entire English curriculum was organized around Pacific writing, which became the beating heart of a reclaimed canon. Correspondingly, the literature that emerges from within the institution in this period was plentiful, engaging not only with the touchstones of European modernism but more especially with the aesthetic traditions of the Pacific: the oral histories, myths, and legends circulating within and across island cultures; the distinct poetic forms and techniques developed within particular societies; the written forms arising from national scenes in Aotearoa, Papua New Guinea, and Fiji.

One way of framing this localizing or recentering in relation to modernism would be to suggest that while European and American writers such as Eliot, Yeats, or Hemingway had helped fledgling Pacific writers find their voice, they had now served their purpose and could be discarded. There is a clear ideological appeal to this narrative, as it finds an aesthetic correspondence to the political independence achieved by many Pacific Island nations in this decolonizing period. Yet such a reading would fundamentally misunderstand both the nature of Oceanian indigenization and the dynamics of modernist literary engagement more generally. As a careful reading of "Mana" against the developing USP curriculum will show, the new regional literature does not move away from modernism, and Pacific writers continued to engage with the canonical modernists in a process that would endure throughout the 1980s and 1990s and into the new millennium.[23] What was different, however, was that writers received and responded to modernism in a more complexly mediated fashion, as well as through a distributed range of channels.

Some writers, such as Vini, wove the modernist texts they encountered at school and university into their writings. Others encountered it less directly or, rather more accurately, from multiple sources at once. Thus, as we will outline, when ni-Vanuatu students attending the 1974 Regional

Creative Writing Workshop at USP set out to establish a poetic voice of political frustration, they did so with reference to the protest poetry of neighboring Papua New Guinea. As we showed in chapters 2 and 4, among that poetry's referents was modernist and modernist-mediated verse from across the African diaspora. Modernism thus enters the ni-Vanuatu register from a complex, enmeshed network of sources, many of which themselves mediated other modernist texts and forms. In the new age of Pacific literature that "Mana" helped usher in, independence lies not in being impervious to other literatures but in the agency and discernment with which it invites and integrates these literatures into the regional court. Such agency, such an ability to choose—that, to invoke a well-turned phrase of Teresia Teaiwa's, is sovereignty.[24]

"FROM ALL OVER THE ISLANDS": PROSE WORKINGS OF PACIFIC STORIES

"Mana" declares its own modernity, but this is no futurist break from the past. As Crocombe states in her opening editorial, the pages were established "to publish works in traditional and modern form," and a substantial part of the project included the transcription and adaptation of oral histories, legends, and myths.[25] These appeared "from all over the Islands," not only USP member countries and the ever-prolific Papua New Guinea but also areas apt to be omitted in Anglophone literary histories, from Palau (Caroline Islands) to Futuna. As would be expected across such a vast geographical range, there are clear local distinctions, from the royal genealogies and histories typical of Tonga, to Fijian itukuni explaining customary relations between vanua and yavusa.[26] Yet beneath these distinctions lie deeper ties, with a cognate mythological grammar and typology across different languages and oral histories linking disparate islands.

To take just one example, Kenneth Fakamuria's "The First Coconut" recounts a Futunan legend explaining the origins of this quintessential Pacific tree. In this story a woman is captured by a snake and bears him a son. Her family members chop up the snake in revenge, and the woman buries his skull, which grows into a tall coconut tree. When the village children eat too many of the tree's coconuts, she throws the remaining nuts to the surrounding islands, which, the story concludes, is why coconuts grow "on all the islands of the New Hebrides."[27] Similar origin stories for the coconut can be found across the Pacific, but—appearing in "Mana"—Fakamuria's account performs an important unifying function.[28] Fiji and Futuna are near neighbors, yet the colonial partitioning of Oceania has severely limited cultural interaction between the islands. Wallis and Futuna remain under French rule, and with the linguistic differences introduced by rival colonial powers, Wallis and Futuna have remained all but invisible in the Anglophone literary mapping of the region. Though Fiji-based, the regional circulation of "Mana" encouraged Fakamuria to publish there, and the pan-Pacific aspects of his story remind readers in Fiji and elsewhere that beneath the colonial compartments remain shared roots. In this way, Fakamuria's decision to publish performs the story's final act: he throws his coconut-as-story to other islands, resowing symbols of concordance, this time using the technologies of print to increase the range of the broadcast.

Reinforcing the shared heritage so invaluable to the regional movement, the writers publishing in "Mana" also discovered the shared aesthetic challenge of finding new ways to articulate this heritage in the motley medium of written English. Different writers met this challenge in different ways. Some presented legendary material through seemingly straightforward translation, as with Jerry Iakavi's ni-Vanuatu custom story "The Mysterious Maidens from the East." This traditional tale tells of a village man's abduction of a mysterious flying woman and her eventual escape, upon which the man and their son are turned to stone. Although variations of the story exist across the Pacific, Iakavi plays an essential role in its transmission through "Mana," most obviously through his composition in a new language. This is an inherently creative act, and there are many Pacific storytelling traditions that show great ingenuity in their play with translations across languages and cultures. In the previous "Mana" issue, for example, Wendt had described the Samoan fāgogo, which interweaves local tales with improvised translations from the Bible, Aesop, and the Brothers Grimm to create new stories "better than the originals."[29] Iakavi's use of the English storytelling formula "once upon a time"—itself used in the first translations of the European fairytales gathered and rewritten by Charles Perrault and the Brothers Grimm—shows his own deployment of heterogeneous sources for his translation and couples his story with iterations of the swan maiden tale at the global scale.[30] Nevertheless, he generally effaces his presence as an active, creative controller of the material, using a restrained narrative voice and an almost total absence of figurative language. Iakavi is content to appear as spokesperson for this "live art" from Tanna, where villagers, as is stated in the introduction, "prefer to be left alone to lead their lives in their own way," free of the colonial administration and its "government schools."[31] By implication, then, some stories stand strongest when hewn close to the original.

Yet even seemingly direct translations reveal complex creative engagements. Leonard Garae's "Beware, the Worst Is Still to Come!" tells the story of a cursed village's self-destruction on the Vanuatu island of Aoba. Garae's account is framed by narrative commentary, opening with a note on the oral transmission of a story "handed down by word of mouth" and closing with archaeological evidence to support the truth of the tale's claims.[32] Yet the narrator subtly interrupts its "authenticity" with a range of devices, shifting between the cues and conventions of oral storytelling ("every day it happened that"; "it is said that"; "I wonder"), figurative devices more literary in tone ("on stormy nights when a dark veil of clouds swept in over the valley and the wind tore through the coconut leaves like angry waves through a fisherman's net"), and unusual metaphors and epithets ("the leading freedom-dreamer") that might be translations of local idioms or might be new phrases, coined, perhaps, in the creative writing classes and workshops where much of the early "Mana" material was written, including Garae's story: though he was not yet enrolled at USP, contemporary records show that Garae attended the 1974 Regional Creative Writing Workshop, where Wendt taught attendants "how traditional story-telling techniques could be used to write modern stories and poems."[33]

And as we have seen with Vini's "The Thing," modern storytelling techniques could also be used to write traditional stories, bringing multiple modes into dialogue to produce new forms. We have already discussed Vini's productive engagement with Conrad, but his conclusion makes clear that the Cook Island author is presenting, among other things, a study in mode and perspective. Having explained that from the many variations of this story circulating on the atoll he has captured the agreed facts, the narrator ends wryly: "One can only speculate upon why the man left the ship to swim ashore. . . . It is also hard to trace his name. Perhaps it is written in some ship's logbook that is preserved somewhere."[34] Quite likely it is. As Thomas Richards has pointed out, power in the later stages of the British Empire consisted more than anything else in "keeping track, and keeping track of keeping track."[35] With increasingly far-flung territories held together by a ramshackle bureaucracy, the imperial office sought to unify by text what could not be done for the territory, assembling what Richards famously terms the "imperial archive," a "paper empire" of information on a scale that historians are still only beginning to comprehend.[36] Vini is right, then, that some archived logbook may name the sailor or stowaway who disappeared nine degrees south of the equator. But for those outside of Tongareva, this is where his story ends—if not wholly lost in the reams of archived paper, then known only to the odd historian. The living record of Penrhyn's oral history, by contrast, preserves for the community the experience of the sailor's encounter on shore and, indeed, his lasting significance in the social transformations that followed: he was the "last to be eaten" on Penrhyn, with the next shipwrecked Europeans to be adopted formally as sons of the island. Yet lest this conclusion imply a victory of the oral over the written that is too absolute, the contrast is encoded here, on the published page, in a written form that itself has its genesis in the colonial encounter the story describes. The Pacific storyteller asserts his perspectival centrality while drawing attention to the foreign entanglements of the material he has mastered.

In short, Vini draws on the range of aesthetic and technical resources available to the Pacific prose writer in the early 1970s. Introducing his story with a concrete location and descriptive setting, he draws mana from the oral history of his island. Taking the techniques of a written mode introduced through the colonial education system, he reconciles the modern short story form to an Indigenous position, extracting and reversing the subject-object codifications that are the formal properties of the genre in the context of the Pacific adventure story. Conrad did not enter the USP curriculum until 1974, the year after Vini graduated with his bachelor of arts and graduate certificate of education, but the author featured on the New Zealand School Certificate in the 1960s—the curriculum sat by Cook Islanders at this time—so he would have encountered the novel in the classroom before learning to teach at USP.[37] Concentrating the prolonged, modernist defamiliarization found in Conrad's texts of Empire, Vini dissolves the aura of the colonizer. Setting up the oral history of his people against the imperial archive of the foreigner, he shows how the Pacific short story, integrating oral and written imperatives, may present the fullest compass of perspectives and experiences. And, most importantly, by publishing in the new "Mana" pages, he embeds his work in a site of regional correspondence that subverts colonial norms. His text not only circulates around the region but is taught, as we will see, as part of the reworked literature program at USP. In the sheer range of written approaches to the oral heritage—from Fakamuria's direct translation, to Iakavi's introduction of English storytelling formulae, to Garae's shifting strategies and Vini's overt intertwining of opposed forms—"Mana" presented to readers and writers, students and teachers, the productive potentials in Pacific orality that Beier had wished for at UPNG in the previous decade.

EXTRACURRICULAR WRITING WORKSHOPS: BLACK POWER ACROSS BORDERS IN NI-VANUATU VERSE

The Vanuatu involvement in the literature of the "Mana" archipelago was a relatively late development: no poems appeared from what was then the New Hebrides in the first year and a half of *Mana*'s *PIM* run. This changed with a late-1974 special issue on Vanuatu writing, with all but one of the contributors USP students. These writers brought a new poetic voice to "Mana," exclamatory and direct in its challenge to colonial occupation and presented on the page so as to emphasize its affinities with orality. While anticolonial writing was prominent from the first issue, there had been little resembling the Black nationalist literature appearing from UPNG. Indeed, in an early editorial Crocombe had rejected a challenge she had received arguing that Pacific writers ought to "focus their attention upon 'protest.'" While "such kinds of writing have a place," she responds, it is "better that they arise naturally than through direction."[38] Crocombe seems to glance at Beier here and certainly draws a distinction between their curatorial attitudes to local literatures. But she is not resistant to this kind of writing when it does arise, celebrating in her special issue editorial the "new voice of the New Hebrides."[39]

The standard mode for this poetry is the short, free-verse poem, addressing from the first-person perspective a figure or concept involved in the colonial situation. The lines are strikingly short—often only three or four words—and they scan as they would sound when read aloud: trochees resound as exclamations. Anger provides the keynote. This can be expressed directly and aggressively, as by Kali Vatoko and Albert Leomala in "Mi stap sori nomo / I Bow in Sorrow": "You wait whiteman / . . . / I'll kick your arse."[40] It appears as indignant complaint in Donald Kalpokas's "Who Am

I?': "My beautiful land was alienated through fraud."[41] It gathers strength through the appeal to custom, as in Leomala's "Culture My Culture": "destroy the western / stop him growing / burn him down."[42] It approaches despair when it is turned back upon the community, as with Mildred Sope's challenging of a metonymic "mother" in "Motherland": "Why did you create me at all."[43] This metonymic address is comparable to Russell Soaba's call to the "Mother of Life" in "Dusk," a poem written for the 1974 Regional Creative Writing Workshop he attended as a special guest alongside the Vanuatu students, and this connection reminds us of the concrete interconnections between the two Pacific university scenes, particularly the way in which the earlier movement served to inspire and instruct the later, at this stage outside of the formal setting of the classroom.[44] Sope's strength is to present this address with an immediacy at once personal and political, without the diffusing effect of a device manifestly figurative.

A similar pathos may be found in Leomala's "Live in Me," where the speaker cries out to his ancestors, trying to understand their part in colonial modernity's betrayals: "What made you sell our land / for sticks of tobacco."[45] Seeking in vain some sign of kinship—"where are your bones / and where are your stories"—Leomala's speaker is frustrated by the inadequacy of contemporary accounts, both the current "oldtime stories" and "the book" of modern learning and religion. Unable to uncover the roots of his political suffering, all that remains in the final stanza is the anguish itself: "fathers of father / and mothers of mother / your sufferings / live in me." When the title of the poem appears here as the poem's final line, its affirmative connotations have given way to something sad and ironic, an inheritance of trauma with neither a clear comprehension of its cause nor a rooted aesthetic form through which to express it. In this sense, the Regional Creative Writing Workshop and the pages of "Mana" provided complementary forums for the construction of an Indigenous written form sufficient to the expression of old traumas and new experiences.

Sope and Leomala remained the most prolific of the Vanuatu set, and Leomala continued to refine the expression of anger as a form in itself. His poems addressing the colonial occupiers are often presented in Bislama alongside the English, exploiting the impression of a direct, vernacular outburst. In "Hoom blong mi," the speaker appeals to the father, mother, sister, and brother who have abandoned him before again directly threatening the occupier: "whiteman go home / i am tired of seeing your face / i am tired of listening to your voice / go home / go home white skin."[46] Leomala ventures toward the figurative in his best-known poem, "Kros / Cross." Personified as proud, belittling, and destructive, "Cross" is a synecdoche for Christianity and, by further extension, colonialism. Yet while the symbol is effective in adding connotative dimensions to Leomala's earlier, denotative approach, he retains his signature rhetorical structure, addressing the figure in direct expostulation: "Cross run away / Run away from me / I hate you / Take your ideas / And your civilisation / And go back / To where you belong."[47]

The exclamatory voice; the direct, sometimes militant statements of protest; the use of simple but powerful symbolism to contain and banish figures of colonial rule; the shared critical reception: all of this suggests engagement with PNG verse by ni-Vanuatu poets. In 1972, K. L. Goodwin wrote of Kasaipwalova's "remarkable" expression of "black anger," praising the poet's ability to "encompass any of the emotions, tender or fierce, that he wants to present."[48] Crocombe appears to intuit a relationship between the style and affect of PNG and ni-Vanuatu writing when she introduced the 1974 special issue in much the same terms, identifying "anger and sensitivity as the new voice of the New Hebrides—and what a remarkable and powerful voice it is."[49] Even more directly, in "Towards a New Oceania," which appeared in the first standalone *Mana* and presented an overview of the literature of the *PIM* era, Wendt connects Leomala's imagery to Kasaipwalova's personification of colonialism as "chill."[50] While the imagery is less elaborately worked out in "Kros / Cross," there are distinct similarities, including the direct address, the violent language, the embodiment of colonialism in an evocative symbol, and the open expression of anger and hatred, though Leomala is perhaps mild in comparison to Kasaipwalova's address in *Reluctant Flame*: "FUCK OFF, WHITE BASTARDRY, FUCK OFF!" (6). There is a sustained resemblance between the two national poetries, suggested by the Soaba example cited earlier, and of all the branches developing in the "Mana" growth phase, it is the ni-Vanuatu alone who adopt the direct, populist register established by PNG poets for their activist verse. It is then, we can surmise, with both ni-Vanuatu and PNG poetry in mind that Wendt refers to the "raw power of innocent anger" in his introduction to the 1980 *Lali* collection, and this description in turn resembles Beier's assessment of the "healthy, exuberant, explosive exposure of colonialism" in PNG verse.[51]

But granting the filiation with PNG verse, where, precisely, did these students find it? As we shall see, 1974 was a watershed year for the undergraduate English program, which for the first time included Pacific literature on the syllabus. The Vanuatu set, however, were Diploma of Education students, sitting applied English courses that emphasized literacy and teaching methods. Only three texts are listed for English III, the final-year paper sat by the students in 1974: Joyce's *Portrait of the Artist as a Young Man* (1914), V. S. Naipaul's *A House for Mr Biswas* (1961), and Wendt's *Sons for the Return Home* (1973). These novels appear to have obtained little purchase with the Vanuatu writers, though the inclusion of Wendt's provocative, sexually explicit novel within the teacher training program reveals a new level of permissiveness at the institution, no doubt appealing for these students of the 1970s. The year 1974 was also when Wendt arrived at USP, fresh off the heels of his founding a strong extracurricular creative writing culture at Samoa College. Sope, at USP from 1972 to 1974, speaks of Wendt as an inclusive, motivating teacher, noting that "he got us to write poems, like a competition in the class. He would pick on each one to go in front and read, and then we would comment. Boys and girls, Albert Wendt took everyone as equal."[52] Thus, while the Diploma of Education curriculum might not have formally included the Yeats and Eliot that were so influential in the main English program or the African and African diasporic verse that was so productive at UPNG, Wendt was evidently weaving poetry into his pedagogy. He was encouraging writing, normalizing conversation and engaged critique, and nurturing expressive talent. Given his repeated praise of Papua New Guinean poetry in print from this time, it is reasonable to speculate that he shared examples of the political verses that so impressed him with his students, particularly those from what was then the New Hebrides (Vanuatu), still very much under colonial rule.

Yet as "Mana" itself shows, USP's literary culture at this stage existed largely outside of the classroom, and we see this even more clearly with the major impact made by the 1974 Regional Creative Writing Workshop. Sponsored by USP and UNESCO, chaired by the Samoan USP director of extension services, and held over two weeks at the main campus, the event brought students together with staff from the university—Wendt, Crocombe, Nacola, Helu Thaman—and other established Pacific writers, including Soaba from PNG and Alistair Te Ariki Campbell, the Aotearoa New Zealand poet of Cook Island Māori descent. With participants from twelve Pacific countries, the writers' workshop was unprecedented in its regional scope. Reporting on the event in "Mana," Crocombe celebrates the coming together of writers hitherto separated by distance and colonial divisions, creating a literature that draws upon "a valued heritage" but also explores "new forms and styles reflecting the changes within the continuity of the unique world of our Island cultures."[53] Praising the members' plans to return to "Samoa, Rarotonga, Tarawa, Tonga, the New Hebrides and elsewhere across the Pacific to carry forward and expand the initiatives begun at the workshop," Crocombe evidently sees the Regional Creative Writing Workshop as part of the broader movement "Mana" documents and helped drive.[54]

Kalpokas, Leomala, Sope, and Vatoko were among the students attending the event (see the detailed USP/UNESCO report cited earlier), and if they possibly encountered in class examples of the Papua New Guinean verse from which they drew, they surely encountered it here. Soaba may seem an unlikely mentor in this direction, given his doubts about overtly political content. But the poetry he wrote for this event, as published in the Workshop Report though not in the "Mana" special issue that arose from it, is closer to the political writing of the Vanuatu poets: his appeal to the "Mother of life"—"Why must you die out on me?"—sounds very much like Sope, and his claim of "my betel nut" has the cultural self-consolation of Leomala. There seems to have been an openly political side to Soaba's writing, even if he ultimately presented the more cynical, questioning aspect in his published fiction. Wendt also led sessions on poetry and prose at the workshop, setting out to "actively foster the development of our own distinctively South Pacific styles" by "following what has and is taking place in ... Papua New Guinea," and defining regional creative writing programs against English secondary curricula dependent on the "literature of alien cultures."[55] Furthermore, he expressly encouraged political writing—on "problems such as migration and emigration, urbanisation, social change, elitism and political corruption," prominent themes in ni-Vanuatu verse as in PNG—and agreed that "these should be some of our main concerns in our writing."[56] In this light, Papua New Guinean examples would have been relevant to the ni-Vanuatu group of teachers and trainees, some of whom were already actively involved in national politics. Kalpokas would go on to serve twice as prime minister of Vanuatu, and while a teacher in 1971 he was a founding member of the New Hebrides Cultural Association, whose publication, *New Hebrides Viewpoints* and later *Vanua'aka Viewpoints*, was published in English, French, and Bislama and included stories and poetry.[57] The Cultural Association became the New Hebrides National Party (NHNP), later the Vanua'aka Pati. In 1974, then, Kalpokas was writing from a position of deep political involvement, in a context where colonization and its many ills were discussed in various political spaces, from nakamal (the traditional ni-Vanuatu meeting place) to church groups, and often in contexts which—like the Regional Creative Writers' Workshop—included delegates from across the Pacific.

Whatever the line of transmission, the direct, vocally oriented style forged at UPNG and adopted by ni-Vanuatu poets is eminently appropriate to their immediate political concerns. Kalpokas's repeated, titular question in "Who Am I?" has a general relevance for all Pacific cultures affected by colonialism, conveying the anxiety of a speaker "lost in the ocean of confusion."[58] But it is more precisely political than that, presenting the oddity of the New Hebrides Condominium, which until the achievement of an independent Vanuatu in 1980 was controlled by not one but two imperial powers, the "two great enemies," as Kalpokas describes them, France and Britain. Defending jealously their own interests against each other—each colonial administration notoriously refused to concede to the other's driving customs, so that the French drove on the right while the British drove on the left—the "so-called government" left the people thoroughly disenfranchised, as Kalpokas complains: "I am stateless and have no right / Of appeal in my country's high court." For this singular situation, Kalpokas invokes the form of a riddle to build toward a bitterly singular answer: "Who am I? / I am that third citizen of my country, / The only condominium in the world."[59] In a short article titled "How to Get Students Writing Poetry," Wendt wrote that it is the task of the teacher to "get students to write about what *they* know, meaning their own cultural/physical/social environment";[60] Kalpokas's poem was published a few months after the July 1974 occupation of the condominium building in Port Vila by members of the NHNP.[61] Wherever they turned for inspiration, the Vanuatu poets wrote about what they knew. The anger and frustration they expressed is not mere style.

But it is mediated. With the formal and informal channeling of PNG writing into USP's literary scene, we see some of the complexity of the routes of both Pacific works and global modernism into the regional literature.

With a few quite distinct exceptions, discussed in what follows, the ni-Vanuatu set are the only "Mana" contributors to take up the rhetoric of blackness utilized by the Papua New Guineans: "white thieves" are challenged for seizing the "black country"; the "black child" sings; the racialized marker is reclaimed in the vernacular, "Mi—mi—blak."[62] As we have seen, PNG poets had already localized this rhetoric and the poetics of Black activism more generally from African American writing and from African négritude. There is no direct reference to these movements by the ni-Vanuatu and none of the cultural signifiers of contemporary blackness that Kasaipwalova had imported, from Chubby Checker to Ray Charles to the Black Panthers. Yet the connection is there: a passage can be traced from the already transnational modernist or modernist-informed movements of the African diaspora, writings that were often in conversation with Anglo-American and Francophone modernisms, to the national scene of Papua New Guinea, to the fledgling anticolonial writing of the ni-Vanuatu, itself part of a regional Pacific movement gyring around USP.

This threading of modernist influence should not be conceptualized as a succession. PNG writers continued to be active during this period, in "Mana" as well as in *Kovave* and *Papua New Guinea Writing*: Aivu Kula's 1975 poem "Black Venture," for example—which presents the barely controlled outburst of a speaker "Gripped by a white whirlpool"—shows that this strain of Papua New Guinean poetry was not extinct.[63] What emerges, rather, is a drawing of transnationally seeded national literatures into regional systems, within which they continued to function, whether in the interplay between African American works and the broader writing of négritude or in the way writing from PNG gave rise to and flowed within the regional literature centered around USP. Finally, though the 1974 workshop was extracurricular, this is a site of literary transmission that cannot be separated from the university space. Entering Papua New Guinea through the UPNG literature curriculum and creative writing program and through the explorations of students overseas on scholarship, these flows of inspiration reached USP students in and outside of the seminar rooms, and their responses appeared in "Mana," which—though bigger than the institution—was nevertheless closely associated with the activities of its staff and students. Crucially, the rising literature would be channeled back to this first generation of homegrown Pacific tertiary students through the inclusion of "Mana" on the USP curriculum from 1974 onward, helping produce the self-sufficient literary culture foundational to Pacific literature as we now know it.

TRANSFORMING CURRICULA: DETERMINING AND OVERDETERMINING INFLUENCES

The writers' workshops brought a rapid exchange of influences, ideas, and styles, and in the texts coming out of these sessions cross-references appear between writers from very different backgrounds. Yet this interplay is only a concentration of the process at work between writers and traditions that the Mana project had created. By late 1974, this project was already well established, and special issues on Samoa, Fiji, Papua New Guinea, Vanuatu, Rotuma, Kiribati and Tuvalu (then the Gilbert and Ellice Islands) had validated local traditions and ventures as part of the regional movement. It is from this time that USP student participation, which, as we have shown, was largely confined to Fiji in the five years from the university's inception, becomes truly regional. Some three-fifths of student contributions to "Mana" came from outside of Fiji, and even *UNISPAC*, all but exclusively Fijian in the period discussed in the previous chapter, began to reflect the diversity of the university's student body: a 1974 double-page spread featuring new student poetry is dominated by pieces from Cook Islanders, Tongans, and Samoans, each of whom had participated at the 1974 USP/UNESCO workshop and many of whom would go on to play bigger roles in Pacific literature in the decades to come.[64]

This academic year also brought an acceleration of changes within the classroom. The previous year had seen the much-desired reorganization of the English program, with literature set alongside linguistics in first- and final-year modules. This reorganization had strengthened the modernist element, and students read texts by Eliot, Joyce, Yeats, D. H. Lawrence, Katherine Mansfield, and many more. In 1974, with Wendt and Nandan now on the faculty, the program was further restructured: with new second-year modules and a new literature-only course in the final year, students for the first time encountered literature at every level. Modernism remained in the ascendancy, and the generic rationalization of texts into modules such as "The Novel and the Short Story" and "Poetry and Prose" encouraged an attention to form supporting the kinds of experiments discussed in this chapter. Paul Sharrad has stressed the innovation of Wendt and his colleagues in introducing African and other postcolonial texts to the undergraduate syllabus,[65] but the most exciting innovation was the inclusion of an ultramodern Pacific literature within the "Commonwealth Literature" module: Ihimaera's *Tangi* (1973), Wendt's "Pepesa and Other Stories"—presumably the collection he would publish as *Flying-Fox in the Freedom Tree* (1974)—and the 1973 *Mana Annual of Creative Writing*.

Here we see the revolutionary nature of the changes now underway within the classroom as well as without, and the coming together of the university's curricular and extracurricular divisions. The *Mana Annual* gathered all of the texts published in *Pacific Islands Monthly* that year, with some new texts besides, including Arvidson's critical overview of Pacific literature and Crocombe's report on the South Pacific Festival of Arts. This meant that alongside Eliot, Hemingway, and Yeats, students read texts by the rising stars of the regional movement: Ihimaera, Wendt, Te Ariki Campbell, Helu Thaman; John Saunana and Mostyn B. Habu of the Solomon Islands; the Samoans Ruperake Petaia and Eti Sa'aga; the iKiribati poet Maunaa Itaia; a new generation of writers from PNG, including Rita Mamavi, Venantius Tapin, and Monica Yadiwalya. They studied works by the Fijian student writers discussed in the previous chapter, Vanessa Griffen, Pillai, and Seri. Indeed, they read most of the specific texts discussed in chapter 5 and elsewhere: Griffen's "Marama," which had been reprinted in the November 1973 *PIM*; Seri's "Prologue"; 'O Helu's "Ko Ha Faka'anau / In a Longing"; Malupo's "Tonga, Blessed Land"; Vini's "The Thing"; Fakamuria's "The First Coconut"; Iakavi's "The Mysterious Maidens from the East"; Helu Thaman's "You, the Choice of My Parents."

What must this experience have been like for students in the classroom? It is hard to conceive a more effective validation of the Pacific literature beginning to flourish across the region. In Wendt and Ihimaera they found novelists of international standing, who proved that the long narrative form could be repurposed to speak to and for Oceanian people. In the *Mana Annual* they saw major new departures in prose and verse, some of it from their own classmates and peers, drawing upon particular national forms and traditions as part of an explicitly regionalist project. For students already aware that they were participating in an unparalleled venture as members of the regional university, this must have been inspiring, and in the years that followed these students contributed substantially to the growing movement, particularly in the periodicals and books appearing through Mana Publications.

Reading "Mana" against the English curriculum of the period, we find the swelling of a self-supporting literary infrastructure hitherto unseen in the Pacific regional context. The Mana project emerged through the establishment of the University of the South Pacific and drew in writers from across the region, each working from and through their national traditions toward a shared literature in English. A radically modern syllabus channeled this shared literature back into classrooms, enabling students to experiment with these traditions for themselves, whether at home, in the extracurricular workshops we have discussed in relation to the Vanuatu set, or in the credit-bearing creative writing courses introduced to the program in 1976. Finally, students were encouraged to feed back into the rising tide of Pacific literature by publishing these experiments for themselves, whether in the student pages of *UNISPAC* or in "Mana," with the massive readership its association with *Pacific Islands Monthly* brought.

Within this interactive and immensely productive literary environment, student writers had access to multiple traditions simultaneously: the oral and other Indigenous traditions of their own communities; the written Pacific literatures engaging these traditions, now foregrounded in their classes; the modernist texts that continued to feature prominently in their university courses; the postcolonial writing introduced in the Commonwealth modules; the English, often colonial writing, upon which they had been examined at school. It is no wonder that in their own literature, student writers shuttle back and forth between these different traditions, experimenting with the new forms that develop in the interaction between older ones. So, from 1974 onward, we see a new diversity of material appearing in the pages of "Mana" and its associated publications.

Many of the earlier modernist touchstones remain. The Solomon Islander Celestine Kulagoe, another 1974 Workshop participant, opens his poem "Peace Signs" with an invocation of the wise men tracking the Star of Bethlehem as it moves "resolutely / across the sky."[66] Their "anxiety" echoes the "Hard and bitter" experience of Eliot's disillusioned wise men in "Journey of the Magi," another staple of the USP curriculum.[67] Yet this is no Christian nativity. As in Yeats's "The Second Coming," reworked to the Pacific context by Seri in the previous year, this is a terrible birth, figuring the nuclear atrocities introduced to the Pacific world by the United States with the Bikini tests in 1946 and maintained across the century with French and British participation. As the atomic star lands in Kulagoe's poem, "A mushroom sprouts from / an arid Pacific atoll," leaving only an "empty tomb": Kulagoe extends his calculated upheaval of Christian imagery with the eruption of a "wooden cross of disgrace."[68] In the final stanza, Eliot's conflicted Magi are replaced by oxymoronic UN military peacekeepers, "men with clenched fists / signing peace treaties."[69]

The modernist intertexts are important, but Kulagoe also seems to take a cue from Seri's "Prologue," part of the curriculum in 1974, which had demonstrated the felicitousness of these poets for mythologizing a catastrophic Pacific encounter. Seri, meanwhile, in the same issue as Kulagoe's "Peace Signs," turns from his vision of Fiji *sub specie aeternitatis* to the concrete hardships of the independent state in "Monday Morning Street Ride." Setting his poem in the newly developed Suva government housing settlement of the "tin-can / reservation Raiwaqa," Seri sets aside the high strain of the Yeatsian seer.[70] In its place he adopts the African American ghetto vernacular of the Black Arts Movement—"black bitches, liquor and crime"—to depict a scene where "nothing seems the same any more," importing even the jazz references characteristic of that poetry: "blowing like an ol' Louis' flat saxophone."[71] Yet as we have seen with the Vanuatu example, this Black vernacular is as likely to have entered USP with Kasaipwalova as with Amiri Baraka or Haki Madhubuti. The strands of influence split, muddle, multiply.

To take just one more poetic example, Peni Tutuʻila Malupo's dedicatory poem to the 1974 writers' gathering, "Creative Arts Workshop," contains all the hallmarks of classical Tongan poetry displayed in his "Tonga, Blessed Land," discussed in chapter 1. It is presented in Tongan and English and again gives prominence to heliaki, figuring Pacific literature as a *"Ngoue Kakala"* ("flower garden") and the workshop as the *"Tauhi"* ("keeper").[72] The characteristic archaisms and inversions in the English version likewise remain: "waters pure"; "My fancy it has captured." Yet while Malupo situates the poem unmistakably in the Tongan tradition, he celebrates the cross-pollination that the regional workshop allows—"Different types you transplant / Little by little / gathering"—and in the final lines completes his flower garden conceit with a reference to Wendt's recently published *Sons for the Return Home* (1973): "gather flowers / To weave our garlands /

for the return home."[73] The traditional technique of indirect allusion moves out from the customary Tongan frame of reference to register this most modern of Samoan novels in English. Again, in the exchange multiple critical frames appear tenable. Shift your lens, and heliaki begins to resemble the modernist intertextuality in which Wendt was so well versed.

In prose, meanwhile, the experimentation in form we found in Garae, Buamai, and Vini both intensifies and diffuses. Intensifies, where the collision of vernacular and literary registers and of oral and written modes become the subject of the narrative and not just the medium, where the background collapses into the frame, and where the experimentation becomes more self-conscious and more explicit. For example, Ata Maʻiaʻi's first-person story "Past the Old Track (An Exploration)" shifts between meditation on the importance of the sunset in a Samoan village and the account of an old village woman. From the first line, the sunset is presented not as a concrete material fact but as an event refracted by the villagers through all manner of narrative forms, "songs and rhetorics . . . burning oratories . . . the sublime folklores mothers told their children before bedtime."[74] Correspondingly, Maʻiaʻi pursues the subject through a range of modes, from prose to poetry to village chant, each interrupting the other. It makes for a strange text, hard to classify and at times hard to follow. But what surfaces is that "Past the Old Track" is not only an exploration of form but a reflection on how form shapes meaning.

The experimentation between modes that we saw in the written treatment of oral history and legend appears more diffusely, by contrast, when oral features are encoded within short stories even though legend and myth play no obvious role. This encoding often appears in the use of song, gossip, or other vocal forms of expression as minor or major devices within an otherwise writerly frame, and examples can be found throughout "Mana." But to take just one example we might end with Crocombe's story, "Bush Beer," which presents a modern, everyday village scene where men meet for their weekly homebrew session. The meeting is necessarily clandestine because of the colonial law prohibiting the consumption of alcohol by Cook Islanders, but as the men drink, raillery and petty grudges flare in outbursts of violence. These are set aside only for the singing of a song, which—temporarily uniting the brawling men in the second half of the story—also interrupts the columns of prose and appears in Cook Islands Māori, with only a general explanation that it follows "the theme of so many songs of the fear of losing one's woman."⁷⁵ "Mana" had from its launch presented Pacific songs in the vernacular, typically as standalone texts, though often with translations, images, or explanations of the dance, custom, or other context that gives it significance in daily life. They are also often printed alongside or within legends and oral histories. Crocombe's innovation is to incorporate a song within a new story, mundane in setting and action, both signifying the living importance of song in Pacific communities and opening up her written narration with an untranslated, untranslatable, oral event.

Crocombe had introduced "Mana" as a space for Pacific "creative writing in all its forms—poetry, plays, chants, short stories, and legends"⁷⁶— and like most of the texts discussed in this chapter, "Bush Beer" shows the porousness of these formal distinctions in the Pacific context. Crocombe made few claims about her own writing, and it is rarely discussed. Yet it comprises an important if minor link in the development of Pacific Island literature, connecting her fellow Cook Islander Florence "Johnny" Frisbie's *Miss Ulysses from Puka-Puka* (1948), which describes the conversion of the events of the postwar period into local oral histories, to Wendt's major novel *Pouliuli* (1977), which performs the transformation of oral imperatives— gossip, myth, recitation of gafa—into a masterfully written text.⁷⁷ Crocombe's story "The Healer"—first published in the UPNG magazine *Kovave*—is still taught in literature courses at the University of the South Pacific, its tale of a skilled village taʻunga turning gossip to stories, stories to reality, used to illustrate the transformative power of narrative.⁷⁸ Crocombe's writing career began in Beier's classes at UPNG, and though it is Wendt who liked to compare his mission at USP to Beier's work at the other university,⁷⁹ Crocombe too—as author, educator and editor—can be seen as an Indigenous, pan-Pacificist counterpart to this influential European figure.

As author, Crocombe's visions of village life reflect both her situated identity as a Cook Islander and her wish to relate this life, full of story and song, to other Pacific communities and readerships. Unassuming as she was in her writing, she took pride in this identity and had no need for the masks and pseudonyms that mar Beier's contributions to the region. As educator, she helped establish the Extension Services, vital to the fulfillment of USP's regional mandate. As editor, she launched and drove the Mana project, without which Pacific literature as we know it is unimaginable. Beier has been accused of silently introducing his own standards through his editorial practice. Crocombe, by contrast, reveals a consistently light touch, encouraging contributors to introduce their own personal and cultural experiences—many, as we have seen, encoding the oral traditions of their community—while fostering interaction in print between writers separated by a vast ocean and a history of colonial division. She praises and prints the political verse of the ni-Vanuatu when it arises in the workshops of the university, but she does not dictate the direction she feels it should take. Finally, then, while Beier's editorial agendas and authorial deceptions compromise his legacy in Papua New Guinean literature, significant as that is, Crocombe's endeavors as writer, teacher, and editor are all complementary and part of her humble but no less significant gift to the region, recognized locally by her affectionate moniker "Mama Marjorie." And so they will be treasured.

THE INSTITUTION FINDS ITS PACIFIC SOUL

Much had changed at the University of the South Pacific in the five years between 1973—the year "Mana" was launched—and 1977, which saw the publication of the last of the Mana annuals. Many of the best-known Pacific writers had joined the USP staff roster, and they continued to make bold changes to the curriculum, strengthening the Pacific component in 1975 to include Eri's *The Crocodile* (1970), Ihimaera's *Pounamu, Pounamu* (1972), Kiki's *Ten Thousand Years*, and poetry from the 1974 *Mana Annual*, continuing the practice of channeling brand new literature by USP affiliates back into the curriculum.

The university now boasted a program divided evenly between modernist, postcolonial, and Pacific literature, already a highly progressive curriculum for 1975. But the changes introduced in the following year were visionary. The two first-year courses strip away all the European and American texts from earlier years and are renamed Commonwealth and South Pacific Literature I and II. The body of available Pacific material is now so substantial that the reading lists for these courses can be divided by mode into prose, drama, and poetry. To the Pacific titles already listed are added Patricia Grace's *Waiariki* (1975), Jo Nacola's *Three Plays* (1976), Ulli Beier's edition of *Five New Guinea Plays* (1971), Helu Thaman's *You, the Choice of My Parents* (1974), Sano Malifa's *Looking Down at Waves* (1975), and selections from Mana Publications. The second-year courses are reserved for "Commonwealth and Third World Literature," and only in the final year would students encounter European texts, mostly modernist, with poetry from Yeats, Eliot, and W. H. Auden; a play by Samuel Beckett; and novels by Conrad, Ellison, and Naipaul alongside Joyce, Lawrence, and Malcolm Lowry.

This program is close to the structure of the UPNG curriculum from the first years of the decade discussed in chapter 2. Many of the postcolonial texts in the UPNG course New Writing in English from Emerging Nations reappear in the USP courses of the 1970s, including works by Tutuola, Achebe, Soyinka, and Naipaul. The third-year modernist courses are also comparable, both featuring Eliot, Kafka, Camus, and Beckett. The main difference is that at USP there is no formal grounding in orature in the first year: this stage is replaced with a written, regional Pacific literature. This shows just how productive the first half-decade of the 1970s was in the rise of Pacific literature. Beier's use of orature demonstrates his belief that a national literature must spring from native soil, but in 1971 he still felt the need to refer to Africa and India for written examples of how decolonizing societies could write toward freedom. At USP, by contrast, thanks in no small part to the work of the Papua New Guineans, there existed a Pacific literature of such quantity and vitality that it could fill whole university courses.

However, while recognizing this great growth in written material, we must be cautious of a developmental view that sees the difference between the two literature programs as a growth away from increasingly outdated oral roots, "a beginning," as Subramani put it, finding "material that could be translated or rewritten."[80] As we have seen repeatedly, the written literature that now filled the USP first-year courses—from the plays collected as *Five New Guinea Plays* to the "Mana" texts discussed in this chapter—is fundamentally rooted in oral texts and traditions. These may be translated or rewritten, but they remain living sources, encoded in the literature in varied and complex ways.

It is also in 1976 that USP at last included creative writing courses within the degree structure, again bringing the English undergraduate program closer to the arrangement that had been so productive at UPNG. Creative Writing in English I and II ran consecutively in the first and second years. In keeping with the surrounding syllabus, the first-year course specifically lists Pacific texts as models, including all available *Mana* annuals and "a selection of poetry/plays/novels etc. from South Pacific writing." Creative Writing in English II, again in keeping with its surrounding second-year courses, sets texts from "Commonwealth and Third World Literature" and concentrates particularly on drama, with attention to oral traditions, but facing fully to the present in teaching the "writing and producing of plays for both stage and radio." Orature, Pacific literature, inspirational postcolonial works, European and American modernism: all ripple through the new literature and are channeled back into USP student writing through formal and informal creative writing classes. We might better appreciate the complexity of Oceanian writers' networks of influence by thinking with archipelagos and oceanic flows rather than with periodization, narratives of development, or national borders.[81]

Finally, 1976 is a signal year in the changes it brought to the Mana project itself. It is in this year that "Mana" broke from *Pacific Islands Monthly*, establishing itself as a separate, locally published periodical, *Mana: A South Pacific Journal of Language and Literature*, which provided an avenue for both the region's creative and critical writing. As the regional project grew, it fed an interest in further strengthening national scenes and, in particular, creative writing in the vernacular.[82] This commitment led Mana Publications to support the creation of smaller, nationally focused periodicals, including *Faikava* in Tonga, *Moana* in Samoa, and *Waswe?* in the Solomon Islands. With vernacular languages privileged, the interactions, adaptations, and indigenizations we have sketched here become ever more complex.

We see from 1973 to 1976 the development of an autonomous literary culture at USP. "Mana" drew in writers from across the region to create a regional project. Prose writers worked through their own national oral traditions to create a storytelling idiom for the region as a whole. As outlined in chapter 1, poets achieved something similar with poetic technique, working national traditions into a contemporary, globally aware style. Other poets turned more recent Pacific forms to their own cultural situations, as with Vanuatu and Papua New Guinea. Together, these examples show the broadening of the USP literary culture, with creative writing workshops and courses, a new regional staffing, and a coursing of the various modernisms—themselves already complexly mediated—into the regional literature. From this expanded scene, Pacific literature poured back into the USP curriculum—again, mediating modernism—which presented a complex network from which Pacific student writers could draw. As "Mana" broke from *PIM* as a standalone periodical, it began to route back into national scenes. Thanks to the labors of local editors, educators, and authors dedicated to Crocombe's regionalist goal, the institution at last had its Pacific soul.

Chapter Seven

SUBRAMANI'S SUGARCANE GOTHIC

Haunting the Regional Dream

The 1976 relaunch of "Mana" was symbolic as a reclamation and expansion of its medium. From an eight-page segment in the colonially rooted, Australia-based *Pacific Islands Monthly*, it reappeared as an eighty-page periodical based at the University of the South Pacific, dedicated to the new regional literature and proudly declaring its independence in the title, *Mana Review: A South Pacific Journal of Language and Literature*. "Mana" had contained Pacific literature; *Mana* was a Pacific journal. Taking on the editorial role and heading the journal for the next three years, Subramani opened the first issue with the now-famous declaration that "the struggle for a South Pacific Literature has more or less been won."[1] The martial metaphor captures the prevailing mood at this turning point in the history of the movement—the commitment to a shared cause, the sense of political importance, and the recognition that this was essentially a struggle for ownership of representation and expression.

As the Indo-Fijian descendant of an indentured laborer, raised far from the capital on the island of Vanua Levu, Subramani has described the loneliness of his early love for literature, fed on the books his father rescued from the trash of the European overseer of a sugarcane plantation—a sublime image of the self-education of a savant in the colonial hinterlands.[2] This love resulted in a distinguished literary career: a series of scholarships at home and abroad led to his appointment as a lecturer at the University of the South Pacific for the 1975 academic year, where he worked alongside Marjorie Tuainekore Crocombe, Albert Wendt, Konai Helu Thaman, Satendra Nandan, Pio Manoa, Mostyn Habu, and others, and his subsequent academic distinctions include a Fulbright Scholarship at Johns Hopkins University and the pro-vice-chancellorship and acting vice-chancellorship of USP. Of the writer-scholar-editors who came to prominence at USP in the 1970s, Subramani boasts an international reputation exceeded only by that of Wendt, and while we opened the book with an account of Wendt's literary genealogy, Subramani has till now played more in the background. Yet to leave him there would be a grave misrepresentation: his story is the indispensable countersign to the university scene's literary passport to modernity.

Subramani the editor participated fully in the custodianship of the regional movement; Subramani the lecturer would teach courses on Pacific literature, in person and via USP's extension services, considering its relation to "oral traditions" and "European fiction";[3] and Subramani the critic did much for its scholarly validation, particularly with his pioneering monograph *South Pacific Literature* (1985). For Subramani the writer, however, a very different mood prevails. His first story, "Sautu," published in the 1974 *Mana Annual*, depicts the mental disintegration of Dhanpat, an old Indo-Fijian man in a remote, postindenture settlement. Poorly situated, hemmed in by an "irregular stretch of unprosperous sugar cane fields," the Indo-Fijian village is cut off from Fiji's postwar development: half a century on from indenture, the village and its villagers are "an aberration, a contortion of history, on that landscape."[4] As a village elder, Dhanpat has experienced each twist of that contortion, but with the departure of his son and the growing inadequacies of his community for solace or purpose, he becomes "rapidly disoriented" within his home (12). This feeling is explicitly connected to the oppressive dreams and memories of indenture, but it is also connected to present unrest, with burned sugarcane fields and looting in nearby villages ominous reminders of Indo-Fijian insecurity, as Dhanpat and his community are accommodated only by sufferance of the landowning iTaukei chiefs. Amid these scenes of discontent, Dhanpat feels "defeaed and humiliated" (12) as he looks around at his life's meager possessions. Picking up a "jagged mirror"—that venerable modernist symbol of fractured identity—he sees the extent to which his "years in the fields had bent his constitution" (10). With his rootless stasis set against his son's equally aimless migration, his "days oscillat[e] between a past order and new anguish" (12), and Dhanpat becomes increasingly alienated.

The alienation characterizing Subramani's English-language fiction reflects an essentially modernist sensibility.[5] However, where modernist writers of the Global North, from Joseph Conrad to Franz Kafka, T. S. Eliot to John Dos Passos, present alienation as an urban affect—"London / Unreal"—Subramani locates it in the rural space of the Fijian sugarcane fields.[6] The metropolis and the plantation, his short stories suggest, are counterparts, two sides of an integral global machinery that functions through the demarcation of uneven dualities—motherland and colony, consumer and laborer, commodity and raw material, refined sugar and bagasse. For the villager in "Sautu," cut off from the "world beyond," disorientation appears a local issue. For the author, perceiving this system in its totality, it is an inescapably global phenomenon. As Subramani writes in "Tropical Traumas," a short story suffused with the haunting ambiguities of E. M. Forster's *A Passage to India* (1924), tourists might flee to Fijian resorts to escape the "disorders of temperate wastelands," but there they encounter the disorders and wasteland of modern Fiji, causing a French-Canadian visitor to complain that "it never works, does it? . . . This bringing together of people. Fijians. Indians."[7] Adapting the "European" modernist techniques that he taught in the USP classroom—techniques developed as the literary expression of one manifestation of an interconnected modernity—and turning them to representations of the plantations underpinning European wealth, Subramani recovers devices to which the son of an indentured laborer under colonial modernity may rightly lay claim.

In his short fiction from this period, Subramani explores the dark recesses that lie beneath the bright tropical sun: in "Sautu" we encounter Dhanpat's "dismal and dark" hut (10), the trees in "various stages of decomposition" (11), the swamp that swallows animals and children whole. Squalor and degeneracy lie all around, from the "mangy dog" licking the open sores of a visitor to the young wife tormenting a disabled villager. Indenture is figured as "a labyrinth full of shadows and memories," and its brutalities, such as the violent death of Dhanpat's wife, appear only in fragmented images: "Ratni's madness, the pool of blood in dry sugarcane leaves, the frightening pursuit by apparitions on horse-back and Ratni's dismembered limbs in the machan" (10). Offering its characters "nowhere else to go," the story is permeated by the sense of claustrophobic confinement, and when Dhanpat is forced finally to leave the village he is confined still more closely in a mental hospital. This survivor of indenture loses his last, attenuated claim to belonging in a climax of failed self-immolation, insanity, and dispossession.

Subramani's Fiji is a haunted country whose modern history is inextricable from the complex monstrosity of colonial violence, a violence that finally subsumes Conrad's Kurtz with his gothic expiration: "The horror!"[8] Conrad loomed large in the early curricula and writing of the Pacific, and in *The Rise of Pacific Literature* we have drawn out his significance in relation to myth, modernity, and postcoloniality. To these we can add the gothic, a mode that rings throughout his works and resonates with Pacific writers such as Subramani. For Eugenia DeLamotte, the horrors belying the march of progress in *Heart of Darkness* render the early modernist novel the culmination of "the century-long racial project which is Gothic romance," and the work is indeed filled with gothic scenes, from the "ominous" atmosphere of the Company office at the start of the book, where the silent women knit black wool "feverishly" and fatally, to Marlow's encounter with the Intended at the close—"all in black, with a pale head, floating towards me in the dusk."[9] Yet as we noted in the last chapter, Conrad reserves his most horrifying imagery for the abased "black shadows of disease and starvation, lying confusedly in the greenish gloom"—colonized figures of abjection upon whose "pain, abandonment, and despair" are shown to depend the English civilization taken for granted by Marlow's (and Conrad's) audience, with "a butcher round one corner, a policeman round another, excellent appetites, and temperature normal."[10]

At the heart of Subramani's aesthetic is a similarly modernist gothic, or gothic modernism, which fuses gothic horror with modernist sensibility—that formal apotheosis of disorientation and alienation—to depict the enduring social and psychological wounds inflicted by indenture upon its victims and their descendants. With stories like "Sautu," "Gamalian's Woman," and especially "Tell Me Where the Train Goes," Subramani modernizes the gothic aspects of Indo-Fijian life and gothicizes Indo-Fijian modernity to develop a prose register that calls to the existentialism of the UPNG writers, the estrangement of the early USP set, and the experimental ambition of Wendt's early work, but whose refinement and political nuances make it wholly his own. In this chapter we offer two ways of conceptualizing the stylistic hallmarks of Subramani's prose. First, as the "sugarcane gothic" of modern Oceanian writing, a genre specific to Indo-Fijians in the Pacific context though linked to a wider network spanning from England to the American South to the Caribbean. Just as the remote sugarcane plantation, though appearing an "aberration" to its alienated laborers, completes the ruthless logic of a global economic system, so Subramani's stories, intensely local on the surface, reveal complex flows of literary exchange. Second, we find in Subramani a poetics of the unwanted guest, where the closed doors and quiet whispers of his exposition never welcome the reader fully into his textual world but restrict entry, thereby requiring the reader, like the Indo-Fijian, to dwell in a space that unsettles.

We illustrate our claims with a detailed analysis of Subramani's 1977 *Mana Annual* story, "Tell Me Where the Train Goes," written while he was teaching at USP. Though indenture is patently the background to "Tell Me Where the Train Goes," by placing it carefully in its literary historical context—not as a story published in Subramani's later collection *The Fantasy Eaters* (1988) but as a story of the Mana project centered at USP—we argue for another important signifying function. Read in the precise moment with which we opened this chapter, as "Mana" triumphantly transitioned into *Mana*, Subramani's despondent tone also expresses the contested place of the Indo-Fijian writer in the growing regionalist movement and university. At this momentous point in the development of Pacific literature, Subramani's story presents a minor-key counterpoint to the major chord of artistic triumph that the Mana project sounds.

"A HEAP OF BROKEN IMAGES": THE MODERNIST GOTHIC

That gothic literature fed into modernism is clear from the sheer number of modernist authors who take up gothic themes and ideas. Indeed, it might be easier to list modernist authors who did not engage with the gothic than to number those who did. But to take just a few prominent instances, we might think of Kafka's transformation of the gothic works of E. T. A. Hoffmann and Fyodor Dostoevsky in *The Metamorphosis* (1915), of James Joyce's gothically tainted stories in *Dubliners* (1914), of William Faulkner's transplantation of the gothic to the fictional Yoknapatawpha County, or of Samuel Beckett's so-called postgothic or gothic minimalism.[11] The annus mirabilis of 1922 saw the publication of *Ulysses*—filled with gothic tropes and images, such as Stephen's *"pale vampire"* on *"swift sail"*—and *The Waste Land*, whose "bats with baby faces ... crawl head downward down a blackened wall."[12] Each of these passages reveal the modernist afterlife of Bram Stoker's fin-de-siècle novel *Dracula* (1897), but 1922 was also the year of F. W. Murnau's *Nosferatu*: the gothic was no atavistic resurgence of a repressed bloodline but an undead contemporary walking among the modernists.

Modernism and the gothic were easy bedfellows for the uneasy sleep of reason. Both were conceived as reactions against the outdated critical standards of their day—the neoclassicism that reigned beyond the Augustan period, the realism retained from the late Victorian age—and both terms drew self-conscious attention to their temporality, with the gothic knowingly anachronistic in its appeal to an imagined preclassical tradition and modernism claiming a contemporaneity always already slipping into the past. Each of these movements were of such massive importance that they diffused almost immediately out from their local contexts (a specific region, a specific set of authors, a fixed set of aesthetic or thematic expectations) and spread over several generations, across geographic and generic lines. And each proved to be endlessly transformable, contributing to the creation of whole national and regional literatures. In each case, then, the limited, periodizing function of these critical categories gives way to something looser and more expansive, something essentially relational.

Modernism played a foundational role in the development of postcolonial literatures, but so too did the gothic, despite or even because of its colonial associations. Though early gothic texts worked with a quickly codified repertoire of tropes and images—many of them Orientalist or Africanist in nature or inflection—it was also from the start a hybrid and malleable form, "stemming ... from an uneasy conflation of genres, styles, and conflicted cultural concerns."[13] It was thus well suited to adaptation, and by the time Subramani put pen to paper he had access to at least a century's worth of examples of this mode being bent to new ends, many amenable to the Fijian colonial situation. John Paul Riquelme implies that the Irish mastery of the gothic in the nineteenth century presents an early example of postcolonial reclamation, though the Anglo-Irish identity of key figures in this turn—Charles Maturin, Joseph Sheridan Le Fanu, Bram Stoker, Oscar Wilde—complicates this picture.[14] But less ambiguous instances abound. Richard Wright's seminal novel *Native Son* (1940) gathers gothic horror tropes into a modernist textual fabric to fit the African American experience, and we have already seen that Wendt includes Wright in his tabernacle of modernist authors who influenced Pacific writers of the 1970s, Subramani among them. Indeed, as Maisha L. Wester's *African American Gothic* (2012) has shown, there was a rich African American gothic tradition going back as far as the slave narratives of the nineteenth century, and Black authors have long sought to "appropriate and revise the genre's tropes" to "make it a capable and useful vehicle for expressing the terrors and complexities of black existence in America."[15]

If the gothic arose, as Riquelme contends, to express "the dark side of modernity," it is an appropriate mode for the literature of a people condemned to servitude for the sake of sugar, a colonial commodity epitomizing, in Sidney W. Mintz's classic account, "the productive thrust and emerging intent of world capitalism."[16] From the first flourishing of the British gothic in the eighteenth century—just the time that sugar was revolutionizing English dietary habits at home and the human labor trade abroad—this literature stood in open defiance of the sureties of the age of reason.[17] With its brazen disregard of neoclassical literary decorum, its overt anachronisms of time and setting, and its celebration of the perverse, the supernatural, the irrational, and the unexplained, the gothic violates post-Enlightenment tenets of clarity, unity, rationalism, and progress.[18] As Fred Botting states, the gothic has from its earliest days "continued to shadow the progress of modernity with counter-narratives displaying the underside of enlightenment and humanist values."[19] In fact, the shadowing function of the gothic may be exactly its appeal. Across a range of contexts, gothic scholars have shown the many ways in which this penumbral form can reveal and accommodate contradictions between social relations and the dogma of the day. In his landmark study of the North American novel, Leslie Fiedler characterizes this national tradition as "almost essentially a gothic one," reading American gothic as a projection of the "special guilts" belying the American dream: "the slaughter of the Indians . . . and the abominations of the slave trade."[20]

Acknowledging this deep association of the gothic and the imperial experience, we can see why Subramani wove this register into modernist-oriented stories portraying the inheritance of colonial plantation trauma. Indeed, other Indo-Fijian writers were dabbling in similar imagery and themes around the same time, albeit to less concentrated effect. Chattur

Singh's "The Final Journey"—published alongside "Sautu" in the 1974 *Mana Annual*—connects the mysterious degenerative illness afflicting a poverty-stricken farmer to an oppressive past, figured in visions of his house in flames, sinister encircling serpents, and the specter of a deceased wife who returns in his dreams, befanged, solemn, and silent, "dashing to bite Singh's face and suck his blood."[21] These are all images that recur in Subramani's writing. Furthermore, as observed recently by Caitlin Vandertop—to our knowledge, the first scholar to recognize in print the gothic turn in Indo-Fijian literature, which she relates to the "vampire crop" of sugarcane—such imagery can be traced back to the earliest writing of indenture.[22] Totaram Sanadhya's first-hand account *Fiji men mere ikkis varsh* [*My Twenty-One Years in the Fiji Islands*] (1919), contributed to the abolition of indenture in India, and with his shorter narrative "Bhut len ki katha" ["The Story of the Haunted Line"] (1922), his writing was foundational to Indo-Fijian literature and indenture scholarship more generally. It may seem incongruous to associate this political Hindi writing with the European gothic tradition, despite the suggestive title of the later work: Sanadhya "knew no English," and the idea of haunting was hardly invented by Horace Walpole.[23] Yet as Vandertop rightly points out, Sanadhya's writing is "filled with nightmares, death, sorcery and spirits," and given Subramani's documented engagement with Sanadhya in his own fiction, these elements no doubt informed his own treatment of the Fijian sugar lines.[24]

Subramani's stylistic gothic influences, however, seem to come primarily from the Anglophone tradition, with distinct shades of the modernist. In an essay published in the inaugural *Mana Review* Subramani connects Conrad to the Pacific context, arguing that his "short time in the South Seas ... altogether transformed" his life and art.[25] Where Herman Melville's contact with the Pacific leads to the "warm affirmation of primitive life," Subramani's Conrad finds only "*horror*, this chasm between man's humane aspirations and the reality of his bestial nature which is at the root of Conrad's alienation."[26] As with Conrad, so with Subramani. Speaking with Sanadhya, conversant with Conrad, and criss-crossing Jean Rhys's *Wide Sargasso Sea* (1966)—another seminal treatment of a dislocated sugarcane plantation colony—Subramani's sugarcane gothic in "Tell Me Where the Train Goes" links a local tale of the girmitiya to a global literature of estrangement.

THE STRANGE ERUPTION OF SUGARCANE GOTHIC: "TELL ME WHERE THE TRAIN GOES"

Set directly in the indenture period, some half a century before "Sautu," "Tell Me Where the Train Goes" presents an adolescent boy whose life is bounded by the dimly seen horror and corruption of the sugarcane plantation. Amid the squalor of the laborers' camp, Manu is caught up in a series of traumatic events, with his father apparently murdered in the cane fields and his mother left vulnerable in the barracks. Now ostracized and unprotected within the indentured community and sensing an increasing threat of violence from the "sinister attention" of his male elders, Manu escapes regularly into the jungle, one day finding himself in the grounds of the colonial bungalow, where he witnesses his mother bathing after an assignation with the Saheb. Resentment in the barracks continues to gather and climaxes in the killing of the Saheb, an orgy of violence that further disrupts Manu's flimsy sense of colonial order.[27] Understanding that he and his mother Kunti are now at serious risk of attack, he flees to warn her but is knocked unconscious by the arriving sugarcane train, and he awakes to the realization that he is stuck at the barracks: in the final scene, echoing Dhanpat's realization in "Sautu," Manu learns there is "nowhere to go" (77).

Subramani uses a number of gothic modernist conventions to establish a fitting atmosphere for this tale of trauma and powerlessness. The "oppressive gloom" of this "nightmarish world" is introduced directly: "The old paraffin lamp flickered, casting shadows which trembled and moved in the corner where Kunti slept" (75). The threat of the supernatural hovers throughout, and danger lurks "in unexpected places in the dark," with "threatening whispers in the rustle of coconut fronds and mango branches" (76). The laborers are haunted by the strange terrors of local Fijian tradition—"there were whispers of Tevoro [the devil] in the lines" (75)—while for Manu, "lonely and afraid" at the "hour of the earth-bound spirits," and cut off from the tutelary gods of his fatherland, the only comfort comes in the "quizzical expression" of an "exiled" Hindu god in a picture pulled from a calendar (75). A morbid sense of decay and grotesquery pervades, from the "sickly wind" that consigns the laborers to their beds, to the Fijian coconut seller, legs swollen with elephantiasis, to the threatening figure of Dhanai, "pigmy-sized and mis-shapened," who frightens Manu as much with the hidden "stump of his leg" (75) as with the cutlass he sharpens menacingly.

Kunti fulfills the gothic archetype of the woman in distress, threatened by the catcalls and leers of the laboring men within the barracks and outside subjected to the will of the Saheb, lord of the manor in the gothic imaginary. But an air of sexual corruption permeates the whole story, from the "mingling of curiosity, excitement and guilt" felt by Manu when he witnesses his mother bathing, to his recollection of the time an older boy "persuaded him into his barrack and exposed himself" (76). As with everything else in this story—the hauntings, the threats of violence, the "secret his father told . . . about his half-brother, Yama"—these sexual stirrings are half-hidden, dimly perceived, and obliquely understood (76). Thus Subramani conjures the sense of foreboding and mystery essential to the gothic genre, augmented through the use of modernist technique—a fragmentary and ambiguous narrative moving between the "meanderings" (76) of Manu's reveries and retreats and events on the barracks, past and present. Beset by "torments and disorder" from the sugar lines, Manu is perpetually on the edge of comprehending the cause of his condition. So he surrenders himself to life on the edge, to "images and echoes which drifted from the obscure regions of his experience . . . always refusing to fall into a pattern" (76).

Like the threat that hangs over Manu throughout the story, the nature of this oppression is felt rather than comprehended by these "humble refugees from impoverished regions of a depressed land" (76). "Brutalised by life in the ghettos," the laborers respond in various ways to their "humiliating captivity"—some "simply wilted"; others were "bored or secretly dreamt of self annihilation"—but the most common reaction is violence (76). This violence is typically turned back toward the oppressed community, in the acts of sexual and domestic violence that pervade the story, in the fights that break out in the fields, in the victimization of the vulnerable Manu and his mother. But in the singular event of this story, it finds its proper channel in the murder of the Saheb, who is pulled into the dark, hissing and wriggling, is pinned down while the women take turns "urinating on the writhing figure," and is finally killed. However temporary a reprieve this "ritual of death and dissolution" may bring (77), it can be read as the awakening of political consciousness, an awareness of the contingency of the laborers' suffering upon the exploitative relations embodied in the sugar plantation.[28] For Manu, however, there is no such relief.

Disorder is the tenor of the laborers' lives, but the transgressive act of violence central to the gothic narrative comes in this desacralization of imperial authority, and while Manu takes no part, it nevertheless completes his detachment from the delusion of colonial order. Seeing the Saheb half-naked in the bungalow after his liaison with Kunti, Manu glimpses briefly through the myth of authority that maintains order on the plantation. Manu is used to seeing the Saheb in the pomp of his rule when he visits the lines, when "labourers cringed and stood in disarray, like frightened minah birds." Here, however, without the trappings of his "khaki tunic and topee, his sunburnt body looked small and vulnerable" (76). This is the vulnerability that the laborers at last perceive and exploit, fighting disgust and degradation with disgusting and degrading acts. Manu, however, is unable to see his insight through to this violent conclusion. Instead, the killing of the Saheb fills him with "muted panic" and the urge to vomit, and sends him running back to the barracks (77). In the final instance, the boy is shown to be as bound psychologically as he is trapped physically. Hit by the sugarcane train on his return to the barracks, he lies drifting in "waves of oblivion," still trying to "create patterns" on the ceiling. The train—that icon of mobility under industrial modernity—is no escape for those on the obverse of the colonial coin. So, as Kunti cries over him and promises that they will "ask for land and go away," Manu meets his bitter epiphany: "He knew she was lying; there was nowhere to go. They were simply shipwrecked in the barracks" (77).

The story thus ends as it begins, in the dark and claustrophobic setting that most directly establishes its gothic atmosphere. Yet the threat in Manu's world is not confined to the derelict nocturnal space, as in much of the cold gothic of the Global North. Instead, we are told, he experiences "a sense of foreboding at noon on a hot day when there wasn't a breath of fresh air," a sense that pertains in "the fields," which seem to be "waiting for some strange eruption" (75). In full sight, under the glaring sun, the horror concealed in the story is shown to inhere in the plantation itself, as Manu and the laborers perceive with their application of Indian myth: "He hated the sugar cane (Jagannath said it was karkotaka—one of the principal serpents from the underworld)" (75). As the barracks were often referred to as narak (hell), visualizing the cash crop that caused indenture in Fiji as a powerful serpent of the underworld is apposite.[29] Connecting the gothic mood of alienation and psychological oppression to the labor represented by the sugar fields, Subramani situates this story of squalor and brutality squarely in the context of Fiji's colonial history of indenture.

GOTHIC, MODERNIST, POSTCOLONIAL: SUBRAMANI AND JEAN RHYS

Lizabeth Paravisini-Gebert has described the Caribbean as the "premiere site of the colonial and postcolonial Gothic since the early nineteenth century."[30] With the plantations utilized first as the backdrop for gothic scenes or a source for grotesque figures, Paravisini-Gebert argues that the gothic was reclaimed by Caribbean-born writers and brought into "a complex interplay with its English and continental counterparts in a colonizer-colonized point-counterpoint whose foremost concern has finally become the very nature of colonialism itself."[31] The watershed moment in this Caribbean interplay came, of course, with Jean Rhys's classic novel *Wide Sargasso Sea* (1966), which Paravisini-Geber calls the "mother text" of Caribbean gothic.[32] Transposing the wintry northern gothic evoked in Charlotte Brontë's *Jane Eyre* (1847) to the brilliant landscape and flora of Jamaica, Rhys presents a model of literary engagement triangulating gothic, modernism, and the postcolonial that has been immensely influential for postcolonial scholars and writers—Subramani included, we contend. When the Australian journal *Kunapipi* launched in 1979, it included writing by Subramani alongside memorial essays on Rhys. Though *Wide Sargasso Sea* was not yet on the USP curriculum when Subramani arrived to teach modules on "Commonwealth Literature" and "Commonwealth and Pacific Literature," he brought a whole raft of new ideas from his postgraduate studies in Canada, and he could surely not have missed this novel, foundational to the growing field of Commonwealth literary studies.[33] As another novel of cultural dislocation in a former British sugar plantation colony, *Wide Sargasso Sea* spoke clearly to the Indo-Fijian context in the decade after its publication, and a comparison of Rhys's novel with "Tell Me Where the Train Goes" reveals suggestive parallels.[34]

Both texts proceed from the limited perspective of a child protagonist, isolated with their mothers in a hostile community from which they see no escape. In each text, the child's loneliness is heightened by the emotional distance of the disturbed mother. With Kunti's retreat into silence, her "self-effacing and secretive" (75) behavior, and her alarming stares into space,

Subramani presents a suffering woman, who—like Annette Cosway in *Wide Sargasso Sea*—passes on generational trauma to the vulnerable child, a "trope often found in the postcolonial Gothic," as Ken Gelder has remarked.[35] A gothic atmosphere is maintained in both texts by hints of folk magic, the "heap of chicken feathers" that whisper of Obeah to Antoinette, the "ball of feathers" left at the door to threaten Kunti and Manu.[36] In Subramani's story as in Rhys's, the uncanny effect of such scenes is heightened by their being brought out into the open. Manu's world is filled with "a sense of foreboding at noon on a hot day," and the "warm fragrance of ripe fruits and flowers" or the "intoxicating scent of frangipani" are no security against such menaces as the discovery of his slaughtered dog, the wound on its back "opened like an ugly and festering mouth" (76). So too for Antoinette in the Jamaican Coulibri Estate, a one-time sugar plantation where Obeah stands revealed in the open sun, beneath "the deep blue colour of the sky and the mango leaves, the pink and red hibiscus," and for whom the neighborly threat also appears first in the shock of a dead animal, with the young girl finding the poisoned family horse "lying down under the frangipani tree. . . . He was not sick, he was dead and his eyes were black with flies."[37] In both texts, the gothic is presented as a product of the sugar colony, not a stylistic overlay.

Most significantly, Subramani follows Rhys in adapting modernist narrative techniques—fragmentariness, interiority, allusiveness—to augment the sense of helplessness that is both a staple of gothic fiction and essential to these tales of colonial alienation. Or, more specifically, to these tales of postcolonial exclusion. For in their different ways, both Rhys and Subramani are concerned with the position of the abject, dispossessed, in-between figure—the white Creole, the Indo-Fijian—at the moment of emancipation or decolonization, unable to identify easily with either the agents of colonization or anticolonial resistance.[38] In each case, the island—to which neither can lay claim—presents both ground and metaphor for the sense of exclusion and isolation. "We are marooned," says the mother at the start of *Wide Sargasso Sea*; Manu and his mother are "simply shipwrecked" at the end of "Tell Me Where the Train Goes" (77).

The similar phrases indicate the comparable contexts of these British sugar island colonies. They also, however, contain very specific situational distinctions. Rhys's character uses the word "marooned" with its normal English sense, suggesting that they are stranded without resources ashore the island. But in the novel's Jamaican context, Rhys also alludes to the Maroons, former slaves who escaped the Spanish plantations when the British took possession in the seventeenth century and who established lasting, independent communities in the mountain regions. The name, which predates the contemporary English sense, is thought to derive from Spanish *cimarrón*—"wild savage," stemming ultimately from "mountain top."[39] Rhys adds a complexly ironic charge in associating this word with Annette Cosway. She is the white wife of a sugar plantation owner and thus in an important sense complicit with the system against which the Maroons fought. Clearly, she is no Maroon. Yet the Maroons themselves have an ambiguous history in relation to the changing orders of Jamaican colonization, having first escaped the Spanish, then maintained prolonged wars of resistance against the incoming British, before forming a pact with the new power that committed them to return newly runaway slaves to plantation owners.[40] Like the historical Maroons, Annette exists in the new, liminal social space that opens between the ligatures of the history of colonial exploitation—the former in the shift between Spanish and British colonization of Jamaica, the latter in the shift from chattel slavery to indentured labor in the British sugar colony.

Subramani's term, "shipwrecked," also carries a precisely local connotation. From 1879 to 1916, the British transported some sixty thousand indentured adults and children from India to Fiji, in ships designed for the traffic in human cargo.[41] Taken from some of the most famine- and poverty-stricken regions of India and beguiled by promises of prosperity from the dubious arkathi (recruiters), many of the laborers on board could not read the contracts they were told to sign; many did not know that they were leaving Indian waters, and contemporary accounts describe instances of outright abduction.[42] As Ahmed Ali put it in an early retrospective essay, "even those who knew that Fiji was outside India did not realize the full impact of their decision until they felt the first toss and roll of the boat."[43] Death from disease was common aboard these ships, and "traumatic experience" was the norm.[44] Subramani was a direct inheritor of this trauma: his father was one of the laborers transported to Fiji under indenture, and he himself grew up in a postindenture sugar barracks before he received the scholarship that would take him to Suva Grammar School for sixth-form study. Subramani also played an immeasurable role in the cultural confrontation of this injury in the 1970s. His important volume *The Indo-Fijian*

Experience (1979) brings together historical, sociological, and literary critical essays with poems and stories by Indo-Fijians, including works by Raymond Pillai and Satendra Nandan, alongside his own stories "Sautu" and "Tell Me Where the Train Goes."[45]

It is in this collection that Brij V. Lal published "The Wreck of the *Syria*, 1884," documenting the sea passage that, of the eighty-seven passages in the indenture period, left the deepest scar in the cultural memory. Setting sail in 1884 with a cargo of almost five hundred adults and children, the *Syria*, once used for Caribbean labor traffic, would not arrive intact.[46] Following a series of errors of judgment from the inexperienced captain and crew, it ran aground on the reef off Nasilai, in the southeast corner of Fiji's largest island, Viti Levu. Five of the six lifeboats were smashed, so as the first mate set off for help, the laborers—housed between deck at the time of the smash and for the most part unable to swim—attempted to cling to the reef or to the broken remains of the boat.[47] The British and Fijian rescue operation was surprisingly successful: it was commended at the time and continues to be celebrated popularly as an instance of iTaukei and Indo-Fijian rapprochement.[48] Yet fifty-six laborers died, including women and children, with a further eleven succumbing to related illness in the weeks that followed.[49] A subsequent inquiry found the captain and first mate culpable; the captain's certificate was suspended for nine months. But for the other survivors there was little reprieve. Taken first to the Nukulau depot and then to Suva, "they were sorted out and allocated to the various plantations."[50]

In a period remembered chiefly for the brutality suffered by the indentured Indians, the shipwreck of the *Syria* stands as an especially potent symbol of loss, horror, and helplessness. Lal himself took recourse to gothic imagery for his description of the historical legacy of the shipwreck—"many incarnations of the *Syria* tragedy are with us today, evoking haunting memories of some of the horrors of Indian immigration to Fiji"[51]—and while there are no first-hand written accounts from the Indian survivors, a contemporary letter from the leader of the rescue operation to the colonial governor Gordon, quoted by Lal, is also gothic in tone: "The scene was simply indescribable, and pictures of it haunt me still like a horrid dream.... People falling, fainting, drowning all around one; the cries for instant help, uttered in an unknown tongue, but emphasized by looks of agony and the horror of impending death, depicted on dark faces rendered ashy grey by terror."[52] Subramani's closing vision of the boy and his mother "simply shipwrecked in the barracks" is not just an echo of Rhys; it evokes the specter of the *Syria* to conclude his gothic tale. While the gothic is often framed as an antirealistic literature of excess, the deep historical correspondence in Subramani's text suggests that, on one level at least, it provides an all-too-realistic depiction of the horrors of indenture, from the suffocating scene of barracks life with which his story opens to the traumatic sea passage submerged in his concluding metaphor.

"THE IN-BETWEEN, THE AMBIGUOUS, THE COMPOSITE": THE POETICS OF THE UNWANTED GUEST

In *Powers of Horror* (1980), Julia Kristeva defines the abject as that which is "opposed to *I*"; those aspects of the self that are "rejected" but "from which one does not part"; that which has been "ejected beyond the scope of the possible, the tolerable, the thinkable."[53] The abject is a border discourse, naming the horror felt at the breakdown of the barriers between the self and other or the subject and the object, which in her later work Kristeva redefined to add "collective, cultural, interpersonal" dimensions.[54] In Jerrold E. Hogle's terms, the gothic abject can be taken to mean the monstrous or outcast figures central to gothic texts, from Maturin's *Melmoth the Wanderer* (1820) to Shelley's *Frankenstein* (1818), Robert Louis Stevenson's *Dr Jekyll and Mr Hyde* (1886) to Stoker's *Dracula* (1897). In either sense, for Hogle, the gothic abject serves as the repository of those "deep social antagonisms" and "unresolved conflicts among competing ideologies" that both cleave and constitute modernity, including along the lines of gender, sexuality, nationalism, and the colonial/postcolonial.[55] Though Gayatri Spivak has questioned the utility of Kristeva's concept for postcolonial thought, given its roots within the "dominant historical narrative" of a Eurocentric psychoanalytic tradition, critics such as Sarah Ilott and Andrew Hock Soon Ng identify postcolonial contexts in which images of the abject have proven powerful tools for the depiction of the colonial subaltern.[56] Such a frame seems appropriate for Subramani's depiction of the girmitiya, "secretly dream[ing] of self annihilation" while laboring in "humiliating captivity" (76), and especially for Manu, born to the sugarcane fields that define his existence and utterly excluded from the modernity that this commodity helps uphold. From this perspective, Subramani's story answers Alison

Rudd's definition of the postcolonial abject as the representation of the "underside of the imperial project."[57] If we consider Kristeva's etymological rooting of the concept as that which is cast off or thrown aside, "abject" also describes Manu quite directly. At the end of the story, when for the first time he tries to take decisive action to avoid the violence of the coolie lines, he is hit by the train that carries the commodity away from the alienated laborers and "thrown over the tramline"—literally abjected—"into a heap of burnt coal" (77). It is one of the bluntest of Subramani's metonymic devices.

If gothic in all its incarnations is the literature of the abject, defined, with Kristeva, as "the in-between, the ambiguous, the composite," it is surely significant that in this triumphant, flourishing phase of early Pacific Island literature it appears in the writing of an Indo-Fijian.[58] In an essay on Indo-Fijian fiction published in Subramani's *The Indo-Fijian Experience*, Vijay Mishra argues that "indenture consciousness" presents the "ideological 'base' against which Indo-Fijian fiction must be evaluated."[59] Importantly, for Mishra, this consciousness results not simply from the trauma of colonial subjection but, more specifically, from the experience of a "failed millennial quest" in the passage from India to Fiji.[60] Connecting early writing by Subramani, Nandan, and Pillai to contemporary accounts of indentured laborers, he finds a shared literature of an indenture experience that leads "to questions about self and identity, about 'purpose,' about . . . psychological and social commitment to the 'new land,' indicat[ing] not only a corrosive *angst* but also a corresponding fragmentation of *psyche*."[61] While Mishra does not refer to the gothic here, his framing of the literature in relation to the specifically Indo-Fijian experience—in terms of psychological suffering, dehumanization, and disillusionment with a millennial, "end-oriented" project—presents suggestive reasons for the appeal of a postcolonial, modernist-veering gothic mode to the Indo-Fijian writer.[62]

Most pressingly, the history of dehumanization and disillusionment was in the process of repeating itself. Postindependence relations in Fiji were initially amicable, but racial antagonism was fermenting. In December 1976, months before Subramani published "Tell Me Where the Train Goes," the nationalist iTaukei politician Sakiasi Butadroka published his party manifesto in the *Fiji Times*, including the pledge that "Indians should be repatriated to India."[63] The shock win of the largely Indo-Fijian Federation Party in the 1977 elections did little to reassure iTaukei voters of the security of Fijian paramountcy, and the governor general, Ratu George Cakobau, intervened to reappoint Ratu Sir Kamisese Mara, leader of the losing Alliance party, as prime minister.[64] Such were the conditions in which Mishra and Subramani wrote, a state of unrest upheld by the anti-Indian sentiment that would culminate in the 1987 coups led by Sitiveni Rabuka. The coups drove one hundred thousand people to emigrate from the country of their birth, the majority of whom were Indo-Fijian: the alienation of the colonial barracks, depicted by Subramani in "Tell Me," was by no means only a thing of the past.[65] The abjection of the indentured laborers continued to haunt the Indo-Fijians, who held an in-between and ambiguous position in the new postcolonial state to which they may commit but not belong. The pessimism and disorientation of Subramani's stories speak not only to the past horror of indenture but to the uncertainty of the postcolonial present.

Returning to the literary movement to which Subramani committed his critical and creative writing, we suggest that his modernist gothic sensibility also reflects an ambiguity in the place of the Indo-Fijian writer within the new regional literary movement, premised, as we have seen, on a rhetoric of Indigenous ownership and reclamation. As seen in chapter 5, Indo-Fijian writers were key drivers of USP's early literary scene, and while writers such as Raymond Pillai transitioned successfully to "Mana," others—Anirudh Singh, Shashikant Nair, Karuna Prasad, Sulochana Devi—did not. Even Subramani, whose work now forms an undisputed part of the early Pacific literary canon, did not publish in the regular *PIM* "Mana" columns: "Sautu" and "Tell Me Where the Train Goes" were collected as supplements in the *Mana Annuals*. The gothic mode that characterizes these stories does not sit easily within the shiny pages of *Pacific Island Monthly*. Though later writing by Wendt and others would introduce gothic elements to create a similarly pessimistic tone, these earlier works brood apart from the congregation enjoying the first flush of Pacific independence writing. They certainly sit uncomfortably within the "confidence," "independence," "cultural vitality," or "integrity" that Crocombe rightly presents as the "keynote[s]" of the artistic movement at this moment.[66]

Instead, Indo-Fijian writers like Subramani were experimenting with an unsettling, unhomely narrative form, which we describe here as a poetics of the unwanted guest. Subramani's allusive, elusive style means that little in his stories lays itself bare for the reader, with the result that the reader can never be fully at home in the text, as so much is hidden and withheld. As such, his stories—like many modernist works—oblige the reader to read provisionally, like a guest uncertain of their reception. As a guest, the reader inhabits the text tentatively, never in full command of the meaning, never sure of their position in relation to the text's implications. The relationship with the text that Subramani creates for his reader is thus a performance of Indo-Fijians' relationship with Fiji: guests in an unsettling space that holds them at a distance and sees them as residents without roots, ambivalently tolerated as visitors on Indigenous land. An integral, modernist aspect of the uncanniness of Subramani's sugarcane gothic, then, is his creation—during a period of agency and independence—of an aesthetics of the unbelonging, a literary form mirroring his understanding of the political position of Indo-Fijians. And if, during the period, writers saw themselves as writing for a Pacific readership, then Subramani's short stories not only provided Pacific readers—many of them Fijian voters—with characters and scenes through which to understand Indo-Fijians' history but a poetics through which Pacific readers could experience a shade of Indo-Fijian alienation for themselves.

It is in this political and literary context that the particular appeal of the gothic and the gothic-modernist to the Indo-Fijian author makes sense. As Botting and others have argued, gothic registers—like many modernist forms—exist for the negotiation of psychological and social contradictions, quandaries, and double binds, of contexts where "ambivalence and uncertainty obscure single meaning."[67] Subramani inscribes this uncertainty throughout his literary works: in "Tell Me" through his fragmentary and partial narrative, with his drawing of social, political, and supernatural mysteries to hover on the limn of Manu's understanding. But in a manner recalling the doubling of classical gothic, he compounds the ambivalence that is fundamental to the genre by splitting certain key archetypes across lines that typically divide within the colonial context of the story.[68] So the haunted house is not just the threatening, shadowy barrack but also the colonial bungalow, overlooking the barracks "in a heavy brooding silence" (76). Hauntings are not restricted to the nocturnal quarters but open out into the sugar fields, under the bright sun. The gothic villain is not just the Saheb, who runs over resting laborers in his truck and enjoys *droit de seigneur* with indentured women, but also his victim Dhanai, the laborer who—implicated in Manu's father's death—menaces the widow and son with his "maniacal glint" and insinuations of further violence (75). The persecuted maiden is not only Kunti but also Manu himself, subject to sinister harassment from the leering men of the barracks. And the deformed colonial victim is not only Dhanai, whose encounter with the Saheb has left him permanently disabled, but the unnamed iTaukei figure who appears with elephantiasis, alternately startling and reassuring Manu. As in the decolonizing Fijian state at large, the threat for this young Indo-Fijian subject comes from both within and outside of the community.

This sense of doubling has implications for the reading of Subramani's literature more generally. In a 1992 retrospective on his account of the girmit ideology, Vijay Mishra identified slippages in Subramani's English-language fiction, pointing out that for all the psychological complexity of his characters, they regularly "'translate' into standard English their innermost feelings."[69] Mishra describes this teetering between registers as a mark of "intractable, deep-seated schizophrenia," an extension of indenture that sees the author "bonded to a kind of literary imprisonment which leads to a general mimicry of the colonizer's discourses."[70] Yet considering Subramani's purposeful channeling of the gothic obsession with madness and self-destructiveness and his intensification of these experiences with the quintessential features of modernist prose—incommensurable registers, decentering, fragmentation, linguistic failure, partial translation—the "schizophrenia" Mishra diagnoses appears not as an unfortunate fault line in Subramani's artistic vision but an expression of his complex relationship with multiple, possibly disjunctive languages, literatures, and worldviews, as well as a performance of the unsettled lives of many Indo-Fijians.

AN UNWANTED GUEST, AN IMPORTANT RELATIVE

By the time Subramani published "Tell Me Where the Train Goes," he was an established scholar, shaping the direction of Oceanian literature not only through his development of a distinctive, contemporary register to express the contradictions of Pacific modernity but in his editorship of *Mana*, his important critical writing on the regional literature, and his teaching at the University of the South Pacific, where students were already turning the lessons offered by Subramani and his colleagues to new and exciting ends. As one of the major characters in our story of the rise of Pacific literature, Subramani joins Wendt and Crocombe as a writer-editor-scholar engaged in a shared, decolonizing project, and he speaks with them when, in the 1976 *Mana* editorial with which we began this chapter, he declares the struggle for a viable Pacific literature to have been effectively won.

As we have argued in *The Rise of Pacific Literature*, this is a struggle that was to a significant degree fought in the educational space. At USP as at UPNG, literature programs of the late 1960s and 1970s coordinated modernist and other world literatures around a Pacific center, teaching students that they were not perching on the outskirts of an unassailable, monolithic European tradition but were the living inheritors of an Oceanian lineage strong enough to absorb outside influences in the continual development of a regional literature. Similarly, in his own writing, Subramani's approach—his drawing in of myriad thematic, stylistic, and tonal traces, many of them of modernist ancestry, to an intensely local text—appears of a piece with the acts of literary adaptation that we have seen again and again in this monograph. Like Kama Kerpi, John Kasaipwalova, and Russell Soaba, like Vanessa Griffen, Seri, and Satendra Nandan, like Nihi Vini, Mildred Sope, and Ata Maʻiaʻi, like Wendt and Crocombe themselves, Subramani channels globally circulating texts and techniques toward new writings of Oceanian modernity.

Rightly, then, Subramani appears integral to the rise of Pacific literature as framed through the pedagogical institution. Yet for all the similarities, the pained sadness of his stories and his poetics of the unwanted guest also speak to a rift within this literature, to fractures and dislocations within the new movement that have still not fully healed. The struggle for a decolonizing literature may have been shared, but the grounds from which it was approached were unstable, and within a decade of the publication of this story, the Fiji coup would remind Subramani, Nandan, Pillai, and the other Indo-Fijian authors discussed in this monograph that for all their endeavors their inclusion was by no means guaranteed. For many of the writers, scholars and students of UPNG and USP, as across much of the Pacific Islands, decolonization meant the reclamation of Indigenous ownership, the celebration of rooted belonging, and the agency to select the materials to be retained and refitted for the return home. As Crocombe put it in her description of the work of the iKiribati poet Maunaa Itaia, these writers set out to "produce something new yet essentially indigenous."[71] Wendt conceives the literary and cultural project in much the same terms, as we detailed in chapter 1, although with his distant German ancestry, even he felt the occasional need to defend his right to belong, and Wendt is careful not to imply that indigeneity precludes mixed heritage.[72] But what about those with no rooted ties to the land, descendants of indentured laborers whose only home was one in which they felt like unwelcome guests? While Subramani's writer-scholarly project was a shared one and while his processes of literary adaptation were technically comparable with those of his contemporaries listed here, it would be misleading to conclude that it was identical. We opened this book by outlining the empowering framework of indigenization, but how could writers indigenize who were not themselves Indigenous, never completely sure of the ground on which they stood?

The rise of Pacific literature was not a solely Indigenous movement, of course, and alongside those whose families were brought to the Pacific through indenture were those whose mobility was facilitated in far less restrictive, disempowering ways, both by ideologies of colonization and processes of decolonization. The universities were populated, particularly in the early days, by large numbers of international staff, some of whom supported local literatures and some who did not. Others, like Ulli Beier, helped and hindered in complex, often contradictory, ways. If Subramani cannot be placed wholly comfortably with Wendt and Crocombe, neither does he sit easily with other non-Indigenous participants of the movement discussed in this book. A traveling editor, teacher, and writer like Beier could embrace a life that moved easily across oceans and continents, and while he might share with Indo-Fijians an ancestry that is not of the ancient Pacific, his blithe border crossings and ready settling in new spaces is very different. Beier's ability to appropriate Indigeneity is rooted in the power that comes from his specific non-Indigenous position: a white man in university spaces whose decolonizing agendas are framed by lingering colonial worldviews. Subramani had no such luxury, and he, alongside other Indo-Fijian writers, had to live at home, unsettled.

For some Pacific writers, the decolonial drive of this period was the return of power and agency to Indigenous peoples, with Indo-Fijians viewed as part of colonization's troubling foreign incursions, while for most Indo-Fijians decolonization was the removal of powers who had brought their ancestors to labor under false promises and entrenched their position as second-class citizens. The decolonization dream for both groups, then, was a Pacific in which their agency, self-determination and flourishing could be realized, but the golden age would end, at least in Fiji, in 1987, when these promises were determined to be in opposition for iTaukei and Indo-Fijians. Read as part of the broader literary, pedagogical, and political context at which we have now arrived, the intense disquiet of Subramani's gothic modernist vision suggests something much bigger than the sad story of a particular boy, even a particular writer. It reveals the tragic afterlife of a colonial nightmare, a register of the unresolved rifts already troubling the regional, cooperative dream.

Coda

THE STORIES
OF MULTITUDES TO COME

Albert Wendt's second novel *Pouliuli* (1977), published the same year that Subramani's "Tell Me Where the Train Goes" appeared in the final *Mana Annual*, ends with a striking image of postcolonial despair. The elderly protagonist Faleasa stands before the village church, his "arms outstretched to the dazzling sky, his mouth fixed in a soundless scream, his long hair and beard as brilliantly white as the whitewashed church walls."[1] Frozen thus, Faleasa becomes an avatar of the voiceless paralysis presented earlier in the novel, when as a young boy he encounters an old man torn between the dictates of a European education and the values of the faʻasāmoa. Arriving mysteriously in Faleasa's village, each night the old man strives for order and wholeness through the creation of stone circles. The young Faleasa, confused by the dizzying changes of the high colonial period, when Samoa was divided and passed among Germany, the United States, Britain, and New Zealand, shatters the old man's ritual in a misdirected outburst, breaking the stone circle and tipping the old man into final, irrevocable madness. "Before you the old man stands," an aged Faleasa recalls, "his head thrown back, his mouth uttering that soundless scream, unable to bear the world's pain any longer" (133). Set some sixty years on from this traumatic event, well into independence, *Pouliuli* opens with Faleasa sickened by the society he leads as a village matai, "vomiting uncontrollably" from the "unbearable feeling of revulsion" at everything that had previously "given

CODA: THE STORIES OF MULTITUDES TO COME

meaning to his existence" (1). In the chapters that follow, he attempts to redeem himself by challenging the institutions of a Samoan modernity disfigured, as he perceives it, by the corruptions of the colonial experience. He fails. His assumption of the old man's broken pose in the climactic scene signals the ultimate defeat of his campaign, his silent scream a symbol of the futility of resistance when the enemy is no longer an occupying power but a way of life. "The centre has held," Faleasa realizes, "but the sickness has invaded that centre and is infecting it cell by cell" (139).

The metaphor, of course, is from W. B. Yeats, and adapted by way of Chinua Achebe it suggests a gloomier figure of modernist inheritance than the genealogical one Wendt presents in *Ancestry*, the example with which we opened this book. Here we encounter reproduction through infection, not procreation, and though the technique may be similar—a surface allusion to a modernist precursor already thoroughly integrated into the postcolonial corpus—the effect seems more comparable to Subramani's adaptation of bitter textual roots for his images of postcolonial despondence. *Pouliuli* is a deeply pessimistic novel, skewing closer to the dark colonial fantasies of "Sautu" and "Tell Me Where the Train Goes" than to the defiant celebrations of Pacific identity and voice in Wendt's earlier works, *Sons for the Return Home* (1973) and *Flying-Fox in a Freedom Tree* (1974). On one level, this pessimistic turn suggests that Subramani's influence had already started to spread into the broader movement; Wendt's figure of the "ancient carcass" (122) screaming silently on the church steps is a stark gothic image. But more broadly, it shows that by the late 1970s there was a Pacific literature of such substance and diversity that it could begin to generate its own intertextuality, overlaying foreign modernist indexes with sources closer to home.

The tableau of the silent scream, to stay with this example, may recall Edvard Munch's *The Scream* (1893), whose archetypal portrait of modernist alienation is a fitting image both for Faleasa's personal despair and, in its visual remove from the vistas of the Pacific Islands, for the expression of anguish at the imposition of foreign norms. Yet there are less obvious references at play. Like *Pouliuli*, the USP student Anirudh Singh's "The Screaming Man" (1970), discussed briefly in chapter 5, opens with a man who has been sickened physically by the corruptions of the "modern age"; as in *Pouliuli*, the "bitterness and the sickness and the frustration" find expression in a prolonged, inaudible cry: "no matter how hard he screamed, he could not make anybody hear him."[2] Unlike *Pouliuli*, which accrued much critical attention from the start and continues to feature on university reading lists in and outside of Oceania, "The Screaming Man" is rarely mentioned in accounts of Pacific literature. Yet when read as an early progenitor of the gothic modernist tradition we have traced in Indo-Fijian writing or as a textual reference for Wendt's popular novel, it emerges as a small but significant sequence in the regional literature's genetic code.

At the time that Pacific literature was growing into a self-sufficient, self-referential literary system, the transformative innovations in curriculum design at the two foundational universities began to falter. By 1980, Beier was decrying the "tragic" failure of UPNG in nurturing new literature.[3] He claimed that staff numbers were so reduced and student enrollment in the humanities so discouraged that only one student took creative writing in the first semester of 1978: there was, he reported, even talk in the university council of "abolishing the Arts Faculty altogether."[4] At USP, a major reorganization of the program in 1977 saw the removal of the creative writing courses, and the literature coverage was substantially reduced, affecting the logic of the program structure. One of the first-year courses gave way to an "Academic English" course, and another removed all Pacific and postcolonial content in favor of texts by William Shakespeare, Emily Brontë, Charles Dickens, and D. H. Lawrence, with stories and poems selected from such anthologies as the *Penguin Book of English Short Stories* (1967) and the *Mentor Book of Major British Poets* (1963). A second-year paper was converted to foreground linguistics content, and the Pacific literature that had featured so prominently in previous years was corralled into a single course. In the following year, the Commonwealth Literature course was removed, and while students still ended the program by studying modernism, the ingenious centrifugal structure that we have described in earlier chapters, which placed Oceania at the heart of an outwardly spiraling curriculum, was lost. Since the staff list remained largely the same for these years, it is not clear what precipitated this recession—whether it came from internal pressures, such as a newly invigorated linguistics staff or a tiring literature faculty, or from external pressures, such as a decline in student numbers. But the effect is that, after the excitement and swell of the mid-1970s, the decade ended as it had begun, with literature in abeyance.

It was also around this time that there began to develop a critical narrative framing Pacific literature in terms of decline, a remarkable turn from the optimism of the previous decade. In the introduction to his influential anthology *Lali* (1980), Wendt observed that despite the early flourishing of Papua New Guinean literature, by the late 1970s, "not long after Independence, it stalled—many of the writers chose to become politicians and bureaucrats."[5] Acknowledging that writers such as Nora Vagi Brash and Benjamin Umba had begun writing after independence and that other institutions such as the National Broadcasting Commission and the National Theatre Company had assumed the university's place of importance, Beier identified a similar downturn, attributing it to UPNG's devolution from "a university to a 'manpower training institution.'"[6] Although Russell Soaba continued to write, joined by others such as Paulias Matane, the contraction of Papua New Guinean literature became a critical truism. As Nigel Krauth put it, writers who had "produced work in creative writing courses at university had received their degrees and stopped writing.... The lone novel of 1970 was still the lone published novel of 1975."[7]

A similar sense of precarity was emerging at USP. Subramani's *South Pacific Literature* (1985) was a landmark critical study, but while its full-length treatment lent critical validation to the regional movement, Subramani's outlook is decidedly cautious. Beginning with the admonition that emerging "jingoistic accent[s]" among some writers "could, in the end, nullify the 'ideology' of regionalism and the Pacific Way," he concluded by listing political factors that risked bringing the new literary development to "stasis."[8] Speaking in the same year, Raymond Pillai argued that the contemporary literary scene of the Pacific Islands was "one of stagnation, with just the occasional convulsions here and there," and spoke critically of a perceived decline in output and quality among many of the writers we have discussed in this book.[9] It is significant that it was within the university space that the account of literary decline took root, and indeed this perceived decline was associated with limitations in the education systems of the decolonizing region. Pillai argued that *Mana* struggled after parting ways with *Pacific Islands Monthly*, at least partly because of its closer association with the university, where the academics who took custodianship of the periodical were "frequently on the move."[10] Paul Sharrad, meanwhile, has claimed that the decline in Papua New Guinean literature reflects the fact that "the optimistic years of decolonisation and the busy years of early independence carried over in different guises the same pattern of colonial thinking about education."[11] Across the education sector, Sharrad concludes, the binding of literary pedagogies to pragmatic ideas about nation building in PNG made it all but inevitable that student writers would leave behind their writing for more profitable activities: "education is schooling; schooling is training; training is for material gain."[12]

Since many of the critical voices around the turn of the 1980s remained involved with the teaching of literature in the universities, it is possible that their frustrations about lost ground in curriculum design spilled out into their commentary on the literature itself. But if we expand beyond the university horizon that limited the vision of what constituted "South Pacific" literature, the image of literary decline is less definite. Both Pillai and Subramani excluded the "literatures of Maori and Aboriginal people" as "belonging to the mainstream of Australian and New Zealand writing," but other Pacific Islanders—from Konai Helu Thaman to Epeli Hauʻofa—rejected this view, recognizing the deep historical, cultural, and literary affinities connecting Māori literature to that of the smaller Pacific Islands.[13] The Māori literary scene was developing apace when Subramani and Pillai were sounding the alarm, such that Witi Ihimaera and D. S. Long could mark 1980 as the turning point for "a second generation of Māori writers" who had "burst beyond the traditional cultural constraints on form and content."[14] Keri Hulme was the giant of this generation, whose Booker Prize–winning novel *the bone people* (1983) brought a new international audience to Pacific writing. The Indigenous literature of the Francophone Pacific had also been growing steadily from the 1960s, with writers such as Henri Hiro helping establish a new literary community, though this remained largely absent from the critical maps of the Anglophone Pacific; as Frank Stewart, Kareva Mateata-Allain, and Alexander Dale Mawyer have pointed out, "even many local Tahitians were unaware" that from the 1980s "a community of writers had answered Hiro's compelling pleas, and that in fact a literary movement was growing."[15] The Hawaiian Renaissance of the 1960s and 1970s, embodied in John Dominis Holt's essay "On Being Hawaiian" (1964), included literary and musical dimensions, and on the front page of the *Honolulu Advertiser* for March 24, 1977, George Kanahele described the renaissance as "the most significant chapter in [Hawaiʻi's] modern history since the overthrow of the monarchy and loss of nationhood in 1893."[16]

Taking the broader view, the regional movement was in full flow by the 1980s, and even within the USP catchment area this decade can be seen as a period of diversification rather than decline. From the late 1970s, a number of smaller periodicals arose to serve particular Pacific Island nations, often in the vernacular, including *Faikava* in Tonga, *Moana* in Samoa, *Purua* in the Cook Islands, and *Waswe?* in the Solomon Islands. Julian Maka'a and Stephen Oxenham's 1985 survey of Solomon Island literature was one of a number of publications recording the breadth of national scenes not captured by the regional overviews of Subramani and others, and the tertiary space remained central to these movements, with Maka'a and Oxenham stating that "university was undoubtedly a terrific stimulus" for Solomon Islands literature.[17] This is also the era when the Tongan titan Hau'ofa came to prominence, with the stories that would be collected as *Tales of the Tikongs* (1988) appearing in *Mana* from the late 1970s and his novel *Kisses in the Nederends* (1987) staking new ground for Oceanian literature in its narrativization of the ribald mockery characteristic of vernacular exchanges in parts of the Pacific.

By the mid-1990s—in cultural contexts transformed by the political traumas of the first Fiji coup (1987) and the Bougainville Civil War (1988)—a new generation of writers, many of them students, would begin to fashion themselves as the next wave. The year 1995 saw the formation of the Niu Waves collective at USP and the publication of *Searching for Nei Nim'anoa* by its founding member Teresia Teaiwa. Their boozy readings on provocative themes in Suva nightclubs drew in writers who had forged their own paths in the preceding decade. Sudesh Mishra's collections *Rahu* (1987), *Tandava* (1992), and *Memoirs of a Reluctant Traveller* (1994) used dexterous turns of perspective and voice to render the concept of "home" difficult, in poems at once lyrical, political, intimate, and satirical. John Pule—whose artwork adorns the cover of this book—followed his poetry volumes of the 1980s with *The Shark That Ate the Sun* (*Ko E Mago Ne Kai E La*) (1992), which articulated the troubles of a diasporic upbringing through a narrative enriched by Niuean myth and verse. Sia Figiel was hugely productive in the 1990s, publishing a novella, a collection of stories and verse, and two novels, including *Where We Once Belonged* (1996), which won the regional Commonwealth Writers' Prize for Best First Book in 1997. Exploring aspects of Samoan culture overlooked by Wendt, including female agency, sexuality, friendship, and girls' education, she forged new narrative forms from Samoan practices such as suifefiloi, "the weaving or the threading of many different songs/tunes to make one long long song."[18]

CODA: THE STORIES OF MULTITUDES TO COME

In Papua New Guinea, writers such as Steven Winduo, Nash Sorariba, and Regis Tove Stella arose to form an important bridge between the formative years covered in this book and the literature of the twenty-first century. The university space remained significant in each case, at home and abroad. Stella, for example, joined UPNG in 1988; he completed his master's and PhD in Australia, each on Pacific literature, and in 1995 traveled for the International Writing Program Fall Residency at the University of Iowa, where he wrote much of the novel that would be published in 1999 by Mana Publications as *Gutsini Posa* (*Rough Seas*). Set during a fictionalized Bougainville Civil War, this novel stages the inner conflict of a former UPNG student—described by Winduo as "a cross between a Joycean breed of Bloom and Camus's Meursault"—who wrestles with questions of literary value in the context of war.[19] The revolutionary figures in the novel look back on UPNG's literature department as a "major influence in the development of their ideas," citing the "cross-fertilization" that came from reading Ngũgĩ wa Thiong'o and Ralph Ellison alongside Russell Soaba and Albert Wendt.[20] This fictional recollection of curricular cross-fertilization has a definite historical basis, as *The Rise of Pacific Literature* makes clear. At the same time, the protagonist Penagi holds a palpable sense of betrayal from the first wave of Papua New Guinean authors: "Where the hell are the authors of 'The Unexpected Hawk' [John Waiko], 'The Ungrateful Daughter' [Leo Hannett]? The writer of 'The Good Woman of Konedobu' [Rabbie Namaliu], he heard, was now a government minister. As for the fiery author of 'The Reluctant Flame,' he had become a businessman."[21] This was not the bold, politicized vocation Penagi and has classmates had been taught to revere in his literature seminars.

Yet if John Kasaipwalova is seen as personally compromised, his work remains a key touchstone for *Gutsini Posi*. As in *Reluctant Flame*, volcanic eruptions are presented as a figure for revolutionary fervor, and the fire metaphor recurs across the narrative: "My people have already lit the fire and all we have to do is keep it alight."[22] Across the text and through the act of the novel's publication, literary resistance is seen as a multigenerational project, a view that Penagi attributes to his education: "As his teachers used to say, 'You are there to form the critical conscience of a democracy. It is a long journey, but if you don't complete it, don't despair. Your children will continue the journey.'"[23] In this sense, Stella's dedication of the book to his "*family . . . past, present and future*" opens out into the genealogical commitment in Pacific literature with which we opened this monograph. And the genealogy remains associated with the university space: among the various university scholarships and fellowships supporting Pacific writing, Iowa's IWP Fall Residency can be seen as an important link between Pacific authors, past and present. From UPNG, Stella was preceded by Prithvindra Chakravarthy and Jack Lahui in the 1970s, he was joined by writers from Fiji in the 1990s, including Seona Smiles and Larry Thomas, and he has been succeeded in recent decades by the Māori writers Hinemoana Baker, Whiti Hereaka, and Briar Grace-Smith. Most recently, the award-winning Fijian author Mary Rokonadravu has returned from her stay in Iowa for the 2023 residency.

With a network of writers linking Pacific texts across time and space, Oceanian artists of the new millennium are less pressed than their literary forebears to delineate or justify a regional literary tradition. They are also supported by the mentorship and networks conceived by earlier generations, and groups such as Ples Singsing in PNG and the Poetry Shop in Fiji are comfortable with the exigencies of the digital age. These are important advantages for writers wrestling with challenges old and new: the tightening of colonial, neocolonial, and neoliberal controls; wrangling among world powers for Pacific territory and resources; political instability, inequality, and violence against women and LGBTQIA+ people; the dislocations of diaspora; the increasingly alarming realities on the frontlines of climate change. In this context and despite these challenges, contemporary Pacific writers are flourishing in and beyond the fields staked out by their predecessors.

Part of the aesthetic genealogy passed on from Wendt and his contemporaries, through Figiel, Mishra, and Pule, is—in keeping with the modernist-informed aesthetics of the first wave of Pacific writers—the art of strengthening tradition through rewriting and disruption. Witi Ihimaera and Tina Makereti's 2017 volume *Black Marks on the White Page* includes a poem by Selina Tusitala Marsh, then New Zealand poet laureate, called "Pouliuli: A Story of Darkness in 13 Lines." Finding a new and literal meaning in the title of *Pouliuli*, usually translated as "darkness," she applies a black marker to darken the lines of Wendt's novel, forming from the remainder a new text that speaks to the concerns of today's modernity. Figiel, meanwhile, in 2023 translated Wendt's novel into Samoan, showing how contemporary Pacific writers may both revere and reframe now-canonical Pacific works.

Receiving the prestigious Ockham Award in 2022 for *Kurangaituku* (2022), a retelling of Hatupatu and the Bird-Woman from the perspective of the maligned "ogress / monster / thing," Hereaka joins a pantheon of Māori winners—including Alan Duff, Patricia Grace, Hulme, and Paula Morris—expanding still further the international readership of the Pacific novel.[24] The Commonwealth Short Story Prize serves a similar function for short fiction: as well as Makereti, recent winners of the Pacific division include the Samoan USP graduate Jenny Bennett-Tuionetoa, while Rokonadravu, another USP graduate who in the last decade taught creative writing on the literature program, has taken it for Fiji twice. Appearing some fifty years on from the university's first cohort of students and drawing into dialogue three generations of Pacific writing—Wendt to Subramani, Hauʻofa to Figiel—these are emblems of a contemporary Oceanian literature ka mua ka muri, walking backward into the future. They are fine texts to end on.

Rokonadravu's "Famished Eels" (2015) presents an Indo-Fijian marine biologist's account of her family history, recovered from scattered archival records and "a few stories told and retold in plantations, kitchens, hospitals, airport lounges."[25] Returning to Fiji when her father suffers an incapacitating stroke, she uncovers a lineage stretching back to an enigmatic matriarch transported from India under indenture. Reconstructing the story from documents in the national archives, the narrator learns that the family memory of her great-grandmother as a "virgin devotee" is a sentimental fiction. She had conducted "liaisons with more than ten men before she is put into the lines" and learned to throw the men around her into deadly, advantageous competition: the one surviving picture shows her "rigid under a cascade of jewellery." It was known that this elder lost many of her children in childbirth, and the narrator has grown up "imagining the digging of little graves at the edge of sugar cane." Instead, she learns, her ancestor killed her first eight children, perhaps as an oblique expression of plantation trauma, perhaps as an act of protofeminist defiance, perhaps through ruthless economic expedience. Her only surviving child, a daughter, is taken in by an orphanage when the woman is "imprisoned for the brutal murder of a Muslim man."[26]

CODA: THE STORIES OF MULTITUDES TO COME

This is sheer sugarcane gothic, straight from the Subramani mode, and it might seem that we have ended with yet another picture of Indo-Fijian alienation. Yet while the narrator's father has endured a "lifetime of being told he was boci"—uncircumcised, a decisive physiological marker of cultural exclusion in Fiji, often used as an insult against Indo-Fijians—"Famished Eels" is really a story of learning to be accommodated rather than living as an unwanted guest. As a marine biologist studying sea life in New Caledonia, the narrator has educated herself into a broader Pacific belonging, and though she recognizes that her studies placed "miles between my father and me," she concludes that they have allowed for deeper, more expansive connections. "I was born to be a bridge," she reflects. "All I see are connections. I bridge between time, people and places." It is as a writer that she does so, learning from her father that a story must "make room for uncertainty" and continual adaptation. Here is not only a connection with the past but with the future too, and the story ends with the promise of a new generation, a niece in Canada who is seen as the next custodian of both the ocean and the family history: "Her handwriting yearns for water. Salt water. Sea. In her milk tooth grin I see the next storyteller."[27]

Bennett-Tuionetoa's "Matalasi" (2018) presents a very different experience of gender-based violence, looking not to the ancestral past but to a present where tradition refuses to bend to the rich variety of human identity and experience. The story opens with a withdrawal, as the eponymous protagonist retreats from loud family voices fussing in preparation for his wedding: "He slammed the door shut and leaned against it. He had to get away."[28] Matalasi looks back on a childhood of proscription—"Stop. Stop. Stop"—which has prohibited him from sharing the experiences of the other boys: climbing the coconut tree, undergoing circumcision, tying his lavalava in the male fashion. Transgression of these restrictions is punished violently, and when Matalasi defies Samoan protocols of tatau—tattooing rites of passage that are rigidly gendered—his father bars the bedroom windows and attacks him with a "fury that had written upon his back with the sapelu's blade." Significantly, Matalasi finds relief only in the classroom, where he falls in love with the pisikoa teacher of English, memorizing *Twelfth Night* to impress her and finding fleeting solace in literary expression: "He started writing poetry; churning out verses by the day. Each more desperate than the last."[29]

As with so many of the texts we have studied in these pages, the liberation afforded through literature and learning is insufficient for the characters within the story: the pisikoa returns to the United States, and the protagonist falls into a depression; soon Matalasi will be forced to marry a man. But the sophistication of the narrative implies a more lasting literary experience for the author. Bennett-Tuionetoa performs the disjunction between Matalasi's inner experience of gender and the expectations of his society through narrative slippage and delayed decoding: the opening word of the story is "he," but the story slowly reveals that Matalasi was born female and is subject to oppressive acts of feminizing socialization and—still more traumatically—physiology. We see this first with his distressing experience of menstruation and again in the moment before the marriage, when Matalasi forces himself to confront the mirror that reveals "full, round breasts. The slender waist. The curved hips." In the final scene, as Matalasi is pushed down the aisle to wed the man his family has arranged for the honor of the āiga, this act of "violation" opens out into a hopeless cycle of constraining tradition: "He saw the two gleaming rings . . . side by side. Circles. . . . Round and round and round and round."[30]

Samoan culture is often celebrated in gender studies for the Indigenous and precolonial social recognition of the faʻafafine, a "third gender" that allows biological males to be acculturated as women, assigned female roles and responsibilities within the āiga.[31] Bennett-Tuionetoa's story—written while she was at USP—complicates the image of Samoa as a nonbinary paradise in a global age of embattled transgender rights, revealing the violence and coercion faced by faʻafātama, whose assumption and embodiment of maleness appears intolerable to the contemporary Christian state. The protagonist's name is thus well chosen: "matalasi" in Samoan means "varied" or "complicated," though it is often mistranslated outside the islands as "beautiful," after the popular song "Samoa Matalasi," which celebrates traditional Samoan culture and identity. In a story of strict gender identity and heteronormativity, the name rings ironically, and "Matalasi" suggests that only some Samoans may be found beautiful, only some varieties tolerated.

Rokonadravu's "The Nightwatch" (2022), the most recent of the short story prize winners, uses the death of an elderly woman at the outbreak of yet another coup as a parable for the losses and potential redemptions of postmillennial Fiji. With her "bright hibiscus sulu and jaba" and her hair

CODA: THE STORIES OF MULTITUDES TO COME

"in the traditional Fijian buiniga," the woman, whose name we never learn, is every inch the iTaukei marama.[32] Leaving her neat village for Suva, she is shocked by the squatter settlement in which her son resides and sets out to stem the "rising filth" of the "degraded salt swamp." She makes arduous headway, and as a group of women and children gather around to help her tidy, some semblance of cleanliness is restored. What she is unequipped to face, however, is her son's new partner, a sex-worker-cum-preacher who bursts from their shack and humiliates the old woman with invective of evangelical proportions: "Spirit of jealousy! . . . I command you to come out in Jesus' name! Out!"[33] With the neighbors jeering and "filming the spectacle on smartphones," the old lady is sent reeling into the city, now suffering its own turmoil with the announcement of a coup. As the parliament building is occupied and gangs take to the streets, as Indo-Fijian shops are looted and taxis stoned, the woman is taken in by the staff of a Chinese bakery. Here, she dies. Yet though one version of Fijian civility comes to an end, something of the marama's grace and compassion is passed on. As chaos fills the city, the small makeshift community inside the shop—the local Chinese owner, the iTaukei staff members, a sheltering Indo-Fijian taxi driver—carry the woman to the morgue. Moved to unaccustomed acts of hospitality and care, these "motley men" form a microcosm of a possible Fijian futurity: urban, multicultural, yet held together by the Indigenous values of the woman laid to rest. It is an apt image for a modern Fijian author of mixed iTaukei, Indo-Fijian, and European heritage.

Rokonadravu credits the "rural Fijian culture of oral storytelling" for her creative gift, supplemented by "the oral storytelling" practiced by her adoptive Indo-Fijian father.[34] But each of these stories also work from the Pacific texts published in the "golden age" that we have examined across *The Rise of Pacific Literature*. The tragedy of "The Nightwatch" is alleviated not only by the kindness of the strangers who come together in the bakery but by scenes of bawdy slapstick in the home of the daurairai (seer), where flatulence and foul language ring in tribute to Hau'ofa's fabulously profane *Kisses in the Nederends*, an ode to the anus that opens with a punning invocation of Eliot's "Little Gidding": "to make an end is to make a beginning."[35] Bennett-Tuionetoa continues a Samoan literary tradition, begun by Wendt and extended by Figiel, of presenting personal suffering under a social order that sacrifices the individual to tradition. Yet the key textual reference here is neither Wendt nor Figiel but Helu Thaman's "You, the Choice of My Parents," discussed in chapter 1. Published in an early installment of "Mana" and a mainstay of Pacific high school classrooms since the 1980s, this poem depicts a girl whose arranged marriage causes her to die "slowly / To family and traditions."[36] Meeting her betrothed at the altar—with his "Western-type education / and second-hand car"—Helu Thaman's speaker is "masked with pretence and obedience / And my smiles tell you that I care; / I have no other choice."[37] So for Matalasi, who "force[s] himself to smile" at the man "resplendent in his American tailored suit': "There was no choice, really. . . . I just had to obey."[38] And the narrator of "Famished Eels" is bolstered not only by the tales of her father but also by the rich Indo-Fijian literary tradition that she carries with her physically, in boxes of "signed copies of diasporic books by names such as Brij Lal, Mohit Prasad, Sudesh Mishra and Subramani."[39]

The Commonwealth Short Story Prize–winning stories of Bennett-Tuionetoa and Rokonadravu, as well as Makereti, demonstrate the new levels of access to global publishing outlets for Pacific writers of the twenty-first century and the presence of an established Oceanian literary canon, which provides mana for its custodians and stands as the principal storehouse for literary influence and allusion. The stories we end with are formally conversant with the techniques of modernist and postcolonial literature, but their intertextual repository is the generative Pacific writing explored in *The Rise of Pacific Literature*. These are texts that have been studied by several generations of Oceanian writers at high school. Wendt, Hauʻofa, Helu Thaman, and Subramani are now central to the Pacific curriculums that they helped inspire with their pedagogies and their literature alike. As educators in the broadest sense, they are nodes in a genealogical network extending back into the Indigenous past and forward into the future to come. We have charted the ways in which a first generation of Pacific writers made modernism, in its varied manifestations, part of the literary bloodline. As we enter the third decade of the twenty-first century, that bloodline continues to flow in these stories of Oceanian modernity. "My story is not mine alone," Rokonadravu's narrator concludes. "It is the story of multitudes and it will become a thread in the stories of multitudes to come."[40]

NOTES

INTRODUCTION: PACIFIC UNIVERSITIES AND MODERNIST LITERATURE

1. Alice Te Punga Somerville, "Inside Us the Unborn: Genealogies, Futures, Metaphors, and the Opposite of Zombies," in *Pacific Futures: Past and Present*, ed. Warwick Anderson, Miranda Johnson, and Barbara Brookes (Honolulu: University of Hawai'i Press, 2018), 70.
2. Albert Wendt, *Ancestry* (Suva: University of the South Pacific Press, 2012), 254.
3. Wendt, *Ancestry*, 29.
4. Karlo Mila, "After Reading *Ancestry*: For Albert Wendt," *Blackmail Press* 40 (July 2015), http://nzpoetsonline.homestead.com/KM40.html.
5. Albert Wendt, ed., *Nuanua: Pacific Writing in English Since 1980* (Honolulu: University of Hawai'i Press, 1995), 4.
6. Te Punga Somerville, "Inside Us the Unborn," 70.
7. Te Punga Somerville, "Inside Us the Unborn," 70.
8. Konai Helu Thaman, "Of Daffodils and *Heilala*: Understanding (Cultural) Context in Pacific Literature," in *Navigating Islands and Continents: Conversations and Contestations in and Around the Pacific: Selected Essays*, ed. Cynthia Franklin, Ruth Hsu, and Suzanne Kosanke (Honolulu: University of Hawai'i; East-West Center, 2000), 42.
9. This institutional reception is not without its problems. As Teresia Teaiwa notes in a chapter on Joseph Veramu and Sia Figiel, two later Pacific writers, if literature were featured in more popular media and consumed more broadly by Pacific Islanders, rather than by "university students and academics on far-flung shores, how much more astute and incisive might our responses to colonialism and imperialism be?" Teresia Teaiwa, "Reading Imperialism in the Pacific: The Prose of Joseph

Veramu and the Poetry of Sia Figiel," in *Anglo-American Imperialism and the Pacific: Discourses of Encounter*, ed. Michelle Keown, Andrew Taylor, and Mandy Treagus (New York: Routledge, 2018), 65.
10. Mark McGurl, *The Program Era: Postwar Fiction and the Rise of Creative Writing* (Cambridge, MA: Harvard University Press, 2009), ix.
11. Ben Conisbee Baer, *Indigenous Vanguards: Education, National Liberation, and the Limits of Modernism* (New York: Columbia University Press, 2019), 43; Rachel Sagner Buurma and Laura Heffernan, *The Teaching Archive: A New History for Literary Study* (Chicago: University of Chicago Press, 2020), 2.
12. Apisai Enos, "Niugini Literature," *Kovave* 4, no. 1 (1972): 46.
13. Albert Wendt, "Tatauing the Post-Colonial Body," *SPAN: Journal of the South Pacific Association for Commonwealth Literature and Language Studies* 42–43 (1996): 18; Emma Emily Ngakuravaru Powell, "'Akapapa'anga Ara Tangata: Genealogising the (Cook Islands) Māori Imaginary," PhD diss., Victoria University of Wellington, 2021, 47.
14. Laura Heffernan, "Axel's Classroom," *Modernist Cultures* 14, no. 3 (2019): 317.
15. Gerald Graff, *Professing Literature: An Institutional History* (Chicago: University of Chicago Press, 1987), 196; Lionel Trilling, "On the Teaching of Modern Literature," in *Beyond Culture: Essays on Literature and Learning* (London: Secker and Warburg, 1966), 3–30.
16. Gail McDonald, *Learning to Be Modern: Pound, Eliot, and the American University* (Oxford: Clarendon, 1993), 139–40.
17. William Carlos Williams, *The Autobiography of William Carlos Williams* (New York: Random House, 1951), 146, 174.
18. McDonald, *Learning to Be Modern*, 138.
19. William F. Pinar, *What Is Curriculum Theory?* (2004; New York: Routledge, 2012), 47.
20. Lesley Le Grange, "The Curriculum Case for Decolonisation," in *Decolonisation in Universities: The Politics of Knowledge*, ed. Jonathan D. Jansen (Johannesburg: Wits University Press, 2019), 40.
21. Walter D. Mignolo and Catherine E. Walsh, *On Decoloniality: Concepts, Analytics, Praxis* (Durham, NC: Duke University Press, 2018).
22. Wendt, *Nuanua*, 4. This point is found too in Chris Tiffin, introduction to *South Pacific Images*, ed. Chris Tiffin (Brisbane: South Pacific Association for Commonwealth Literature and Language Studies, 1978), 4.
23. Albert Wendt, ed., *Lali: A Pacific Anthology* (Auckland: Longman Paul, 1980), xv–xvi.
24. Mignolo and Walsh, *On Decoloniality*, 81; Linda Tuhiwai Smith, *Decolonizing Methodologies: Research and Indigenous Peoples*, 3rd ed. (1999; London: Zed, 2021), 38.
25. Wendt, *Nuanua*, 4.
26. Subramani, "The Oceanic Imaginary," *Contemporary Pacific* 13, no. 1 (2001): 155. For an alternative reading of Wendt's postmodernism, see Elizabeth M. DeLoughrey, *Roots and Routes: Navigating Caribbean and Pacific Island Literatures* (Honolulu: University of Hawai'i Press, 2007), 225.
27. Subramani, "The Oceanic Imaginary," 156.
28. Konai Helu Thaman, "Decolonizing Pacific Studies: Indigenous Perspectives, Knowledge and Wisdom in Higher Education," *Contemporary Pacific* 15, no. 1 (2003): 11–12.

29. Postmodernist authors were there to draw on. Vladimir Nabokov's *Pale Fire* was published in 1962; Thomas Pynchon's *The Crying of Lot 49*, in 1965; John Barth's "The Literature of Exhaustion," in 1967; and J. G. Ballard's *The Atrocity Exhibition*, in 1970, alongside novels by Kurt Vonnegut, Philip K. Dick, John Fowles, and B. S. Johnson. The reading lists at UPNG and USP contained recently published works, yet there is no sign of authors we would consider postmodern, nor do Oceanian authors of the period often mention them as sources of inspiration.
30. See Damon Salesa, "Cowboys in the House of Polynesia," *Contemporary Pacific* 22, no. 2 (2010): 330–48.
31. The neatest introduction to this shifting view of modernism remains Douglas Mao and Rebecca L. Walkowitz, "The New Modernist Studies," *PMLA* 123, no. 3 (2008): 737–48. For a fuller, more recent exploration, see Douglas Mao, ed., *The New Modernist Studies* (New York: Cambridge University Press, 2021). On modernism's soft borders, see Paul Saint-Amour, "Weak Theory, Weak Modernism," *Modernism/modernity* 25, no. 3 (2018): 437–59.
32. Matthew Hayward and Maebh Long, "Towards an Oceanian Modernism," *Modernism/modernity* 28, no. 2 (2021): 209–28.
33. Matthew Hayward, "'Our Own Identity': Albert Wendt, James Joyce, and the Indigenisation of Influence," in *New Oceania: Modernisms and Modernities in the Pacific*, ed. Matthew Hayward and Maebh Long (New York: Routledge, 2019), 97.
34. Kirby Brown, Stephen Ross, and Alana Sayer, *The Routledge Handbook of North American Indigenous Modernisms* (New York: Routledge, 2023), 2. Similar projects in art history include Elizabeth Harney and Ruth B. Philips, *Mapping Modernisms: Art, Indigeneity, Colonialism* (Durham, NC: Duke University Press, 2018).
35. Teresia Teaiwa, "The Ancestors We Get to Choose: White Influences I Won't Deny," in *Theorizing Native Studies*, ed. Audra Simpson and Andrea Smith (Durham, NC: Duke University Press, 2014), 43–55.
36. Lewis R. Gordon and Jane Anna Gordon, "Introduction: Not Only the Master's Tools," in *Not Only the Master's Tools: African-American Studies in Theory and Practice*, ed. Lewis R. Gordon and Jane Anna Gordon (2006; London: Routledge, 2016), ix.
37. Quito Swan, *Pasifika Black: Oceania, Anti-Colonialism, and the African World* (New York: New York University Press, 2022); Michelle Keown, *Pacific Islands Writing: The Postcolonial Literatures of Aotearoa/New Zealand and Oceania* (Oxford: Oxford University Press, 2007); Elizabeth DeLoughrey, *Routes and Roots: Navigating Caribbean and Pacific Island Literatures* (Honolulu: University of Hawai'i Press, 2007); Sina Va'ai, *Albert Wendt and Samoan Identity* (Apia: National University of Samoa Publications, 1997).
38. Nauru (1968), Fiji (1970), Tonga (shed its official position of "protected state" by the United Kingdom in 1970), Papua New Guinea (1975), the Solomon Islands (1978), Tuvalu (1978), Kiribati (1979), Vanuatu (1980).
39. In 1986, the Marshall Islands and the Federated States of Micronesia became independent, followed by Palau in 1994, all under compact of free association with the United States. The Cook Islands and Niue retain citizenship links with New Zealand but became states in free association in 1965 and 1974 respectively, with the Cook Islands recognized as a state under international law by the UN in 1992, and Niue in 1994.

40. See Lyndon Megarrity, "Indigenous Education in Colonial Papua New Guinea: Australian Government Policy 1945–1975," *History of Education Review* 34, no. 2 (2005): 41–58; John Lynch, "The Papua New Guinea System," in *Pacific Universities: Achievements, Problems, and Prospects*, ed. Ron Crocombe and Malama Meleisea (Suva: Institute of Pacific Studies, 1988); Penelope S. Murphy, "Universities, Government Intervention and the Commission for Higher Education in Papua New Guinea," *International Journal of Educational Development* 9, no. 3 (1989): 175–82. For a history of Pacific decolonization that focuses on Indigenous involvement and insistence, see Tracey Banivanua Mar, *Decolonisation and the Pacific: Indigenous Globalisation and the Ends of Empire* (Cambridge: Cambridge University Press, 2016).
41. *Report of the Commission on Higher Education in Papua and New Guinea* (1964), 9.
42. *Report of the Commission*, vi.
43. *Report of the Commission*, 24.
44. *Report of the Commission*, 5. J. T. Gunther, one of the authors of the report, would become UPNG's vice-chancellor and would sustain his dismissal of Tok Pisin. See J. T. Gunther, "More English, More Teachers: Putting a Cat Among the Pidgins," *New Guinea* 4, no. 2 (1969): 43–53.
45. K. S. Inglis, "Education on the Frontier: The First Ten Years of the University of Papua New Guinea," *Critical Studies in Education* 22, no. 1 (1980): 68. The university was founded in 1965, but classes began in 1966.
46. University of the South Pacific Calendar (1970), 13.
47. C. Morris et al., *Report of the Higher Education Mission to the South Pacific* (London: Her Majesty's Stationery Office, 1966), 5.
48. Tupeni Baba, Ron Crocombe, and Malama Meleisea, "The Development of Higher Education in the Pacific Islands," in *Pacific Universities: Achievements, Problems, Prospects*, ed. Ron Crocombe and Malama Meleisea (Suva: Institute of Pacific Studies, University of the South Pacific, 1988), 29.
49. Colin M. Aikman, "Establishment: 1968–74," in *Pacific Universities: Achievements, Problems, Prospects*, ed. Ron Crocombe and Malama Meleisea (Suva: Institute of Pacific Studies, University of the South Pacific, 1988), 43.
50. University of the South Pacific Calendar (1971): 17–18.
51. Aikman, "Establishment: 1968–74," 41.
52. Inglis, "Education on the Frontier," 69.
53. Russell Soaba, "The Victims," *Kovave* 4, no. 1 (1972): 16–20.
54. "Exploitation," *UNISPAC* 7, no. 2 [1974]: 1, 20.
55. Alan Wendt, "A Poem for USP," *UNISPAC* (April 1978): 10.
56. Ron Crocombe and Malama Meleisea, "Achievements, Problems and Prospects: The Future of University Education in the South Pacific," in *Pacific Universities: Achievements, Problems, Prospects*, ed. Ron Crocombe and Malama Meleisea (Suva: Institute of Pacific Studies, University of the South Pacific, 1988), 342.
57. In 1952, the Territorial College of Guam was founded as a two-year teaching-training school and by 1968 had become the University of Guam, a four-year, degree-granting institution. Fiji College of Agriculture had opened in 1954, and Fiji Institute of Technology was established in 1963 for vocational and technical training. The College of Micronesia–FSM began in 1963 as the Micronesian Teacher Education Centre, and

also in 1963 the 'Atenisi Institute in Tonga was founded by Futa Helu as a night school for members of the civil service. It then opened a secondary school, and in 1975 lectures began at 'Atenisi's university division. The Pacific Theological College opened in Suva in 1966 and offered degree-level courses in theology, in 1970 the American Samoa Community College was established and offered two-year programs, and the National University of Samoa was established in 1984.

58. The first four issues came out under the name *New Guinea Writing*.
59. See Evelyn Ellerman, "Literary Institutions in Papua New Guinea," PhD diss., University of Alberta, 1994, for a thorough account of this literary and institutional history. Also Evelyn Ellerman, "The Literature Bureau: African Influence in Papua New Guinea," *Research in African Literatures* 26, no. 4 (1995): 206–15.
60. Joseph Waleanisia, "Writing I," in *Ples Blong Iumi: Solomon Islands, the Past Four Thousand Years*, ed. Hugh Laracy (Suva: Institute of Pacific Studies, University of the South Pacific, 1989), 31–40.
61. Crocombe and Meleisea, "Achievements, Problems and Prospects," 342.
62. Robert M. Kamins and Robert E. Potter, *Malamalama: A History of the University of Hawai'i* (Honolulu: University of Hawai'i Press, 1998), 74, 91.
63. Haunani-Kay Trask, *From a Native Daughter: Colonialism and Sovereignty in Hawai'i* (1993; Honolulu: Latitude 20, 1999), 152.
64. Kamins and Potter, *Malamalama: A History of the University of Hawai'i*, 97.
65. See, for example, Steven Winduo, "Indigenous Pacific Fiction in English: The 'First Wave,'" 499–510; and Mohit Prasad, "Indigenous Pacific Fiction in English: The 'Niu Wave,'" 511–23; both in *The Novel in Australia, Canada, New Zealand, and the South Pacific Since 1950*, ed. Coral Ann Howells, Paul Sharrad, and Gerry Turcotte (Oxford: Oxford University Press, 2017).
66. Marjorie Crocombe, "Mana and Creative Regional Cooperation," *Mana Annual*, 1977, 5.
67. This point has been made by numerous Pacific scholars, with Teresia Teaiwa calling in 2010 for the necessary acknowledgment of "almost a century of prior literary production and publication in the form of vernacular newspapers throughout the Pacific region." Teresia Teaiwa, "What Remains to Be Seen: Reclaiming the Visual Roots of Pacific Literature," *PMLA* 125, no. 2 (2010): 731. Wanda Ieremia-Allan presented her research on *O le Sulu Samoa* at the Pacific History Association 24th Biennial Conference, University of the South Pacific, Suva, Fiji, in 2021.
68. Similarly, although outside our period of focus, the foundational Pacific studies text "Our Sea of Islands" (1993) would not exist without Hau'ofa's teaching, as it arose from the sorrow he felt when witnessing his students' reactions to narratives of Pacific islands' smallness. See Epeli Hau'ofa, "Our Sea of Islands," in *A New Oceania: Rediscovering Our Sea of Islands*, ed. Eric Waddell, Vijay Naidu, and Epeli Hau'ofa (Suva: University of the South Pacific School of Social and Economic Development, in association with Beake House, 1993), 5.
69. Paul Sharrad, "Literary Legacies: Faltering Feet; Dancing a Pen to a National Beat," in *Lines Across the Sea: Colonial Inheritance in the Post Colonial Pacific*, ed. Brij V. Lal and Hank Nelson (Brisbane: Pacific History Association, 1995), 199.
70. Ruperake Petaia, "Kidnapped," *Pacific Islands Monthly* 46, no. 1 (January 1975): 49.
71. Venantius Tapin, "Where Have All the Young Men Gone?," *Pacific Islands Monthly* 44, no. 8 (August 1973): 72; Maunaa Itaia, "My Educated Son," *Pacific Islands Monthly*

44, no. 5 (May 1973): 73; Vili Vete, "For Change," *Pacific Islands Monthly* 46, no. 11 (November 1975): 56; Rejieli Racule, "The Gift," *Pacific Islands Monthly* 46, no. 12 (December 1975): 50.
72. Futa Helu, Epeli Hauʻofa, Thomas Schneider, and Konai Helu Thaman, "Foreword," *Faikava* 1 (1978): 1.
73. Crocombe, "Mana and Creative Regional Cooperation," 5.
74. Editorial, *Kovave* 1 (1968): 4; Editorial Board note, *Sinnet* 1, no. 1 (1980): 4.
75. In the chapters that follow, "Mana" refers to the literary section of the magazine *Pacific Islands Monthly*, while references to the various *Mana* periodicals and annuals will specify the iteration by title and year and/or volume number. On the complicated print history of Mana publications, see chapter 6, note 14.
76. Many of the writers covered in Winduo's essay came to prominence in the 1990s, but the "writer scholar" label is equally apt for the earlier generation; Steven Edmund Winduo, "Unwriting Oceania: The Repositioning of the Pacific Writer Scholars Within a Folk Narrative Space," *New Literary History* 31, no. 3 (2000): 608.
77. See, for example, Albert Wendt, "The Artist and the Reefs Breaking Open," *Mana* 3, no. 1 (1978): 119; "Editorial," *Papua New Guinea Writing* 23 (September 1976): 2.

1. MODERNISM, PEDAGOGY, AND PACIFIC WRITER-SCHOLARS

1. W. H. Auden to Gabriel Carritt, qtd. in H. Carpenter, *W. H. Auden: A Biography* (London: Allen & Unwin, 1981), 110.
2. Rachel Sagner Buurma and Laura Heffernan, "The Classroom in the Canon: T. S. Eliot's Modern English Literature Extension Course for Working People and *The Sacred Wood*," *PMLA* 133, no. 2 (2018): 264–81.
3. A. P. Porter, *Jump at de Sun: The Story of Zora Neale Hurston* (Minneapolis, MN: Twenty-First Century, 1992), 66.
4. James Joyce, *Letters of James Joyce*, ed. Richard Ellmann (London: Faber, 1966), 2:322.
5. Beth Rigel Daugherty, "The Streets of London: Virginia Woolf's Development of a Pedagogical Style," in *Woolf and the City*, ed. Elizabeth F. Evans and Sarah E. Cornish (Liverpool: Liverpool University Press, 2010), 191.
6. In the Anglo-American context, see Lawrence Rainey, *Institutions of Modernism: Literary Elites and Public Culture* (New Haven, CT: Yale University Press, 1998).
7. See, e.g., Peter Howarth, ed., "Modernism and/as Pedagogy," special issue, *Modernist Cultures* 14, no. 3 (2019).
8. D. H. Lawrence, *The Rainbow, Part 2*, ed. Mark Kinkead-Weekes (Cambridge: Cambridge University Press, 2002), 355.
9. Langston Hughes, "Cowards from the Colleges," *The Crisis* 41, no. 8 (1934): 227.
10. W. H. Auden, "Private Pleasures," *Scrutiny* (September 1932): 192–93.
11. Wyndham Lewis, *The Art of Being Ruled*, ed. Reed Way Dasenbrock (Santa Rosa, CA: Black Sparrow, 1989), 106.
12. Virginia Woolf, *A Room of One's Own & Three Guineas* (New York: Oxford University Press, 1992), 199.
13. Woolf, *A Room of One's Own*, 199.
14. Woolf, *A Room of One's Own*, 199.

1. MODERNISM, PEDAGOGY, AND PACIFIC WRITER-SCHOLARS

15. "Preliminary Announcement of the College of Arts," *The Egoist* 21, no. 1 (1914): 414.
16. C. E. Beeby, *The Biography of an Idea: Beeby on Education* (Wellington: New Zealand Council for Educational Research, 1992), 261.
17. Beeby, *The Biography of an Idea*, 214.
18. Beeby, *The Biography of an Idea*, 263.
19. C. E. Beeby, *The Quality of Education in Developing Countries* (Cambridge, MA: Harvard University Press, 1966), blurb, dust jacket.
20. Beeby, *The Biography of an Idea*, 265.
21. Albert Wendt, "A Sermon on National Development, Education, and the Rot in the South Pacific," in *Education in Melanesia*, ed. J. Brammall and Ronald J. May (Canberra: Australian National University and University of Papua New Guinea, 1975), 378; Albert Wendt, "Samoa's Albert Wendt: Poet and Author," interview by Marjorie Crocombe, *Mana Annual*, 1973, 46.
22. Wendt, "A Sermon on National Development," 373, 379.
23. Ulli Beier to Michael Josselson, June 12, 1974, Michael Josselson Papers 1914–1991, 19.5, Harry Ransom Center, University of Texas at Austin.
24. Wendt, "A Sermon on National Development," 373, 378.
25. Howarth, "Introduction: Modernism and/as Pedagogy," 261.
26. Hugh Kenner, "Poets at the Blackboard," in *Ezra Pound and William Carlos Williams*, University of Pennsylvania Conference Papers (Philadelphia: University of Pennsylvania Press, 1983), 3–13; William Carlos Williams, *The Autobiography of William Carlos Williams* (New York: Random House, 1951), 148.
27. Herbert J. Muller, *Modern Fiction: A Study of Values* (New York: Funk and Wagnalls, 1937).
28. Richard Ellmann and Charles Feidelson, preface to *The Modern Tradition: Backgrounds of Modern Literature* (New York: Oxford University Press, 1965), vi. There are similar ideas in Frank Kermode and John Hollander, *Modern British Literature* (New York: Oxford University Press, 1973).
29. Frank Kermode, *Continuities* (New York: Random House, 1968), 26.
30. Harry Levin, "What Was Modernism?," in *Refractions: Essays in Comparative Literature* (New York: Oxford University Press, 1966), 284. See the section titled "Modernism" in A. Alvarez, *Beyond All This Fiddle: Essays 1955–1967* (London: Allen Lane, 1968).
31. Irving Howe, "The Culture of the Modern," in *Decline of the New* (London: Victor Gollancz, 1971), 6.
32. Howe, "The Culture of the Modern," 21–22.
33. Trilling, "On the Teaching of Modern Literature," 3.
34. The University of the South Pacific Calendar (1977), 120.
35. Gerald Graff, *Professing Literature: An Institutional History* (Chicago: University of Chicago Press, 1987), 183, 241.
36. Rachel Sagner Buurma and Laura Heffernan, *The Teaching Archive: A New History for Literary Study* (Chicago: University of Chicago Press, 2020); Alice Te Punga Somerville, "English by Name, English by Nature," in *Ngā Kete Māturanga: Māori Scholars at the Research Interface*, ed. Jacinta Ruru and Linda Waimarie Nikoa (Dunedin, NZ: Otago University Press, 2021), 90–104. See too Andy Hones, *Outside Literary Studies: Black Criticism and the University* (Chicago: University of Chicago Press, 2022).

37. Joanne Wodak, e-mail message to Maebh Long, December 9, 2021.
38. Alan Barker, "Education and the Critic," *Mana: A South Pacific Journal of Language and Literature* 2, no. 2 (1978): 60–77; responses in "Mana Forum," *Mana: A South Pacific Journal of Language and Literature* 3, no. 1 (1978): 5–16. See too John Docker, "The Neocolonial Assumption in University Teaching of English," in *South Pacific Images*, ed. Chris Tiffin (Brisbane: South Pacific Association for Commonwealth Literature and Language Studies, 1978), 28.
39. "Mana Forum," 12.
40. Levin, "What Was Modernism?," 287.
41. Stephen Spender, *The Struggle of the Modern* (London: Hamish Hamilton, 1963), 71, 78.
42. Mostyn Habu, "Creative Writing in the Solomons," *Mana* 4, no. 1 (1979): 3.
43. "Mana Forum," 14.
44. Muller, *Modern Fiction*, 14.
45. See the essays collected in Georg Lukács, *Essays on Realism*, ed. Rodney Livingston, trans. David Fernbach (Cambridge, MA: MIT Press, 1981); Alick West, *Crisis and Criticism* (London: Lawrence and Wishart, 1937).
46. Bertold Brecht, "Against Lukács," trans. Stuart Hood, in *Aesthetics and Politics*, ed. Ronald Taylor (1977; London: Verso, 1980), 68–85; Richard Wright, "Blueprint for Negro Writing," *New Challenge* 2 (1937): 53–65.
47. Vincent Sherry, "Introduction: A History of Modernism," in *The Cambridge History of Modernism* (Cambridge: Cambridge University Press, 2016), 13.
48. See Alan Filres, *Counter-Revolution of the Word: The Conservative Attack on Modern Poetry, 1945–1960* (Chapel Hill: University of North Carolina Press, 2012).
49. Hugh Kenner, *Dublin's Joyce* (London: Chatto & Windus, 1955), 235.
50. Kermode, *Continuities*, 5; Howe, "The Culture of the Modern," 3.
51. See, for example, Greg Barnhisel, *Cold War Modernists: Art, Literature, and American Cultural Diplomacy* (New York: Columbia University Press, 2015); Greg Barnhisel, "Modernism and the MFA," in *After the Program Era: The Past, Present, and Future of Creative Writing in the University*, ed. Loren Glass (Iowa: University of Iowa Press, 2016), 55–66.
52. Howe, "The Culture of the Modern," 10.
53. UPNG Course Handbook (1971), 269.
54. F. Abiola Irele, *The African Imagination: Literature in Africa and the Black Diaspora* (New York: Oxford University Press, 2001); Simon Gikandi, *Writing in Limbo: Modernism and Caribbean Literature* (Ithaca, NY: Cornell University Press, 1992).
55. Selina Tusitala Marsh, "The Body of Pacific Literature," *Mai Review* 1 (2010): 2.
56. Howarth, "Introduction: Modernism and/as Pedagogy," 271–73.
57. On the history of modernism in Fiji's colonial curriculum, see Maebh Long and Matthew Hayward, "For I Have Fed on Foreign Bread: Modernism, Colonial Education, and Fijian Literature," *Modernist Cultures* 15, no. 3 (2020): 377–98.
58. Satendra Nandan, email message to Maebh Long, November 9, 2023.
59. Felicia Dorothea Hemans, *The Poetical Works of Felicia Dorothea Hemans* (London: Oxford University Press, 1914), 396. For more on "Casabianca" in relation to the history of recitation in British and American schools, see Catherine Robson, *Heart Beats: Everyday Life and the Memorized Poem* (Princeton, NJ: Princeton University Press, 2012).

1. MODERNISM, PEDAGOGY, AND PACIFIC WRITER-SCHOLARS

60. Elizabeth Bishop, "Casabianca," in *North and South* (Boston: Houghton Mifflin, 1946), 4.
61. Joseph Conrad, *Heart of Darkness*, ed. Paul B. Armstrong (New York: Norton, 2006), 5.
62. T. S. Eliot, *For Lancelot Andrewes; Essays on Style and Order* (London: Faber and Gwyer, 1928), 27.
63. T. S. Eliot, "The Metaphysical Poets," in *Selected Essays* (London: Faber and Faber, 1953), 289.
64. Edward Kamau Brathwaite, *History of the Voice: The Development of Nation Language in Anglophone Caribbean Poetry* (London: New Beacon, 1984), 30–31; Brij V. Lal, "Primary Texts," in *Bittersweet: The Indo-Fijian Experience*, ed. Brij V. Lal (Canberra: Pandanus, 2004), 248.
65. Sia Figiel, *To a Young Artist in Contemplation: Poetry and Prose* (Suva: Pacific Writing Forum, USP, 1998), 40.
66. Michelle Cliff, *Abeng* (New York: The Crossing, 1984), 85; Jamaica Kincaid, *Lucy: A Novel* (London: Cape, 1991), 7.
67. Ivan Illich also spoke at UPNG, at the 1972 Waigani seminar entitled Priorities in Melanesian Development. His *Deschooling Society* (1971) influenced both faculty and students. Listen, for example, to Stephen Pokawin, interview by Ian Kemish and Jonathan Ritchie, *PNG Speaks*, May 10, 2016, https://pngspeaks.com/stephen-pokawin.
68. Rod C. Taylor, "Narrow Gates and Restricted Paths: The Critical Pedagogy of Virginia Woolf," *Woolf Studies Annual* 20 (2014): 57.
69. Paulo Freire, *The Pedagogy of the Oppressed* (1968), trans. Myra Bergman Ramos (New York: Continuum, 2005), 72.
70. Jonathan Heron and Nicholas Johnson, "Beckettian Pedagogies: Learning Through Samuel Beckett," *Journal of Beckett Studies* 29, no. 1 (2020): 55.
71. Chinua Achebe, "An Image of Africa," *Massachusetts Review* 18, no. 4 (1977): 788.
72. James Joyce, *Ulysses: A Critical and Synoptic Edition*, ed. Hans Walter Gabler with Wolfhard Steppe and Claus Melchior (New York: Garland, 1984), 8.744–47; for the Fiji connection, see Harald Beck, "Salty Missionaries," *James Joyce Online Notes* 8 (2015), https://www.jjon.org/joyce-s-environs/missionaries.
73. D. H. Lawrence, "Herman Melville's *Typee* and *Omoo*," in *Selected Critical Writings*, ed. Michael Herbert (Oxford: Oxford University Press, 1998), 115, 118.
74. Virginia Woolf, *The Common Reader: Second Series* (London: Hogarth, 1953), 258. Of course, Woolf's suggestion to take no advice is followed by a stream of further advice.
75. Pio Manoa, "Recall," reprinted in *Waves: An Anthology*, ed. Vijay Mishra (1975; Auckland: Heinemann Education, 1979), 111.
76. Manoa, "Recall," 111.
77. Manoa, "Recall," 111.
78. Pio Manoa, "Singing in Their Genealogical Trees," *Mana Review: A South Pacific Journal of Language and Literature* 1, no. 1 (1976): 64.
79. Pio Manoa, "Recollect," *Dreadlocks* 6–7 (2010–11): 263.
80. On Fijian modernist challenges to the rote learning of the secondary education system, including that of Manoa, see Long and Hayward, "For I Have Fed on Foreign Bread."

1. MODERNISM, PEDAGOGY, AND PACIFIC WRITER-SCHOLARS

81. Nathan Suhr-Sytsma, "Ibadan Modernism: Poetry and the Literary Present in Mid-Century Nigeria," *Journal of Commonwealth Literature* 48, no. 1 (2013): 43.
82. Alan Natachee, "My Worthy Warning" and "Advance Atomic Age," in "Mekeo Poems and Legends," *Oceania* 2, no. 2 (1951): 148, 149.
83. Elizabeth Wood-Ellem, ed., *Songs and Poems of Queen Sālote*, trans. Melenaite Taumoefolau (Nukuʻalofa: Vavaʻu Press, 2004).
84. We are grateful to Tilisi Bryce for her guidance on the use and importance of heliaki in Tongan composition. For a printed account in English, see Melenaite Taumoefolau, "The Translation of Queen Sālote's poetry," in *For Better or Worse: Translation as a Tool for Change in the South Pacific*, ed. Sabine Fenton (2003; London: Routledge, 2014), 255.
85. Tēvita O. Kaʻili, *Marking Indigeneity: The Tongan Art of Sociospatial Relations* (Tucson: University of Arizona Press, 2016), 61.
86. Peni Tutuʻila Malupo, "Tonga, Blessed Land," *Pacific Islands Monthly* 44, no. 9 (September 1973): 68.
87. Tutuʻila Malupo, "Tonga, Blessed Land," 68.
88. Futa Helu, "The Kakala," *Pacific Islands Monthly* 44, no. 3 (March 1973): 70.
89. Helu, "The Kakala," 70.
90. Tevita ʻO. Helu, "Ko ha fakaʻanau / In a Longing," *Pacific Islands Monthly* 44, no. 12 (December 1973): 64.
91. Gerald Moore and Ulli Beier, introduction to *Modern Poetry from Africa*, ed. Gerald Moore and Ulli Beier (1963; Harmondsworth: Penguin, 1966), 30.
92. Tutuʻila Malupo, "Tonga, Blessed Land," 68.
93. Salochana Devi, "Man," *Pacific Islands Monthly* 44, no. 4 (April 1973): 66.
94. Long and Hayward, "For I Have Fed on Foreign Bread," 383–84.
95. Harry Ivaiti, "Tangaroa," *Mana Annual* (1973): 100.
96. Joseph W. Sukwianomb, "Where Are the Green Leaves," *Pacific Islands Monthly* 46, no. 3 (March 1975): 52.
97. Konai Helu Thaman, "Resistance," *Pacific Islands Monthly* 45, no. 1 (January 1974): 61.
98. Helu Thaman, "Resistance," 61.
99. Konai Helu Thaman, "You, the Choice of My Parents," *Pacific Islands Monthly* 44, no. 7 (July 1973): 72.
100. Helu Thaman, "You, the Choice of My Parents," 72.
101. Helu Thaman, "You, the Choice of My Parents," 72.
102. Konai Helu Thaman, "Of Daffodils and *Heilala*: Understanding (Cultural) Context in Pacific Literature," in *Navigating Islands and Continents: Conversations and Contestations in and Around the Pacific: Selected Essays*, ed. Cynthia Franklin, Ruth Hsu, and Suzanne Kosanke (Honolulu, HA: University of Hawaiʻi; East-West Center, 2000), 46.
103. Helu Thaman, "Of Daffodils and *Heilala*," 46.
104. Paul Sharrad, "Breaks, Gaps, Waves: Pacific Literature and (Re)Making History," in *Encyclopédie des historiographies: Afriques, Amériques, Asies*, vol. 1, *Sources et genres historiques*, ed. Nathalie Kouamé, Éric P. Meyer, and Anne Viguier (Paris: Presses de l'Inalco, 2020), 139–50.
105. Helu Thaman, "Of Daffodils and *Heilala*," 41.

2. DECOLONIZING THE LITERATURE PROGRAM

106. Satendra Nandan, *In Diaspora: Theories, Histories, Texts* (New Delhi: Indialog, 2001), 302.
107. John Waiko, "The Place of Literature in Papua New Guinea Education," *Teaching Literature in Papua New Guinea*, ed. Elton Brash and Mike Greicus (Port Moresby: UPNG, 1972), 4.
108. Helu Thaman, "Decolonizing Pacific Studies," 10–11.
109. Tuhiwai Smith, *Decolonizing Methodologies*.
110. Albert Wendt, "Towards a New Oceania," *Mana Review: A South Pacific Journal of Language and Literature* 1, no. 1 (1976): 51, 56.
111. Wendt, "Towards a New Oceania," 52, 53.
112. Wendt, "Towards a New Oceania," 53.
113. Wendt, "Towards a New Oceania," 58.
114. Wendt, "Towards a New Oceania," 58.
115. Albert Wendt, "An Interview with Albert Wendt," by John Beston and Rose Marie Beston, *World Literature Written in English* 16, no. 1 (1977): 158.
116. Wendt, "A Sermon on National Development," 380.

2. DECOLONIZING THE LITERATURE PROGRAM, GENERATING THE NIUGINIAN LITERARY SCENE

1. Kama Kerpi, "Kulpu's Daughter," *Kovave* 5, no. 1 (1975): 12. Subsequent citations will be made parenthetically within the text.
2. Quito Swan, *Pasifika Black: Oceania, Anti-Colonialism, and the African World* (New York: New York University Press, 2022), 131.
3. Okot p'Bitek, "Interview with Okot p'Bitek," *Kunapipi* 1, no. 1 (1979): 89.
4. Jahan Ramazani, *A Transnational Poetics* (Chicago: University of Chicago Press, 2009), 7–8. See too Oga A. Ofuani, "The Traditional and Modern Influences in Okot p'Bitek's Poetry," *African Studies Review* 28, no. 4 (1985): 87–99. For Taban Lo Liyong, however, the English version is decidedly inferior. From his perspective Okot wrote two poems—a "deep, philosophical book in Acholi" and a "second, light book, *Song of Lawino*." Taban Lo Liyong, "On Translating the 'Untranslated': Chapter 14 of 'Wer pa Lawino' by Okot p'Bitek," *Research in African Literatures* 24, no. 3 (1993): 88.
5. "Drama & Arts—a Lively Afterlife?," *Nilaidat* 2, no. 3 (1969): 14.
6. Tim Allen, "The Rage of Okot p'Bitek: Colonial Perspectives and a Failed Oxford Doctorate," *LSE Blogs*, April 12, 2019, https://blogs.lse.ac.uk/africaatlse/2019/07/12/rage-okot-pbitek-colonial-perspectives/.
7. Kirsty Powell, "The First Papua New Guinean Playwrights and Their Plays," master's thesis, University of Papua New Guinea, 1975. Kirsty Powell was a promising student whose master's thesis remains a valuable piece of scholarship. Tragically, Powell was killed in a car accident as she was in the final stages of research. The thesis, which she was upgrading to a PhD before her death, was submitted posthumously.
8. Ulli Beier, *In a Colonial University* (Bayreuth: Iwalewa-haus, University of Bayreuth, 1993), 13–14.

2. DECOLONIZING THE LITERATURE PROGRAM

9. Ulli Beier, *Decolonising the Mind: The Impact of the University on Culture and Identity in Papua New Guinea, 1971–74* (Canberra: Pandanus, 2000), 8, 2.
10. In 1967, for example, the offerings were very limited, comprising only two courses—a course on Traditions of Oral Literature and one on the Literature of Developing Countries in English. Modern Literature was then added, and from there course offerings grew.
11. See too Evelyn Ellerman, "Learning to Be a Writer in Papua New Guinea," *History of Intellectual Culture* 8, no. 1 (2008–2009): 1–16.
12. Ngũgĩ wa Thiong'o, Henry Owuor-Anyumba, and Taban Lo Liyong, "On the Abolition of the English Department," in *The Postcolonial Studies Reader*, ed. Bill Ashcroft, Gareth Griffiths, and Helen Tiffin (London: Routledge, 1995), 438–42. For context of the progressive nature of this course structure, in 1966 the English department at the University of Sydney was preoccupied with splits over approaches to Leavis. See William Christie, "'The Essential Cambridge in Spite of Cambridge': F. R. Leavis in the Antipodes," *Australian Humanities Review* 68 (2021).
13. A. Aleper's *Maori Myths and Tribal Legends* (1964) was on the recommended reading list.
14. UPNG Course Handbook (1970), 198.
15. UPNG Course Handbook (1971), 259.
16. UPNG Course Handbook (1971), 269.
17. John Kadiba, "Elites and Education: John Kadiba on Ulli Beier," *Sumatin: A Magazine of Papua New Guinean Writing* 2 (2022): 17.
18. Ulli Beier, introduction to *When the Moon Was Big: Legends from New Guinea* (Sydney: Collins, 1972).
19. Ulli Beier, preface to *Words of Paradise: Poetry of Papua New Guinea*, ed. Ulli Beier (Melbourne: Sun, 1972), 11. Emphasis in original.
20. Arthur Jawodimbari, "The Sun," *Kovave* 2, no. 1 (1970): 48.
21. Powell, "The First Papua New Guinean Playwrights and Their Plays," 203.
22. Addie Odai, untitled, *Kovave* 2, no. 1 (1970): 20.
23. Russell Soaba, "The Villager's Request," *Mana Annual* (1974), 72.
24. Soaba, "The Villager's Request," 72.
25. Dan Izevbaye, "West African Literature in English: Beginnings to the Mid-Seventies," in *The Cambridge History of African and Caribbean Literature*, ed. F. Abiola Irele and Simon Gikandi (Cambridge: Cambridge University Press, 2004), 479.
26. Amos Tutuola, *The Palm-Wine Drinkard* (London: Faber and Faber, 1977), 65–73; Matthew Omelsky, "The Creaturely Modernism of Amos Tutuola," *Cultural Critique*, 99 (2018): 84–87.
27. John Kadiba, "Growing Up in Mailu," *Kovave* pilot (1968): 18–25.
28. Beier, *Decolonising the Mind*, 66.
29. Namaliu is unusual in that he was the third generation in his family to be educated; see Powell, "The First Papua New Guinean Playwrights and Their Plays," 161.
30. For more on the background to the protest, see Powell, "The First Papua New Guinean Playwrights and Their Plays," 374–75; and Ian Howie-Willis, *A Thousand*

2. DECOLONIZING THE LITERATURE PROGRAM

Graduates: Conflict in University Development in Papua New Guinea, 1961–1976 (Canberra: Australian National University, 1980), 107.
31. John Kasaipwalova, "Betel Nut Is Bad Magic for Aeroplanes," in *Through Melanesian Eyes: An Anthology of Papua New Guinea Writing*, ed. Ganga Powell (Melbourne: Macmillan, 1987), 69.
32. Kasaipwalova, "Betel Nut is Bad Magic for Aeroplanes," 77.
33. Kasaipwalova, "Betel Nut is Bad Magic for Aeroplanes," 69.
34. Kasaipwalova, "Betel Nut is Bad Magic for Aeroplanes," 69, 76.
35. Report of the Commission on Higher Education in Papua and New Guinea (1964), 5.
36. For more on code-switching and language use in Pacific writing, see Steven Winduo, "Pidgin Poetics in Oceania," *Oxford Research Encyclopedia of Literature* (2020), https://doi.org/10.1093/acrefore/9780190201098.013.198.
37. Enos, "Niugini Literature," 47.
38. Selina Tusitala Marsh, "Theory 'versus' Pacific Islands Writing: Toward a Tamaʻitaʻi Criticism in the Works of Three Pacific Islands Woman Poets," in *Inside Out: Literature, Cultural Politics, and Identity in the New Pacific*, ed. Vilsoni Hereniko and Rob Wilson (Lanham, MD: Rowman & Littlefield, 1999), 340.
39. Tusitala Marsh, "Theory 'Versus' Pacific Islands Writing," 340. See too Elizabeth M. DeLoughrey, *Roots and Routes: Navigating Caribbean and Pacific Island Literatures* (Honolulu: University of Hawaiʻi Press, 2007).
40. Caroline Sinavaiana Gabbard, "Samoan Literature and the Wheel of Time: Cartographies of the Vā," *symplokē* 26, nos. 1–2 (2018): 34. See too, for example, Albert Wendt, "Tatauing the Post-Colonial Body," *SPAN: Journal of the South Pacific Association for Commonwealth Literature and Language Studies* 42–43 (1996): 41.
41. Terrance Borchard and Philip Gibbs, "Parallelism and Poetics in Tindi Narratives Sung in the Ipili Language," in *Sung Tales from the Papua New Guinea Highlands: Studies in Form, Meaning, and Sociocultural Context*, ed. Don Niles and Alan Rumsey (Canberra: Australian National University, 2011), 165.
42. John D. Waiko, "'Head' and 'Tail': The Shaping of Oral Traditions Among the Binandere in Papua New Guinea," *Oral Tradition* 5, no. 2–3 (1990): 340.
43. John D. Waiko, "Oral Traditions Among the Binandere: Problems of Method in a Melanesian Society," *Journal of Pacific History* 21, no. 1 (1986): 21–38. See too Don Niles and Alan Rumsey, "Introducing Highlands Sung Tales," in *Sung Tales from the Papua New Guinea Highlands: Studies in Form, Meaning, and Sociocultural Context*, ed. Don Niles and Alan Rumsey (Canberra: Australian National University, 2011), 19.
44. For more on the publishing history of *The Palm-Wine Drinkard*, see Gail Low, "The Natural Artist: Publishing Amos Tutuola's *The Palm-Wine Drinkard* in Postwar Britain," *Research in African Literatures* 37, no. 4 (2006): 15–33.
45. T. S. Eliot, "Ulysses, Order, and Myth," in *Selected Prose of T. S. Eliot*, ed. Frank Kermode (Orlando, FL: Harcourt, 1975), 177–78.
46. Robert Hampson, "Joseph Conrad," in *The Cambridge Companion to English Novelists*, ed. Adrian Poole (Cambridge: Cambridge University Press, 2009), 299–300.

2. DECOLONIZING THE LITERATURE PROGRAM

47. Cary Snyder, "'When the Indian Was in Vogue': D. H. Lawrence, Aldous Huxley, and Ethnological Tourism in the Southwest," *Modern Fiction Studies* 53, no. 4 (2007): 662–96.
48. Shanyn Fiske, "From Ritual to the Archaic in Modernism: Frazer, Harrison, Freud, and the Persistence of Myth," in *A Handbook of Modernism Studies*, ed. Jean-Michel Rabaté (London: Wiley, 2013), 173–91.
49. Ulli Beier, introduction to *The Origin of Life and Death: African Creation Myths*, ed. Ulli Beier (London: Heinemann, 1966), vii.
50. Beier, introduction to *The Origin of Life and Death: African Creation Myths*, x, vii.
51. Much has been written on genealogy and Pacific literature; see, for example, Caroline Sinavaiana Gabbard, "Amerika Samoa: Writing Home," in *The Oxford Handbook of Indigenous American Literature*, ed. James H. Cox and Daniel Heath Justice (Oxford: Oxford University Press, 2014), 589–607; Tina Makereti, "Māori Writing: Speaking with Two Mouths," *Journal of New Zealand Studies* 26 (2018): 57–65; Nālani Wilson-Hokowhitu, ed., *The Past Before Us: Moʻokūʻauhau as Methodology* (Honolulu: University of Hawaiʻi Press, 2019).
52. Russell Soaba, "Scattered by the Wind," *Kovave* 4, no. 1 (1972): 34.
53. Lewis Nkosi, "Lewis Nkosi on Black Atlanticism and (Southern) African Writing," interview by Stephan Meyer, *Current Writing: Text and Reception in Southern Africa* 16, no. 2 (2004): 121.
54. Nkosi, "Lewis Nkosi on Black Atlanticism," 121.
55. Kumalau Tawali, "An Interview with Kumalau Tawali," interview by Don Maynard, *New Guinea Writing* 2 (1970): 13.
56. Peter Abrahams, *A Wreath for Udomo* (London: Faber and Faber: 1956), 22.
57. Simon Gikandi, "Cultural Translation and the African Self: A (Post)colonial Case Study," *Interventions* 3, no. 3 (2001): 355–75.
58. Kumalau Tawali, "The Bush Kanaka Speaks," *Kovave* 1, no. 2 (1970): 17.
59. Ferdinand Oyono, *Houseboy* (1956, trans. 1966); Peter Abrahams, *A Wreath for Udomo* (1956); Aimé Césaire, *Notebook of a Return to the Native Land* (1939, trans. 1969); Chinua Achebe, *A Man of the People* (1966); Wole Soyinka, *Kongi's Harvest* (1965); Wole Soyinka, *The Road* (1965); Ferdinand Oyono, *The Old Man and the Medal* (1974); Okot p'Bitek, *Song of Lawino* (1966); Gabriel Okara, *The Voice* (1964); Alex La Guma, *A Walk in the Night* (1962).
60. Moore and Beier, introduction to *Modern Poetry from Africa*, 30.
61. Simon Gikandi, "Foreword: On Afropolitanism," in *Negotiating Afropolitanism: Essays on Borders and Spaces in Contemporary African Literature and Folklore*, ed. Jennifer Wawrzinek and J. K. S. Makokha (Leiden: Brill Rodopi, 2011), 9–11.
62. Arthur Jawodimbari, qtd. in Powell, "The First Papua New Guinean Playwrights and Their Plays," 235.
63. Marjorie Crocombe, "The Healer," *Kovave* 2, no. 1 (1970): 5–12.
64. F. Abiola Irele, *The African Imagination: Literature in Africa and the Black Diaspora* (New York: Oxford University Press, 2001), 57.
65. Chinweizu, Onwuchekwa Jemie, and Ihechukwu Madubuike, *Toward the Decolonization of African Literature*, vol. 1, *African Fiction and Poetry and Their Critics* (Washington, DC: Howard University Press, 1983), 173.

2. DECOLONIZING THE LITERATURE PROGRAM

66. Roger Field, "'Across the River and Into the Trees, I Thought': Hemingway's Impact on Alex La Guma," in *Hemingway and the Black Renaissance*, ed. Gary Edward Holcomb and Charles Scruggs (Columbus: Ohio State University Press, 2010), 214–28.
67. Simon Gikandi, "African Literature and Modernity," in *Texts, Tasks, and Theories: Versions and Subversions in African Literatures*, ed. Tobias Robert Klein, Ulrike Auga, and Viola Prüschenk (Matatu 35; Amsterdam; New York: Editions Rodopi, 2007), 3:9.
68. Nkosi, "Lewis Nkosi on Black Atlanticism," 121.
69. Irele, *The African Imagination*, 64.
70. Ngũgĩ wa Thiong'o, *Moving the Centre: The Struggle for Cultural Freedoms* (London: James Currey, 1993), 23.
71. Gikandi, "African Literature and Modernity," 3.
72. Martin Esslin, *The Theatre of the Absurd* (London: Eyre Methuen, 1974), 350.
73. John Kadiba, "Tax," *Kovave* 1, no. 1 (1969): 9–13; John Kasaipwalova, "The Magistrate and My Grandfather's Testicles," *Kovave* 3, no. 2 (1972): 9–15.
74. Russell Soaba, "A Portrait of the Odd Man Out," *Kovave* 2, no. 2 (1971): 7–11.
75. Russell Soaba, "A Glimpse of the Abyss," *Kovave* 3, no. 2 (1972): 6–8.
76. Soaba, "The Victims," 16, emphasis in original; T. S. Eliot, *The Waste Land* [1922], Norton Critical Edition, ed. Michael North (New York: Norton, 2001), 19.
77. Soaba, "The Victims," 20.
78. John Kasaipwalova, "Kanaka's Dream," *Kovave* 3, no. 1 (1971): 47, 57.
79. Esslin, *The Theatre of the Absurd*, 352.
80. Allen Ginsberg, *Howl and Other Poems* (San Francisco: City Lights, 1973), 9.
81. C. L. R. James, "Appendix: From Toussaint L'Ouverture to Fidel Castro," in *The Black Jacobins: Toussaint L'Ouverture and the San Domingo Revolution* (New York: Vintage, 1963), 402.
82. Mara de Gennaro, "A Return to *The Waste Land* After Césaire's *Cahier*," *Comparative Literature Studies* 52, no. 3 (2015): 479–509.
83. James Kaputin, "Tolai Songs," *Kovave* 1, no. 1 (1969): 35.
84. Kama Kerpi, "Song of Lament," *Kovave* 4, no. 2 (1974): 16.
85. Nigel Krauth, "Interpreting the Signs," *Kovave* 3, no. 1 (1971): 43.
86. Kalyan Chatterjee, "Papua New Guinea Literature: Innocence and Self-Knowledge," *Pacific Islands Communication Journal* 14, no. 1 (1985): 6.
87. Paul Sharrad, "A Map of PNG Short Stories in English," *Bikmaus* 5, no. 2 (1984): 9.
88. Although we lack the space for a detailed exposition, the oral form of drama, on the whole, tends to marry contrasting narrative and ontological expectations more smoothly.
89. Enos, "Nuigini Literature," 49.
90. Leo Hannett, "The Church and Nationalism," in *The Politics of Melanesia: Papers Delivered at the Fourth Waigani Seminar*, ed. Marion W. Ward (Canberra and Port Moresby: ANU and UPNG, 1970), 654–65.
91. Arthur Jawodimbari, qtd. in Powell, "The First Papua New Guinean Playwrights and Their Plays," 235.

3. TRAVELING EDITORS AND INDIGENOUS MASKS: THE TEACHINGS OF ULLI BEIER

1. John Waiko, "The Unexpected Hawk," *Kovave* 1, no. 1 (1969): 56–57.
2. Maurice Thompson, "Seduction," *Kovave* 2, no. 1 (1970): 14.
3. Ken Goodwin, "Bulls and Prophets in Papua New Guinea," *Journal of Postcolonial Writing* 16, no. 1 (1977): 169.
4. Albert Maori Kiki, *Kiki: Ten Thousand Years in a Lifetime* (London: Pall Mall, 1968), 69.
5. K. S. Inglis, "Education on the Frontier: The First Ten Years of the University of Papua New Guinea," *Critical Studies in Education* 22, no. 1 (1980): 79; Christine Stewart, "Not a *Misis*," in *Australians in Papua New Guinea, 1960–1975*, ed. Ceridwen Spark, Seumus Spark, and Christina Twomey (St. Lucia: University of Queensland Press, 2014), 258.
6. Leo Hannett, "Niugini Black Power," *Nilaidat*, May 1971, 1; Hank Nelson, *Papua New Guinea: Black Unity or Black Chaos?* (Harmondsworth: Penguin, 1974), 183. Other members included Martin Buluna and Mekere Morauta.
7. Quito Swan, *Pasifika Black: Oceania, Anti-Colonialism, and the African World* (New York: New York University Press, 2022), 122.
8. Renagi R. Lohia, "Your First Year at University," *Nilaidat* 2, no. 1 (April 1969): 13.
9. Regis Stella, "Reluctant Voyages Into Otherness: Practice and Appraisal in Papua New Guinean Literature," in *Inside Out: Literature, Culture, Politics, and Identity in the New Pacific*, ed. Vilsoni Hereniko and Rob Wilson (Lanham, MA: Rowman and Littlefield, 1999), 222.
10. Tracey Banivanua Mar, *Decolonisation and the Pacific: Indigenous Globalisation and the Ends of Empire* (Cambridge: Cambridge University Press, 2016), *Decolonisation and the Pacific*; Evelyn Ellerman, "Literary Institutions in Papua New Guinea," PhD diss., University of Alberta, 1994, 1–2.
11. Ulli Beier, *In a Colonial University* (Bayreuth: Iwalewa-haus, University of Bayreuth, 1993), 14.
12. Steven Edmund Winduo, "Cultural Invasion, Negative Knowledge, Self-Expression and the Prose Narratives of Papua New Guinea," master's thesis, University of Canterbury, 1991, 3.
13. Marjorie Crocombe, "Mana and Creative Regional Cooperation," *Mana Annual*, 1977, 5; Epeli Hau'ofa, "'We Were Still Papuans': An Interview with Epeli Hau'ofa," interview by Nicholas Thomas, *Contemporary Pacific* 24, no. 1 (2012): 123–24. Wendt praises the Beiers' contributions to art in Albert Wendt, "The Artist and the Reefs Breaking Open," *Mana* 3, no. 1 (1978): 111.
14. Kirsty Powell, "The First Papua New Guinean Playwrights and Their Plays," master's thesis, University of Papua New Guinea, 1975, 42.
15. Ulli Beier, *Decolonising the Mind: The Impact of the University on Culture and Identity in Papua New Guinea, 1971–74* (Canberra: Pandanus, 2000), 2; Beier, *In a Colonial University*, 14.
16. Elton Brash, "Creative Writing, Literature and Self Expression in Papua New Guinea," in *Teaching Literature in Papua New Guinea*, ed. E. Brash and M. Greicus (Port Moresby: UPNG, 1972), 35.
17. Brash, "Creative Writing," 36–37.

3. TRAVELING EDITORS AND INDIGENOUS MASKS

18. W. Hurrey, "The Demonstration," *Nilaidat* 1, no.7 (1968): 5.
19. D. P. Sheekey, Head of Special Branch to the Commissioner of Police, Konedobu, October 1, 1969, qtd. in Banivanua Mar, *Decolonisation and the Pacific*, 184.
20. Secret, M. A. Beasley to R. Whitrod, 1969, qtd. in Banivanua Mar, *Decolonisation and the Pacific*, 184.
21. Beier, *In a Colonial University*, 17.
22. Ulli Beier, "Review: Yirawala: Artist and Man, by Sandra Le Brun Holmes," *Kovave* 4, no. 2 (1973): 55.
23. Powell, "The First Papua New Guinean Playwrights and Their Plays," 41.
24. John Kadiba, "Elites and Education: John Kadiba on Ulli Beier," *Sumatin: A Magazine of Papua New Guinean Writing* 2 (2022): 17.
25. Marjorie Tuainekore Crocombe, "Mana Forum," *Mana* 3, no. 1 (1978): 9.
26. Powell, "The First Papua New Guinean Playwrights and Their Plays," 39, 47n1.
27. Russell Soaba, "An Interview with Russell Soaba by Chris Tiffin," *Span* 8 (1979): 15; Powell, "The First Papua New Guinean Playwrights and Their Plays," 44.
28. Beier, *In a Colonial University*, 13.
29. Beier, *Decolonising the Mind*, 52.
30. Evelyn Ellerman, "Learning to Be a Writer in Papua New Guinea," *History of Intellectual Culture* 8, no. 1 (2008–2009): 10.
31. Paul Sharrad, "A Map of PNG Short Stories in English," *Bikmaus* 5, no. 2 (1984): 5–6.
32. Ulli Beier, "Literature in New Guinea," *Hudson Review* 24, no. 1 (1971): 119, 123.
33. Beier, *Decolonising the Mind*, 16–17. For a more nuanced reading of Natachee, see Paul Sharrad, "Literary Legacies: Faltering Feet; Dancing a Pen to a National Beat," in *Lines Across the Sea: Colonial Inheritance in the Post Colonial Pacific*, ed. Brij V. Lal and Hank Nelson (Brisbane: Pacific History Association, 1995).
34. Beier, *Decolonising the Mind*, 17.
35. Beier, *Decolonising the Mind*, 17.
36. Editorial, *Kovave*, 1969, 4.
37. William Wyckom Jr., "Letters," *African Arts* 8, no. 3 (1975): 7.
38. Michele V. Gilbert, "Letters," *African Arts* 9, no. 2 (1976): 2–3.
39. Peter Livingston, "From the Emotions of Ulli to a Simple Descriptive Paulias," *Pacific Islands Monthly*, June 1973, 78.
40. Kirsty Powell, "Ulli Beier's Role," *Pacific Islands Monthly*, August 1973, 23.
41. Abiola Irele, "'Papuan Parallels,' review of *Kiki: Ten Thousand Years in a Lifetime* by Albert Maori Kiki, *Reluctant Flame* by John Kasaipwalova, *High Water* by Apisai Enos, *The Crocodile* by Vincent Eri, *Kovave, a Journal of New Guinea Literature, Five New Guinea Plays* ed. Ulli Beier," *Transition* 44 (1974): 51.
42. Paul Sharrad, "A Map of PNG Short Stories," 6.
43. Peter Benson, *Black Orpheus, Transition, and Modern Cultural Awakening in Africa* (Berkeley: University of California Press, 1986), 93.
44. Peter Kalliney, "Modernism, African Literature, and the Cold War," *Modern Language Quarterly* 76, no. 3 (2015): 339n5.
45. Fredric Jameson, *A Singular Modernity* (London: Verso, 2012).
46. Qtd. in Benson, *Black Orpheus*, 95.
47. Paul Lyons, "Africana Calls, Pasifika Responses: Ellison's Invisible Man, Soaba's Wanpis, and Oceanian Literary Modernism," in *New Oceania: Modernisms and Modernities in the Pacific*, ed. Matthew Hayward and Maebh Long (New York:

Routledge, 2020), 118–35; Kalliney, "Modernism, African Literature, and the Cold War," 335–36.

48. Beier claims that Soyinka knew he was Ijimere, though this would make Soyinka's comments about his "authentic Yoruba perspectives" hard to understand. Ulli Beier, *The Return of Shango: The Theatre of Duro Ladipo* (Bayreuth: Iwalewa-Haus, 1994), 67.

49. Beier confirms that he is the author behind these names in a letter to Bernth Lindfors. Beier's reply is undated, but he responds to a letter from Lindfors sent March 7, 1967. Research in African Literatures Records ca. 1966–1990, 26, HRC B.108:25:005:06, Harry Ransom Center, University of Texas at Austin.

50. Wole Ogundele, *Omoluabi: Ulli Beier, Yoruba Society, and Culture* (Bayreuth: Bayreuth African Studies, 2003), 112.

51. Beier, *Decolonising the Mind*, 66.

52. Powell, "The First Papua New Guinean Playwrights and Their Plays," 239.

53. Powell, "The First Papua New Guinean Playwrights and Their Plays," 241.

54. Beier, *Decolonising the Mind*, 66.

55. Beier, *Return of Shango*, 67.

56. Ogundele, *Omoluabi*, 255.

57. UPNG Handbook (1968), 100, 105.

58. Christopher L. Miller, *Impostors: Literary Hoaxes and Cultural Authenticity* (Chicago: University of Chicago Press, 2018), 90–104.

59. Miller, *Impostors*, 1–2.

60. Beier, *Decolonising the Mind*, 25.

61. Ed Brumby, "Ulli Beier: A Personal Recollection," *Sumatin: A Magazine of Papua New Guinean Writing* 2 (2022): 15.

62. Kiki, *Kiki: Ten Thousand Years*, 164–65.

63. Ogundele, *Omoluabi*, 239–40.

64. Charles R. Larson, "Ulli Beier—African Playwright?," *Books Abroad* 46, no. 3 (1972): 395.

65. Ulli Beier to Diana Speed of the Transcription Centre, February 6, 1965, The Transcription Centre Records, 1931–1986, 14.5 HRC B. 108:30:002:02, Harry Ransom Center, University of Texas at Austin.

66. Emphasis in original. As stated in note 49 to this chapter, Beier's reply is undated, but he responds to a letter from Lindfors sent March 7, 1967.

67. James Gibbs to the Transcription Centre, June 3, 1970, The Transcription Centre Records, 1931–1986, 14.5 HRC B. 108:30:002:02, Harry Ransom Center, University of Texas at Austin. See too James Gibbs, *Nkyin-Kyin: Essays on the Ghanaian Theatre* (Leiden: Brill, 2009), 197.

68. Ulli Beier, ed., *Three Nigerian Plays* (London: Longmans, Green and Co., 1967), xiv; Ulli Beier to Maxine Lautré of the Transcription Centre, undated, The Transcription Centre Records, 1931–1986, 14.5 HRC B. 108:30:002:02, Harry Ransom Center, University of Texas at Austin.

69. Ulli Beier, ed., *Five New Guinea Plays* (Milton, Queensland: Jacaranda, 1971), viii.

70. John Kasaipwalova, *Reluctant Flame* (Ife: Papua Pocket Poets, 1971), 1.

71. Ellerman, "Learning to Be a Writer," 7.

72. Beier, *Decolonising the Mind*, 27.

73. Ulli Beier, "The Cultural Dilemma of Papua New Guinea," *Meanjin Quarterly* 34, no. 3 (1975): 307–8.
74. Oyekan Owomoyela, "Obotunde Ijimere, the Phantom of Nigerian Theatre," *African Studies Review* 22, no. 1 (1979): 46.
75. D. Laycock, "Pulling the Punches on Papuan Plays," *Kovave* 1, no. 2 (1970): 55.
76. Judith H. McDowell, "The Embryonic Literature of New Guinea," *Journal of Postcolonial Writing* 12, no. 2 (1973): 300.
77. Irele, "'Papuan Parallels,'" 51.
78. Toby Forward, "Being Rahila Khan," *London Review of Books*, February 4, 1988, https://www.lrb.co.uk/the-paper/v10/n03/toby-forward/diary.
79. Philippe Lejeune, *On Autobiography*, trans. Katherine Margaret Leary (Minneapolis: University of Minnesota Press, 1989).
80. Jaime Hanneken, "Scandal, Choice and the Economy of Minority Literature," *Paragraph* 34, no. 1 (2011): 49.
81. Albert Wendt, "Samoa's Albert Wendt: Poet and Author," interview by Marjorie Crocombe, *Mana Annual*, 1973, 47.
82. Powell, "Ulli Beier's Role," 23.

4. BLACK POWER AND PACIFIC EXISTENTIALISM: JOHN KASAIPWALOVA AND RUSSELL SOABA

1. *Kovave* 2, no. 2 featured Soaba's short story "A Portrait of the Odd Man Out" and Kasaipwalova's theatrical script "Rooster in the Confessional," *Kovave* 2, no. 2 (1971): 42–47. See also Kirsty Powell, "The First Papua New Guinean Playwrights and Their Plays," master's thesis, University of Papua New Guinea, 1975, 459, 467.
2. John Kasaipwalova, "The Role of the Educated Elite," *Nilaidat* (1971), reprinted in *Papua New Guinea Education*, ed. E. Barrington Thomas (Melbourne: Oxford University Press, 1976), 130, 131.
3. Ulli Beier, "The Beginnings of Literature in New Guinea," in *Black Writing from New Guinea*, ed. Ulli Beier (St Lucia: University of Queensland Press, 1973), xiii.
4. Ian Howie-Willis, *A Thousand Graduates: Conflict in University Development in Papua New Guinea, 1961–1976* (Canberra: Australian National University, 1980), 208.
5. John Kasaipwalova, "Problems of Unity in Niugini," *Nilaidat* 3, no. 1 (1970): 8.
6. John Kasaipwalova, *Reluctant Flame* (Ife: Papua Pocket Poets, 1971), 7. Subsequent citations will be made parenthetically within the text.
7. Albert Camus, *The Myth of Sisyphus*, trans. Justin O'Brien (Harmondsworth: Penguin, 1979), 58.
8. Powell, "The First Papua New Guinean Playwrights and Their Plays," 22.
9. Powell, "The First Papua New Guinean Playwrights and Their Plays," 373.
10. Jerry W. Leach, "Socio-Historical Conflict and the Kabisawali Movement in the Trobriand Islands," in *Micronationalist Movements in Papua New Guinea*, ed. R. J. May (Canberra: Research School of Pacific Studies, Australia National University, 1982), 264.
11. Quito Swan, *Pasifika Black: Oceania, Anti-Colonialism, and the African World* (New York: New York University Press, 2022), 112.

12. Powell, "The First Papua New Guinean Playwrights and Their Plays," 407.
13. Some of his ideas on a politics of creativity can be found in John Kasaipwalova, "'Modernising' Melanesian Society—Why, and for Whom?," in *Priorities in Melanesian Development: Papers Delivered at the Sixth Waigani Seminar*, ed. Ronald J. May (Canberra and Port Moresby: Australia National University and the University of Papua New Guinea, 1973), 451–54.
14. Greg Murphy, introduction to *Sail the Midnight Sun* by John Kasaipwalova (Credit Melanesia, Trobriands, 1980), 2.
15. J. A. Ballard, "Students and Politics: Papua New Guinea," *Journal of Commonwealth and Comparative Politics* 15, no. 2 (1977): 118; Norman Simms, "John Kasaipwalova," in *Writers from the South Pacific: A Bio-Bibliographical Critical Encyclopaedia* (Washington, DC: Three Continents, 1991), 73–74; R. J. May's "Editor's Note" addendum to Leach, "Socio-Historical Conflict," 289. There are some irregularities between these accounts, such as the year—1976 or 1977—and the amount of time in jail—eight or nine months.
16. Powell, "The First Papua New Guinean Playwrights and Their Plays," 377.
17. Ulli Beier, *Decolonising the Mind: The Impact of the University on Culture and Identity in Papua New Guinea, 1971–74* (Canberra: Pandanus, 2000), 49.
18. Kasaipwalova, "The Role of the Educated Elite," 130–34.
19. On PNG poets and gender, see Laura Zimmer-Tamakoshi, "Passion, Poetry, and Cultural Politics in the South Pacific," *Ethnology* 34, no. 2 (1995): 113–27.
20. John Kasaipwalova, "What Is 'Cultural Reconstruction'???," *New Guinea Writing* 3 (1971): 16, 15.
21. Leo Hannett, "Niugini Black Power," in *Racism: The Australian Experience. A Study of Race Prejudice in Australia*, ed. F. S. Stevens (Sydney: Australia and New Zealand Book Company, 1972), 41.
22. Beier, *Decolonising the Mind*, 56.
23. Ben Conisbee Baer, *Indigenous Vanguards: Education, National Liberation, and the Limits of Modernism* (New York: Columbia University Press, 2019), 104.
24. John Waiko, "The Place of Literature in Papua New Guinea Education," *Teaching Literature in Papua New Guinea*, ed. Elton Brash and Mike Greicus (Port Moresby: UPNG, 1972), 5, 6.
25. Hannett, "Niugini Black Power," in *Racism: The Australian Experience*, 48.
26. Leo Hannett, "The Niugini Black Power," in *Tertiary Students and the Politics of Papua New Guinea: Papers Delivered at the Second Seminar of Papua New Guinea Tertiary Students, Held at the Papua New Guinea Institute of Technology, Lae, 23rd–25th August, 1971* (Lae: Papua New Guinea Institute of Technology, 1971), 5–6.
27. Hannett, "The Niugini Black Power," in *Tertiary Students and the Politics of Papua New Guinea*, 3.
28. Hannett, "Niugini Black Power," in *Racism: The Australian Experience*, 43.
29. Hannett, "Niugini Black Power," in *Racism: The Australian Experience*, 44.
30. Baer, *Indigenous Vanguards*, 139–88.
31. Abiola Irele, "Aimé Césaire: An Approach to His Poetry," in *Introduction to African Literature: An Anthology of Critical Writing on African and Afro-American Literature and Oral Tradition*, ed. Ulli Beier (London: Longmans Green and Co., 1967), 62.
32. Irele, "Aimé Césaire: An Approach to His Poetry," 66.

4. BLACK POWER AND PACIFIC EXISTENTIALISM

33. Aimé Césaire, *The Original 1939 Notebook of a Return to the Native Land*, ed. and trans. A. James Arnold and Clayton Eshleman (Middleton, CT: Wesleyan University Press, 2013), 55. See too Powell, "The First Papua New Guinean Playwrights and Their Plays," 384.
34. Abiola Irele, "'Papuan Parallels,' review of *Kiki: Ten Thousand Years in a Lifetime* by Albert Maori Kiki, *Reluctant Flame* by John Kasaipwalova, *High Water* by Apisai Enos, *The Crocodile* by Vincent Eri, *Kovave, a Journal of New Guinea Literature, Five New Guinea Plays* ed. Ulli Beier," *Transition* 44 (1974): 50.
35. Chinua Achebe, *Things Fall Apart* [1958] (London: Penguin, 2010), 166.
36. Peter Abrahams, *A Wreath for Udomo* (London: Faber and Faber: 1956), 74.
37. James Baldwin, *The Fire Next Time* (London: Michael Joseph, 1968), 112.
38. Richard Wright, *Native Son* [1940] (New York: Harper Perennial Classics, 1988), 298, 387.
39. Wright, *Native Son*, 362.
40. Eldridge Cleaver, *Soul on Ice* [1968] (New York: Delta, 1992), 24.
41. Allen Ginsberg, *Howl and Other Poems* (San Francisco: City Lights, 1973), 9, 13; Chris Tiffin, introduction to *South Pacific Images*, ed. Chris Tiffin (Brisbane: South Pacific Association for Commonwealth Literature and Language Studies, 1978), 8.
42. John Beston, "Chill and the Flame: The Poetry of John Kasaipwalova," *Meanjin Quarterly* 40, no. 4 (1981): 485.
43. Lynda Thomas, "Volcano," *Kovave* 2, no. 2 (1971): 29.
44. Nigel Krauth, "A Postmortem of Papua New Guinea Poetry," *Papua New Guinea Writing* 25 (1977): 19.
45. K. L. Goodwin, "No Stagnant Neutrality: John Kasaipwalova's Poems," *Kovave* 4, no. 1 (1972): 52; K. L. Goodwin, "Invective and Obliqueness in Political Poetry: Kasaipwalova, Brathwaite, and Soyinka," in *Awakened Consciousness: Studies in Commonwealth Literature*, ed. C. D. Narasimhaiah (New Delhi: Sterling, 1978), 253.
46. Qtd. in M. Buluna, "The Role of the Student in Niugini Politics," in *The Politics of Melanesia: Papers Delivered at the Fourth Waigani Seminar*, ed. Marion W. Ward (Canberra and Port Moresby: Australian National University and the University of Papua New Guinea, 1970), 309.
47. Powell, "The First Papua New Guinean Playwrights and Their Plays," 462.
48. Russell Soaba, "Russell Soaba: An Interview," interview by Kirpal Singh, *Westerly* 29, no. 2 (1984): 49.
49. Powell, "The First Papua New Guinean Playwrights and Their Plays," 465–66.
50. Russell Soaba, "The Next Resort," *Mana Annual*, 1974, 70; Russell Soaba, "Natives Under the Sun," in *Black Writing from New Guinea*, ed. Ulli Beier (Brisbane: Queensland University Press, 1973), 87.
51. Soaba, "Russell Soaba: An Interview," 50.
52. Russell Soaba, "Interview with Russell Soaba," interview by Gilian Gorle, *New Literatures Review* 26 (1993): 68–72.
53. Soaba, "Russell Soaba: An Interview," 50.
54. Hannett, "Niugini Black Power," in *Racism: The Australian Experience*, 42.
55. Russell Soaba, *Wanpis* [1977] (Port Moresby: University of Papua New Guinea Press and Bookshop, 2012), 164. Subsequent citations will be made parenthetically within the text.

56. See Johnson's remarks in Elton Brash, "Creative Writing, Literature and Self Expression in Papua New Guinea," in *Teaching Literature in Papua New Guinea*, ed. E. Brash and M. Greicus (Port Moresby: UPNG, 1972), 38.
57. Paul Lyons, "Africana Calls, Pasifika Responses: Ellison's Invisible Man, Soaba's Wanpis, and Oceanian Literary Modernism," in *New Oceania: Modernisms and Modernities in the Pacific*, ed. Matthew Hayward and Maebh Long (New York: Routledge, 2020).
58. Ralph Ellison, *Invisible Man* (New York: Random House, 1952), 268.
59. Cameron Duodo, *The Gab Boys* (Bungay: Richard Clay, 1967), 174.
60. Laura Doyle, "Geomodernism, Postcoloniality, and Women's Writing," in *The Cambridge Companion to Modernist Women Writers*, ed. Maria Tova Linett (Cambridge: Cambridge University Press, 2010), 130. For more on Wendt and Camus see the Michelle Keown citation in the next note, as well as Faʻalafua L. Auvaʻa, "The Cultural Perspective of Albert Wendt's Novel *Pouliuli*," master's thesis, Utah State University, 1997; Evelyn Ellerman, "Intertextuality and the Fiction of Camus and Wendt," in *Comparative Literature East and West: Traditions and Trends: Selected Conference Papers*, ed. Cornelia N. Moore and Raymond Moody (Honolulu: University of Hawaiʻi College of Languages, Linguistics, and Literature, and the East-West Center, 1989), 43–50; Paul Sharrad, *Albert Wendt and Pacific Literature: Circling the Void* (Auckland: Auckland University Press, 2003).
61. Michelle Keown, "The Samoan Sisyphus: Camus and Colonialism in Albert Wendt's *Leaves of the Banyan Tree*," *Journal of Commonwealth Literature* 37, no. 1 (2002): 50.
62. Albert Wendt, "Discovering *The Outsider*," in *Camus's "L'Etranger": Fifty Years On*, ed. Adele King (New York: Palgrave Macmillan, 1992), 48–49.
63. Wendt, "Discovering *The Outsider*," 49.
64. Soaba, "Russell Soaba: An Interview," 55.
65. Soaba, "Russell Soaba: An Interview," 55.
66. Soaba, "Russell Soaba: An Interview," 55.
67. "Lus Man" is also a poem by Jerry Kavop, which features in *Kovave* 4, no. 1 (1972): 14. But while Soaba's lusman has the aura of one who chooses to resist the system, Kavop's lus man has been beaten by it.
68. Russell Soaba, "A Glossary of Words," in *Kwamra: A Season of Harvest* (Port Moresby: Anuki Country, 2000), 59.
69. Soaba, "An Interview with Russell Soaba," interview by Chris Tiffin, 23.
70. Soaba, "A Portrait of the Odd Man Out," 11.
71. Regis Stella argues that, in fact, St. Nativeson faked his death. Dead or gone, St. Nativeson's absence enables the literature that follows; Stella, "Reluctant Voyages Into Otherness," 224.
72. Steven Edmund Winduo, "Cultural Invasion, Negative Knowledge, Self-Expression and the Prose Narratives of Papua New Guinea," master's thesis, University of Canterbury, 1991, 74.
73. Soaba, "An Interview with Russell Soaba," interview by Chris Tiffin, 27–28.
74. Soaba, "An Interview with Russell Soaba," interview by Chris Tiffin, 24.
75. Soaba, "An Interview with Russell Soaba," interview by Chris Tiffin, 25.
76. Paul Lyons notes James St. Nativeson's tendency to return within the works of Papua New Guinean writers; Lyons, "Africana Calls, Pasifika Responses," 118.

5. PRELIMINARIES AND PROLOGUES

77. Russell Soaba, "Return of St. Nativeson," in *Kwamra: A Season of Harvest* (Port Moresby: Anuki Country, 2000), 1. There are overtones of C. P. Cavafy's "Waiting for the Barbarians" in Soaba's poem.
78. Soaba, "An Interview with Russell Soaba," interview by Chris Tiffin, 22.
79. "Saying What You Think on NG," *Pacific Islands Monthly* 41, no. 7 (July 1970): 45; Leach, "Socio-Historical Conflict," 265.
80. Soaba, "An Interview with Russell Soaba," interview by Chris Tiffin, 26.
81. Soaba, "Russell Soaba: An Interview," 52.
82. Soaba, "An Interview with Russell Soaba," interview by Chris Tiffin, 15.
83. See Soaba in Powell, "The First Papua New Guinean Playwrights and Their Plays," 39, 47n1.
84. Beier mentions these parties in *Decolonising the Mind*, 8.
85. Ellison, *Invisible Man*, 72.

5. PRELIMINARIES AND PROLOGUES: A NATIONAL SCENE IN A REGIONAL UNIVERSITY

1. Vanessa Griffen, "A Double Life," *Mana: A South Pacific Journal of Language and Literature* 4, no. 2 (1979): 15–16. Subsequent citations will be made parenthetically within the text.
2. Brij V. Lal, "Primary Texts," in *Bittersweet: The Indo-Fijian Experience*, ed. Brij V. Lal (Canberra: Pandanus, 2004), 248.
3. There was also a three-year Diploma in Education, which included English as one of its teaching streams and included a compulsory English component for each year of study. Writing by students in this program will be discussed in chapter 6.
4. "Exploitation," *UNISPAC* 7, no. 2 [1974]: 20; The University of the South Pacific Calendar (1970), 36.
5. The University of the South Pacific Calendar (1970), 36–37.
6. The University of the South Pacific Calendar (1971), 45–48.
7. The University of the South Pacific Calendar (1972), 59.
8. The University of the South Pacific Calendar (1970), 37.
9. Sr. M. Stella, "In Support of the USP!," *UNISPAC* [1969]: 4–5.
10. *UNISPAC* 3, no. 3 (1970): 15.
11. Brij V. Lal, *Broken Waves: A History of the Fiji Islands in the Twentieth Century* (Honolulu: University of Hawai'i Press, 1992), 228.
12. Steven Ratuva, *Politics of Preferential Development: Trans-Global Study of Affirmative Action and Ethnic Conflict in Fiji, Malaysia and South Africa* (Canberra: Australian National University Press, 2013), 35.
13. See, e.g., Aiyub Khan, "Gold Etched Independence?," *UNISPAC* 3, no. 2 (1970): 13.
14. Marjorie Crocombe, "Mana and Creative Regional Cooperation," *Mana Annual*, 1977, 6.
15. *UNISPAC* 4, no. 2 (1971); John Steinbeck, *"The Pearl" and "Burning Bright"* (London: Heinemann, 1954), 26.
16. Steinbeck, *The Pearl*, 22; Anirudh Singh, "The Screaming Man," *UNISPAC* 3, no. 3 (1970): 15.

17. Steinbeck, *The Pearl*, 58.
18. Singh, "The Screaming Man," 15, 16.
19. Shashikant Nair, "That Hour," *UNISPAC* 3, no. 1 (1970): 6.
20. Steinbeck, *The Pearl*, 6.
21. Ana Madigibuli, "Back in Time: Lecturer Recounts Abduction," *Fiji Times*, November 4, 2020, 6.
22. Raymond Pillai, "Prose Fiction in Fiji—a Question of Direction," *Mana: A South Pacific Journal of Language and Literature* 4, no. 2 (1979): 8–9.
23. Raymond Pillai, "Muni Deo's Devil," *UNISPAC* 4, no. 3 (1971): 24.
24. Griffen's engagement with Hemingway in preliminary studies was a return to the text, as she had already studied his work at high school. For a fuller account of the Fijian secondary curriculum in the mid-twentieth century, specifically in relation to modernist literature, see Maebh Long and Matthew Hayward, "For I Have Fed on Foreign Bread: Modernism, Colonial Education, and Fijian Literature," *Modernist Cultures* 15, no. 3 (2020).
25. Vanessa Griffen, "Marama," *UNISPAC* 4, no. 3 (1971): 25.
26. Griffen, "Marama," 25.
27. Vanessa Griffen, e-mail message to Maebh Long, November 1, 2018.
28. Betty Schutz, Hira Lal, Lognada, et al., "Individual Development vs National Development: Creativity vs Utility," *UNISPAC* 4, no. 3 (1971): 21.
29. Schutz, Lal, Lognada, et al., "Individual Development," 21.
30. L. F. Brosnahan, letter, *UNISPAC* 4, no. 4 (1971): 4–6.
31. *New Zealand Universities Arts Festival Yearbook* (Wellington: New Zealand Universities Publications, 1963); *Landfall* 17, no. 4 (1963); The University of the South Pacific Calendar (1972), 85, 88.
32. Pillai, "Prose Fiction in Fiji," 6.
33. There are gaps in the Pacific Collection archive in the library of the University of the South Pacific.
34. See our discussion of Manoa's poem "Recall" in chapter 1.
35. Seri, "Prologue," *Pacific Islands Monthly* 44, no. 4 (April 1973): 69.
36. Seri, "Prologue," 69.
37. Seri, "Prologue," 69; W. B. Yeats, *The Collected Poems*, ed. Richard J. Finneran, rev. 2nd ed. (New York: Scribner, 1996), 187.
38. Seri, "Prologue," 69; Yeats, *The Collected Poems*, 187.
39. The University of the South Pacific Calendar (1973), 97; The University of the South Pacific Calendar (1972), 88; T. S. Eliot, *Selected Poems* (London: Faber, 1954); W. B. Yeats, *Selected Poetry of W. B. Yeats*, ed. A. Norman Jeffares (London: Macmillan, 1962), incorrectly titled *Selected Poems* in the 1971 USP Calendar.
40. K. O. Arvidson, "Aspects of Writing in the South Pacific," *Mana Annual* (1973): 8; citing W. B. Yeats, *Letters to the New Island* (Cambridge, MA: Harvard University Press, 1934), 174.
41. Arvidson, "Aspects of Writing in the South Pacific," 6.
42. Lawrence Jones, *Picking up the Traces: The Making of a New Zealand Literary Culture, 1932–1945* (Wellington, NZ: Victoria University Press, 2003), 158; Paul Sharrad, "No Ordinary Modernism: Hone Tuwhare's First Book of Verse," in *New Oceania: Modernisms and Modernities in the Pacific*, ed. Matthew Hayward and Maebh Long (New York: Routledge, 2019), 68–70.

43. Satendra Nandan, "My Father's Son," *Pacific Islands Monthly* 45, no. 8 (August 1974): 64.
44. Nandan, "My Father's Son," 64.
45. Nandan, "My Father's Son," 64.
46. Nandan, "My Father's Son," 65.
47. Nandan, "My Father's Son," 64, 65.
48. T. S. Eliot, *The Waste Land* [1922], Norton Critical Edition, ed. Michael North (New York: Norton, 2001), 16, 5.
49. Eliot, *The Waste Land*, 20.
50. Pillai, "Prose Fiction in Fiji," 1.

6. MANA ON CAMPUS: NEW FORMS IN PACIFIC POETRY AND PROSE

1. Nihi Vini, "The Thing," *Pacific Islands Monthly* 44, no. 4 (April 1973): 67.
2. Vini, "The Thing," 67.
3. Vini, "The Thing," 67.
4. Vini, "The Thing," 67.
5. R. M. Ballantyne, *The Coral Island: A Tale of the Pacific Ocean* (1857; London: Ward, Lock & Co., 1901), 188.
6. Ballantyne, *The Coral Island*, 193, 194, 196.
7. Viktor Shklovsky, "Art as Technique," trans. Lee T. Lemon and Marion J. Reis, in *Russian Formalist Criticism: Four Essays*, ed. Lee T. Lemon and Marion J. Reis (Lincoln: University of Nebraska Press, 1965), 3–24; Ezra Pound, *Make It New* (London: Faber, 1934).
8. Ian Watt, *Conrad in the Nineteenth Century* (Berkeley: University of California Press, 1979), 175.
9. Vini, "The Thing," 67.
10. Joseph Conrad, *Heart of Darkness*, ed. Paul B. Armstrong (New York: Norton, 2006), 17.
11. Chinua Achebe, "An Image of Africa," *Massachusetts Review* 18, no. 4 (1977): 788.
12. Marjorie Crocombe, "Introducing Mana," *Pacific Islands Monthly* 44, no. 3 (March 1973): 69.
13. *Pacific Islands Monthly* 48, no. 2 (February 1977): 7; 46, no. 3 (March 1975): 1; 46, no. 8 (August 1975): 1.
14. "Mana" ran in this form from March 1973 to February 1976, with three annuals collecting and adding to this material in 1973, 1974, and 1977 (covering 1975–1976). In January 1976, just before the split from *Pacific Islands Monthly* (*PIM*), an affiliated journal was launched, edited by Subramani and titled *Mana Review: A South Pacific Journal of Language and Literature*. Designed as the critical arm of the South Pacific Creative Arts Society and publishing in its first issue such influential essays as Wendt's "Towards a New Oceania," it adapted quickly to fill the creative gap left by the seemingly unforeseen removal of "Mana" from *PIM*, and the second issue, in December of the same year, was almost entirely creative. In 1977 it rebranded accordingly, dropping "Review" from the title and continuing as such for the remainder of its print life, until 2003. As stated in note 75 of the introduction, "Mana" refers to

the literary section of *PIM*, while references to the various *Mana* periodicals and annuals will specify the iteration by title and year and/or volume number.

15. Marjorie Crocombe, "Mana and Creative Regional Cooperation," *Mana Annual*, 1977, 5.
16. Crocombe, "Mana and Creative Regional Cooperation," 6; Marjorie Crocombe, "Nero," *Kovave* 1, no. 1 (1969): 37–42; Marjorie Crocombe, "The Healer," *Kovave* 2, no. 1 (1970): 5–12.
17. Crocombe, "Mana and Creative Regional Cooperation," 6.
18. Marjorie Crocombe, "The South Pacific Festival of Arts," *Mana Annual*, 1973, 70.
19. Crocombe, "Introducing Mana," 69.
20. Crocombe, "Mana and Creative Regional Cooperation," 6.
21. Crocombe, "Mana and Creative Regional Cooperation," 6.
22. On the significance of SPCAS in the formation of the Pacific literature, see Emma Emily Ngakuraevaru Powell, introduction to *Mana: Fifty Years of Cook Islands Creative Writing in English and Cook Islands Māori*, ed. Joan Gragg, Patricia Thompson, Ngavaevae Papatua, and Rod Dixon (Rarotonga, Cook Islands: USP Press, 2018), 4.
23. For examples of this engagement, see the essays gathered in Matthew Hayward and Maebh Long, eds., *New Oceania: Modernisms and Modernities in the Pacific* (New York: Routledge, 2019).
24. Teresia Teaiwa, "The Ancestors We Get to Choose: White Influences I Won't Deny," in *Theorizing Native Studies*, ed. Audra Simpson and Andrea Smith (Durham, NC: Duke University Press, 2014), 52.
25. Crocombe, "Introducing Mana," 69.
26. For Tonga, see, e.g., Tevita 'O. Helu, "Ko ha fakaʻanau / In a Longing," *Pacific Islands Monthly* 44, no. 12 (December 1973): 64; Atunaisa Havea Katoa, "The Legend of Sangone the Turtle and the Royal Mats," *Pacific Islands Monthly* 46, no. 2 (February 1975): 44–46. For Fiji, see, e.g., Jo Nacola, "Living Under the Authority of a Myth in Ra," *Pacific Islands Monthly* 44, no. 5 (May 1973): 72–73; Mele Nasalivata, "A Legend of Love and Death," *Pacific Islands Monthly* 44, no. 11 (November 1973): 63–64.
27. Kenneth Fakamuria, "The First Coconut," *Pacific Islands* 44, no. 9 (September 1973): 62.
28. Raden S. Roosman, "Coconut, Breadfruit and Taro in Pacific Oral Literature," *Journal of the Polynesian Society* 79, no. 2 (1970): 222.
29. Albert Wendt, "Samoa's Albert Wendt: Poet and Author," interview by Marjorie Crocombe, *Mana Annual*, 1973, 75.
30. Jerry Iakavi, "The Mysterious Maidens from the East," *Pacific Islands Monthly* 44, no. 7 (July 1973): 70. See, for example, Steven Edmund Winduo, "Reconstituting Indigenous Oceanic Folktales," paper presented at Folktales and Fairy Tales: Translation, Colonialism, and Cinema, University of Hawaiʻi at Mānoa International Symposium, Honolulu, September 2010, http://hdl.handle.net/10125/16460.
31. Anne Stamford, "Custom Stories of the New Hebrides," *Pacific Islands Monthly* 44, no. 7 (July 1973): 70.
32. Leonard Garae, "Beware, the Worst Is Still to Come," *Pacific Islands Monthly* 45, no. 9 (September 1974): 60.

6. MANA ON CAMPUS

33. "Regional Creative Writing Workshop," USP/UNESCO Report, August 26–September 6, 1974, 16.
34. Vini, "The Thing," 67.
35. Thomas Richards, *The Imperial Archive: Knowledge and the Fantasy of Empire* (London: Verso, 1993), 3.
36. Richards, *The Imperial Archive*, 4.
37. Mike Murtagh and Michael Steer, "New Zealand Examining Bodies in the South Pacific," in *Examination Systems in Small States: Comparative Perspectives on Policies, Models and Operations*, ed. Mark Bray and Lucy Steward (London: Commonwealth Secretariat, 1998), 210.
38. Marjorie Crocombe, "Mana," *Pacific Islands Monthly* 44, no. 7 (July 1973): 65.
39. Marjorie Crocombe, "Mana," *Pacific Islands Monthly* 45, no. 9 (September 1974): 60.
40. Kali Vatoko and Albert Leomala, "Mi stap sori nomo / I Bow in Sorrow," *Pacific Islands Monthly* 45, no. 9 (September 1974): 62.
41. Donald Kalpokas, "Who Am I?," *Pacific Islands Monthly* 45, no. 9 (September 1974): 61.
42. Albert Leomala, "Culture My Culture," *Pacific Islands Monthly* 45, no. 9 (September 1974): 64.
43. Mildred Sope, "Motherland," *Pacific Islands Monthly* 45, no. 9 (September 1974): 64.
44. "Regional Creative Writing Workshop," 31.
45. Albert Leomala, "Live in Me," *Pacific Islands Monthly* 46, no. 12 (December 1975): 48.
46. Albert Leomala, "Hoom blong mi," *Mana Annual*, 1974, 38.
47. Albert Leomala, "Kros / Cross," in *Some Modern Poetry from the New Hebrides*, ed. Albert Wendt (Suva: Mana Publications, 1975), 18–19.
48. Goodwin, "No Stagnant Neutrality," 52.
49. Marjorie Crocombe, "Mana," *Pacific Islands Monthly* 45, no. 9 (September 1974): 60.
50. Albert Wendt, "Towards a New Oceania," *Mana Review: A South Pacific Journal of Language and Literature* 1, no. 1 (1976): 50.
51. Ulli Beier, *Decolonising the Mind: The Impact of the University on Culture and Identity in Papua New Guinea, 1971–74* (Canberra: Pandanus, 2000), 49.
52. Mildred Sope, interview with Mikaela Nyman, in Mikaela Nyman, "Sado—a Novel and Expressions of Creativity and Rhetorical Alliance: Ni-Vanuatu Women's Voices," PhD diss., Victoria University of Wellington, 2020, 246.
53. Marjorie Crocombe, "Writers Workshop," *Pacific Islands Monthly* 45, no. 11 (November 1974): 60.
54. Crocombe, "Writers Workshop," 60.
55. "Regional Creative Writing Workshop," 17.
56. "Regional Creative Writing Workshop," 16–17.
57. He studied in the Solomon Islands, New Zealand, and Fiji. See "A Secret Agent for Change—Donald Kalpokas," *Daily Post*, July 12, 2020, https://www.dailypost.vu/news/a-secret-agent-for-change-donald-kalpokas/article_a3ef01ca-cad5-11ea-9dc7-b3e20b284faa.html.
58. Kalpokas, "Who Am I?," 61.
59. Kalpokas, "Who Am I?," 61.
60. Albert Wendt, "How to Get Students Writing Poetry," *Multi-cultural School* 3 (1976): 18.

61. James Jupp, "The Development of Party Politics in the New Hebrides," *Journal of Commonwealth and Comparative Politics* 17, no. 3 (1979): 269.
62. Albert Leomala, "Niuhebridis," *Pacific Islands Monthly* 45, no. 9 (September 1974): 63; Albert Leomala, "Thieves," *Pacific Islands Monthly* 46, no. 7 (July 1975): 46; Vatoko and Leomala, "Mi stap sori nomo / I Bow in Sorrow," 62.
63. Aivu Kula, "Black Venture," *Pacific Islands Monthly* 46, no. 1 (January 1975): 51.
64. "A Creative Vein of Things," *UNISPAC* 7, no. 2 [1974]: 6–7; "Regional Creative Writing Workshop," 60–61.
65. Paul Sharrad, "Out of Africa: Literary Globalization in the Winds of Change," *South Atlantic Quarterly* 100, no. 3 (2001): 726.
66. Bro. C. Kulagoe, "Peace Signs," *Pacific Islands Monthly* 45, no. 7 (July 1974): 66.
67. Kulagoe, "Peace Signs," 66; T. S. Eliot, *Selected Poems* (London: Faber, 1954), 98.
68. Kulagoe, "Peace Signs," 66.
69. Kulagoe, "Peace Signs," 66.
70. Seri, "Monday Morning Street Ride," *Pacific Islands Monthly* 45, no. 7 (July 1974): 65.
71. Seri, "Monday Morning Street Ride," 65.
72. Peni Tutu'ila Malupo, "Creative Arts Workshop," *Pacific Islands Monthly* 45, no. 11 (November 1974): 61.
73. Tutu'ila Malupo, "Creative Arts Workshop," 61.
74. Ata Ma'ia'i, "Past the Old Track (An Exploration)," *Pacific Islands Monthly* 45, no. 2 (February 1974): 60.
75. Marjorie Crocombe, "Bush Beer," *Mana Annual*, 1974, 57.
76. Crocombe, "Introducing Mana," 69.
77. Florence (Johnny) Frisbie, *Miss Ulysses from Puka-Puka: The Autobiography of a South Sea Trader's Daughter* (New York: Macmillan, 1948); Albert Wendt, *Pouliuli* (1977; Hawaii: University of Hawai'i Press, 1980).
78. Crocombe, "The Healer."
79. Albert Wendt, "An Interview with Albert Wendt," by John Beston and Rose Marie Beston, *World Literature Written in English* 16, no. 1 (1977): 161.
80. Subramani, *South Pacific Literature: From Myth to Fabulation* (Suva: Institute of Pacific Studies, University of the South Pacific, 1985), 45, 72.
81. In a global context, see, for example, Susan Stanford Friedman, *Planetary Modernisms: Provocations on Modernity Across Time* (New York: Columbia University Press, 2015); Wai Chee Dimock, *Through Other Continents: American Literature Across Deep Time* (Princeton, NJ: Princeton University Press, 2008).
82. See Wendt, "An Interview with Albert Wendt," 160–61.

7. SUBRAMANI'S SUGARCANE GOTHIC: HAUNTING THE REGIONAL DREAM

1. Subramani, "Editor's Page," *Mana Review: A South Pacific Journal of Language and Literature* 1, no. 1 (1976): 5.
2. Subramani, *Wild Flowers* (Suva: University of the South Pacific Press, 2017), 266.
3. Course outline, "Pacific Literature in English," 1987, enclosed with letter from Subramani to Norman Ware, August 18, 1987, Donald E. Herdeck Records of Three

7. SUBRAMANI'S SUGARCANE GOTHIC

Continents Press and Passeggiata Press 1941–2007, 35.3, Harry Ransom Center, University of Texas at Austin.
4. Subramani, "Sautu," *Mana Annual*, 1974, 10. Subsequent citations will be made parenthetically within the text.
5. Maebh Long and Matthew Hayward, "For I Have Fed on Foreign Bread: Modernism, Colonial Education, and Fijian Literature," *Modernist Cultures* 15, no. 3 (2020): 395.
6. T. S. Eliot, *Selected Poems* (London: Faber, 1954), 65. Half a century on, the classic account of the modernist city remains Malcolm Bradbury, "The Cities of Modernism" (1976), in *Modernism*, ed. Malcolm Bradbury and James McFarlane (Harmondsworth: Penguin, 1986), 96–104. The classic account of urban alienation in European modernism remains chapter 20 of Raymond Williams, *The Country and the City* (New York: Oxford University Press, 1973).
7. Subramani, *The Fantasy Eaters* (Washington, DC: Three Continents, 1988), 26–27.
8. Joseph Conrad, *Heart of Darkness*, ed. Paul B. Armstrong (New York: Norton, 2006), 69.
9. Eugenia DeLamotte, "White Terror, Black Dreams: Constructions of Race in the Nineteenth Century," in *The Gothic Other: Racial and Social Constructions of the Literary Imagination*, ed. Ruth Bienstock Anolik and Douglas L. Howard (Jefferson, NC: McFarland, 2004), 26; Conrad, *Heart of Darkness*, 11, 73.
10. Conrad, *Heart of Darkness*, 17, 47.
11. On these specific authors, see Patrick Bridgwater, *Kafka, Gothic, and Fairytale* (Amsterdam: Rodopi, 2003); Dolores Flores-Silva and Keith Cartwright, "Faulkner and Modernist Gothic," in *The New William Faulkner Studies*, ed. Sarah Gleeson-White and Pardis Dabashi (Cambridge: Cambridge University Press, 2022), 36–50; Kelly Anspaugh, "'Three Mortal Hour[i]s': Female Gothic in Joyce's 'The Dead,'" *Studies in Short Fiction* 31, no. 1 (1994): 1–12; James F. Wurtz, "Scarce More a Corpse: Famine Memory and Representations of the Gothic in *Ulysses*," *Journal of Modern Literature* 29, no. 1 (2005): 102–17; Hannah Simpson, "'Strange Laughter': Post-Gothic Questions of Laughter and the Human in Samuel Beckett's Work," *Journal of Modern Literature* 40, no. 4 (2017): 1–19; Graham Fraser, "'No More Than Ghosts Make': The Hauntology and Gothic Minimalism of Beckett's Late Work," *Modern Fiction Studies* 46, no. 3 (2000): 772–85.
12. James Joyce, *Ulysses: A Critical and Synoptic Edition*, ed. Hans Walter Gabler with Wolfhard Steppe and Claus Melchior (New York: Garland, 1984), 7.522–24; T. S. Eliot, *The Waste Land* [1922], Norton Critical Edition, ed. Michael North (New York: Norton, 2001), 18.
13. Jerrold E. Hogle, "Introduction: The Gothic in Western Culture," in *The Cambridge Companion to Gothic Fiction*, ed. Jerrold E. Hogle (New York: Cambridge University Press, 2002), 2.
14. John Paul Riquelme, "Toward a History of Gothic and Modernism: Dark Modernity from Bram Stoker to Samuel Beckett," *Modern Fiction Studies* 46, no. 3 (2000): 586. A number of scholars have explored the specifically Anglo-Irish complexities of this gothic literature; in a modernist context, see, e.g., Jim Hansen, *Terror and Irish Modernism: The Gothic Tradition from Burke to Beckett* (Albany: State University of New York Press, 2009).

15. Maisha L. Wester, *African American Gothic: Screams from Shadowed Places* (New York: Palgrave Macmillan, 2012), 1–2.
16. Riquelme, "Toward a History of Gothic and Modernism," 585; Sidney W. Mintz, *Sweetness and Power: The Place of Sugar in Modern History* (New York: Viking Penguin, 1985), xxix.
17. Mintz, *Sweetness and Power*, 78.
18. On the relationship between early gothic and the Enlightenment, see David Punter, *The Literature of Terror: A History of Gothic Fictions from 1765 to the Present Day* (London: Longmans, 1980), chap. 2. For an introduction to the overlapping gothic and postcolonial challenges to post-Enlightenment tenets, see Andrew Smith and William Hughes, "Introduction: The Enlightenment Gothic and Postcolonialism," in *Empire and the Gothic: The Politics of Genre*, ed. Andrew Smith and William Hughes (Basingstoke: Palgrave Macmillan, 2003), 1–12.
19. Fred Botting, *Gothic* (London: Routledge, 1996), 1.
20. Leslie A. Fiedler, *Love and Death in the American Novel* (New York: Criterion, 1960), 125, 127.
21. Chattur Singh, "The Final Journey," *Mana Annual*, 1974, 28.
22. Caitlin Vandertop, "Ghosts of the Plantation: Sugar, Narrative Energetics, and Gothic Ecologies in Fiji," *Green Letters: Studies in Ecocriticism* 24, no. 2 (2020): 160.
23. Brij V. Lal and Barry Shineberg, "The Story of the Haunted Line: Totaram Sanadhya Recalls the Labour Lines in Fiji," *Journal of Pacific History* 26, no. 1 (1991): 107.
24. Vandertop, "Ghosts of the Plantation," 159. On Subramani's literary engagement with Sanadhya, see John O'Carroll, "Totaram's Ghost," *Australia Humanities Review* 52 (2012): 91–106.
25. Subramani, "The Mythical Quest: Literary Responses to the South Seas," *Mana Review* 1, no. 1 (1976): 7.
26. Subramani, "The Mythical Quest," 14.
27. Subramani, "Tell Me Where the Train Goes," *Mana Annual*, 1977, 77. Subsequent citations will be made parenthetically within the text.
28. For a historical account of the emergence of this political consciousness, including the act of urinating on the overseer, see Margaret Mishra, "A History of Fijian Women's Activism (1900–2010)," *Journal of Women's History* 24, no. 2 (2012): 118.
29. See, for example, Ahmed Ali, *Girmit: The Indenture Experience in Fiji* (Suva: Fiji Museum, 1979); and Ahmed Ali, *Plantations to Politics: Studies on Fiji Indians* (Suva: University of the South Pacific, 1980).
30. Lizabeth Paravisini-Gebert, "Colonial and Postcolonial Gothic: The Caribbean," in *The Cambridge Companion to Gothic Fiction*, ed. Jerrold E. Hogle (New York: Cambridge University Press, 2002), 233.
31. Paravisini-Gebert, "Colonial and Postcolonial Gothic," 233.
32. Paravisini-Gebert, "Colonial and Postcolonial Gothic," 253.
33. For example, the *Journal of Commonwealth Literature*, founded in 1966, gave prominence to Jean Rhys's writing, particularly *Wide Sargasso Sea*.
34. John O'Carroll spots similarities between Subramani's story and *Wide Sargasso Sea*—two tales of "a generational legacy contextualized by an event"—in an essay on Sanadhya's legacy in Indo-Fijian writing. O'Carroll, "Totaram's Ghost," 99.
35. Ken Gelder, "The Postcolonial Gothic," in *The Cambridge Companion to Modern Gothic*, ed. Jerrold E. Hogle (New York: Cambridge University Press, 2014), 195.

7. SUBRAMANI'S SUGARCANE GOTHIC

36. Jean Rhys, *Wide Sargasso Sea* (1966; New York: Norton, 1992), 106.
37. Rhys, *Wide Sargasso Sea*, 16.
38. On the relationship between Rhys's writing and her identity as a white Creole woman, with particular emphasis upon *Wide Sargasso Sea*, see Veronica Marie Gregg, *Jean Rhys's Historical Imagination: Reading and Writing the Creole* (Chapel Hill: University of North Carolina Press, 1995).
39. Several critics have noted this reference; see, e.g., Mary Lou Emery, "The Politics of Form: Jean Rhys's Social Vision in *Voyage in the Dark* and *Wide Sargasso Sea*," *Twentieth Century Literature* 28, no. 4 (1982): 425–27; Angelita Reyes, *Mothering Across Cultures: Postcolonial Representations* (Minneapolis: University of Minnesota Press, 2002), 105. On the etymology of "maroon," see *Dictionary of Caribbean Usage*, ed. Richard Allsopp (Oxford: Oxford University Press, 1996), s.v. "maroon."
40. On this complicated colonial history, see Mavis Christine Campbell, *The Maroons of Jamaica, 1655–1796: A History of Resistance, Collaboration, and Betrayal* (Granby, MA: Bergin & Garvey, 1988).
41. Brij V. Lal, "The Wreck of the *Syria*, 1884," in *The Indo-Fijian Experience*, ed. Subramani (St. Lucia, Queensland: University of Queensland Press, 1979), 28. The account here is drawn from Lal's authoritative history of the event.
42. Totaram Sanadhya, *My Twenty-One Years in the Fiji Islands, and The Story of the Haunted Line*, trans. John Dunham Kelly and Uttra Kumari Singh (1991; Suva: Fiji Museum, 2003), 35–37.
43. Ahmed Ali, "Indians in Fiji: An Interpretation," in *The Indo-Fijian Experience*, ed. Subramani (St. Lucia, Queensland: University of Queensland Press, 1979), 3.
44. Ali, "Indians in Fiji: An Interpretation," 3.
45. Subramani, ed., *The Indo-Fijian Experience* (St. Lucia, Queensland: University of Queensland Press, 1979).
46. Lal, "The Wreck of the *Syria*," 28.
47. Lal, "The Wreck of the *Syria*," 32, 34.
48. Though see also the qualifier to this received account, in Sudesh Mishra's recovery of forgotten acts of Fijian looting from the wreckage; Sudesh Mishra, "Acts of Rememory in Oceania," *symplokē* 26, no. 1–2 (2018): 28–30.
49. Lal, "The Wreck of the *Syria*," 35.
50. Lal, "The Wreck of the *Syria*," 38.
51. Lal, "The Wreck of the *Syria*," 27.
52. Qtd. in Lal, "The Wreck of the *Syria*," 36.
53. Julia Kristeva, *Powers of Horror: An Essay on Abjection*, trans. Leon S. Roudiez (New York: Columbia University Press, 1982), 2, 4, 1.
54. Jerrold E. Hogle, "Abjection as Gothic and the Gothic as Abjection," in *The Gothic and Theory: An Edinburgh Companion*, ed. Jerrold E. Hogle and Robert Miles (Edinburgh: Edinburgh University Press, 2019), 111.
55. Hogle, "Abjection as Gothic and the Gothic as Abjection," 112.
56. Gayatri Spivak, "Extreme Eurocentrism," *Lusitania* 1, no. 4 (1992): 59. On the postcolonial abject, see Sarah Ilott, *New Postcolonial British Genres: Shifting the Boundaries* (Basingstoke: Palgrave Macmillan, 2015), chap. 2; Andrew Hock Soon Ng, *Interrogating Interstices: Gothic Aesthetics in Postcolonial Asian and Asian American Literature* (Bern: Peter Lang, 2007).

57. Alison Rudd, "Postcolonial Gothic in and as Theory," in *The Gothic and Theory: An Edinburgh Companion*, ed. Jerrold E. Hogle and Robert Miles (Edinburgh: Edinburgh University Press, 2019), 75.
58. Kristeva, *Powers of Horror*, 4.
59. Vijay C. Mishra, "Indo-Fijian Fiction and the *Girmit* Ideology," in *The Indo-Fijian Experience*, ed. Subramani (St. Lucia, Queensland: University of Queensland Press, 1979), 171.
60. Mishra, "Indo-Fijian Fiction and the *Girmit* Ideology," 171.
61. Mishra, "Indo-Fijian Fiction and the *Girmit* Ideology," 172.
62. Mishra, "Indo-Fijian Fiction and the *Girmit* Ideology," 172.
63. Qtd. in Brij V. Lal, *Islands of Turmoil: Elections and Politics in Fiji* (Canberra: Australian National University Press, 2006), 41.
64. Lal, *Islands of Turmoil: Elections and Politics in Fiji*, 38.
65. Lal, *Islands of Turmoil: Elections and Politics in Fiji*, 189.
66. Marjorie Crocombe, "The South Pacific Festival of Arts," *Mana Annual*, 1973, 69.
67. Botting, *Gothic*, 2.
68. As an entry point to gothic doubling, see Dale Townshend, "Doubles," in *The Encyclopedia of the Gothic*, ed. William Hughes, David Punter, and Andrew Smith (Oxford: Blackwell, 2013), 189–95.
69. Vijay Mishra, "The Girmit Ideology Revisited," in *Reworlding: The Literature of the Indian Diaspora*, ed. Emmanuel S. Nelson (New York: Greenwood, 1992), 7.
70. Mishra, "The Girmit Ideology Revisited," 6.
71. Marjorie Crocombe, letter, *Pacific Islands Monthly* 44, no. 6 (June 1973): 30.
72. Albert Wendt, "Towards a New Oceania," *Mana Review: A South Pacific Journal of Language and Literature* 1, no. 1 (1976): 53.

CODA: THE STORIES OF MULTITUDES TO COME

1. Albert Wendt, *Pouliuli* (1977; Hawaii: University of Hawai'i Press, 1980), 144. Subsequent citations will be made parenthetically within the text.
2. Anirudh Singh, "The Screaming Man," *UNISPAC* 3, no. 3 (1970): 15.
3. Ulli Beier, "Papua New Guinea: The Voices of Independence," in *Voices of Independence: New Black Writing from Papua New Guinea*, ed. Ulli Beier (St. Lucia: University of Queensland Press, 1980), xii.
4. Beier, "Papua New Guinea: The Voices of Independence," xii–xiii.
5. Albert Wendt, ed., *Lali: A Pacific Anthology* (Auckland: Longman Paul, 1980), xvii.
6. Beier, "Papua New Guinea: The Voices of Independence," xii–xiii.
7. Nigel Krauth, "'Unfolding Like Petals': The Developing Definition of the Writer's Role in Modern Papua New Guinean Literature," in *Readings in Pacific Literature*, ed. Paul Sharrad (Wollongong: New Literatures Research Centre, 1993), 52.
8. Subramani, *South Pacific Literature: From Myth to Fabulation* (Suva: Institute of Pacific Studies, University of the South Pacific, 1985), xiv, 153.
9. Raymond Pillai, "Directions in Fiji and Pacific Literature," in *Class and Culture and the South Pacific*, ed. Antony Hooper, Steve Britton, Ron Crocombe, Judith Huntsman, and Cluny Macpherson (Suva: Centre for Pacific Studies, University of Auckland and Institute of Pacific Studies, University of the South Pacific: 1987), 106.

CODA: THE STORIES OF MULTITUDES TO COME

10. Pillai, "Directions in Fiji and Pacific Literature," 109.
11. Paul Sharrad, "Literary Legacies: Faltering Feet; Dancing a Pen to a National Beat," in *Lines Across the Sea: Colonial Inheritance in the Post Colonial Pacific*, ed. Brij V. Lal and Hank Nelson (Brisbane: Pacific History Association, 1995), 200.
12. Sharrad, "Literary Legacies, Faltering Feet," 204.
13. Subramani, *South Pacific Literature*, xi; Konai Helu Thaman, "Interview with Konai Helu Thaman," *Mana: A South Pacific Journal of Language and Literature* 9, no. 2 (1992): 9–10; Epeli Hauʻofa, "Our Sea of Islands," in *A New Oceania: Rediscovering Our Sea of Islands*, ed. Eric Waddell, Vijay Naidu, and Epeli Hauʻofa (Suva: University of the South Pacific School of Social and Economic Development, in association with Beake House, 1993), 9.
14. Witi Ihimaera, ed., *Te Ao Mārama: Contemporary Māori Writing*, vol. 3, *Te Puawaitanga o te korero: The Flowering* (Auckland: Reed, 1993), 15.
15. Frank Stewart, Kareva Mateata-Allain, and Alexander Dale Mawyer, eds., *Varua Tupu: New Writing from French Polynesia* (Honolulu: University of Hawaiʻi Press, 2006), xviii.
16. Qtd. in George H. Lewis, "Da Kine Sounds: The Function of Music as Social Protest in the New Hawaiian Renaissance," *American Music* 2, no. 2 (1984): 41.
17. Julian Makaʻa and Stephen Oxenham, "The Voice in the Shadow: A Survey of Writing in Solomon Islands," *Pacific Moana Quarterly* 9, no. 1 (1985): 6.
18. Sia Figiel, *The Girl in the Moon Circle* (Suva: Mana Publications, 1996), 126.
19. Steven Winduo, review of *Gutsini Poasa (Rough Seas)* by Regis Stella, *Contemporary Pacific* 12, no. 2: 551.
20. Regis Stella, *Gutsini Posa (Rough Seas)* (Suva: Mana Publications, 1999), 22, 23.
21. Stella, *Gutsini Posa*, 56.
22. Stella, *Gutsini Posa*, 41.
23. Stella, *Gutsini Posa*, 32.
24. Whiti Hereaka, *Kurangaituku* (Wellington: Huia, 2022).
25. Mary Rokonadravu, "Famished Eels," *Granta*, online edition, April 28, 2015, https://granta.com/famished-eels/.
26. Rokonadravu, "Famished Eels."
27. Rokonadravu, "Famished Eels."
28. Jenny Bennett-Tuionetoa, "Matalasi," *Granta*, online edition, June 27, 2018, https://granta.com/matalasi/.
29. Bennett-Tuionetoa, "Matalasi."
30. Bennett-Tuionetoa, "Matalasi."
31. See, e.g., Niko Besnier and Kalissa Alexeyeff, eds., *Gender on the Edge: Transgender, Gay, and Other Pacific Islanders* (Honolulu: University of Hawaiʻi Press, 2014). For an Indigenous view, see Dan Taulapapa McMullin and Yuki Kihara, eds., *Samoan Queer Lives* (Auckland: Little Island, 2018).
32. Mary Rokonadravu, "The Nightwatch," *Granta*, online edition, May 24, 2022, https://granta.com/the-nightwatch/.
33. Rokonadravu, "The Nightwatch."
34. Mary Rokonadravu, "An Interview with Mary Rokonadravu, Winner of the Commonwealth Short Story Prize for the Pacific Region," Pacific Cooperation Foundation, https://www.pcf.org.nz/news/ns7r6lwrnpdlrzz-h82c8-wg6js-r7d27-fmyxz.

35. Epeli Hau'ofa, *Kisses in the Nederends* (1987; Honolulu: University of Hawai'i Press, 1995), v.
36. Konai Helu Thaman, "You, the Choice of My Parents," *Pacific Islands Monthly* 44, no. 7 (July 1973): 72.
37. Helu Thaman, "You, the Choice of My Parents," 72.
38. Bennett-Tuionetoa, "Matalasi."
39. Rokonadravu, "Famished Eels."
40. Rokonadravu, "Famished Eels."

BIBLIOGRAPHY

"A Creative Vein of Things." *UNISPAC* 7, no. 2 [1974]: 6–7.
Abrahams, Peter. *A Wreath for Udomo*. London: Faber and Faber, 1956.
Achebe, Chinua. "An Image of Africa." *Massachusetts Review* 18, no. 4 (1977): 782–94.
———. *Things Fall Apart*. 1958. London: Penguin, 2010.
Aikman, Colin M. "Establishment: 1968–74." In *Pacific Universities: Achievements, Problems, Prospects*, ed. Ron Crocombe and Malama Meleisea, 35–52. Suva: Institute of Pacific Studies; University of the South Pacific, 1988.
Ali, Ahmed. *Girmit: The Indenture Experience in Fiji*. Suva: Fiji Museum, 1979.
———. "Indians in Fiji: An Interpretation." In *The Indo-Fijian Experience*, ed. Subramani, 3–25. St Lucia: University of Queensland Press, 1979.
———. *Plantations to Politics: Studies on Fiji Indians*. Suva: University of the South Pacific, 1980.
Allen, Tim. "The Rage of Okot p'Bitek: Colonial Perspectives and a Failed Oxford Doctorate." *LSE Blogs*, April 12, 2019. https://blogs.lse.ac.uk/africaatlse/2019/07/12/rage-okot-pbitek-colonial-perspectives/.
Alvarez, A. *Beyond All This Fiddle: Essays, 1955–1967*. London: Allen Lane, 1968.
Anspaugh, Kelly. "'Three Mortal Hour[i]s': Female Gothic in Joyce's 'The Dead.'" *Studies in Short Fiction* 31, no. 1 (1994): 1–12.
Arvidson, K. O. "Aspects of Writing in the South Pacific." *Mana Annual*, 1973, 5–8.
Auden, W. H. "Private Pleasures." *Scrutiny*, September 1932, 191–94.
Auvaʻa, Faʻalafua L. "The Cultural Perspective of Albert Wendt's Novel *Pouliuli*." Master's thesis, Utah State University, 1997.
Baba, Tupeni, Ron Crocombe, and Malama Meleisea. "The Development of Higher Education in the Pacific Islands." In *Pacific Universities: Achievements, Problems, Prospects*, ed. Ron Crocombe and Malama Meleisea, 20–29. Suva: Institute of Pacific Studies; University of the South Pacific, 1988.

BIBLIOGRAPHY

Baer, Ben Conisbee. *Indigenous Vanguards: Education, National Liberation, and the Limits of Modernism.* New York: Columbia University Press, 2019.
Baldwin, James. *The Fire Next Time.* London: Michael Joseph, 1968.
Ballantyne, R. M. *The Coral Island: A Tale of the Pacific Ocean.* 1857. London: Ward, Lock & Co., 1901.
Ballard, J. A. "Students and Politics: Papua New Guinea." *Journal of Commonwealth and Comparative Politics* 15, no. 2 (1977): 112–26.
Banivanua Mar, Tracey. *Decolonisation and the Pacific: Indigenous Globalisation and the Ends of Empire.* Cambridge: Cambridge University Press, 2016.
Barker, Alan. "Education and the Critic." *Mana: A South Pacific Journal of Language and Literature* 2, no. 2 (1978): 60–77.
Barnhisel, Greg. *Cold War Modernists: Art, Literature, and American Cultural Diplomacy.* New York: Columbia University Press, 2015.
———. "Modernism and the MFA." In *After the Program Era: The Past, Present, and Future of Creative Writing in the University*, ed. Loren Glass, 55–66. Iowa City: University of Iowa Press, 2016.
Beck, Harald. "Salty Missionaries." *James Joyce Online Notes* 8 (2015), https://www.jjon.org/joyce-s-environs/missionaries.
Beeby, C. E. *The Biography of an Idea: Beeby on Education.* Wellington: New Zealand Council for Educational Research, 1992.
———. *The Quality of Education in Developing Countries.* Cambridge, MA: Harvard University Press, 1966.
Beier, Ulli. "The Beginnings of Literature in New Guinea." In *Black Writing from New Guinea*, ed. Ulli Beier, xii–xiv. St Lucia: University of Queensland Press, 1973.
———. "The Cultural Dilemma of Papua New Guinea." *Meanjin Quarterly* 34, no. 3 (1975): 307–8.
———. *Decolonising the Mind: The Impact of Culture and Identity in Papua New Guinea, 1971–1974.* Canberra: Pandanus, 2005.
———, ed. *Five New Guinea Plays.* Milton, Queensland: Jacaranda, 1971.
———. *In a Colonial University.* Bayreuth: Iwalewa-Haus, 1993.
———. "Literature in New Guinea." *Hudson Review* 24, no. 1 (1971): 119–27.
———, ed. *The Origin of Life and Death: African Creation Myths.* London: Heinemann, 1966.
———, ed. "Papua New Guinea: The Voices of Independence." In *Voices of Independence: New Black Writing from Papua New Guinea*, ed. Ulli Beier, vi–xvi. St. Lucia: University of Queensland Press, 1980.
———. *The Return of Shango: The Theatre of Duro Ladipo.* Bayreuth: Iwalewa-Haus, 1994.
———. "Review: Yirawala: Artist and Man, by Sandra Le Brun Holmes." *Kovave* 4, no. 2 (1973): 55–56.
———, ed. *Three Nigerian Plays.* London: Longmans, Green and Co., 1967.
———, ed. *When the Moon Was Big: Legends from New Guinea.* Sydney: Collins, 1972.
———, ed. *Words of Paradise: Poetry of Papua New Guinea.* Melbourne: Sun, 1972.
Bennett-Tuionetoa, Jenny. "Matalasi." *Granta*, online ed. June 27, 2018. https://granta.com/matalasi/.
Benson, Peter. *Black Orpheus, Transition, and Modern Cultural Awakening in Africa.* Berkeley: University of California Press, 1986.

BIBLIOGRAPHY

Besnier, Niko, and Kalissa Alexeyeff, eds. *Gender on the Edge: Transgender, Gay, and Other Pacific Islanders*. Honolulu: University of Hawai'i Press, 2014.
Beston, John. "Chill and the Flame: The Poetry of John Kasaipwalova." *Meanjin Quarterly* 40, no. 4 (1981): 480-90.
Bishop, Elizabeth. *North and South*. Boston: Houghton Mifflin, 1946.
Borchard, Terrance, and Philip Gibbs. "Parallelism and Poetics in Tindi Narratives Sung in the Ipili Language." In *Sung Tales from the Papua New Guinea Highlands: Studies in Form, Meaning, and Sociocultural Context*, ed. Don Niles and Alan Rumsey, 165-95. Canberra: Australian National University, 2011.
Botting, Fred. *Gothic*. London: Routledge, 1996.
Bradbury, Malcolm. "The Cities of Modernism." 1976. In *Modernism*, ed. Malcolm Bradbury and James McFarlane, 96-104. Harmondsworth: Penguin, 1986.
Brash, Elton. "Creative Writing, Literature and Self Expression in Papua New Guinea." In *Teaching Literature in Papua New Guinea*, ed. E. Brash and M. Greicus, 35-42. Port Moresby: UPNG, 1972.
Brathwaite, Edward Kamau. *History of the Voice: The Development of Nation Language in Anglophone Caribbean Poetry*. London: New Beacon, 1984.
Brecht, Bertold. "Against Lukács." 1977. In *Aesthetics and Politics*, ed. Ronald Taylor, trans. Stuart Hood, 68-85. London: Verso, 1980.
Bridgwater, Patrick. *Kafka, Gothic, and Fairytale*. Amsterdam: Rodopi, 2003.
Brosnahan, L. F. Letter. *UNISPAC* 4, no. 4 (1971): 4-6.
Brown, Kirby, Stephen Ross, and Alana Sayer. *The Routledge Handbook of North American Indigenous Modernisms*. New York: Routledge, 2023.
Brumby, Ed. "Ulli Beier: A Personal Recollection." *Sumatin: A Magazine of Papua New Guinean Writing* 2 (2022): 15-16.
Buluna, M. "The Role of the Student in Niugini Politics." In *The Politics of Melanesia: Papers Delivered at the Fourth Waigani Seminar*, ed. Marion W. Ward, 303-14. Canberra and Port Moresby: Australian National University and the University of Papua New Guinea, 1970.
Buurma, Rachel Sagner, and Laura Heffernan. "The Classroom in the Canon: T. S. Eliot's Modern English Literature Extension Course for Working People and *The Sacred Wood*." *PMLA* 133, no. 2 (2018): 264-81.
———. *The Teaching Archive: A New History for Literary Study*. Chicago: University of Chicago Press, 2020.
Campbell, Mavis Christine. *The Maroons of Jamaica, 1655-1796: A History of Resistance, Collaboration, and Betrayal*. Granby, MA: Bergin & Garvey, 1988.
Camus, Albert. *The Myth of Sisyphus*. Trans. Justin O'Brien. Harmondsworth: Penguin, 1979.
Carpenter, H. W. H. Auden: A Biography. London: Allen & Unwin, 1981.
Césaire, Aimé. *The Original 1939 Notebook of a Return to the Native Land*. Ed. and trans. A. James Arnold and Clayton Eshleman. Middleton, CT: Wesleyan University Press, 2013.
Chatterjee, Kalyan. "Papua New Guinea Literature: Innocence and Self-Knowledge." *Pacific Islands Communication Journal* 14, no. 1 (1985): 1-11.
Chinweizu, Onwuchekwa Jemie, and Ihechukwu Madubuike. *Toward the Decolonization of African Literature*. Vol. 1: *African Fiction and Poetry and Their Critics*. Washington, DC: Howard University Press, 1983.

Christie, William. "'The Essential Cambridge in Spite of Cambridge': F. R. Leavis in the Antipodes." *Australian Humanities Review* 68 (2021): 1–15.
Cleaver, Eldridge. *Soul on Ice*. 1968. New York: Delta, 1992.
Cliff, Michelle. *Abeng*. New York: Crossing, 1984.
Conrad, Joseph. *Heart of Darkness*. 1899. Ed. Paul B. Armstrong. New York: Norton, 2006.
Crocombe, Marjorie. "Bush Beer." *Mana Annual*, 1974, 57.
———. "The Healer," *Kovave* 2, no. 1 (1979): 5–12.
———. "Introducing Mana." *Pacific Islands Monthly* 44, no. 3 (March 1973): 69.
———. Letter. *Pacific Islands Monthly* 44, no. 6 (June 1973): 30.
———. "Mana." *Pacific Islands Monthly* 44, no. 7 (July 1973): 65.
———. "Mana." *Pacific Islands Monthly* 45, no. 9 (September 1974): 60.
———. "Mana and Creative Regional Cooperation." *Mana Annual* (1977): 5–6.
———. "Mana Forum." *Mana* 3, no. 1 (1978): 8–11.
———. "Nero." *Kovave* 1, no. 1 (1969): 37–42.
———. "The South Pacific Festival of Arts." *Mana Annual* (1973): 69–70.
———. "Writers Workshop." *Pacific Islands Monthly* 45, no. 11 (November 1974): 60.
Crocombe, Ron, and Malama Meleisea. "Achievements, Problems and Prospects: The Future of University Education in the South Pacific." In *Pacific Universities: Achievements, Problems, Prospects*, ed. Ron Crocombe and Malama Meleisea, 341–87. Suva: Institute of Pacific Studies, 1988.
Daugherty, Beth Rigel. "The Streets of London: Virginia Woolf's Development of a Pedagogical Style." In *Woolf and the City*, ed. Elizabeth F. Evans and Sarah E. Cornish, 191–94. Liverpool: Liverpool University Press, 2010.
de Gennaro, Mara. "A Return to *The Waste Land* After Césaire's *Cahier*." *Comparative Literature Studies* 52, no. 3 (2015): 479–509.
DeLamotte, Eugenia. "White Terror, Black Dreams: Constructions of Race in the Nineteenth Century." In *The Gothic Other: Racial and Social Constructions of the Literary Imagination*, ed. Ruth Bienstock Anolik and Douglas L. Howard, 17–31. Jefferson, NC: McFarland, 2004.
DeLoughrey, Elizabeth. *Routes and Roots: Navigating Caribbean and Pacific Island Literatures*. Honolulu: University of Hawai'i Press, 2007.
Demata, Massimiliano. "Discovering Eastern Horrors: Beckford, Maturin and the Discourse of Travel Literature." In *Empire and the Gothic: The Politics of Genre*, ed. Andrew Smith and William Hughes, 13–34. Basingstoke: Palgrave Macmillan, 2003.
Devi, Salochana. "Man." *Pacific Islands Monthly* 44, no. 4 (April 1973): 66.
Dictionary of Caribbean Usage. Ed. Richard Allsopp. Oxford: Oxford University Press, 1996.
Dimock, Wai Chee. *Through Other Continents: American Literature Across Deep Time*. Princeton, NJ: Princeton University Press, 2008.
Docker, John. "The Neocolonial Assumption in University Teaching of English." In *South Pacific Images*, ed. Chris Tiffin, 26–31. Brisbane: South Pacific Association for Commonwealth Literature and Language Studies, 1978.
Doyle, Laura. "Geomodernism, Postcoloniality, and Women's Writing." In *The Cambridge Companion to Modernist Women Writers*, ed. Maria Tova Linett, 129–45. Cambridge: Cambridge University Press, 2010.
"Drama & Arts—A Lively Afterlife?" *Nilaidat* 2, no. 3 (June 1969): 13–14.

BIBLIOGRAPHY

Duodo, Cameron. *The Gab Boys*. Bungay: Richard Clay, 1967.
"Editorial." *Kovave* 1 (1968): 4.
"Editorial." *Papua New Guinea Writing* 23 (September 1976): 2.
"Editorial Board note." *Sinnet* 1, no. 1 (1980): 4.
Eliot, T. S. *For Lancelot Andrewes: Essays on Style and Order*. London: Faber and Gwyer, 1928.
Eliot, T. S. "The Metaphysical Poets." In *Selected Essays*. London: Faber and Faber, 1953.
Eliot, T. S. *Selected Poems*. London: Faber, 1954.
Eliot, T. S. "Ulysses, Order, and Myth." In *Selected Prose of T. S. Eliot*, ed. Frank Kermode, 177–78. New York: Harcourt Brace Jovanovich, 1975.
Eliot, T. S. *The Waste Land*. 1922. Ed. Michael North. New York: Norton, 2001.
Ellerman, Evelyn. "Intertextuality and the Fiction of Camus and Wendt." In *Comparative Literature East and West: Traditions and Trends: Selected Conference Papers*, ed. Cornelia N. Moore and Raymond Moody, 43–50. Honolulu: University of Hawai'i College of Languages, Linguistics, and Literature, and the East-West Center, 1989.
———. "Learning to be a Writer in Papua New Guinea." *History of Intellectual Culture* 8, no. 1 (2008–2009): 1–16.
———. "Literary Institutions in Papua New Guinea." PhD diss., University of Alberta, 1994.
———. "The Literature Bureau: African Influence in Papua New Guinea." *Research in African Literatures* 26, no. 4 (1995): 206–15.
Ellison, Ralph. *Invisible Man*. New York: Random House, 1952.
Ellmann, Richard, and Charles Feidelson. Preface to *The Modern Tradition: Backgrounds of Modern Literature*, v–ix. New York: Oxford University Press, 1965.
Emery, Mary Lou. "The Politics of Form: Jean Rhys's Social Vision in *Voyage in the Dark* and *Wide Sargasso Sea*." *Twentieth Century Literature* 28, no. 4 (1982): 425–27.
Enos, Apisai. "Niugini Literature." *Kovave* 4, no. 1 (1972): 46–49.
Esslin, Martin. *The Theatre of the Absurd*. London: Eyre Methuen, 1974.
"Exploitation." *UNISPAC* 7, no. 2 [1974]: 1, 20.
Fakamuria, Kenneth. "The First Coconut." *Pacific Islands* 44, no. 9 (September 1973): 62.
Fiedler, Leslie A. *Love and Death in the American Novel*. New York: Criterion, 1960.
Field, Roger. "'Across the River and Into the Trees, I Thought': Hemingway's Impact on Alex La Guma." In *Hemingway and the Black Renaissance*, ed. Gary Edward Holcomb and Charles Scruggs, 214–28. Columbus: Ohio State University Press, 2010.
Figiel, Sia. *The Girl in the Moon Circle*. Suva: Mana Publications, 1996.
———. *To a Young Artist in Contemplation: Poetry and Prose*. Suva: Pacific Writing Forum, USP, 1998.
Filres, Alan. *Counter-Revolution of the Word: The Conservative Attack on Modern Poetry, 1945–1960*. Chapel Hill: University of North Carolina Press, 2012.
Fiske, Shanyn. "From Ritual to the Archaic in Modernism: Frazer, Harrison, Freud, and the Persistence of Myth." In *A Handbook of Modernism Studies*, ed. Jean-Michel Rabaté, 173–91. London: John Wiley and Sons, 2013.
Flores-Silva, Dolores, and Keith Cartwright. "Faulkner and Modernist Gothic." In *The New William Faulkner Studies*, ed. Sarah Gleeson-White and Pardis Dabashi, 36–50. Cambridge: Cambridge University Press, 2022.

BIBLIOGRAPHY

Forward, Toby. "Being Rahila Khan," *London Review of Books*, February 4, 1988. https://www.lrb.co.uk/the-paper/v10/n03/toby-forward/diary.

Fraser, Graham. "'No More Than Ghosts Make': The Hauntology and Gothic Minimalism of Beckett's Late Work." *Modern Fiction Studies* 46, no. 3 (2000): 772–85.

Freire, Paulo. *The Pedagogy of the Oppressed*. Trans. Myra Bergman Ramos. New York: Continuum, 2005.

Friedman, Susan Stanford. *Planetary Modernisms: Provocations on Modernity Across Time*. New York: Columbia University Press, 2015.

Frisbie, Florence (Johnny). *Miss Ulysses from Puka-Puka: The Autobiography of a South Sea Trader's Daughter*. New York: Macmillan, 1948.

Garae, Leonard. "Beware, The Worst Is Still to Come." *Pacific Islands Monthly* 45, no. 9 (September 1974): 60.

Gelder, Ken. "The Postcolonial Gothic." In *The Cambridge Companion to Modern Gothic*, ed. Jerrold E. Hogle, 191–207. New York: Cambridge University Press, 2014.

Gibbs, James. *Nkyin-Kyin: Essays on the Ghanaian Theatre*. Leiden: Brill, 2009.

Gikandi, Simon. "African Literature and Modernity." In *Texts, Tasks, and Theories: Versions and Subversions in African Literatures*, ed. Tobias Robert Klein, Ulrike Auga, and Viola Prüschenk, 3:3–19. New York: Rodopi, 2007.

Gikandi, Simon. "Cultural Translation and the African Self: A (Post)colonial Case Study." *Interventions* 3, no. 3 (2001): 355–75.

———. "Foreword: On Afropolitanism." In *Negotiating Afropolitanism: Essays on Borders and Spaces in Contemporary African Literature and Folklore*, ed. Jennifer Wawrzinek and J. K. S. Makokha, 9–11. Leiden: Brill Rodopi, 2011.

———. *Writing in Limbo: Modernism and Caribbean Literature*. Ithaca, NY: Cornell University Press, 1992.

Gilbert, Michele V. "Letters." *African Arts* 9, no. 2 (1976): 2–3.

Ginsberg, Allen. *Howl and Other Poems*. San Francisco: City Lights, 1973.

Goodwin, Ken. "Bulls and Prophets in Papua New Guinea." *Journal of Postcolonial Writing* 16, no. 1 (1977): 169–78.

———. "Invective and Obliqueness in Political Poetry: Kasaipwalova, Brathwaite, and Soyinka." In *Awakened Consciousness: Studies in Commonwealth Literature*, ed. C. D. Narasimhaiah, 251–60. New Delhi: Sterling, 1978.

———. "No Stagnant Neutrality: John Kasaipwalova's Poems." *Kovave* 4, no. 1 (1972): 52.

Gordon, Lewis R., and Jane Anna Gordon. "Introduction: Not Only the Master's Tools." 2006. In *Not Only the Master's Tools: African-American Studies in Theory and Practice*, ed. Lewis R. Gordon and Jane Anna Gordon, ix–xii. London: Routledge, 2016.

Graff, Gerald. *Professing Literature: An Institutional History*. Chicago: University of Chicago Press, 1987.

Gregg, Veronica Marie. *Jean Rhys's Historical Imagination: Reading and Writing the Creole*. Chapel Hill, NC: University of North Carolina Press, 1995.

Griffen, Vanessa. "A Double Life." *Mana: A South Pacific Journal of Language and Literature* 4, no. 2 (1979): 15–16.

———. "Marama." *UNISPAC* 4, no. 3 (1971): 25.

Gunther, J. T. "More English, More Teachers: Putting a Cat Among the Pidgins." *New Guinea* 4, no. 2 (1969): 43–53.

Habu, Mostyn. "Creative Writing in the Solomons." *Mana* 4, no. 1 (1979): 1–3.

BIBLIOGRAPHY

Hampson, Robert. "Joseph Conrad." In *The Cambridge Companion to English Novelists*, ed. Adrian Poole, 290–308. Cambridge: Cambridge University Press, 2009.
Hanneken, Jaime. "Scandal, Choice and the Economy of Minority Literature." *Paragraph* 34, no. 1 (2011): 48–65.
Hannett, Leo. "The Church and Nationalism." In *The Politics of Melanesia: Papers Delivered at the Fourth Waigani Seminar*, ed. Marion W. Ward, 654–65. Canberra and Port Moresby: ANU and UPNG, 1970.
———. "Niugini Black Power." *Nilaidat*, May 1971, 1.
———. "Niugini Black Power." In *Racism: The Australian Experience. A Study of Race Prejudice in Australia*, ed. F. S. Stevens, 41–51. Sydney: Australia and New Zealand Book Company, 1972.
———. "The Niugini Black Power." In *Tertiary Students and the Politics of Papua New Guinea: Papers Delivered at the Second Seminar of Papua New Guinea Tertiary Students, Held at the Papua New Guinea Institute of Technology, Lae, 23rd–25th August, 1971*, 1–7. Lae: Papua New Guinea Institute of Technology, 1971.
Hansen, Jim. *Terror and Irish Modernism: The Gothic Tradition from Burke to Beckett*. Albany: State University of New York Press, 2009.
Harney, Elizabeth, and Ruth B. Philips. *Mapping Modernisms: Art, Indigeneity, Colonialism*. Durham, NC: Duke University Press, 2018.
Hauʻofa, Epeli. *Kisses in the Nederends*. 1987. Honolulu: University of Hawaiʻi Press, 1995.
———. "Our Sea of Islands." In *A New Oceania: Rediscovering Our Sea of Islands*, ed. Eric Waddell, Vijay Naidu, and Epeli Hauʻofa, 2–17. Suva: University of the South Pacific School of Social and Economic Development, in association with Beake House, 1993.
———. "'We Were Still Papuans': An Interview with Epeli Hauʻofa." Interviewed by Nicholas Thomas. *Contemporary Pacific* 24, no. 1 (2012): 120–32.
Hayward, Matthew. "'Our Own Identity': Albert Wendt, James Joyce, and the Indigenisation of Influence." In *New Oceania: Modernisms and Modernities in the Pacific*, ed. Matthew Hayward and Maebh Long, 81–99. New York: Routledge, 2019.
Hayward, Matthew, and Maebh Long, eds. *New Oceania: Modernisms and Modernities in the Pacific*. New York: Routledge, 2019.
———. "Towards an Oceanian Modernism." *Modernism/modernity* 28, no. 2 (2021): 209–28.
Heffernan, Laura. "Axel's Classroom." *Modernist Cultures* 14, no. 3 (2019): 316–36.
Helu Thaman, Konai. "Decolonizing Pacific Studies: Indigenous Perspectives, Knowledge and Wisdom in Higher Education." *Contemporary Pacific* 15, no. 1 (2003): 1–17.
———. "Interview with Konai Helu Thaman." *Mana: A South Pacific Journal of Language and Literature* 9, no. 2 (1992): 5–10.
———. "Of Daffodils and *Heilala*: Understanding (Cultural) Context in Pacific Literature." In *Navigating Islands and Continents: Conversations and Contestations in and Around the Pacific: Selected Essays*, ed. Cynthia Franklin, Ruth Hsu, and Suzanne Kosanke, 40–50. Honolulu: University of Hawaiʻi; East-West Center, 2000.
———. "Resistance." *Pacific Islands Monthly* 45, no. 1 (January 1974): 61.
———. "You, the Choice of My Parents." *Pacific Islands Monthly* 44, no. 7 (July 1973): 72.
Helu, Futa, Epeli Hauʻofa, Thomas Schneider, and Konai Helu Thaman. "Foreword." *Faikava* 1 (1978): 1.

Helu, Futa. "The Kakala." *Pacific Islands Monthly* 44, no. 3 (March 1973): 70–71.
Helu, Tevita 'O. "Ko ha faka'anau / In a Longing." *Pacific Islands Monthly* 44, no. 12 (December 1973): 64.
Hemans, Felicia Dorothea. *The Poetical Works of Felicia Dorothea Hemans.* London: Oxford University Press, 1914.
Hereaka, Whiti. *Kurangaituku.* Wellington, NZ: Huia, 2022.
Heron, Jonathan, and Nicholas Johnson. "Beckettian Pedagogies: Learning Through Samuel Beckett." *Journal of Beckett Studies* 29, no. 1 (2020): 42–62.
Hogle, Jerrold E. "Abjection as Gothic and the Gothic as Abjection." In *The Gothic and Theory: An Edinburgh Companion*, ed. Jerrold E. Hogle and Robert Miles, 108–25. Edinburgh: Edinburgh University Press, 2019.
———. "Introduction: The Gothic in Western Culture." In *The Cambridge Companion to Gothic Fiction*, ed. Jerrold E. Hogle, 2. New York: Cambridge University Press, 2002.
Hones, Andy. *Outside Literary Studies: Black Criticism and the University.* Chicago: University of Chicago Press, 2022.
Howarth, Peter. "Introduction: Modernism and/as Pedagogy." *Modernist Cultures* 14, no. 3 (2019): 261–90.
———, ed. "Modernism and/as Pedagogy." *Modernist Cultures* 14, no. 3 (2019).
Howe, Irving. "The Culture of the Modern." In *Decline of the New.* London: Victor Gollancz, 1971.
Howie-Willis, Ian. *A Thousand Graduates: Conflict in University Development in Papua New Guinea, 1961–1976.* Canberra: Australian National University, 1980.
Hughes, Langston. "Cowards from the Colleges." *Crisis* 41, no. 8 (1934): 226–28.
Hurrey, W. "The Demonstration." *Nilaidat* 1, no.7 (1968): 5–6.
Iakavi, Jerry. "The Mysterious Maidens from the East." *Pacific Islands Monthly* 44, no. 7 (July 1973): 70.
Ihimaera, Witi, ed. *Te Ao Mārama: Contemporary Māori Writing.* Vol. 3: *Te Puawaitanga o te korero: The Flowering.* Auckland: Reed, 1993.
Ilott, Sarah. *New Postcolonial British Genres: Shifting the Boundaries.* Basingstoke: Palgrave Macmillan, 2015.
Inglis, K. S. "Education on the Frontier: The First Ten Years of the University of Papua New Guinea." *Critical Studies in Education* 22, no. 1 (1980): 61–92.
Irele, F. Abiola. *The African Imagination: Literature in Africa and the Black Diaspora.* New York: Oxford University Press, 2001.
———. "Aimé Césaire: An Approach to his Poetry." In *Introduction to African Literature: An Anthology of Critical Writing on African and Afro-American Literature and Oral Tradition*, ed. Ulli Beier, 59–68. London: Longmans Green and Co., 1967.
———. "'Papuan Parallels,' Review of *Kiki*, by Albert Maori Kiki, *Reluctant Flame* by John Kasaipwalova, *High Water* by Apisai Enos, *The Crocodile* by Vincent Eri, *Kovave*, *Five New Guinea Plays* ed. by Ulli Beier." *Transition* 9, no. 44 (1974): 50–51.
Itaia, Maunaa. "My Educated Son." *Pacific Islands Monthly* 44, no. 5 (May 1973): 73.
Ivaiti, Harry. "Tangaroa." *Mana Annual*, 1973, 100.
Izevbaye, Dan. "West African Literature in English: Beginnings to the Mid-Seventies." In *The Cambridge History of African and Caribbean Literature*, ed. F. Abiola Irele and Simon Gikandi, 472–503. Cambridge: Cambridge University Press, 2004.

BIBLIOGRAPHY

James, C. L. R. "Appendix: From Toussaint L'Ouverture to Fidel Castro." In *The Black Jacobins: Toussaint L'Ouverture and the San Domingo Revolution*, 391–418. New York: Vintage, 1963.
Jameson, Fredric. *A Singular Modernity*. London: Verso, 2012.
Jawodimbari, Arthur. "The Sun." *Kovave* 2, no. 1 (1970): 46–57.
Jones, Lawrence. *Picking up the Traces: The Making of a New Zealand Literary Culture, 1932–1945*. Wellington: Victoria University Press, 2003.
Joyce, James. *Letters of James Joyce*. Vol. 2. Ed. Richard Ellmann. London: Faber, 1966.
———. *Ulysses: A Critical and Synoptic Edition*. Ed. Hans Walter Gabler with Wolfhard Steppe and Claus Melchior. New York: Garland, 1984.
Jupp, James. "The Development of Party Politics in the New Hebrides." *Journal of Commonwealth and Comparative Politics* 17, no. 3 (1979): 269.
Ka'ili, Tēvita O. *Marking Indigeneity: The Tongan Art of Sociospatial Relations*. Tucson: University of Arizona Press, 2016.
Kadiba, John. "Elites and Education: John Kadiba on Ulli Beier." *Sumatin: A Magazine of Papua New Guinean Writing* 2 (2022): 17.
———. "Growing Up in Mailu." *Kovave* pilot (1968): 18–25.
———. "Tax." *Kovave* 1, no. 1 (1969): 9–13.
Kalliney, Peter. "Modernism, African Literature, and the Cold War." *Modern Language Quarterly*, 76, no. 3 (2015): 333–68.
Kalpokas, Donald. "Who Am I?" *Pacific Islands Monthly* 45, no. 9 (September 1974): 61.
Kamins, Robert E., and Robert E. Potter. *Malamalama: A History of the University of Hawai'i*. Honolulu: University of Hawai'i Press, 1998.
Kaputin, James. "Tolai Songs." *Kovave* 1, no. 1 (1969): 35–36.
Kasaipwalova, John. "Betel Nut Is Bad Magic for Aeroplanes." In *Through Melanesian Eyes: An Anthology of Papua New Guinea Writing*, ed. Ganga Powell, 69–77. Melbourne: Macmillan, 1987.
———. "Kanaka's Dream." *Kovave* 3, no. 1 (1971): 47–58.
———. "The Magistrate and My Grandfather's Testicles." *Kovave* 3, no. 2 (1972): 9–15.
———. "'Modernising' Melanesian Society—Why, and for Whom?" In *Priorities in Melanesian Development: Papers Delivered at the Sixth Waigani Seminar*, ed. Ronald J. May, 451–454. Canberra and Port Moresby: The Australia National University and the University of Papua New Guinea, 1973.
———. "Problems of Unity in Niugini." *Nilaidat* 3, no. 1 (1970): 8.
———. *Reluctant Flame*. Ife: Pan African Pocket Poets, 1971.
———. "The Role of the Educated Elite." In *Papua New Guinea Education*, ed. E. Barrington Thomas, 130–34. Melbourne: Oxford University Press, 1976.
———. "Rooster in the Confessional." *Kovave* 2, no. 2 (1971): 42–47.
———. "What Is 'Cultural Reconstruction'???" *New Guinea Writing* 3 (1971): 14–16.
Katoa, Atunaisa Havea. "The Legend of Sangone the Turtle and the Royal Mats." *Pacific Islands Monthly* 46, no. 2 (February 1975): 44–46.
Kavop, Jerry. "Lus Man." *Kovave* 4, no. 1 (1972): 14.
Kenner, Hugh. *Dublin's Joyce*. London: Chatto & Windus, 1955.
———. "Poets at the Blackboard." In *Ezra Pound and William Carlos Williams*, 3–13. Philadelphia: University of Pennsylvania Press, 1983.

BIBLIOGRAPHY

Keown, Michelle. *Pacific Islands Writing: The Postcolonial Literatures of Aotearoa/New Zealand and Oceania*. Oxford: Oxford University Press, 2007.
———. "The Samoan Sisyphus: Camus and Colonialism in Albert Wendt's *Leaves of the Banyan Tree*." *Journal of Commonwealth Literature* 37, no. 1 (2002): 49–65.
Kermode, Frank. *Continuities*. New York: Random House, 1968.
Kermode, Frank, and John Hollander. *Modern British Literature*. New York: Oxford University Press, 1973.
Kerpi, Kama. "Kulpu's Daughter." *Kovave* 5, no. 1 (1975): 7–13.
———. "Song of Lament." *Kovave* 4, no. 2 (1974): 15–16.
Khan, Aiyub. "Gold Etched Independence?" *UNISPAC* 3, no. 2 (1970): 13.
Kiki, Albert Maori. *Kiki: Ten Thousand Years in a Lifetime*. London: Pall Mall, 1968.
Kincaid, Jamaica. *Lucy: A Novel*. London: Cape, 1991.
Krauth, Nigel. "Interpreting the Signs." *Kovave* 3, no. 1 (1971): 43–46.
———. "A Postmortem of Papua New Guinea Poetry." *Papua New Guinea Writing* 25 (1977): 18–22.
———. "'Unfolding Like Petals': The Developing Definition of the Writer's Role in Modern Papua New Guinean Literature." In *Readings in Pacific Literature*, ed. Paul Sharrad, 52–62. Wollongong: New Literatures Research Centre, 1993.
Kristeva, Julia. *Powers of Horror: An Essay on Abjection*. Trans. Leon S. Roudiez. New York: Columbia University Press, 1982.
Kula, Aivu. "Black Venture." *Pacific Islands Monthly* 46, no. 1 (January 1975): 51.
Kulagoe, Bro. C. "Peace Signs." *Pacific Islands Monthly* 45, no. 7 (July 1974): 66.
Lal, Brij V. *Broken Waves: A History of the Fiji Islands in the Twentieth Century*. Honolulu: University of Hawai'i Press, 1992.
———. *Islands of Turmoil: Elections and Politics in Fiji*. Canberra: Australian National University Press, 2006.
———. "Primary Texts." In *Bittersweet: The Indo-Fijian Experience*, ed. Brij V. Lal, 239–49. Canberra: Pandanus, 2004.
———. "The Wreck of the *Syria*, 1884." In *The Indo-Fijian Experience*, ed. Subramani, 26–40. St. Lucia: University of Queensland Press, 1979.
Lal, Brij V., and Barry Shineberg. "The Story of the Haunted Line: Totaram Sanadhya Recalls the Labour Lines in Fiji." *Journal of Pacific History* 26, no. 1 (1991): 10–7.
Larson, Charles R. "Ulli Beier—African Playwright?" *Books Abroad* 46, no. 3 (1972): 393–96.
Lawrence, D. H. "Herman Melville's *Typee* and *Omoo*." In *Selected Critical Writings*, ed. Michael Herbert, 113–25. Oxford: Oxford University Press, 1998.
———. *The Rainbow: Part 2*. Ed. Mark Kinkead-Weekes. Cambridge: Cambridge University Press, 2002.
Laycock, D. "Pulling the Punches on Papuan Plays." *Kovave* 1, no. 2 (1970): 54–56.
Le Grange, Lesley. "The Curriculum Case for Decolonisation." In *Decolonisation in Universities: The Politics of Knowledge*, ed. Jonathan D. Jansen, 229–47. Johannesburg: Wits University Press, 2019.
Leach, Jerry W. "Socio-Historical Conflict and the Kabisawali Movement in the Trobriand Islands." In *Micronationalist Movements in Papua New Guinea*, ed. R. J. May, 249–90. Canberra: Research School of Pacific Studies, Australia National University, 1982.

BIBLIOGRAPHY

Lejeune, Philippe. *On Autobiography*. Trans. Katherine Margaret Leary. Minneapolis: University of Minnesota Press, 1989.
Leomala, Albert. "Culture My Culture." *Pacific Islands Monthly* 45, no. 9 (September 1974): 64.
———. "Hoom blong mi." *Mana Annual*, 1974, 38.
———. "Kros / Cross." In *Some Modern Poetry from the New Hebrides*, ed. Albert Wendt, 18–19. Suva: Mana Publications, 1975.
———. "Live in Me." *Pacific Islands Monthly* 46, no. 12 (December 1975): 48.
———. "Niuhebridis." *Pacific Islands Monthly* 45, no. 9 (September 1974): 63.
———. "Thieves." *Pacific Islands Monthly* 46, no. 7 (July 1975): 46.
Levin, Harry. *Refractions: Essays in Comparative Literature*. New York: Oxford University Press, 1966.
Lewis, George H. "Da Kine Sounds: The Function of Music as Social Protest in the New Hawaiian Renaissance." *American Music* 2, no. 2 (1984): 38–52.
Lewis, Wyndham. *The Art of Being Ruled*. Ed. Reed Way Dasenbrock. Santa Rosa, CA: Black Sparrow, 1989.
Livingston, Peter. "From the Emotions of Ulli to a Simple Descriptive Paulias." *Pacific Islands Monthly*, June 1973, 78–79.
Liyong, Taban Lo. "On Translating the 'Untranslated': Chapter 14 of 'Wer pa Lawino' by Okot p'Bitek." *Research in African Literatures* 24, no. 3 (1993): 88–92.
Lohia, Renagi R. "Your First Year at University." *Nilaidat* 2, no. 1 (April 1969): 11–13.
Long, Maebh, and Matthew Hayward. "For I Have Fed on Foreign Bread: Modernism, Colonial Education, and Fijian Literature." *Modernist Cultures* 15, no. 3 (2020): 377–98.
Low, Gail. "The Natural Artist: Publishing Amos Tutuola's 'The Palm-Wine Drinkard' in Postwar Britain." *Research in African Literatures* 37, no. 4 (2006): 15–33.
Lukács, Georg. *Essays on Realism*. Ed. Rodney Livingston. Trans. David Fernbach. Cambridge, MA: MIT Press, 1981.
Lynch, John. "The Papua New Guinea System." In *Pacific Universities: Achievements, Problems and Prospects*, ed. Ron Crocombe and Malama Meleisea, 176–87. Suva: Institute of Pacific Studies, 1988.
Lyons, Paul. "Africana Calls, Pasifika Responses: Ellison's *Invisible Man*, Soaba's *Wanpis*, and Oceanian Literary Modernism." In *New Oceania: Modernisms and Modernities in the Pacific*, ed. Matthew Hayward and Maebh Long, 118–35. London: Routledge, 2020.
Maʻiaʻi, Ata. "Past the Old Track (An Exploration)." *Pacific Islands Monthly* 45, no. 2 (February 1974): 60.
Madigibuli, Ana. "Back in Time: Lecturer Recounts Abduction." *Fiji Times*, November 4, 2020.
Makaʻa, Julian, and Stephen Oxenham. "The Voice in the Shadow: A Survey of Writing in Solomon Islands." *Pacific Moana Quarterly* 9, no. 1 (1985): 5–13.
Makereti, Tina. "Māori Writing: Speaking with Two Mouths." *Journal of New Zealand Studies* 26 (2018): 57–65.
Malupo, Peni Tutuʻila. "Creative Arts Workshop." *Pacific Islands Monthly* 45, no. 11 (November 1974): 61.
———. "Tonga, Blessed Land." *Pacific Islands Monthly* 44, no. 9 (September 1973): 68.

"Mana Forum." *Mana: A South Pacific Journal of Language and Literature* 3, no. 1 (1978): 5–16.
Manoa, Pio. "Recall." 1975. In *Waves: An Anthology*, ed. by Vijay Mishra. Auckland: Heinemann Education, 1979.
———. "Recollect." *Dreadlocks* 6–7 (2010–2011): 261–82.
———. "Singing in Their Genealogical Trees." *Mana Review: A South Pacific Journal of Language and Literature* 1, no. 1 (1976): 64.
Mao, Douglas, ed. *The New Modernist Studies*. New York: Cambridge University Press, 2021.
Mao, Douglas, and Rebecca L. Walkowitz. "The New Modernist Studies." *PMLA* 123, no. 3 (2008): 737–48.
May, R. J. "Editor's Note." Addendum to Jerry W. Leach, "Socio-Historical Conflict and the Kabisawali Movement in the Trobriand Islands." In *Micronationalist Movements in Papua New Guinea*, ed. R. J. May, 249–90. Canberra: Research School of Pacific Studies, Australia National University, 1982.
McDonald, Gail. *Learning to Be Modern: Pound, Eliot, and the American University*. Oxford: Clarendon, 1993.
McDowell, Judith H. "The Embryonic Literature of New Guinea." *Journal of Postcolonial Writing* 12, no. 2 (1973): 299–303.
McGurl, Mark. *The Program Era: Postwar Fiction and the Rise of Creative Writing*. Cambridge, MA: Harvard University Press, 2009.
Megarrity, Lyndon. "Indigenous Education in Colonial Papua New Guinea: Australian Government Policy 1945–1975." *History of Education Review* 34, no. 2 (2005): 41–58.
Mignolo, Walter D., and Catherine E. Walsh. *On Decoloniality: Concepts, Analytics, Praxis*. Durham, NC: Duke University Press, 2018.
Mila, Karlo. "After Reading *Ancestry*: For Albert Wendt." *Blackmail Press* 40 (July 2015), http://nzpoetsonline.homestead.com/KM40.html.
Miller, Christopher L. *Impostors: Literary Hoaxes and Cultural Authenticity*. Chicago: University of Chicago Press, 2018.
Mintz, Sidney W. *Sweetness and Power: The Place of Sugar in Modern History*. New York: Viking Penguin, 1985.
Mishra, Margaret. "A History of Fijian Women's Activism (1900–2010)." *Journal of Women's History* 24, no. 2 (2012): 115–43.
Mishra, Sudesh. "Acts of Rememory in Oceania." *Symplokē* 26, no. 1–2 (2018): 28–30.
Mishra, Vijay. "The Girmit Ideology Revisited." In *Reworlding: The Literature of the Indian Diaspora*, ed. Emmanuel S. Nelson, 1–12. New York: Greenwood, 1992.
———. "Indo-Fijian Fiction and the *Girmit* Ideology." In *The Indo-Fijian Experience*, ed. Subramani, 171–83. St. Lucia: University of Queensland Press, 1979.
Moore, Gerald, and Ulli Beier, eds. *Modern Poetry from Africa*. Harmondsworth: Penguin, 1966.
Morris, C. R., F. R. G. Aitken, H. M. Collins, P. W. Hughes, and D. H. Christie. *Report of the Higher Education Mission to the South Pacific*. London: Her Majesty's Stationery Office 1966.
Muller, Herbert J. *Modern Fiction: A Study of Values*. New York: Funk and Wagnalls, 1937.
Murphy, Greg. "Introduction." In *Sail the Midnight Sun*, by John Kasaipwalova, 1–7. Credit Melanesia: Trobriands, 1980.

BIBLIOGRAPHY

Murphy, Penelope S. "Universities, Government Intervention and the Commission for Higher Education in Papua New Guinea." *International Journal of Educational Development* 9, no. 3 (1989): 175–82.
Murtagh, Mike, and Michael Steer. "New Zealand Examining Bodies in the South Pacific." In *Examination Systems in Small States: Comparative Perspectives on Policies, Models and Operations*, ed. Mark Bray and Lucy Steward. London: Commonwealth Secretariat, 1998.
Nacola, Jo. "Living Under the Authority of a Myth in Ra." *Pacific Islands Monthly* 44, no. 5 (May 1973): 72–73.
Nair, Shashikant. "That Hour." *UNISPAC* 3, no. 1 (1970): 6.
Nandan, Satendra. *In Diaspora: Theories, Histories, Texts*. New Delhi: Indialog, 2001.
———. "My Father's Son." *Pacific Islands Monthly* 45, no. 8 (August 1974): 64.
Nasalivata, Mele. "A Legend of Love and Death." *Pacific Islands Monthly* 44, no. 11 (November 1973): 63–64.
Natachee, A. P. Alan. "Mekeo Poems and Legends." *Oceania* 2, no. 2 (1951): 148–61.
Nelson, Hank. *Papua New Guinea: Black Unity or Black Chaos?* Harmondsworth: Penguin, 1974.
New Zealand Universities Arts Festival Yearbook. Wellington: New Zealand Universities Publications, 1963.
Ng, Andrew Hock Soon. *Interrogating Interstices: Gothic Aesthetics in Postcolonial Asian and Asian American Literature*. Bern: Peter Lang, 2007.
Ngũgĩ wa Thiong'o. *Moving the Centre: The Struggle for Cultural Freedoms*. London: James Currey, 1993.
Ngũgĩ wa Thiong'o, Henry Owuor-Anyumba, and Taban Lo Liyong. "On the Abolition of the English Department." In *The Postcolonial Studies Reader*, ed. Bill Ashcroft, Gareth Griffiths, and Helen Tiffin, 438–42. London: Routledge, 1995.
Niles, Don, and Alan Rumsey. "Introducing Highlands Sung Tales." In *Sung Tales from the Papua New Guinea Highlands: Studies in Form, Meaning, and Sociocultural Context*, ed. Don Niles and Alan Rumsey, 1–38. Canberra: Australian National University, 2011.
Nkosi, Lewis. "Lewis Nkosi on Black Atlanticism and (Southern) African Writing." Interview by Stephan Meyer. *Current Writing: Text and Reception in Southern Africa* 16, no. 2 (2004): 121–30.
Nyman, Mikaela. "Sado—a Novel and Expressions of Creativity and Rhetorical Alliance: Ni-Vanuatu Women's Voices." PhD diss., Victoria University of Wellington, 2020.
O'Carroll, John. "Totaram's Ghost." *Australia Humanities Review* 52 (2012): 91–106.
Odai, Addie. Untitled. *Kovave* 2, no. 1 (1970): 20.
Ofuani, Oga A. "The Traditional and Modern Influences in Okot p'Bitek's Poetry." *African Studies Review* 28, no. 4 (1985): 87–99.
Ogundele, Wole. *Omoluabi: Ulli Beier, Yoruba Society and Culture*. Bayreuth: Bayreuth African Studies, 2003.
Omelsky, Matthew. "The Creaturely Modernism of Amos Tutuola." *Cultural Critique* 99 (2018): 66–96.
Owomoyela, Oyekan. "Obotunde Ijimere, the Phantom of Nigerian Theatre." *African Studies Review* 22, no. 1 (1979): 43–50.
p'Bitek, Okot. "Interview with Okot p'Bitek." *Kunapipi* 1, no. 1 (1979): 89–93.

BIBLIOGRAPHY

Paravisini-Gebert, Lizabeth. "Colonial and Postcolonial Gothic: The Caribbean." In *The Cambridge Companion to Gothic Fiction*, ed. Jerrold E. Hogle, 229–58. New York: Cambridge University Press, 2002.
Petaia, Ruperake. "Kidnapped." *Pacific Islands Monthly* 46, no. 1 (January 1975): 49.
Pillai, Raymond. "Directions in Fiji and Pacific Literature." In *Class and Culture and the South Pacific*, ed. Antony Hooper, Steve Britton, Ron Crocombe, Judith Huntsman, and Cluny Macpherson, 104–15. Suva: Centre for Pacific Studies, University of Auckland and Institute of Pacific Studies, University of the South Pacific, 1987.
———. "Muni Deo's Devil." *UNISPAC* 4, no. 3 (1971): 24.
———. "Prose Fiction in Fiji—a Question of Direction." *Mana: A South Pacific Journal of Language and Literature* 4, no. 2 (1979): 8–9.
Pinar, William F. *What Is Curriculum Theory?* New York: Routledge, 2012.
Pokawin, Stephen. Interview by Ian Kemish and Jonathan Ritchie. *PNG Speaks*, May 10, 2016. https://pngspeaks.com/stephen-pokawin.
Porter, A. P. *Jump at de Sun: The Story of Zora Neale Hurston*. Minneapolis, MN: Twenty-First Century Books, 1992.
Pound, Ezra. *Make It New*. London: Faber, 1934.
Powell, Emma Emily Ngakuraevaru. "'Akapapa'anga Ara Tangata: Genealogising the (Cook Islands) Māori Imaginary." PhD diss., Victoria University of Wellington, 2021.
———. "Introduction." In *Mana: Fifty Years of Cook Islands Creative Writing in English and Cook Islands Māori*, ed. Joan Gragg, Patricia Thompson, Ngavaevae Papatua, and Rod Dixon, 4. Rarotonga, Cook Islands: USP Press, 2018.
Powell, Kirsty. "The First Papua New Guinean Playwrights and Their Plays." Master's thesis, University of Papua New Guinea, 1975.
———. "Ulli Beier's Role." *Pacific Islands Monthly*, August 1973, 21–23.
Prasad, Mohit. "Indigenous Pacific Fiction in English: The 'Niu Wave.'" In *The Novel in Australia, Canada, New Zealand, and the South Pacific Since 1950*, ed. Coral Ann Howells, Paul Sharrad, and Gerry Turcotte, 511–23. Oxford: Oxford University Press, 2017.
"Preliminary Announcement of the College of Arts." *The Egoist* 21, no. 1 (1914): 413–14.
Punter, David. *The Literature of Terror: A History of Gothic Fictions from 1765 to the Present Day*. London: Longmans, 1980.
Racule, Rejieli. "The Gift." *Pacific Islands Monthly* 46, no. 12 (December 1975): 50.
Rainey, Lawrence. *Institutions of Modernism: Literary Elites and Public Culture*. New Haven, CT: Yale University Press, 1998.
Ramazani, Jahan. *A Transnational Poetics*. Chicago: University of Chicago Press, 2009.
Ratuva, Steven. *Politics of Preferential Development: Trans-Global Study of Affirmative Action and Ethnic Conflict in Fiji, Malaysia and South Africa*. Canberra: Australian National University Press, 2013.
"Regional Creative Writing Workshop." USP/UNESCO Report, August 26–September 6, 1974.
Report of the Commission on Higher Education in Papua and New Guinea. 1964.
Reyes, Angelita. *Mothering Across Cultures: Postcolonial Representations*. Minneapolis: University of Minnesota Press, 2002.
Rhys, Jean. *Wide Sargasso Sea*. 1966. New York: Norton, 1992.

BIBLIOGRAPHY

Richards, Thomas. *The Imperial Archive: Knowledge and the Fantasy of Empire*. New York: Verso, 1993.
Riquelme, John Paul. "Toward a History of Gothic and Modernism: Dark Modernity from Bram Stoker to Samuel Beckett." *Modern Fiction Studies* 46, no. 3 (2000): 585.
Robson, Catherine. *Heart Beats: Everyday Life and the Memorized Poem*. Princeton, NJ: Princeton University Press, 2012.
Rokonadravu, Mary. "Famished Eels," *Granta*, online edition, April 28, 2015. https://granta.com/famished-eels/.
———. "An Interview with Mary Rokonadravu, Winner of the Commonwealth Short Story Prize for the Pacific Region." Pacific Cooperation Foundation. https://www.pcf.org.nz/news/ns7r6lwrnpdlrzz-h82c8-wg6js-r7d27-fmyxz.
———. "The Nightwatch." *Granta*, online edition, May 24, 2022. https://granta.com/the-nightwatch/.
Roosman, Raden S. "Coconut, Breadfruit and Taro in Pacific Oral Literature." *Journal of the Polynesian Society* 79, no. 2 (1970): 219–32.
Rudd, Alison. "Postcolonial Gothic in and as Theory." In *The Gothic and Theory: An Edinburgh Companion*, ed. Jerrold E. Hogle and Robert Miles. Edinburgh: Edinburgh University Press, 2019.
Saint-Amour, Paul. "Weak Theory, Weak Modernism." *Modernism/modernity* 25, no. 3 (2018): 437–59.
Salesa, Damon. "Cowboys in the House of Polynesia." *Contemporary Pacific* 22, no. 2 (2010): 330–48.
Sanadhya, Totaram. *My Twenty-One Years in the Fiji Islands, and The Story of the Haunted Line*. Trans. John Dunham Kelly and Uttra Kumari Singh. Suva: Fiji Museum, 2003.
"Saying What You Think on NG." *Pacific Islands Monthly* 41, no.7 (1970): 45.
Schutz, Betty, Hira Lal, Lognada, Vanessa Griffen, Nawal Maharaj, G. Anoop, Cama, V. Deo, Claire Slatter, Joan Yee, R. Pillai, P. Murti, P. Harak, and E. Baro. "Individual Development vs National Development: Creativity vs Utility." *UNISPAC* 4, no. 3 (1971): 21.
Seri. "Monday Morning Street Ride." *Pacific Islands Monthly* 45, no. 7 (July 1974): 65.
———. "Prologue." *Pacific Islands Monthly* 44, no. 4 (April 1973): 69.
Sharrad, Paul. *Albert Wendt and Pacific Literature: Circling the Void*. Auckland: Auckland University Press, 2003.
———. "Breaks, Gaps, Waves: Pacific Literature and (Re)Making History." In *Encyclopédie des historiographies: Afriques, Amériques, Asies*. Vol. 1: *Sources et genres historiques*, ed. Nathalie Kouamé, Éric P. Meyer, and Anne Viguier, 139–50. Paris: Presses de l'Inalco, 2020.
———. "Literary Legacies: Faltering Feet; Dancing a Pen to a National Beat." In *Lines Across the Sea: Colonial Inheritance in the Post Colonial Pacific*, ed. Brij V. Lal and Hank Nelson, 199–212. Brisbane: Pacific History Association, 1995.
———. "A Map of PNG Short Stories in English." *Bikmaus* 5, no. 2 (1984): 1–16.
———. "No Ordinary Modernism: Hone Tuwhare's First Book of Verse." In *New Oceania: Modernisms and Modernities in the Pacific*, ed. Matthew Hayward and Maebh Long, 68–70. New York: Routledge, 2019.
———. "Out of Africa: Literary Globalization in the Winds of Change." *South Atlantic Quarterly* 100, no. 3 (2001): 717–28.

BIBLIOGRAPHY

Sherry, Vincent. "Introduction: A History of Modernism." In *The Cambridge History of Modernism*, 1–26. Cambridge: Cambridge University Press, 2016.
Shklovsky, Viktor. "Art as Technique." In *Russian Formalist Criticism: Four Essays*, ed. and trans. Lee T. Lemon and Marion J. Reis, 3–24. Lincoln: University of Nebraska Press, 1965.
Simms, Norman. "John Kasaipwalova." In *Writers from the South Pacific: A Bio-Bibliographical Critical Encyclopaedia*, 73–74. Washington, DC: Three Continents, 1991.
Simpson, Hannah. "'Strange Laughter': Post-Gothic Questions of Laughter and the Human in Samuel Beckett's Work." *Journal of Modern Literature* 40, no. 4 (2017): 1–19.
Sinavaiana Gabbard, Caroline. "Amerika Samoa: Writing Home." In *The Oxford Handbook of Indigenous American Literature*, ed. James H. Cox and Daniel Heath Justice, 589–607. Oxford: Oxford University Press, 2014.
——. "Samoan Literature and the Wheel of Time: Cartographies of the Vā." *symplokē* 26, no. 1–2 (2018): 33–49.
Singh, Anirudh. "The Screaming Man." *UNISPAC* 3, no. 3 (1970): 15.
Singh, Chattur. "The Final Journey." *Mana Annual*, 1974, 28.
Smith, Andrew, and William Hughes. "Introduction: The Enlightenment Gothic and Postcolonialism." In *Empire and the Gothic: The Politics of Genre*, ed. Andrew Smith and William Hughes, 1–12. Basingstoke: Palgrave Macmillan, 2003.
Snyder, Cary. "'When the Indian Was in Vogue': D. H. Lawrence, Aldous Huxley, and Ethnological Tourism in the Southwest." *MFS: Modern Fiction Studies* 53, no. 4 (2007): 662–96.
Soaba, Russell. "A Glimpse of the Abyss." *Kovave* 3, no. 2 (1972): 6–8.
——. "A Glossary of Words." In *Kwamra: A Season of Harvest*, 59. Port Moresby: Anuki Country, 2000.
——. "An Interview with Russell Soaba." Interview by Chris Tiffin. *Span* 8 (1979): 23.
——. "Interview with Russell Soaba." Interview by Gilian Gorle. *New Literatures Review* 26 (1993): 68–72.
——. *Kwamra: A Season of Harvest*. Port Moresby: Anuki Country, 2000.
——. "Natives Under the Sun." In *Black Writing from New Guinea*, ed. Ulli Beier, 87. Brisbane: Queensland University Press, 1973.
——. "The Next Resort." *Mana Annual*, 1974, 69–70.
——. "A Portrait of the Odd Man Out." *Kovave* 2, no. 2 (1971): 7–11.
——. "Return of St. Nativeson." In *Kwamra: A Season of Harvest*. Port Moresby: Anuki Country, 2000.
——. "Russell Soaba: An Interview." Interview by Kirpal Singh. *Westerly* 29, no. 2 (1984): 49–60.
——. "Scattered by the Wind." *Kovave* 4, no. 1 (1972): 30–42.
——. "The Victims." *Kovave* 4, no. 1 (1972): 16–20.
——. "The Villager's Request." *Mana Annual*, 1974, 72.
——. *Wanpis*. 1977. Port Moresby: University of Papua New Guinea Press and Bookshop, 2012.
Sope, Mildred. "Motherland." *Pacific Islands Monthly* 45, no. 9 (September 1974): 64.
Spender, Stephen. *The Struggle of the Modern*. London: Hamish Hamilton, 1963.
Spivak, Gayatri. "Extreme Eurocentrism." *Lusitania* 1, no. 4 (1992): 59.

BIBLIOGRAPHY

Stamford, Anne. "Custom Stories of the New Hebrides." *Pacific Islands Monthly* 44, no. 7 (July 1973): 70.
Steinbeck, John. *'The Pearl' and 'Burning Bright.'* London: Heinemann, 1954.
Stella, Regis. *Gutsini Posa (Rough Seas)*. Suva: Mana Publications, 1999.
———. "Reluctant Voyages Into Otherness: Practice and Appraisal in Papua New Guinean Literature." In *Inside Out: Literature, Culture, Politics, and Identity in the New Pacific*, ed. Vilsoni Hereniko and Rob Wilson, 221–30. Lanham, MA: Rowman and Littlefield, 1999.
Stella, Sr. M. "In Support of the USP!" *UNISPAC* (1969): 4–5.
Stewart, Christine. "Not a *Misis*." In *Australians in Papua New Guinea 1960–1975*, ed. Ceridwen Spark, Seumus Spark, and Christina Twomey, 248–61. St. Lucia: University of Queensland Press, 2014.
Stewart, Frank, Kareva Mateata-Allain, and Alexander Dale Mawyer, eds. *Varua Tupu: New Writing from French Polynesia*. Honolulu: University of Hawai'i Press, 2006.
Subramani. "Editor's Page." *Mana Review: A South Pacific Journal of Language and Literature* 1, no. 1 (1976): 5.
———. *The Fantasy Eaters*. Washington, DC: Three Continents, 1988.
———, ed. *The Indo-Fijian Experience*. St. Lucia: University of Queensland Press, 1979.
———. "The Mythical Quest: Literary Responses to the South Seas." *Mana: A South Pacific Journal of Language and Literature* 1, no. 1 (1976): 6–27.
———. "The Oceanic Imaginary." *Contemporary Pacific* 13, no. 1 (2001): 149–62.
———. "Sautu." *Mana Annual*, 1974, 10.
———. *South Pacific Literature: From Myth to Fabulation*. Suva: Institute of Pacific Studies, University of the South Pacific, 1985.
———. "Tell Me Where the Train Goes." *Mana Annual*, 1977, 77.
———. *Wild Flowers*. Suva: University of the South Pacific Press, 2017.
Suhr-Sytsma, Nathan. "Ibadan Modernism: Poetry and the Literary Present in Mid-Century Nigeria." *The Journal of Commonwealth Literature* 48, no. 1 (2013): 41–59.
Sukwianomb, Joseph W. "Where Are the Green Leaves." *Pacific Islands Monthly* 46, no. 3 (March 1975): 52.
Swan, Quito. *Pasifika Black: Oceania, Anti-Colonialism, and the African World*. New York: New York University Press, 2022.
Tapin, Venantius. "Where Have All the Young Men Gone?" *Pacific Islands Monthly* 44, no. 8 (August 1973): 72.
Taulapapa McMullin, Dan, and Yuki Kihara, eds. *Samoan Queer Lives*. Auckland: Little Island, 2018.
Taumoefolau, Melenaite. "The Translation of Queen Sālote's Poetry." In *For Better or Worse: Translation as a Tool for Change in the South Pacific*, ed. Sabine Fenton, 241–72. London: Routledge, 2014.
Tawali, Kumalau. "The Bush Kanaka Speaks." *Kovave* 1, no. 2 (1970): 17.
———. "An Interview with Kumalau Tawali." Interview by Don Maynard. *New Guinea Writing* 2 (1970): 12–13.
Taylor, Rod C. "Narrow Gates and Restricted Paths: The Critical Pedagogy of Virginia Woolf." *Woolf Studies Annual* 20 (2014): 55–81.
Te Punga Somerville, Alice. "English by Name, English by Nature." In *Ngā Kete Māturanga: Māori Scholars at the Research Interface*, ed. Jacinta Ruru and Linda Waimarie Nikoa, 90–104. Dunedin: Otago University Press, 2021.

BIBLIOGRAPHY

———. "Inside Us the Unborn: Genealogies, Futures, Metaphors, and the Opposite of Zombies." In *Pacific Futures: Past and Present*, ed. Warwick Anderson, Miranda Johnson, and Barbara Brookes. Honolulu: University of Hawai'i Press, 2018.

Teaiwa, Teresia. "The Ancestors We Get to Choose: White Influences I Won't Deny." In *Theorizing Native Studies*, ed. Audra Simpson and Andrea Smith, 43–55. Durham, NC: Duke University Press, 2014.

———. "Reading Imperialism in the Pacific: The Prose of Joseph Veramu and the Poetry of Sia Figiel." In *Anglo-American Imperialism and the Pacific: Discourses of Encounter*, ed. Michelle Keown, Andrew Taylor, and Mandy Treagus. London: Routledge, 2018.

———. "What Remains to Be Seen: Reclaiming the Visual Roots of Pacific Literature." *PMLA* 125, no. 2 (2010): 730–36.

Thomas, Lynda. "Volcano." *Kovave* 2, no. 2 (1971): 29.

Thompson, Maurice. "Seduction." *Kovave* 2, no. 1 (1970): 13–19.

Tiffin, Chris. Introduction to *South Pacific Images*, ed. Chris Tiffin, 1–10. Brisbane: South Pacific Association for Commonwealth Literature and Language Studies, 1978.

Townshend, Dale. "Doubles." In *The Encyclopedia of the Gothic*, ed. William Hughes, David Punter, and Andrew Smith, 189–95. Oxford: Blackwell, 2013.

Trask, Haunani-Kay. *From a Native Daughter: Colonialism and Sovereignty in Hawai'i*. Honolulu: Latitude 20, 1999.

Trilling, Lionel. "On the Teaching of Modern Literature." In *Beyond Culture: Essays on Literature and Learning*, 3–30. London: Secker and Warburg, 1966.

Tuhiwai Smith, Linda. *Decolonizing Methodologies: Research and Indigenous Peoples*. 3rd ed. London: Zed, 2021.

Tusitala Marsh, Selina. "The Body of Pacific Literature." *Mai Review* 1 (2010): 1–6.

———. "Theory 'Versus' Pacific Islands Writing: Toward a Tama'ita'i Criticism in the Works of Three Pacific Islands Woman Poets." In *Inside Out: Literature, Cultural Politics, and Identity in the New Pacific*, ed. Vilsoni Hereniko and Rob Wilson, 337–56. Lanham, MD: Rowman & Littlefield, 1999.

Tutuola, Amos. *The Palm-Wine Drinkard and His Dead Palm-Wine Tapster in the Deads' Town*. London: Faber and Faber, 1977.

Va'ai, Sina. *Albert Wendt and Samoan Identity*. Apia: National University of Samoa Publications, 1997.

Vandertop, Caitlin. "Ghosts of the Plantation: Sugar, Narrative Energetics, and Gothic Ecologies in Fiji." *Green Letters: Studies in Ecocriticism* 24, no. 2 (2020): 160.

Vatoko, Kali, and Albert Leomala. "Mi stap sori nomo / I Bow in Sorrow." *Pacific Islands Monthly* 45, no. 9 (September 1974): 62.

Vete, Vili. "For Change." *Pacific Islands Monthly* 46, no. 11 (November 1975): 56.

Vini, Nihi. "The Thing." *Pacific Islands Monthly* 44, no. 4 (April 1973): 67.

Waiko, John D. "'Head' and 'Tail': The Shaping of Oral Traditions Among the Binandere in Papua New Guinea." *Oral Tradition* 5, no. 2–3 (1990): 334–53.

———. "Oral Traditions Among the Binandere: Problems of Method in a Melanesian Society." *Journal of Pacific History* 21, no. 1 (1986): 21–38.

———. "The Place of Literature in Papua New Guinea Education." In *Teaching Literature in Papua New Guinea*, ed. Elton Brash and Mike Greicus, 4–6. Port Moresby: UPNG, 1972.

BIBLIOGRAPHY

———. "The Unexpected Hawk." *Kovave* 1, no. 1 (1969): 56–57.
Waleanisia, Joseph. "Writing I." In *Ples Blong Iumi: Solomon Islands, the Past Four Thousand Years*, ed. Hugh Laracy. 31–40. Suva: Institute of Pacific Studies, University of the South Pacific, 1989.
Watt, Ian. *Conrad in the Nineteenth Century*. Berkeley: University of California Press, 1979.
Wendt, Alan. "A Poem for USP." *UNISPAC*, April 1978, 10.
Wendt, Albert. *Ancestry*. Suva: University of the South Pacific Press, 2012.
———. "The Artist and the Reefs Breaking Open." *Mana* 3, no. 1 (1978): 107–21.
———. "Discovering *The Outsider*." In *Camus's 'L'Etranger': Fifty Years On*, ed. Adele King, 48–51. New York: Palgrave Macmillan, 1992.
———. "How to Get Students Writing Poetry." *Multi-cultural School* 3 (1976): 18.
———. "An Interview with Albert Wendt." Interview by John Beston and Rose Marie Beston. *World Literature Written in English* 16, no. 1 (1977): 151–62.
———, ed. *Lali: A Pacific Anthology*. Auckland: Longman Paul, 1980.
———, ed. *Nuanua: Pacific Writing in English Since 1980*. Honolulu: University of Hawai'i Press, 1995.
———. *Pouliuli*. 1977. Honolulu: University of Hawai'i Press, 1980.
———. "Samoa's Albert Wendt: Poet and Author." Interview by Marjorie Crocombe. *Mana Annual*, 1973, 46.
———. "A Sermon on National Development, Education, and the Rot in the South Pacific." In *Education in Melanesia*, ed. J. Brammall and Ronald J. May, 373–80. Canberra: Australian National University and University of Papua New Guinea, 1975.
———. "Tatauing the Post-Colonial Body." *SPAN: Journal of the South Pacific Association for Commonwealth Literature and Language Studies* 42–43 (1996): 15–29.
———. "Towards a New Oceania." *Mana Review: A South Pacific Journal of Language and Literature* 1, no. 1 (1976): 49–60.
West, Alick. *Crisis and Criticism*. London: Lawrence and Wishart, 1937.
Wester, Maisha L. *African American Gothic: Screams from Shadowed Places*. New York: Palgrave Macmillan, 2012.
Williams, Raymond. *The Country and the City*. New York: Oxford University Press, 1973.
Williams, William Carlos. *The Autobiography of William Carlos Williams*. New York: Random House, 1951.
Wilson-Hokowhitu, Nālani, ed. *The Past Before Us: Moʻokūʻauhau as Methodology*. Honolulu: University of Hawai'i Press, 2019.
Winduo, Steven Edmund. "Cultural Invasion, Negative Knowledge, Self-Expression and the Prose Narratives of Papua New Guinea." Master's thesis, University of Canterbury, 1991.
———. "Indigenous Pacific Fiction in English: The 'First Wave.'" In *The Novel in Australia, Canada, New Zealand, and the South Pacific Since 1950*, ed. Coral Ann Howells, Paul Sharrad, and Gerry Turcotte, 499–510. Oxford: Oxford University Press, 2017.
———. "Pidgin Poetics in Oceania." In *Oxford Research Encyclopedia of Literature*, 2020. https://doi.org/10.1093/acrefore/9780190201098.013.198.
———. "Reconstituting Indigenous Oceanic Folktales." Paper presented at Folktales and Fairy Tales: Translation, Colonialism, and Cinema, University of Hawai'i Manoa

International Symposium, Honolulu, September 2010. http://hdl.handle.net/10125/16460.

———. Review of *Gutsini Poasa (Rough Seas)* by Regis Stella. *Contemporary Pacific* 12, no. 2: 551–54.

———. "Unwriting Oceania: The Repositioning of the Pacific Writer Scholars Within a Folk Narrative Space." *New Literary History* 31, no. 3 (2000): 599–613.

Wood-Ellem, Elizabeth, ed. *Songs and Poems of Queen Sālote.* Trans. Melenaite Taumoefolau. Nukuʻalofa: Vavaʻu Press, 2004.

Woolf, Virginia. *The Common Reader: Second Series.* London: Hogarth, 1953.

———. *A Room of One's Own & Three Guineas.* New York: Oxford University Press, 1992.

Wright, Richard. "Blueprint for Negro Writing." *New Challenge* 2 (1937): 53–65.

———. *Native Son.* 1940. New York: Harper Perennial Classics, 1988.

Wurtz, James F. "Scarce More a Corpse: Famine Memory and Representations of the Gothic in *Ulysses*." *Journal of Modern Literature* 29, no. 1 (2005): 102–17.

Wyckom Jr., William. "Letters." *African Arts* 8, no. 3 (1975): 7.

Yeats, W. B. *The Collected Poems.* Ed. Richard J. Finneran. Rev. 2nd ed. New York: Scribner, 1996.

———. *Letters to the New Island.* Cambridge, MA: Harvard University Press, 1934.

———. *Selected Poetry of W. B. Yeats.* Ed. A. Norman Jeffares. London: Macmillan, 1962.

Zimmer-Tamakoshi, Laura. "Passion, Poetry, and Cultural Politics in the South Pacific." *Ethnology* 34, no. 2 (1995): 113–27.

INDEX

abjection, 204–6
Abraham, Peter, 78–79, 120
absurdism, 25, 80, 84–86, 128
Achebe, Chinua, 5, 11, 48, 62, 115, 163, 212
aesthetics, 3, 16, 28–29, 167–68, 192, 207; colonialism and, 11; English language and, 169–70; Indigenous, 25, 29, 35, 94; Kasaipwalova on, 114–15; linear progressions of, 7; modernist, 12, 14, 17, 64, 126, 219; traditionalism, 81; of Vini, 171; Western, 101
Africa, 13–14, 18, 29, 100, 149, 163; African modernist literature, 3, 16–17, 37, 65–66, 78–83, 119; African writers, 66, 69, 79–83, 91, 97, 144; diaspora, 121, 168, 175, 178. *See also specific countries*
African American gothic (Wester), 195
African Americans, 33–34, 82, 121–22, 178, 182, 194–95
agency, 49, 63, 66, 124, 163, 168, 207, 209–11
agriculture, 57–58, 118
alcohol, restrictions on, 183

Ali, Ahmed, 202
alienation, 14, 17, 56, 63, 91, 124, 126, 196; colonial, 79, 116, 146, 201, 206–7; gothic, 199–200; Indo-Fijian, 190–93, 220–21; modernist, 25, 39, 82–83, 90, 191, 213
Alliance party, 205–6
Alvarez, A., 39
ambiguity, 11, 120, 201, 204–11
American modernism, 7, 37, 87, 91, 119, 158
American Samoa Community College, 228n57
anachronism, 38, 52–53, 194–95
Ancestry (Wendt), 1–2, 213
anticolonialism, 10, 23, 96–97, 138, 143, 178, 201; of Kasaipwalova, 30, 115, 118; national literatures and, 30
Aotearoa New Zealand. *See* New Zealand
art, Pacific, 11
Arvidson, Ken, 20, 150–51, 154–55
assimilation, 12, 62, 67, 110, 120; Christianity and, 77; modernism and, 28–29, 44
Auden, W. H., 33–35, 45–46
Australia, 17, 22, 96–97, 114, 124, 136

INDEX

authenticity, 79, 103, 105, 107–8, 122–23, 135, 170
authoritarianism, 125, 129
authority, 68, 163; white, 29–30, 107, 121, 136
autobiography, 23–24, 73, 95, 105, 109
Autobiography of a Native Minister in the South Seas, The (Bulu), 23
Axel's Castle (Wilson), 42

Baker, Hinemoana, 219
Baldwin, James, 133
Ballantyne, R. M., 161
Baraka, Amiri, 121
Barker, Alan, 40–41
Beckett, Samuel, 34, 48, 162, 193
Beeby, Clarence, 35–36
Beier, Ulli, 13–14, 43, 77, 143, 210, 242n49; Crocombe and, 172; decolonization and, 29–30, 97, 101–2, 135–37, 186; Josselson and, 36–37; on négritude, 118; Soaba on, 135–36; as a teacher-editor, 29, 95, 99–102, 135–36; at University of Ibadan, 51, 67, 95–96; at UPNG, 20, 29, 32, 67–71, 80, 94–111, 112–13, 115, 150, 158, 165, 184–86, 214. *See also* M. Lovori; Obotunde Ijimere; Omidiji Aragbabalu; Sangodare Akanji
Being and Nothingness (Sarte), 127
belonging, 25, 31, 56, 102, 145, 209, 221
Bennett-Tuionetoa, Jenny, 220–24
Benson, Peter, 101
Beston, John, 121–22
"Beware, the Worst Is Still to Come!" (Garae), 170
"Bhut len ki katha" ("The Story of the Haunted Line") (Sanadhya), 196
Biafran War, 95
Bikini nuclear tests, 181–82
bildungsroman, 24, 127, 133
Bishop, Elizabeth, 44–45
Bislama (language), 173, 176–77
Black: anger, 122, 172–174; authors, 102, 112, 195; blackness, 178; consciousness, 119–20; existentialism, 17, 30, 126; internationalism, 16, 113; nationalism, 114, 121, 172
Black Arts Movement, 182
Black Fire (Jones and Neal), 70, 121
Black Marks on the White Page (Ihimaera and Makereti), 219
Black Orpheus (periodical), 69, 95, 99–103, 105–6
Black Panther Party, 121, 178
Black Power movement, 30, 107, 128–31, 133, 172, 178; at UPNG, 30, 113–23, 125, 172
"Black Venture" (Kula), 178
Black Writing from New Guinea (Sharrad), 98
boarding schools, 24, 72, 114, 127
bone people, the (Hulme), 216
Boschman, Roger, 21
Botting, Fred, 195
Bougainville Civil War (1988), 217–18
Brash, Elton, 96
Brathwaite, Kamau, 46
bricolage, 7, 12, 75, 122, 136
Britain, 110–11, 177, 181–82, 212; sugar island colonies, 155, 200–202. *See also* United Kingdom
Brontë, Charlotte, 200
Brosnahan, Frank, 20, 149
Brumby, Ed, 105
Bryce, Tilisi, 234n84
Bulu, Joel, 23
"Bush Beer" (Crocombe), 183–84
"Bush Kanaka Speaks, The" (Tawali), 79
Butadroka, Sakiasi, 205–6

Cakobau, Ratu George, 205–6
Cambridge University, 8
Cameroon, 80–81
Campbell, Alistair Te Ariki, 22
Camus, Albert, 85, 102, 113, 124, 126–27, 135
Cannibals and Converts (Maretu and Crocombe), 165
canon, 16–17, 83, 206, 224; modernist, 24, 66, 85–86; Western, 7, 65, 68, 96

INDEX

Cantos, The (Pound), 120
capitalism, 13, 73, 101, 116, 195
Caribbean, 16, 200–203
"Casabianca" (Bishop), 44–45
"Casabianca" (Hemans), 44–45
Casanova, Pascale, 51
castaways, European, 160–63, 171
Catholicism, 114
Celebration, The (Pillai), 147
Césaire, Aimé, 12, 82, 87, 115, 118–20
Chakravarthy, Prithvindra, 68–69, 219
Chatterjee, Kalyan, 90
Christianity, 77, 79–80, 147, 156, 174, 182, 222–23
Cleaver, Eldridge, 121
Cold War, 42, 101
collectivity, 23, 43, 124–25, 165, 204
College of Micronesia-FSM, 228n57
colonial law, 74, 183–84
colonialism and colonization, 7, 14–15, 23, 31, 225n9; alienation, 79, 116, 146, 201, 206–7; curricula and, 9, 44, 66; education and, 9–11, 16–20, 24–29, 36, 58–59, 63, 98, 101, 135–36, 141, 171; in Fiji, 140, 144–45, 147, 155, 189–92, 194; gothic literature and, 194–206; humiliations of, 19, 81; identity and, 25, 127; "Mana" addressing, 172; modernity, 53–54, 73, 86–87, 115–16, 153, 173, 191; paternalism, 17, 79–80; plantation trauma and, 195, 220; in PNG, 74, 79, 115–20, 124–25, 136; power and, 69, 74, 94, 115, 130, 169; Samoa and, 212–13; unlearning and, 28; Vini reframing, 160–63; violence and, 191–92, 197–99, 207–8
communism, 41–42
Congress for Cultural Freedom (CCF), 36–37, 101
Conisbee Baer, Ben, 5
Conrad, Joseph, 45, 48, 76, 162, 170–71, 192, 196; imperialism and, 82–83
consciousness: Black, 119–20; "indenture," 205; individual, 113, 124–34, 162; national, 113, 125–26; political, 93, 198

consumerism and consumption, 56, 109, 141, 156, 191
Cook Islands, 160–63, 217, 227n39; colonial law on, 183–84
Coral Island, The (Ballantyne), 161
corruption, 79, 125, 212–13
counterculture, modernism and, 8, 13, 42
coups, Fijian, 146, 206, 209, 217
critical pedagogy, 10–11, 60
Crocodile, The (Eri), 24, 95
Crocombe, Marjorie Tuainekore, 23, 27, 32, 145, 180, 209–10; "Mana" spearheaded by, 95, 164–66, 168, 172, 174, 176, 184–85, 188. *See also specific works*
cultural: identity, 140; loss, 20, 124
"Culture My Culture" (Leomala), 173
curricula, Pacific, 3–8, 31–32, 179–85, 214–16, 224; colonizing, 9, 44, 66; foreign, 141–42; modernist literature in, 7–10, 31–32, 37–54, 65–67, 75–76, 84, 90–91, 141, 158, 214; regional literature and, 163–64
curricula, UPNG, 6, 13–14, 22, 30, 37, 61–71, 121; Beier on, 67–71, 214; orality in, 22, 29, 65–69, 71–78, 141, 186
curricula, USP, 7, 11, 26, 30, 37, 141, 162, 167, 171, 179–82, 186–87; Diploma of Education, 175; limitations of, 158–59; "Mana" in, 178–81, 185–88; orality in, 22, 186–87, 190; students impacting, 142–50
Currie Report, UN, 17–18, 75

Daugherty, Beth, 34
Davis, Lydia, 24
Davis, Tom, 24
death, 156–57, 160, 191–92, 195–96, 202–4, 223; alienation and, 124; in "Kulpu's Daughter," 61–62; Soaba on, 127–28, 132, 134–35; in sugarcane gothic, 197–98, 201. *See also* murder
decoloniality, 10–11
Decolonising the Mind (Beier), 98, 103–4

INDEX

decolonization, 4–8, 24–25, 35, 73, 78, 126, 201; Beier and, 29–30, 97, 101–2, 135–37, 186; faculty and, 20–21; modernism and, 3, 7, 28–30, 49, 62, 101; self-determination and, 165; Subramani and, 208–10; universities and, 9–12, 17–18, 20–21, 58, 65, 70, 127, 209–10, 215

Decolonizing Methodologies (Tuhiwai Smith), 58

defamiliarization, 123, 161–63, 171

DeLamotte, Eugenia, 192

delayed decoding, 162

DeLoughrey, Elizabeth, 16

Department of Language and Literature, UPNG, 6–7, 10, 62, 67–71, 84, 90–91, 94, 144

Devi, Salochana, 53

diaspora, 13–14, 217; African, 121, 168, 175, 178

"Disillusionment with the Priesthood" (Hannett), 77

Doctor to the Islands (Davis and Davis), 24

domestic violence, 145, 147, 198

Dostoevsky, Fyodor, 193

"Double Life, A" (Griffen), 138–42, 151, 159

doubling, 63, 138–42, 207–8

Doyle, Laura, 126

Dracula (Stoker), 194, 204

Dubliners (Joyce), 193

Duodo, Cameron, 126

"Dusk" (Soaba), 173

educators. *See* teachers and teaching approaches

Eliot, T. S., 8, 11–12, 76–77, 86–87, 151, 157–58, 223; Hannett on, 119; on poetry, 45; at University of London, 33. *See also specific works*

elite, educated, 35–36, 61–62, 113, 129, 132–33

Ellison, Ralph, 98, 106–7, 126, 218

Ellmann, Richard, 38

emotion, 41, 91, 113, 140, 174, 200

Engledow, Neal, 147

English departments, 8–9, 37; UPNG, 6–7, 10, 67–71, 75, 122, 218; USP, 11, 140–50, 175, 179–81, 186–87, 220. *See also* literature programs

English language, 16, 173, 181–82, 191, 207–8; aesthetics and, 169–70; Africanized, 64; Kasaipwalova addressing, 122; Soaba on, 124; Tongan poetry and, 56–57; translation, 80–81; at USP, 140–41

Enos, Apisai, 5, 75

Eri, Vincent, 24, 27, 95

essentialism, 139

Esslin, Martin, 84

estrangement, 31, 51, 162, 192–93, 196

Eurocentrism, 12–13, 18, 29, 36, 78, 204

European: castaways, 160–63, 171; modernism, 1, 3, 7, 17, 32, 67, 76, 83, 87, 91, 119, 155, 167, 191

exclusion, 70, 98–99, 141, 147, 201, 221

existentialism, 5, 24–25, 127–28, 131, 135, 192–93; Black, 17, 30, 126; of Soaba, 85, 102

expatriate faculty, 19–21, 32, 143–44, 210

exploitation, 56, 63, 96, 116, 123, 202

faʻafafine, 222

faculty. *See* teachers and teaching approaches

fāgogo, 29, 169

Faikava (periodical), 26, 187, 217

Fakamuria, Kenneth, 168–69, 172

"Famished Eels" (Rokonadravu), 220–21, 224

Fantasy Eaters, The (Subramani), 193

Farrago (periodical), 24

Faulkner, William, 193

Federated States of Micronesia, 227n39

Feidelson, Charles, 38

feminism, 21, 148

Fiedler, Leslie, 195

Figiel, Sia, 47, 217, 219–20, 223–24

Fiji, 14, 25, 44, 150–54, 156–59, 219, 222–23; colonialism and, 140, 144–45, 147, 155, 189–92, 194; coups, 146, 206, 209, 217; decolonization of, 207–11; indenture in, 31, 144–45, 189–93,

INDEX

195–200, 202–8, 210, 220; Indigenous, 50, 145, 151, 155; modernism, 30, 140–41, 145, 155; Morris Report impacting, 19; postindependence, 145, 182, 205; stereotypes, 48–49, 140; students from, 30, 138–42, 179–80
Fiji College of Agriculture, 228n57
Fiji coup (1987), 217
Fiji men mere ikkis varsh (*My Twenty-One Years in the Fiji Islands*) (Sanadhya), 196
Fiji Times, 205–6
"Final Journey, The" (C. Singh), 196
"First Coconut, The" (Fakamuria), 168–69
Five New Guinea Plays (Beier), 104–6, 108, 186
Flying-Fox in a Freedom Tree (Wendt), 213
Forster, E. M., 33, 191
Forward, Toby, 109
France, 177, 181–82
Frazer, J. G., 77–78
free-verse poetry, 49–50. 56–57, 54, 172
Freire, Paulo, 10, 47–48
Frisbie, Florence "Johnny," 184
futurity, 3, 57, 223

Gab Boys, The (Duodo), 126
Gabbard, Caroline Sinavaiana, 76
Gadd, Bernard, 26
gafa, literary, 1–3, 6
"Gamalian's Woman" (Subramani), 192
Garae, Leonard, 170, 172
Gelder, Ken, 201
gender, 25, 56, 140–42, 149, 217, 220–24; exclusion and, 70, 98–99; students and, 98, 147–48; in sugarcane gothic, 197–98, 200–201, 207–8
genealogy, literary, 1–3, 10–11, 13, 218–19, 224; Wendt on, 190, 213
generational trauma, 200–202
genre, 13, 23–24, 194–95, 207. *See also specific genres*
Germany, 95, 212
"Gift, The" (Racule), 25
Gigibori (periodical), 95
Gikandi, Simon, 79, 82, 84

Gilbert, Michele, 99–100
Ginsberg, Allen, 121
"Glimpse of the Abyss, The" (Soaba), 85
global modernism, 4–7, 14, 31, 177
Global Modernists on Modernism (Ross and Moody), 58
Global North, 8, 14, 20, 99, 191, 199
globalization, 13, 58, 141
Golden Bough, The (Frazer), 77
Goodwin, K. L., 122, 174
Gordon, Jane Anna, 15
Gordon, Lewis R., 15
Goroka Teachers College, 21
Gothic: alienation, 199–200; colonialism, 194–206; minimalism, 193; modernism, 192–93, 195–96, 200, 214, 220–21; postcolonial, 200–206. *See also* sugarcane gothic
Grace, Patricia, 27–28
Grace-Smith, Briar, 219
graduates, Pacific, 21–22; UPNG, 36–37, 93–94; USP, 148, 160–61, 171, 220–22
Graff, Gerald, 40
Griffen, Vanessa, 20, 27, 30, 138–42, 151, 180, 248n24; in *UNISPAC*, 147–49
Guma, Alex La, 82
Gunther, J. T., 228n44
Gutsini Posa (*Rough Seas*) (Stella), 218–19

Habu, Mostyn, 27, 41
Hamilton, Thomas H., 22
Hampson, Robert, 76
Hanneken, Jaime, 109
Hannett, Leo, 71, 73–74, 77, 91, 118–19, 125
hauntings, 191, 196, 198, 203, 207
Hauʻofa, Epeli, 27–28, 95, 217, 229n68
Hawaiʻi, 17, 21–22, 216
"Healer, The" (Crocombe), 81, 184
Heart of Darkness (Conrad), 76, 162, 192
Heffernan, Laura, 5
heliaki, 5, 29, 182, 234n84
Helu Thaman, Konai, 3–4, 12–13, 21, 27, 29, 142, 223–24
Hemans, Felicia, 44–45
Hemingway, Ernest, 11, 19–20, 141, 148–49, 158, 248n24
Hereaka, Whiti, 219–20

Heron, Jonathan, 48
hierarchies, 49, 62, 64–65, 75–78, 94; educational, 10, 36; village, 25, 138
higher education, 4–5, 18–19. *See also* universities, Pacific; *specific institutions*
Higher Education Mission to the South Pacific, 18–19
Hiro, Henri, 216
Hoffmann, E. T. A., 193
Hogle, Jerrold E., 204
Holt, John Dominis, 216
Honiara, Solomon Islands, 19
Honolulu Advertiser, 216
"Hoom blong mi" (Leomala), 173–74
"How to Get Students Writing Poetry" (Wendt), 177
Howarth, Peter, 37, 44
Howie-Willis, Ian, 113
Howl (Ginsberg), 86, 121
Hughes, Langston, 33–34
Hulme, Keri, 216
Huxley, Aldous, 33

Iakavi, Jerry, 169–70, 172
identity, 1–2, 14–15, 90, 102, 124, 126, 213; Anglo-Irish, 194; colonization and, 25, 127; Cook Islander, 184; crisis of, 83; cultural, 140; Indigenous, 69, 110; Indo-Fijian, 190–91, 205–7; national, 94–95; power structures and, 93; pseudonyms and, 29, 94–95, 98–99, 105–11, 184; Samoan, 221–22
Ihimaera, Witi, 27–28, 216, 219
Illich, Ivan, 10, 233n67
imperialism, 10–11, 16, 82–83, 115, 170–71, 177, 225n9; encounter tales, 161–63; medical memoirs, 24; paternalism and, 129; representation and, 204–5
impersonating, Indigenous pseudonyms as, 29, 94–95, 98–99, 103–11, 184
indenture, 25; in Fiji, 31, 144–45, 189–93, 195–200, 202–8, 210, 220
independence, 10, 22, 28, 66, 110–11, 126, 227n39; aesthetics and, 167–68; decolonization and, 17; Fijian, 30, 155; Papua New Guinean, 215; Samoan, 212

India, 69, 156–57, 196, 202–3, 205–6. *See also* Indo-Fijians
indigenization, 82, 167, 187, 210
Indigenous and indigeneity, 127, 141–42, 152, 181, 195, 209–10; Aboriginal people, 216; aesthetics, 25, 29, 35, 94; artists, 5, 11, 97, 165; belonging, 31; decolonization and, 17; Fijians, 50, 145, 151, 155; identity, 69, 110; Kānaka Maoli, 22; languages, 80, 94; missionaries, 23; pseudonyms, 29, 68–69, 94–95, 98–99, 103–11, 184; sovereignty, 20
Indigenous Vanguards (Conisbee Baer), 5
Indigenous writers, 12–16, 22–24, 94, 101, 164–66, 209–10, 216; in "Mana," 173
individual consciousness, 113, 124–34, 162
individuality and individualism, 38, 49, 103, 113, 123, 126, 131; self-determination and, 28; of Wendt, 11
Indo-Fijian Experience, The (Subramani), 202–3, 205
Indo-Fijian Federation Party, 205–6
Indo-Fijians, 12, 15, 25, 30–31, 57–58, 223–24; alienation, 190–93, 220–21; gothic modernism of, 192–93, 195–96, 200, 214, 220–21; identity, 190–91, 205–7; plantation trauma of, 195–96, 220; at USP, 144–49, 151, 155–59, 206. *See also* indenture
Inglis, Ken, 19
"Inside Us the Dead" (Wendt), 2
International Writing Program, University of Iowa, 218–19
intertextuality, 17, 87, 148, 213, 224
Introduction to African Literature (Beier), 120
Invisible Man (Ellison), 126, 129
Irele, Abiola, 81–82, 100, 120
Itaia, Maunaa, 25, 209
iTaukei. *See* Indigenous Fijians
Ivaiti, Harry, 54
Izavbaye, Dan, 73

Jamaica, 200–202
James, C. L. R., 87
Jane Eyre (Brontë), 200

INDEX

Jawodimbari, Arthur, 71–72, 80–81, 91
Jewish people, 110–11, 136
Johnson, Leslie, 125
Johnson, Nicholas, 48
Jones, LeRoi, 70, 121
Josselson, Michael, 36–37
Joyce, James, 1–2, 34, 162, 193–94

Kabisawali Association, 114–15
Kadiba, John, 73, 97
Kafka, Franz, 29, 85, 193
Kalpokas, Donald, 172–73, 176–77
Kanahele, George, 216
Kanaka's Dream (Kasaipwalova), 86
Kaputin, James, 87–88
Kasaipwalova, John, 30, 32, 74–75, 116–36, 174, 218; on limitations of universities, 112–13; plays by, 86; Sopi Arts School established by, 36, 114–15. *See also specific works*
Kenner, Hugh, 37, 42
Keown, Michelle, 16, 127
Kermode, Frank, 38
Kerpi, Kama, 61–64, 88–89
"Kidnapped" (Petaia), 24
Kiki, Albert Maori, 93, 95, 105, 107
kinship, 2, 13, 25, 108, 173
Kiribati, Micronesia, 22
Kisses in the Nederends (Hau'ofa), 217, 223
Kovave (periodical), 5, 20, 22, 26, 29, 86–89, 122; Beier and, 71–72, 95, 99–102; Crocombe in, 81, 165, 184; Hannett in, 73–74; Kerpi in, 63; Soaba in, 85, 112; Thompson in, 92–93
Krauth, Nigel, 88–89, 122, 215
Kristen Pres competitions, 21
Kristeva, Julia, 204–5
"Kros / Cross" (Leomala), 174
Kula, Aivu, 178
Kulagoe, Celestine, 181–82
"Kulpu's Daughter" (Kerpi), 61–64
Kunapipi (periodical), 200
Kurangaituku (Hereaka), 220

Lahui, Jack, 219
Lal, Brij V., 141, 144–45, 203
Lali (Wendt), 11, 174, 215

languages, 23, 149, 168, 187; Anglophone, 169, 196, 216; Bislama, 173, 176–77; Indigenous, 80, 94; local, 122, 129; PNG, 5, 18–19, 28, 132–33; Samoan, 219–20; Tok Pisin, 18, 74–75, 94; Tongan, 182; translation and, 72, 87–88, 103, 106, 169, 172, 186, 219–20, 222. *See also* English language
Larson, Charles, 105–6
Lawrence, D. H., 33–34, 48–49
Laycock, Don, 108
Lejeune, Phillipe, 109
Leomala, Albert, 172–73, 176
L'Étudiant Noir (Césaire), 118
Levin, Harry, 39–41
Lewis, Wyndham, 35
liberation, 17, 119–20, 222
Lindfors, Bernth, 108
linguistics, 141–43, 149–50, 169, 214; curricula focused on, 6–7, 21, 179
literacy, 28, 105, 175
literary: production, 5–6, 21–22, 87, 229n67; resistance, 51, 218
Literature Bureau, Papua New Guinean, 21
literature programs, 15, 29, 39, 209; UPNG, 10, 61–67, 72–91, 96–111, 112–13; USP, 10, 20, 50, 58, 143–59, 171–72. *See also* curricula, Pacific
"Little Gidding" (Eliot), 223
"Live in Me" (Leomala), 173
Livingston, Peter, 100
Liyong, Taban Lo, 10, 68, 80
local: languages, 122, 129; teachers, 57, 143, 151, 158–59
Lohia, Renagi R., 93–94
Long, D. S., 216
Lord Jim (Conrad), 162
loss, 14; cultural, 20, 124
"Lus Man" (Kavop), 246n67
lusman (Soaba), 127, 132, 246n67

M. Lovori (pseudonym). *See* Beier, Ulli
magazines, 24–26. *See also specific periodicals*
"Magistrate and My Grandfather's Testicles, The" (Kasaipwalova), 74–75

INDEX

Maʻiaʻi, Ata, 147, 183
Makaʻa, Julian, 217
Makereti, Tina, 219–20, 224
Makutu (Davis and Davis), 24
"Man" (Devi), 53
Man of the People, A (Achebe), 62
Mana (periodical), 26, 50, 187–88, 189, 196, 217, 249n14; USP connections, 26, 30–31, 151, 215, 249n14
"Mana and Creative Regional Cooperation" (Crocombe), 164
Mana Annual (periodical), 180, 185–87, 190–91, 193, 195–96, 206, 212
"Mana," *PIM*, 26, 180–81, 193, 206, 224, 230n75, 249n14; Crocombe spearheading, 95, 164–66, 168, 172, 174, 176, 184–85, 188; launch of, 25, 142, 145, 159; ni-Vanuatu poetry in, 172–79; Pillai in, 147; regional literature and, 163–72; relaunch outside of *PIM*, 187, 189; vernacular in, 183–84
Mangubhai, Francis, 26
Manoa, Pio, 21, 27, 40–41, 46, 49–51, 152
Māori literature, 155, 216, 219–20
Mar, Tracey Banivanua, 94
Mara, Ratu Kamisese, 205–6
"Marama" (Griffen), 148–49, 180
Maree, Johan, 96
"Marigolds" (Subramani), 25
Maroons (former slaves), 202
marriage, 56, 61–63, 222, 224
Marshall Islands, 227n39
Marxism, 41–42
masculinity, 34, 122, 148
Mataira, Kāterina, 22
"Matalasi" (Bennett-Tuionetoa), 221–22, 224
Matane, Paulias, 215
McDonald, Gail, 8
McDowell, Judith, 108
McGurl, Mark, 5
Melville, Herman, 196
Metamorphosis, The (Kafka), 193
"Mi stap sori nomo / I Bow in Sorrow" (Vatoko and Leomala), 172–73
Micronesia, 22

Mignolo, Walter D., 19
Mintz, Sidney W., 195
Mishra, Sudesh, 217
Mishra, Vijay, 26, 205–6, 208
Miss Ulysses from Puka-Puka (Frisbie), 184
mission schools, 49, 124
missionaries, 78–79, 164–65
Moana (periodical), 187, 217
Modern Tradition, The (Feidelson and Ellmann), 38
modernism and modernity, 8–10, 45–47, 74, 132, 199; aesthetics, 12, 14, 17, 64, 126, 219; alienation and, 25, 39, 82–83, 90, 191, 213; Anglo-American, 141, 158; colonial, 53–54, 73, 86–87, 115–16, 153, 173, 191; counterculture and, 8, 13, 42; in curricula, 7–10, 31–32, 37–54, 65–67, 75–76, 84, 90–91, 141, 158, 214; decolonizing, 3, 7, 28–30, 49, 62, 101; Fijian, 30, 140–41, 145, 155; global, 4–7, 14, 31, 177; gothic, 25, 31, 192–211, 214, 220–21; Indigenous, 15, 117; literary canon, 24, 66, 85–86; orality and, 71–78; Pacific, 10–12, 14–16, 24, 29, 208–9, 224; pedagogy and, 28–29, 37–48; postcolonial, 63, 67, 83, 155, 205; Samoan, 213; Western, 7, 66, 70
modernist literature, 5, 10–13, 30–32, 113–14, 224; African, 3, 16–17, 37, 65–66, 78–83, 119; American, 7, 37, 87, 91, 119, 158; in curricula, 7–10, 31–32, 37–54, 65–67, 75–76, 84, 90–91, 141, 158, 214; defamiliarization and, 161–62, 171; European, 1, 3, 7, 17, 32, 67, 76, 83, 87, 91, 119, 155, 167, 191
Moore, Gerald, 80
Morris Report, Higher Education Mission to the South Pacific, 18–19
Moving the Centre (Ngũgĩ), 82
Muller, Herbert J., 38, 41
Munch, Edvard, 213
"Muni Deo's Devil" (Pillai), 147–48
Murau, Clement, 23
murder, 104, 195, 220; in sugarcane gothic, 147, 197–98
Murnau, F. W., 194

INDEX

"My Father's Son" (Nandan), 155–58
"Mysterious Maidens from the East, The" (Iakavi), 169

Nacola, Jo, 27, 143–44, 166
Nair, Shashikant, 146–47
Namaliu, Rabbie, 27, 73–74, 95–96, 236n29
Nandan, Satendra, 27, 30, 57–58, 142–44, 155–56, 202–3; Pillai on, 158–59; USP curriculum and, 179
Narokobi, Bernard, 27
Natachee, Alan, 52
national: consciousness, 113, 125–26; literature, 28, 30–31, 164–65; literature competitions, 21
National Broadcasting Commission, PNG, 215
National Theatre Company, PNG, 215
National Writers' Day, PNG, 21, 125
Native Son (Wright), 121, 133, 194–95
"Natives Under the Sun" (Soaba), 124
Neal, Larry, 70, 121
négritude, 5, 30, 113, 118, 122, 130–31, 178
neoclassicism, 194
neomodernism, 38–39
New Hebrides, 19, 168–72, 174–77. *See also* Vanuatu
New Hebrides National Party (NHNP), 177
New Hebrides Viewpoints (periodical), 176–77
New Left Movement, 114
New Plymouth Boys High School, 24
New Poetry, The (Alvarez), 39
newspapers, 21–22, 103, 229n67
New Writing in English from Emerging Nations, UPNG, 69, 78, 80, 186
New Zealand, 17–19, 21–22, 24, 27–28, 212, 227n29
New Zealand Scheme of Cooperation, 20, 143
New Zealand University Entrance Examination, 143
"Next Resort, The" (Soaba), 124
Ngũgĩ wa Thiong'o, 10, 68, 82–83, 218
Nigeria, 13, 29, 94–95, 99–100, 107–10
Night Warrior and Other Stories, The (Beier), 100, 111

"Nightwatch, The" (Rokonadravu), 222–23
Nilaidat (periodical), 64, 93, 96, 116, 123
Niugini Black Power movement, 93, 118
Nkosi, Lewis, 78, 82
Noonuccal, Oodgeroo (Kath Walker), 22, 70
Nosferatu (Murnau), 194
Notebook of a Return to the Native Land (Césaire), 115, 119–20
Notes from a Native Son (Baldwin), 133
Nuanua (Wendt), 10
Nukuʻalofa, Tonga, 19, 26

obedience, 34, 45, 224
objectification, 161
Obotunde Ijimere (pseudonym). *See* Beier, Ulli
O'Carroll, John, 243n34
Odai, Addie, 72
Ogundele, Wole, 104–5, 110
Okara, Gabriel, 82
Okigbo, Christopher, 63–64, 102
"Old Man and the Balus, The" (Waiko), 72
Old Man and the Medal, The (Oyono), 80–81
Old Man and the Sea, The (Hemingway), 19–20, 148–49
Old Man's Reward, The (Jawodimbari), 80–81, 85
O le Sulu Samoa (newspaper), 24
Omidiji Aragbabalu (pseudonym). *See* Beier, Ulli
"On Being Hawaiian" (Holt), 216
"On the Abolition of the English Department" (Ngũgĩ wa Thiong'o, Owuor-Anyumba, and Liyong), 10, 68
oppression, 47, 86, 117–119123
orality and orature, 6, 14, 64, 103, 170, 181, 239n88; Fijian, 147, 223; Indigenous, 151–52; in "Mana," 168, 172; modernity and, 43–48, 71–78; oral histories, 23, 26, 31, 160–63, 171–72, 184–85; in UPNG curricula, 22, 29, 65–69, 71–78, 141, 186; in USP curricula, 22, 186–87, 190

INDEX

originality, 11, 107, 123, 142
Orwell, George, 33, 136
Owuor-Anyumba, Henry, 10, 68
Oxenham, Stephen, 217
Oyono, Ferdinand, 29, 80–81

Pacific Islands Monthly (PIM), 100, 189, 206, 215, 230n75, 249n14. See also "Mana"
Pacific literature. See specific topics
Pacific modernism, 10–12, 14–16, 24, 29, 208–9, 224
Pacific Theological College, 228n57
Pacific writers. See specific topics
Palm-Wine Drinkard, The (Tutuola), 73, 76, 84
Pan African Pocket Poets, 80, 112
Papua New Guinea (PNG), 13, 31, 112–13, 215; colonialism of, 74, 79, 115–20, 124–25, 136; languages in, 5, 18–19, 28, 132–33; Ples Singsing, 219; poetry, 174–75, 178; Port Moresby, 13, 18, 21, 30, 107, 113; UN in, 17–18. See also specific institutions
Papua New Guinea Writers Conference (1976), 22, 62, 70
Papua New Guinea Writing (periodical), 21, 178
Papua New Guinean literature, 21, 96–97, 135, 185, 215–16, 218
Papua Pocket Poets, UPNG, 6, 68–69, 86–89, 95, 98, 112, 136
Papuan Villager, The (newspaper), 24
Paravisini-Gebert, Lizabeth, 200
Passage to India, A (Forster), 191
"Past the Old Track (An Exploration)" (Ma'ia'i), 183
paternalism, 110, 129; colonial, 17, 79–80
patriarchy, 140, 147
p'Bitek, Okot, 62–65, 73, 86
"Peace Signs" (Kulagoe), 181
Pearl, The (Steinbeck), 141, 146
pedagogy, 2–3, 7, 49–60, 68, 98, 104, 155–56; Beier on, 36–37; critical, 10–11, 60; hierarchies and, 65; Indigenous,

29; modernist, 28–29, 37–48; Pacific, 3–4, 58, 209
Pedagogy of the Oppressed, The (Freire), 47
Petaia, Ruperake, 24
Pillai, Raymond, 27, 166, 180, 202–3, 206, 215–16; on Nandan, 158–59; in UNISPAC, 147–49
PIM. See Pacific Islands Monthly
Pinar, William F., 9–10
Pinongo, Avaisa, 98–99
plagiarism, 38, 131, 134
plantations: sugarcane, 189–93, 196–201, 204–7; trauma, 195–200, 220
plays and playwrights, 4, 67, 71–72, 86, 92, 103–8, 165–66
Ples Singsing, PNG, 219
PNG. See Papua New Guinea
poetry and poets, 15–16, 51–53, 58–60, 71–72, 86–89, 217, 223–24; Fijian, 150–59; free-verse, 49–50, 54, 56–57, 172; Indigenous, 4, 15–1630; modernist, 45–47; ni-Vanuatu, 172–79; PNG, 174–75, 178; protest, 167–68; Tongan, 52–57, 182
political activism, 17, 74; of students, 4, 93, 114–15, 125, 134, 146
political consciousness, 93, 198
polygamy, 61, 118
Port Moresby, Papua New Guinea, 13, 18, 21, 30, 107, 113
postcolonial, 16, 36, 51, 156; abjection, 204–6; despair, 212–14; educational, 36, 140; gothic, 200–206; literature, 7, 10–12, 83, 151, 179–80, 186, 194, 224; modernism, 63, 67, 83, 155, 205
postgothic, 193
postindependence, 79, 145, 182, 205
postmodernism, 12–13, 227n29
"Pouliuli" (Tusitala Marsh), 219
Pouliuli (Wendt), 184, 212–14, 219
Pound, Ezra, 35, 37, 120, 162
Powell, Emma, 5–6
Powell, Kirsty, 67, 100, 104, 106–7, 111, 235n7

power, 92, 99, 109–10, 115, 134, 184; colonial, 69, 74, 94, 115, 130, 169; imperial, 170–71, 177; structures, 25, 81, 85, 93, 102, 163; white, 22, 29–30, 119, 121
Powers of Horror (Kristeva), 204
precolonial, 23, 164–65, 222
primitivism, 73, 88, 122–23
Program Era, The (McGurl), 5
"Prologue" (Seri), 152–55
prose, 4, 71–72, 151–52, 168–72, 183
"Prose Fiction in Fiji" (Pillai), 151
pseudonyms, Indigenous, 29, 94–95, 98–99, 103–11, 184
psychological oppression, 192, 199–200, 205
Pule, John, 217
Purua (periodical), 217

Quality of Education in Developing Countries, The (Beeby), 36
Queensland, Australia, 114

Rabuka, Sitiveni, 206
race, 18, 93, 104, 121, 123, 145
racial antagonism, 205
racialization, 148–49, 178
racism, 107, 110, 119
Racule, Rejieli, 25
Rainbow, The (Lawrence), 34
realism, 82, 86, 89, 100–101, 194
"Recall" (Manoa), 49–51
Regional Creative Writing Workshop (1974), USP, 22, 24, 60, 167–68, 170, 173, 175–79, 181
regional literature, 3, 31, 193, 214–19; Beier and, 102; in "Mana," 163–72, 177–79; in the *Mana Annual*, 180; *Mana* on, 187, 189; Subramani and, 190, 208–9; USP and, 142–43, 145, 155, 159
relationality, 6, 14–16, 76, 123
religion, 23, 78, 116, 120, 145–46, 164–65, 173; Christianity and, 77, 79–80, 147, 156, 174, 182, 222–23
Reluctant Flame (Kasaipwalova), 30, 112–24, 133–34, 174, 218

representation, 22, 103, 110, 189, 204–5; faculty and, 163–64; of sexuality, 1, 221–22
"Return of St. Nativeson" (Soaba), 133–34
Rhys, Jean, 196, 200–204, 254n33
Richards, I. A., 40
Richards, Thomas, 170
Riquelme, John Paul, 194–95
rituals, 43, 77–78, 136, 156–57, 160, 198, 212
Rokonadravu, Mary, 219–24
roman à clef, 134–38
rote learning, 9, 28–29, 35–36, 44, 47, 50
Rudd, Alison, 205–6

Samoa, 35–36, 212, 217 175, 222
Samoa College, 27, 36
Sanadhya, Totaram, 195
Sangodare Akanji (pseudonym). *See* Beier, Ulli
Sartre, Jean-Paul, 127, 132
Saunana, John, 27
"Sautu" (Subramani), 190–92, 195–96, 197, 202–3, 213
Scattered by the Wind (Soaba), 77
Scream, The (Munch), 213
"Screaming Man, The" (A. Singh), 146, 213–14
Searching for Nei Nim'anoa (Teaiwa), 217
"Second Coming, The" (Yeats), 152–54, 181–82
"Seduction" (Thompson), 92–93
self: determination, 28, 59, 83, 165, 210–11; education, 44, 48–49; government, 118, 163; immolation, 192
Senghor, Léopold, 118
Seri, 30, 152–55, 158–59, 180–82
sex workers, 136, 223
sexuality, 1–2, 217, 221–22; in sugarcane gothic, 197–98, 207–8
Shark That Ate the Sun, The (*Ko E Mago Ne Kai E La*) (Pule), 217
Sharrad, Paul, 24, 57, 90, 98, 100, 215–16
Sherry, Vincent, 42
shipwrecks, 179–80, 201–4

silence, 200–201, 207
Singh, Anirudh, 30, 146–47, 213–14
Singh, Chattur, 146, 195–96
Sinnet (periodical), 26
slavery and slave trade, 194–95, 202–3
Smiles, Seona, 219
Soaba, Russell, 20, 24–25, 30, 32, 112, 124–36, 215; on Beier, 97; existentialism of, 85, 102; on orality, 72–73; at Regional Creative Writing Workshop, 175–76; Sope compared to, 173. *See also specific works*
sociology, 27, 139–40
Solomon Islands, 27, 217
"Song of Lament" (Kerpi), 88
Song of Lawino (p'Bitek), 62–65, 86
Sons for the Return Home (Wendt), 24–25, 182–83, 213
Sope, Mildred, 173, 176
Sopi Arts School, 36, 114–15
Sorariba, Nash, 218
Soul on Ice (Cleaver), 121
South Pacific Creative Arts Society (SPCAS), 166, 180
South Pacific Literature (Subramani), 190, 215
sovereignty, 18, 20, 110, 168
Soyinka, Wole, 63–64, 73, 82, 103, 108
Spain, 202
SPCAS. *See* South Pacific Creative Arts Society
Spender, Stephen, 41
Spivak, Gayatri, 109, 204
staff. *See* teachers and teaching approaches
Steinbeck, John, 141, 146
Stella, Regis Tove, 218–19
stereotypes, 48–49, 140
Stoker, Bram, 194, 204
Story of a Melanesian Deacon (Murau), 23
Stranger, The (Camus), 127
Student Representative Council (SRC), UPNG, 114
students, Pacific, 9, 21–22, 27–28, 30, 166, 174–75; female, 98, 147–48; Fijian, 30, 138–42, 179–80; Indigenous, 22;

ni-Vanuatu, 167–68, 173; political activism of, 4, 93, 114–15, 125, 134, 146; Samoan, 165; UPNG, 19–20, 69–78, 92–94, 112–37, 214; USP, 19, 31, 142–50, 175–76, 180–81, 214
students, undergraduate, 11, 30, 141–50, 179–80, 186–87
subaltern, 109, 204
Subramani, 12, 27, 145, 186, 249n14; in *Mana Review*, 189; sugarcane gothic of, 31, 195–207; in *UNISPAC*, 147. *See also specific works*
suffering, 133, 162, 173, 198, 200–201, 205, 223
sugar island colonies, British, 155, 200–202
sugarcane gothic, 31, 85–86, 147, 193, 196–207, 220–21
Suhr-Sytsma, Nathan, 51
Sukwianomb, Joseph W., 54–55
Suva, Fiji, 19
Swan, Quito, 16, 93
syllabi. *See* curricula
Syria (ship), 203–4

Tahiti, 216
Tales of the Tikongs (Hauʻofa), 217
"Tangaroa" (Ivaiti), 54
Tapin, Venantius, 25
Taranakian, The (periodical), 24
Tarawa, Kiribati, 19
Tawali, Kumalau, 27, 71, 78–79, 88–89
Tawali, Soaba, 27
Taylor, Rod, 48
Te Punga Somerville, Alice, 2–3, 40
teacher-editors, 4, 26, 112, 137, 166; Beier as a, 29, 95, 99–102, 135–36; Subramani as a, 208–109
teachers and teaching approaches, 3–5, 9–10, 25, 39–41, 44; expatriate, 19–21, 32, 143–44, 210; local, 57, 143, 151, 158–59; pedagogy of, 28–29; UPNG, 68–71, 214; USP, 20, 57–58, 138–43, 149–59, 166, 175, 185. *See also* writer-scholars; *specific teachers*
Teaching Archive, The (Buurma and Heffernan), 5

INDEX

Teaiwa, Teresia, 15, 168, 217, 225n9, 229n67
technologies, print, 23, 169
"Tell Me Where the Train Goes" (Subramani), 192–93, 196–203, 205, 212–13
Territorial College of Guam, 228n57
"Thing, The" (Vini), 160–63, 168
Things Fall Apart (Achebe), 115
Thomas, Larry, 219
Thomas, Lynda, 122
Thompson, Maurice, 92–93
Tiffin, Chris, 97, 121, 132–34
Tok Pisin, 18, 74–75, 122, 288n44
Tonga, 25, 52–57, 182, 217
Tongareva, Cook Islands, 160–63, 171
Tongia, Makiuti, 27–27
torture, military, 146
"Towards a New Oceania" (Wendt), 24, 58–60, 149n14, 164
transgender, 222
translation, 87–88, 169, 172, 186, 219–20, 222; by Beier, 103, 106; by Odai, 72
Trask, Haunani-Kay, 22
trauma, 31, 84, 127, 212, 217, 221–22; generational, 200–202; of indenture, 189–92, 202–4; plantation, 195–200, 220
Trilling, Lionel, 8, 39–40
Trobriand Islands, 36, 114–15, 124
"Tropical Traumas" (Subramani), 191
Tuhiwai Smith, Linda, 11, 58
Tusitala Marsh, Selina, 43, 75–76, 219
Tutuʻila Malupo, Peni, 182
Tutuola, Amos, 73, 84
Tuwhare, Hone, 22

Ulysses (Joyce), 34, 48, 76, 193–94
Under Western Eyes (Conrad), 162
undergraduate students, 11, 30, 141–50, 179–80, 186–87
underrepresentation, 22, 145
Unexpected Hawk, The (Waiko), 92 m85
UNISPAC (periodical), 20, 144–49, 166, 179, 181
United Kingdom, 18–19. *See also* Britain

United Nations (UN), 17–18, 118, 182, 227n29
United States, 181–82, 212, 227n39; American modernism, 7, 37, 87, 91, 119, 158; slavery in, 194–95
universities, Pacific, 2–8, 11–12, 31–32, 33–48, 55, 193, 214–17; decolonization and, 9–12, 17–18, 20–21, 58, 65, 70, 127, 209–10, 215; enrollment in, 22, 150, 154, 214; founding of, 16–19, 21–25; literary genealogy and, 218–19. *See also* curricula; literature programs; *specific universities*
University of Auckland, 27–28
University of Exeter, 144
University of Fiji, 27
University of Ghana, 106
University of Guam, 21, 228n57
University of Hawaiʻi, 21–22
University of Ibadan, 51, 67, 95–96
University of Iowa, 218–19
University of Leeds, 144
University of London, 33, 95
University of Papua New Guinea (UPNG), 3–4, 29; Black Power movement, 30, 113–23, 125, 172; Crocombe and, 166; Department of Language and Literature, 6–7, 10, 62, 67–71, 75, 84, 90–91, 94, 122, 144, 218; founding of, 16–19, 21–26, 125–26; graduates, 36–37, 93–94; in "Kulpu's Daughter," 61–64; literature programs, 10, 61–67, 72–91, 96–111, 112–13; Modern World Literature I, 69, 78–79, 84; Modern World Literature II, 70, 84, 121; as a national university, 28, 215; New Writing in English from Emerging Nations, 69, 78, 80, 186; Papua Pocket Poets, 6, 68–69, 86–89, 95, 98, 112, 136; students, 19–20, 69–78, 92–94, 112–37, 214; teachers, 68–71, 214; Waigani seminar, 24, 36, 47, 60, 70, 93; in *Wanpis*, 30, 112–13, 124–35. *See also* curricula, UPNG; *specific publications*
University of Queensland, 114

University of the South Pacific (USP),
3–4, 6–7, 185–88, 237n3;
Commonwealth Literature course,
151, 179–80, 200, 214; Crocombe at, 32,
164–66; Diploma of Education, 19,
175; in "A Double Life," 139–42;
Extension Service, 27, 184; founding
of, 17, 19–26, 30, 181; graduates, 148,
160–61, 171, 220–22; Indo-Fijian
writers at, 144–49, 151, 155–59, 206;
linguistics at, 141–43, 149–50, 179, 214;
literature program, 10–11, 20, 50, 58,
140–59, 171–72, 175, 179–81, 186–87,
220; as a multinational institution,
28, 180–81, 215; Niu Waves collective,
217; Oceania Centre for Arts, 27;
School of Education, 27, 150; South
Pacific Arts Festival, 165; students, 19,
31, 142–50, 175–76, 180–81, 214;
Subramani at, 189–90, 208–9;
teachers, 20, 57–58, 138–43, 149–59,
166, 175, 185; Wendt at, 27, 142, 175,
179–80; writing workshops, 22, 31,
163–64, 172–79. *See also* curricula,
USP
University of Waikato, 143
unwanted guests, 31, 193, 206–11, 221
UPNG. *See* University of Papua New
Guinea
urgency, 64, 113, 145
USP. *See* University of the South Pacific

Va'ai, Sina, 16
Vandertop, Caitlin, 196
Vanua'aka Viewpoints (periodical),
176–77
Vanuatu, 167–68, 170, 172–79
Vatoko, Kali, 172–73
vernacular, 118, 173, 178, 182–84, 187, 217,
229n67
Vete, Vili, 25
"Victims, The" (Soaba), 20, 85
Victoria, Australia, 124
Victoria University of Wellington, 24, 28
Victorian age, 44, 89, 194
"Village Idiot, The" (Soaba), 112
"Villager's Request, The" (Soaba), 72–73

Vini, Nihi, 160–62, 167, 170–72
violence, 92, 130, 132, 146; colonial,
191–92, 197–99, 207–8; domestic, 145,
147, 198; gender-based, 121, 220–22;
sexual, 121
Voice, The (Okara), 82

Waigani seminar, UPNG, 24, 36, 47, 60,
70, 93
Waigani Writing Competition, 21
Waiko, John, 27, 58, 72, 76, 103–4, 118
Waleanisia, Joseph, 21
Walsh, Catherine E., 10
Wanpis (Soaba), 24–25, 30, 112–13, 124–35
Waste Land, The (Eliot), 8, 15–16, 120,
152, 154, 157, 193–94
Waswe? (periodical), 187, 217
Watt, Ian, 162
Wells, H. G., 18
Wendt, Albert, 1–2, 20, 21, 26, 212,
223–24, 249n14; on anger, 174; on
Barker, 41; Camus and, 127;
contributing to *Taranakian*, 24;
Freire and, 48; on the genealogy of
Oceanian writing, 10–11; on
indigeneity, 209–10; in "Mana," 169;
modernist pedagogy of, 29; at
Regional Creative Writing
Workshop, 175–76; at Samoa College,
27; Subramani compared to, 190;
translation of works by, 219–20; on
vā, 5–6; at Waigani Seminar, 36;
Wright and, 194–95
Wester, Maisha L., 195
Western: canon, 7, 65, 68, 96;
modernism, 7, 66, 70
Western Samoa, 17, 35
Westernization, 15, 61, 127, 154
"Where Are the Green Leaves"
(Sukwianomb), 54–55
Where We Once Belonged (Figiel), 217
white: authority, 29–30, 107, 121, 136;
power, 22, 29–30, 119, 121; supremacy,
75, 116–17; whiteness, 115–16, 122
"Who Am I?" (Kalpokas), 172–73, 177
"Why We Should Hate Whites"
(Kasaipwalova), 134

INDEX

Wide Sargasso Sea (Rhys), 196, 200–202, 254nn33–34
Williams, William Carlos, 8, 37
Wilson, Edmund, 42
Winduo, Steven, 26–27, 95, 132, 218, 230n76
Wodak, Joanne, 40
Woolf, Virginia, 34–35, 48–49, 162
Words of Paradise (Beier), 71
Works of Taʻunga, The (Crocombe), 164–65
workshops, writing, 4, 21; USP, 22, 31, 163–64, 172–79
world literatures, 7–8, 32, 63, 209
World War I, 81

World War II, 8, 42, 81, 127
Wreath for Udomo, A (Abraham), 78–79, 120
"Wreck of the *Syria*, 1884, The" (Lal), 203
Wright, Richard, 11–12, 42, 121, 133, 194–95
writer-scholars, 4, 21, 26–29, 32, 230n76
Wyckom, William, Jr., 99

Yeats, William, 11–12, 120, 141, 151–55, 181–82, 212
"You, the Choice of My Parents" (Helu Thaman), 56, 223–24

GPSR Authorized Representative: Easy Access System Europe, Mustamäe tee 50, 10621 Tallinn, Estonia, gpsr.requests@easproject.com